Perspectives on Asian Tourism

Series editors
Catheryn Khoo-Lattimore
Griffith University
Nathan, Queensland, Australia

Paolo Mura
Taylor's University
Subang Jaya, Selangor, Malaysia

While a conspicuous body of knowledge about tourism in Asia is emerging, Western academic ontologies and epistemologies still represent the dominant voice within tourism circles. This series provides a platform to support Asian scholarly production and reveals the different aspects of Asian tourism and its intricate economic and socio-cultural trends.

The books in this series are aimed to pave the way for a more integrated and multifaceted body of knowledge about Asian tourism. By doing so, they contribute to the idea that tourism, as both phenomenon and field of studies, should be more inclusive and disentangled from dominant (mainly Western) ways of knowing.

More specifically, the series will fill gaps in knowledge with regard to:

- the ontological, epistemological, and methodological assumptions behind Asian tourism research;
- specific segments of the Asian tourist population, such as Asian women, Asian backpackers, Asian young tourists, Asian gay tourists, etc;
- specific types of tourism in Asia, such as film-induced tourism, adventure tourism, beauty tourism, religious tourism, etc;
- Asian tourists' experiences, patterns of behaviour, and constraints to travel;
- Asian values that underpin operational, management, and marketing decisions in and/or on Asia (travel);
- external factors that add to the complexities of Asian tourism studies.

More information about this series at http://www.springer.com/series/15382

Sangkyun Kim • Stijn Reijnders
Editors

Film Tourism in Asia

Evolution, Transformation, and Trajectory

 Springer

Editors
Sangkyun Kim
School of Business and Law
Edith Cowan University
Joondalup, WA, Australia

Stijn Reijnders
Erasmus University Rotterdam
Rotterdam, The Netherlands

ISSN 2509-4203   ISSN 2509-4211   (electronic)
Perspectives on Asian Tourism
ISBN 978-981-10-5908-7   ISBN 978-981-10-5909-4   (eBook)
DOI 10.1007/978-981-10-5909-4

Library of Congress Control Number: 2017952952

Printed on acid-free paper

This Springer imprint is published by Springer Nature
The registered company is Springer Nature Singapore Pte Ltd.
The registered company address is: 152 Beach Road, #21-01/04 Gateway East, Singapore 189721, Singapore

Contents

Part III   The Film Tourist Experience

Part IV   Transcontinental Film Tourism

Contributors

Sue Beeton William Angliss Institute, Melbourne, VIC, Australia

Torsha Bhattacharya School of Travel Industry Management, University of Hawaii, Manoa, Honolulu, HI, USA

Joydeep Biswas KIIT School of Management (KSOM), KIIT University, Bhubaneswar, India

Glen Croy Department of Management, Monash Business School, Monash University, Caulfield East, VIC, Australia

Oxford School of Hospitality Management, Oxford Brookes University, Oxford, UK

Yun-An Olivia Dung Institute for Area Studies, Leiden University, Leiden, The Netherlands

Warwick Frost La Trobe University, Melbourne, VIC, Australia

Ulrike Gretzel Annenberg School of Communication and Journalism, University of Southern California, Los Angeles, USA

Sangkyun Kim School of Business and Law, Edith Cowan University, Joondalup, WA, Australia

Seongseop (Sam) Kim School of Hotel & Tourism Management, Hong Kong Polytechnic University, Kowloon, Hong Kong

Jennifer Laing La Trobe University, Melbourne, VIC, Australia

Eerang Park School of Management, Victoria University of Wellington, Wellington, New Zealand

Stijn Reijnders Erasmus University Rotterdam, Rotterdam, The Netherlands

Chris Ryan The China-New Zealand Tourism Research Unit, Waitako Management School, University of Waikato, Hamilton, New Zealand

Elisabeth Scherer University of Dusseldorf, Dusseldorf, Germany

Philip Seaton Hokkaido University, Sapporo, Japan

Jun Shao School of Landscape Architecture, Beijing Forestry University, Beijing, China

Gregorius Suri Tourism Department, Government of Belu Regency, East Nusa Tenggara, Indonesia

Faye Taylor Nottingham Trent University, Nottingham, UK

Aaron Tham School of Business, University of the Sunshine Coast, Sippy Downs, QLD, Australia

Timo Thelen University of Dusseldorf, Dusseldorf, Germany

Desmond Wee Karlshochschule International University, Karlsruhe, Germany

Min Xu Erasmus University Rotterdam, Rotterdam, The Netherlands

Xiaoyu (Nancy) Zhang Tourism College, Beijing Union University, Beijing, China

Chapter 1
Asia on My Mind: Understanding Film Tourism in Asia

Sangkyun Kim and Stijn Reijnders

1.1 Introduction

The popularity of film tourism, the phenomenon of people travelling to locations or sites because of their association with a movie or TV series, has risen dramatically over the last decade. Arguably, this is not a new phenomenon, as the film and TV industries, with their integral system of stardom and fandom, have influenced people's mobility and tourism practically from the advent of cinema. The rise of the film industry and its stars in the 1920s led to a similar fascination with film locations and the film stars' Hollywood mansions. Also, groups of tourists have visited locations they associate with popular novels and authors since at least the late nineteenth century. Literary tourism is often considered a precursor to film tourism (Herbert 2001; Seaton 1998; Watkins and Herbert 2003). Since the late twentieth century in particular, the majority of TV and film scripts have been inspired by or directly based upon classic literature. Some examples include *The Lord of the Rings* (2001–2003), *Harry Potter* (2001–2011) and *Jane Eyre* (2006, 2011).

Following the release of the movie adaptations of *The Lord of the Rings* (*LOTR*), the impact of the *LOTR* film trilogy (2001–2003) on New Zealand's tourism industry has been widely documented in academic literature (Buchmann et al. 2010; Carl et al. 2007; Roesch 2009; Tzanelli 2004). The exact net worth of the economic impact is difficult to measure accurately because of the complexities and dynamics of the film tourism phenomenon itself. According to Tourism New Zealand, 6% of international tourists to New Zealand cite *LOTR* as being one of their main

S. Kim (✉)
School of Business and Law, Edith Cowan University,
270 Joondalup Drive, Joondalup, WA 6027, Australia
e-mail: s.kim@ecu.edu.au

S. Reijnders
Erasmus University Rotterdam, Rotterdam, The Netherlands
e-mail: reijnders@eshcc.eur.nl

© Springer Nature Singapore Pte Ltd. 2018
S. Kim, S. Reijnders (eds.), *Film Tourism in Asia*, Perspectives on Asian Tourism, DOI 10.1007/978-981-10-5909-4_1

motivations for visiting the country. Since 2004, New Zealand has attracted an average of 47,000 international tourists per year, specifically to film locations associated with *LOTR* (www.tourismnewzealand.com), resulting in an enormous boost to the country's second largest economic sector (Roesch 2009).

Another example concerns the Louvre Museum in Paris, which received a record number of visitors in 2006. This interest was not generated by a famous exhibition but by the fact that the museum figured prominently in the popular thriller *The Da Vinci Code* (2006), a blockbuster movie adaptation of the bestselling novel *The Da Vinci Code* (2005). Thousands of tourists made their way to the Louvre in order to see and confirm with their own eyes the location where the fictional murder had taken place. A similar phenomenon has been experienced by the little Rosslyn Chapel in Scotland, which became one of the most popular tourist destinations in Europe, also as a result of *The Da Vinci Code* (Johnston 2006). Two more recent examples are the *Games of Thrones* tour in Dubrovnik, Croatia (Waysdorff and Reijnders in press), and the Millennium Tour in Stockholm, Sweden (Van Es and Reijnders 2016).

It is hardly surprising that film tourism has attracted considerable academic attention. The phenomenon has been labelled film-induced tourism (Beeton 2005), movie-induced tourism (Riley et al. 1998), television-induced tourism (Connell 2005; Riley et al. 1998; Su et al. 2011), film tourism (Yen and Croy 2016), cinematic tourism (Tzanelli 2004, 2013), media-related tourism (Busby and Klug 2001), media tourism (Reijnders 2011), media pilgrimage (Couldry 1998) and screen tourism (Kim 2010).

Varied as these terms and disciplinary approaches may be, current film tourism literature appears 'very broad and inclusive in its coverage by conflating many different genres of media programmes' (Kim and Long 2012, p. 174). Thus, the apparent interchangeability of Hollywood blockbusters with niche arthouse 'foreign'-language productions has been a point of criticism.

Despite the above-mentioned criticism, the generic term *film tourism* defined as 'visitation to sites where movies and TV programmes have been filmed as well as tours to production studios, including film-related theme parks' (Beeton 2005, p. 11), is the definition adopted in this book. The reasons for this are that the term is widely used in related literature and appreciation of the complexities and dynamics of the film tourism phenomenon as a distinctive field of research.

As highlighted by Beeton (2010), Reijnders (2011) and Connell (2012), film tourism is a true testimonial to an interdisciplinary or multidisciplinary research area that involves work from psychology, media and audience studies, cultural studies, cultural geography, cultural heritage, marketing and environmental studies. The time and effort that both scholars and stakeholders have invested in the study of film tourism have led to a much better understanding of the phenomenon in recent years.

While there has been a welcome growth in academic attention to the topic of film tourism, some critical gaps remain in the knowledge about this phenomenon. Five pressing questions have been identified. In the following sections, these five concerns will be outlined one by one. This exposition will be followed by a focus on the particulars of film tourism in Asia, before finishing the chapter with an overview of the separate contributions that comprise this book. This will clarify how the authors and other contributors have tried to tackle the gaps in knowledge mentioned below.

1.2 Studying Film Tourism: Gaps and Challenges

First, little is known about the dimensional aspect of film tourism relating to media content: why do some films and TV series lead to film tourism while others do not? Film scholars such as Bruno (2002) and Ruoff (2006) have highlighted the strong links between film and notions of space. But how is this expressed in terms of tourism? Do different genres possibly lead to various subtypes of film tourism? These questions have been partly posed in previous studies (Kim and Long 2012; Roesch 2009; Reijnders 2011), but no satisfactory answers have yet been given. How are the selected shooting locations represented, and what significance does this representation have for the theme and the development of the plot? How do these representations differ from genre to genre and from country to country, and what role does this representation have in influencing whether or not the landscape becomes popular (cf. Reijnders 2011)? Instead of using either a text-based or location-based approach, along the lines of the disciplinary divides between media studies and tourism studies, this book advocates a combination of both approaches, integrating content and tourism behaviour.

Secondly, few studies have been conducted on film tourism as a government strategy or policy from a critical cultural policy study approach (Kim and Nam 2016; Lewis and Miller 2003). While attracting, hosting and promoting film and TV productions have become important government strategies in an increasing number of countries, including developing ones, little research has closely examined film tourism policies and their effects on cultural policy, media economies, tourism and creative industries and host communities (cf. Martens 2013: 26). For example, whereas Nollywood tourism is mainly based on individual entrepreneurship, as the Nigerian government lacks control, this turns out to be the opposite in Brazil, where the national government is actively engaged in promoting film tourism, often associated with Latin American versions of daily TV soap operas, especially 'telenovelas'.

In a similar vein, this field of tourism policy and regulation research seems to be more marginal in Asian contexts where the notion of creativity and connections with tourism is very recent and still in its infancy. Some exceptions include existing studies such as the *Hallyu* phenomenon and its impact on tourism growth and new tourism patterns (e.g. film tourism) in South Korea (Kim et al. 2009; Kim and Nam 2016) and Japanese studies examining contents tourism and popular culture related to Japanese animation or manga (Beeton et al. 2013; Ng 2008; Seaton et al. 2017). It is noteworthy that Hong Kong, Singapore, Thailand and Taiwan have also positioned themselves as leading nations in cultural and creative industries and formulated and implemented supportive government policies promoting the development of cultural and creative industries in conjunction with the tourism industry as a vehicle for creative development (Chang and Lee 2015; Hui 2006; Ooi 2007). The Thai government's national support and master plans and polices for the development of the creative economy in the tourism sector also exemplify this trend (Wattanacharoensil and Schuckert 2016).

Thirdly, existing academic knowledge about film tourism is still highly fragmented and mostly focuses on destination marketing and a management perspective, often leading to narrowly focused findings that fail to provide a holistic understanding of the impact of film tourism. While this narrow approach has enhanced our understanding of destination image, destination choice and film tourist motivations (e.g. Beeton 2010; Connell 2012; Croy and Heitmann 2011; Kim 2012b; Kim and O'Connor 2011), there has been little research on the impact of film tourism, in particular on local or host communities and residents of film tourism locations (Connell 2012; Yoon et al. 2015). Of particular note is the scarcity of film tourism impact research from a multiple stakeholder perspective.

This lack of existing relevant literature exclusively focusing on residents' perceptions of film tourism impact has meant that little scholarly attention has been expended on advancing the conceptual understanding of how tourists perceive and evaluate their impact on the communities and place/space changes of film tourism destinations. Similarly, little is known about governments' perceptions and evaluations of the impact of film tourism on host communities, even though governments at all levels are widely acknowledged as the most influential stakeholders in tourist destination development and regional competitiveness (Liu 2003; Ruhanen 2013). Indeed, governments control most tourism planning tools and take a large amount of responsibility for any issues related to tourism development and its impact. In this regard, it is tourists as users and governments as policymakers and/or developers that are seen as the prime source of the 'problem' or 'issue', yet to date, they have rarely been regarded as part of the 'solution' or a subject of investigation within the context of film tourism. It appears to be most scarce in the Asian context.

As such, a holistic understanding of the perceived impact of film tourism on host communities among tourists, governments and local communities will help build a stronger foundation for management strategies targeting film tourists and is designed to reduce its negative impact and maximise its positive effects. In addition, the current literature on the impact of film tourism still heavily relies on previous studies on community perceptions of the impact of tourism and attitudes towards associated tourism development in the context of *general* tourism destinations. The specific characteristics of film tourism, however, need to be taken into account to conduct more accurate research on the impact of film tourism. One such characteristic is that the general public's fixation with films or TV programmes can be short lived. This means that there are considerable risks for potential film tourism locations seeking to develop film tourism products in a more sustainable manner. It is therefore assumed that the potential impact of short-term film tourism will not be completely identical to the impact generated by often longer-term general tourism.

Fourthly, another important concern that to date remains largely unanswered is the significance of film tourism to the tourists themselves. It is remarkable that we know so little about this, for it is precisely their personal experiences and the significance they ascribe to the events that form the crux of the phenomenon. Some studies (Kim 2012a; Reijnders 2016) have suggested that audiences develop a form of familiarity with the filmed locations. From the perspective of human geography and environmental psychology, Tuan (1974) defined this as *topophilia*, or love of a particular place. According to Reijnders (2016, p. 675), stories have the potential to create new, or contribute to, existing forms of topophilia, associating certain narrative sites with 'positive values such as security, nostalgia, happiness, freedom and safety'.

Thus, film tourists' experiences can go beyond the tangible cognitive dimension of the filmed locations (Couldry 1998). They can be appreciated as a memory or nostalgic structure in which this appreciation can elevate the filmed locations to become more symbolic and ritual places (Couldry 1998; Kim 2010), a 'sacred site' (Seaton et al. 2017) or 'imagined landscape' (Reijnders 2016). This is because audience involvement is the centre of the audience viewing experience that will then lead to and contextualise a personalised film tourism experience (Kim 2012a). In this respect, Connell (2012, p. 1019) states that 'emerging research on the social psychology of film tourism is a welcome step forward in producing more in-depth explanations of the link between film and tourism'. However, this concern is not sufficiently addressed, and theory in this field of research is still less developed than might be hoped (Connell 2012).

Last but not the least, and partly related to the concerns stated above, is the striking fact that the great majority of existing studies on film tourism focus exclusively on Western examples, predominantly from the UK, Ireland, Australia and the USA, with a handful of exceptions (Dung and Reijnders 2013; Kim et al. 2009; Kachipande 2013; Kim and Nam 2016). In this regard, Kim et al. (2009, p. 311) correctly state that 'the longstanding pervasiveness and power of Hollywood as a source of global imagery is generally unchallenged in much of the work carried out on film tourism'. It is also related to 'the hegemony of the English language as the foremost mechanism of narrating what is on the screen (Kim et al. 2009, p.311)'. However, this Western focus and paradigm tend to overlook the fact that the face of the media industry, including the creative industry as well as the tourism industry, has been undergoing an unprecedented rapid and radical change on a global scale.

At the same time, there are other centres and sources of screen imagery and narrative, for example, in Asian cinema and media production, from countries such as China, India, Hong Kong, South Korea and Japan. Therefore, it would be inaccurate and problematic to presuppose audience reactions and tourist behaviours associated with film tourism if future film tourism research were restricted to the immediacy of the English language and the recognisable histories and traditions of Western screen production. More in particular, due to the fixation on Western examples, little to no attention has been paid to cross-cultural differences in cinematographic, musical or literary traditions and their possible effect on film tourism. For example, Bollywood cinema is well known for featuring songs, referred to as 'filmi songs', as an integral feature of the plot. How do these popular song-and-dance routines affect the film tourist experience, which is, in a Western context, said to be mainly *visual* (Roesch 2009)?

Also, the global tourist flows can no longer be characterised as a (neo-)colonial phenomenon in which the white, Western tourist consumes the 'exotic otherness' in the non-West. Instead, people from the BRIC countries are increasingly present in the global tourist flows (Matusitz and Payano 2012; Smith 2009), partly driven by images from their own film industries. It is also noteworthy that the rise of the middle classes in several countries in Southeast Asia will lead to the creation of a new pool of potential film tourism. These developments call for a broader, more global approach to film tourism that takes into account possible commonalities and differences in the development and experience of film tourism in different cultural settings.

The question arises as to how a global approach to film tourism can be advocated while at the same time limiting the analysis in this edited volume to one specific continent: Asia. From a global perspective, one could indeed criticise such a geographic focus and question whether there is something typically 'Asian' about the different case studies collected in this volume. On the one hand, it is obviously true that film tourism in India is quite different from film tourism in Japan or Indonesia. There are so many differences between these national media cultures that it is hard to maintain the idea of a single univocal 'Asian' film tourism. Certainly, looking at the chapters collected in this volume, the diversity is more striking than the few similarities found. Furthermore, in most examples that are described in this book, a strong influence of 'non-Asian' factors from the West and beyond can be detected – be it Western tourists, cinematic traditions from Hollywood or global financial flows affecting the face of film tourism in Asian countries.

On the other hand, as will hopefully be demonstrated in the next section, it is safe to say that Western hegemony in film and TV production has been challenged in recent decades. Across the Asian continent (as well as in Africa and South America), we can see new media centres popping up, producing more and more movies and catering to a larger audience than the average Hollywood blockbuster. These 'new' media centres became popular in the 1990s and the first decade of the new millennium. They usually produce films and TV series that are firmly rooted in local or regional cinematic traditions, policy configurations and audience perceptions. At the same time, industries like Bollywood make abundant use of film conventions and genre characteristics borrowed from European/American cinema – remodelled for local uses and preferences. In that sense, Asian film cultures are prime examples of hybrid, multi-faceted cultures consisting of both global and local elements. As such, Asia offers a promising point of departure for exploring contemporary film cultures and related examples of film tourism from a global perspective.

1.3 Film Tourism in Asia

It should be acknowledged that these gaps form a very useful context and starting point for this edited volume. This is the first in-depth examination of the breadth, scope and trajectory of the film tourism phenomenon in Asia. It is timely and crucial to a more comprehensive understanding of film tourism from the Asian tourism perspective, as described above, particularly in light of the increased volume of media production and consumption in the pan-Asian regions of the world and the consequent potential film tourism destination development that will ensue. In this context, the significance of India (e.g. Bollywood), Japan (e.g. contents tourism) and South Korea (e.g. *Hallyu* or Korea Wave) as leading exporters of popular media content including films, TV dramas and animations has, to a limited extent, been documented in relevant literature.

For instance, India provides a relevant example for studying processes of globalisation and film tourism in non-Western contexts, since its film industry, comprised primarily of Bollywood, has grown into the world's largest film economy, surpassing Hollywood in terms of production and viewership since 2004 (Kavoori 2008) (see Chap. 2 in this book). Recent figures show that 1827 digital Indian feature films were issued certification in 2014–2015 (Central Board of Film Certification 2015). Bollywood productions set in India boost tourism to a large degree by commodifying 'Indianness' and (re)producing cultural stereotypes through the essentialist perspective of an internalised Western 'mediatised gaze' (Urry 2002). These productions contain self-representations of popular Indian clichés such as spirituality, timelessness, exotic colours, etc., reminiscent of *Lonely Planet* visual aesthetics (see Chap. 14 in this book). Bollywood constructs and brands 'Indian spatial and cultural identity' in conjunction with Western stereotypes of 'the Orient', leading to practices of 'self-Orientalism' (Yan and Santos 2009).

The effects of Indian Bollywood films on Indian diasporic communities around the world have also been noted in the context of film tourism (Bandyopadhyay 2008) (see Chap. 10 in this book). It is certainly an important subject area to be investigated further, considering the vast diasporic Indian community and the rise of the Indian middle class in global tourist streams. However, there has been scant research on film tourism related to Indian films and how this affects tourism to and in the country. However, strategic efforts to leverage the potential of film tourism in India have recently emerged at national, state and corporate levels.

Though very little attention has been paid to the film tourism phenomenon in Japan in the English-language literature, Japan offers a fascinating new perspective on film tourism in general and the convergence of tourism and popular culture in particular. This comes from the introduction of a new term, *contents tourism*, in the early twenty-first century. The term represents tourism induced by various creative elements of Japanese popular culture forms such as animation and manga (Beeton et al. 2013; Seaton and Yamamura 2015; Seaton et al. 2017) (also refer to Chap. 4). The continuity of both the domestic popularity and the global appeal of Japanese popular culture triggered this development, and the Japanese government has actively promoted a national branding strategy associated with contents tourism. Prior to that, anime tourism and *Taiga drama* tourism, a popular historical series format of TV drama, mainly involving domestic tourists, have been examined in various studies addressing Japanese sensibilities and comprehension (Okamoto 2015; Seaton 2015).

In comparison, the popularity and influence of Korean popular culture are not relatively new. The phenomenon has been labelled *Korean Wave* or *Hallyu* since the 1990s and is often described as a 'cultural tsunami' (Dator and Seo 2004). With no consensus on its definition and scope, it generally encapsulates Korean TV dramas, movies, variety TV shows, pop music (K-pop), computer games, fashion and cosmetics and food (Kim et al. 2009). The spin-off effect of the *Hallyu* phenomenon has been noted in a variety of ways. For example, about 60% of international inbound tourists claim that their decision to visit Korea was mainly influenced by the *Hallyu* phenomenon. It is estimated there are more than 3.3 million enthusiastic *Hallyu* fans around the world (KNTO 2014), and *Hallyu* is worth US$5.6 billion in economic value and US$95 billion in asset value (Hallyu Future Strategy Forum 2012).

While there have been ongoing debates on the continuing popularity and sustainability of *Hallyu*, both industry practitioners and academic researchers across multiple disciplines have addressed its significance and thus examined this social and cultural phenomenon through various lenses, including cultural studies (e.g. Cho 2011; Huang 2011; Joo 2011), fandom studies (e.g. Kim 2015; Madrid-Morales and Lovric 2015) and media studies (e.g. Hanaki et al. 2007; Oh 2009; Ryoo 2009; Shim 2006). Another important concern is tourism studies associated with its broader impact on Korean tourism and creative industries. Korean TV dramas, referred to as K-dramas, are the centre of the previous studies (e.g. Kim 2012a, b; Kim et al. 2007; Kim et al. 2009; Kim et al. 2010; Kim and Nam 2016; Lee and Yoo 2011; Su et al. 2011; see Chap. 11 in this book).

Despite its faded popularity and diminishing momentum, Hong Kong is – and at least has been for quite some time – another important geographical location in the context of film tourism in Asia. Hong Kong used to be the centre of Asian cinema and has catered to the Asian film markets that include mainland China, Taiwan, Singapore, South Korea, Japan and Malaysia since the 1970s. Prior to the new millennium, Hong Kong films gained unrivalled popularity as the hub of the Asian film industry (Wong and McDonogh 2001). It reached its pinnacle of production in the 1990s with an average of 150 films per year (Hong Kong Film Archive 2011). This led to an era of cultural renaissance for Hong Kong cinema until the late 1990s. The momentum was often termed 'harbour wave' (Jang 2011) and 'Hollywood in Asia' (Weng 2008) and was described as a 'social syndrome' in many countries, including Taiwan and South Korea.

In those days, it was no exaggeration to assert that watching a Hong Kong film in a theatre was a luxury, a prime leisure and an entertainment activity. Asian film audiences grew up watching many film celebrities in Hong Kong films of diverse genres, such as Chinese martial arts, action, culture, history and romance. For example, Bruce Lee is second to none as the iconic star of Hong Kong films in his collection of martial arts films such as *The Big Boss* (1971) and *Enter the Dragon* (1973). Also, Hong Kong movie stars such as Chow Yun-Fat, Andy Lau, Tony Leung Chiu Wai, Stephen Chow and Maggie Cheung enjoyed immense popularity (Hong Kong Film Archive 2011).

Hong Kong films and their stars have now become a trigger for memory and nostalgia of the Asian audiences who were exposed to and grew up with Hong Kong films in those days. In the wake of their memories of these films, middle-aged people in particular often visit the Hong Kong Heritage Museum and *Avenue of Stars* associated with Bruce Lee's memorabilia. Also, avid fans of *Chungking Express* (1994) wander through the Central-Mid-Levels escalator, which was used as one of its filmed locations, listening to *Dreams* originally sung by The Cranberries and *California Dreaming* by The Mamas and The Papas. This shows a notably different perspective and dimension of film tourism in the context of Hong Kong (see Chap. 9 in this book).

While India, Japan, South Korea and Hong Kong are currently the most important centres in terms of (potential) film tourism in Asia, the following chapters are not restricted to these four national contexts. All chapters of this book draw together empirical research across a range of contemporary examples of film tourism in Asia, sometimes from a comparative perspective. This provides a holistic picture of the phenomenon of film tourism in Asia. It encompasses case studies from around the pan-Asia regions such as China, India, Japan, South Korea, Thailand, Hong Kong, Indonesia and Singapore.

1.4 Chapter Overview

1.4.1 Part I: Histories and Current Developments

While many of contributions of this edited volume touch upon the themes of evolution, transformation and trajectory in the Asian contexts of film tourism, the first part entitled 'Histories and Current Developments' constitutes three key chapters that all offer a historical perspective of the interrelation of tourism and cinema in, respectively, India (Chaps. 2 and 3) and China (Chap. 4). In Chap. 2, Jennifer Laing and Warwick Frost show how Western cinematic representations of Asia for a long time mainly focused on the nineteenth century, emphasising a romanticised imperial past. This dominance of the past has been challenged in more recent film productions. As Laing and Frost show, based on an in-depth textual analysis of movies set in India, films like the American *The Darjeeling Limited* (2007), the British *The Best Exotic Marigold Hotel* (2011) and the Australian/Indian co-production *UnIndian* (2015). These films deal in more or less similar ways with representing contemporary Indian society. In these films, India and Indian culture are portrayed as attractive and accessible to Westerners, without being blind to the contradictions and conflicts that are part of the current modernisation process in India. The protagonists of these movies are shown having difficulty with adapting to the Indian environment and seem to be caught in their tourist bubble, but in the end, their journey through modern India turns out to be a valuable, longed-for stage for personal transformation.

In Chap. 3, 'Film Tourism in India: An Emergent Phenomenon', Biswas and Croy likewise start with an overview of the emergence of film tourism in India by acknowledging both key determinant opportunities and challenges that may influence the potential of film tourism to and in the country. According to the authors, India is arguably one of the largest film production nations in the world and would therefore be expected to be one of the largest film tourism destinations. Indeed, there are key determinant factors to support this hypothesis. These factors include (1) the diversity of Indian films characterised by the linguistically and culturally diverse Indian audiences in as many as 40 languages, (2) the increased use of India as the background and foreground of internationally produced films, (3) the rapid transition or transformation from family-run domestic film production to more co-production with international production firms and (4) the increased efforts to capitalise on the potential of film tourism at national, state and corporate levels. This is in line with the increased focus of the Indian Ministry of Tourism on film tourism as one of the ten prioritised tourism domains. However, the current infrastructure bottlenecks, the absence of a national film commission and the scant research on film tourism related to Indian films from various perspectives are identified as key challenges that will play a role in the future growth and prospects of film tourism in India. Thus, Biswas and Croy, in Chap. 3, recommend an urgent and timely call for further research on film tourism in India. This will enhance the current limited understanding and knowledge of the complexity, multiplicity and dynamics behind the potential of film tourism in India.

In Chap. 4, Zhang and Ryan attempt to introduce a historical overview of the emergence of literary and film tourism phenomenon in the context of China by addressing the social, cultural and political changes and their impact on the tourism and film industries. In this chapter, the past, present and future of film tourism in China are presented chronologically with selected examples and supportive material. These materials include the case of Grant View Garden, a constructed film set where a Chinese TV series based on the classical novel *The Dream of the Red Chamber* was filmed. The authors also highlight that film tourism has come to require both local administrations and film industries to make popular films and TV series that can serve as an effective marketing tool to promote destinations in ways consistent with local and national policies in the Chinese context.

1.4.2 Part II: The Impact of Film Tourism

The second part, covering Chaps. 5, 6, 7 and 8, specifically tackles the third critical gap identified above in the current literature of film tourism. This part aims to provide a more holistic understanding of film tourism impact from various stakeholders' perspectives. Scherer and Thelen, in Chap. 5, introduce a domestic touristic phenomenon induced by the Japanese morning drama, known as the *asadora*. This is a very popular and unique format of Japanese TV drama genre that originated in the early 1960s. Based on the case study of *Mare* set in Ishikawa Prefecture located in the central part of Japan's main island Honshū, Chap. 5 investigates the impact of film tourism from a multi-stakeholder perspective, bringing to the fore the voices from the fans, the media producers as well as the local communities. The involvement of multiple stakeholders in this case lies in the common belief that film tourism can contribute to the economic revitalisation and regeneration of their region. The authors, however, highlight the complex and multilayered nature of networks and actions of various parties with different interests and goals in terms of film tourism development and promotion. For that reason, it is noteworthy that mere interpretation of film tourism as a strategic planning option for local governments would bear various risks, in particular for the local community. This is because of the fact that an increase in tourists visiting filming locations never appears to be a quasi-automatic effect as expected. The authors also thoughtfully offer general insights on the opportunities and risks of film tourism that would make their specific case study more relevant beyond the Japanese context.

In Chap. 6, Taylor brings to our attention and revisits a relatively well-known film tourism destination associated with a blockbuster film *The Beach* (2000). This film is arguably one of the most significant factors influencing the development of tourism on Phi Phi Island, Thailand. *The Beach*, based upon the novel by Alex Garland in 1996, describes a backpackers' quest for a utopian island. However, the novel was not intended to celebrate backpacker culture but to criticise it. Regardless, the book and the subsequent film immediately opened the floodgates to millions more backpackers joining the multitude already making their way along the well-trodden tourist trail to the island. *The Beach* forms the core of Phi Phi's tourist product, recognising and capitalising upon the economic benefits associated with fulfilling the desire to visit and be photographed in the same location as Leonardo DiCaprio, even though it is saddening and disappointing when the islands have so much else to offer. As expected from the chapter's title '*The Beach* goes full circle?', Taylor intelligently attempts to explore the debates and controversies surrounding the multilayered impacts of *The Beach* (2000) on Phi Phi Island and map out the nature of tourism development from the point of filming to the present day, based on her longitudinal ethnographic research. It also considers the long-term impact of the film. Her approach is welcomed and appreciated, given that much of the previous research on film tourism impacts is descriptive and involves one-off cases, which means that longitudinal studies are still very limited. Potential readers will be welcomed to challenge themselves to answer her primary question, 'has the Beach gone full circle?'.

The common denominator of Chaps. 7 and 8 is the case study of the Hollywood film *Eat Pray Love* (2010), based on a book written by Elizabeth Gilbert. This film is primarily set and filmed in Ubud, Bali, which is selected by the authors of both chapters. The Indonesian government has recently realised the great potential of film tourism for the nation following the unprecedented pulling power of this particular film and the original book – which was published in 2006 and has sold over 10 million copies worldwide. Bali as a tourism destination is now strongly associated with the *EPL* phenomenon. As described by Mowbray (2012), "It is impossible to ignore the *Eat Pray Love* pilgrims in Ubud. Solo female travellers in their forties and fifties, wearing sun-proof clothing and seen cycling Dutch-style gearless bikes up impossibly steep hills …To call *Eat Pray Love* an 'industry' is not an exaggeration".

Despite the growth of film tourism associated with *Eat Pray Love* (2010), there has been a paucity of academic attention for this unique case study, given that tourism was already an established industry prior to the release of the *EPL* book and film. However, since their release, the tourism products offered in Ubud have been significantly transformed by an influx of tourists seeking to have their own *Eat Pray Love* experience (O'Connor and Kim 2014). In Chap. 7, Park aims to analyse and discuss how the tourist experience has been transformed over time in Ubud, Bali, in part by the impact of the Hollywood film *Eat Pray Love* (*EPL*). Similar to Taylor's chapter on *The Beach* (2000), Park also adopted a longitudinal study, but this time, an auto-ethnographic approach was employed, using direct observations and experiences, informal conversations with locals and other tourists, photographs and field accounts of the tours in June 2010, July 2013 and April 2016. According to Park, a sudden influx of *Eat Pray Love*-motivated tourists has resulted in dramatic and long-lasting changes to the existing tourism products and activities offered in loco. The two most significant changes that have taken place as a result of the impact of the film *EPL* are the commodification of agricultural places and the commodification of social practices and sacred rituals. During this process, new hybrid forms of tourism experiences have been created, which have in turn led to the enrichment of the tourism experiences on offer in Ubud. What is important in Chap. 7 is a shift in the research perspective, in theoretical terms, from traditional triple bottom-line assessments of tourism impact (i.e. socio-cultural, environmental and economic) towards tapping into the different ways tourism contributes to and detracts from the change in role and function of places by adopting the typology of places in a destination (i.e. tourism places, shared places and non-tourism places) from the study of McKercher et al. (2015).

In comparison, in Chap. 8, Kim, Suri and Park address a research paucity in the field of film tourism from a local community perspective. Since current film tourism literature predominantly focuses on development, marketing and management of potential and actual film tourism locations, this leaves vast scope for future research on local community's perceptions and attitudes towards film tourism impact. Similar to Park's research presented in Chap. 7, the authors adopted a longitudinal approach to examine and discuss how, and the extent to which, local residents' perceptions and attitudes towards the impacts of film tourism at a film tourism destination have changed, been transformed and/or adjusted over time. Kim et al., in Chap. 8, summarise that during the film production stage, local communities generally had positive perceptions and attitudes towards the impacts of film tourism and anticipated further positive indirect effects of the film's production in the future. However, their generally positive perceptions and attitudes gradually began to change during the post-production effect (PPEF) phase, leaving them with mixed perceptions and attitudes. The authors also raise issues about the role of government and self-efficacy in place identity in the Indonesian context, which will be applicable in a wider context.

1.4.3 Part III: The Film Tourist Experience

The third part introduces and discusses various psychological aspects and dimensions of tourist behaviours and experiences associated with film tourism from multiple case studies. To a large extent, Chaps. 9, 10, 11 and 12 in this part collectively aim to critically and synthetically respond to the aforementioned fourth critical gap in current film tourism literature. To do this, in Chap. 9, Kim and Kim correctly postulate that the role of nostalgia has, until now, not been fully theorised and integrated in related theories on film tourism. Nostalgia on its own plays a crucial role not only in stimulating perceived familiarity with certain locations but also in motivating tourists to visit the locations and satisfying on-site experiences in the context of film tourism. Chap. 9 has a particular focus on those Korean audiences who were exposed to Hong Kong films produced from the 1970s until the late 1990s. It examines and identifies the role of nostalgia in the development of future film tourism products and activities in Hong Kong. Kim and Kim conclude that stronger feelings of nostalgia and sentimentality, particularly associated with film content, film stars and film backdrops, are crucial to the support needed for the development of Hong Kong film tourism-related tour programmes.

While the great majority of previous film tourism studies have been devoted to understanding factors influencing likelihood of an audience's future intention to visit filmed locations (e.g. familiarity, cultural proximity, audience involvement), Tham and Kim, in Chap. 10, address a critical gap in our current understanding as to the determinants that actually *hinder* tourist intentions to visit film tourism locations. Chapter 11 thus attempts to elucidate some of these factors using the case of the Korean TV drama series *Descendants of the Sun* (DOTS). This successful Korean TV series was filmed across several locations in Korea and Greece. Chapter 10 identifies three important mitigating factors that have affected the propensity of the audience to visit Greece: safety, affordability and accessibility and familiarity. These hindering factors were dramatically diminished when participants assessed Korea as a potential film tourism destination associated with DOTS, showing how participants cognitively appraised destinations that were concurrently featured in media programme(s). Knowing more about these hindering factors will lead to better informed theory and practice in seeking out destinations to take advantage of the potential of film tourism demand.

The film tourism experience is further explored and conceptually expanded upon in Chaps. 11 and 12. In Chap. 11, Xu and Reijnders introduce China's Hengdian World Studios, the world's largest outdoor film studio that is called the 'Hollywood of the East'. Here, more than 20, 000 people have registered with the actors' union. This chapter focuses on the motivations and experiences of extras from Hengdian who immerse in film studios as constructed or built filmed locations for a longer period. This is in contrast to previous studies on motivations and experiences of film tourists that mainly concern *short-term* tourists, for example, those participating in a 2-hour tour or visiting film locations individually as part of a day trip. Xu and Reijnders also postulate that the extras' motivations and experiences will likely differ from those of short-term film tourists and have the potential to deepen our understanding of the close relationships between film, experience and place. By shedding light on the meanings behind extras' experiences, Chap. 11 also offers an original perspective on both the symbolic and practical power structures of the Chinese film industry.

Shao and Gretzel's Chap. 12 on a cross-cultural comparison of volunteerism between the Chinese and Americans, motivated by popular local TV dramas, is in an ideal position to identify research gaps of current film tourism literature: neither the connection between film tourism and volunteerism nor the differences between Chinese and American film-induced voluntarists have been adequately studied. Based on a qualitative 'netnographic' study of online fan conversations, they examined the phenomenon of voluntourism among fans of two very popular TV dramas in China and the USA, *Soldier Sortie* (2007) and *Lost* (2004–2010), respectively. They suggest that *Soldier Sortie* fans in China act more like a virtual charity organisation, while *Lost* fans engage with an existing charity organisation. Volunteering programmes initiated by *Soldier Sortie* fans have taken on an important role in propelling the development of some tourist destinations in rural areas of the province where the series was shot. Moreover, *Soldier Sortie* fans act not only as donors but also as organisers and auditors, choosing and determining which school to help. This reflects the much stronger level of connectivity and activism among Chinese fans. Shao and Gretzel highlight how film tourism can be more than just visiting film locations – for some of these tourists, simply checking the boxes is not enough.

1.4.4   Part IV: Transcontinental Film Tourism

In our discussion of the gaps and challenges in the field of film tourism (see above), we advocated a global approach to film tourism. This challenge is taken up explicitly – but not exclusively – in the fourth and final part of the book. The final part of this book looks at examples of film tourism that include either tourists or films from other continents and, where possible, include the perspective of diasporic audiences. Chapters 13, 14, 15 and 16 offer a fresh perspective on transcontinental cultural exchanges between film tourism hosts and guests. For example, in Chap. 13, Dung and Reijnders examine how Chinese and Taiwanese tourists imagine Europe and how these imaginations are being realised, challenged and modified during their concrete tourist experiences of Paris, France. According to Dung and Reijnders, the Chinese and Taiwanese experience of Paris is characterised by an ongoing negotiation between media-inspired fantasies – dominated by American movies – and personal experiences of the 'real' Paris. As a result, the way these tourists imagined Europe before their visit is reinforced but also challenged. Also, Chinese tourists tend to develop a hybrid perspective, which means that they learn to re-appreciate Paris in its complexity while reconstituting their own cultural identity vis-a-vis the European Other.

The Euro-Asian perspective is further explored in Chap. 14. It centres on the German Village in Namhae, South Korea, which was built over a decade ago as a tribute to the Korean workers who lived in Germany as *Gastarbeiter*. The author, Desmond Wee, explores the question of identities of the 'locals' as portrayed in the film *Endstation der Sehnsüchte* and juxtaposes this alongside the huge influx of 'tourists' indulging in the photographing of experiences on the film set of the Korean TV drama *Couple or Trouble*. What emerges from this research is a mediation of experiences that explores the nexus between the impact of film and television on the cultural heritage of residents in film tourism locations on the one hand and the convergence of mediatisation, globalisation and identity through film on the other.

Questions of cultural heritage and nostalgia within the context of a specific diasporic community return in Chap. 15. Based on the case of the Indian diaspora in Hawaii and their consumption of Bollywood films, Bhattacharya tries to elucidate how the Indian diaspora located on an isolated island maintains its connection with its homeland. What sustains their nostalgia, in a place thousands of miles away from home? Bhattacharya argues that Bollywood films serve as an active medium through which the distance between the diaspora and the homeland is erased. The diaspora population remains physically away from their country but constantly attempts to be connected with their homeland emotionally and psychologically while watching Bollywood films. Bhattacharya's analysis presents the social and cultural impact of Bollywood films on the Indian diaspora in Hawaii in terms of their travel decisions and social interactions.

The final chapter of this book considers the ways that elements of Japanese heritage have been incorporated into the contemporary Hollywood theme parks of Disney (Tokyo) and Universal Studios (Osaka), resulting in an attraction quite different from their US counterparts. This presents a significant change to the way in which these places have been traditionally developed, resulting in a 'glocalised' tourist attraction that appeals to both Japanese and foreign visitors. By taking a cultural landscape approach, Sue Beeton and Philip Seaton uncover the cultural layers of these two theme parks, resulting in a deeper understanding of the relationship between Western and Asian culture, presenting a popular culture phenomenon that transcends the traditional monocultural approach. Beeton and Seaton conclude that theme parks should be seen as more than bland, 'placeless' places of Western cultural imperialism.

References

Bandyopadhyay, R. (2008). Nostalgia, identity and tourism: Bollywood in the Indian diaspora. *Journal of Tourism and Cultural Change, 6*(2), 79–100.

Beeton, S. (2005). *Film-induced tourism*. Clevedon: Channel View Publications.

Beeton, S. (2010). The advance of film tourism. *Tourism and Hospitality Planning & Development, 7*(1), 1–6.

Beeton, S., Yamamura, T., & Seaton, P. (2013). The mediatisation of culture: Japanese contents tourism and pop culture. In J. Lester & C. Scarles (Eds.), *Mediating the tourist experience: From brochures to virtual encounters* (pp. 13–32). Surrey: Ashgate Publishing.

Bruno, G. (2002). *Atlas of emotion: Journeys in art, architecture, and film*. New York: Verso.

Buchmann, A., Moore, K., & Fisher, D. (2010). Experiencing film tourism: Authenticity and fellowship. *Annals of Tourism Research, 37*(1), 229–248.

Busby, G., & Klug, J. (2001). Movie-induced tourism: The challenge of measurement and other issues. *Journal of Vacation Marketing, 7*(4), 316–332.

Carl, D., Kindon, S., & Smith, K. (2007). Tourists' experience of film locations: New Zealand as 'Middle-Earth'. *Tourism Geographies, 9*(1), 49–63.

Central Board of Film Certification [CBFC] (2015). Annual Report from April 2014 to March 2015. Retrieved November 15, 2016, from http://cbfcindia.gov.in/html/uniquepage.aspx?unique_page_id=30

Chang, W. S., & Lee, Y. (2015). Policy momentum for the development of Taiwan's cultural creative industries. *Current Issues in Tourism, 18*(11), 1088–1098.

Cho, Y. (2011). Desperately seeking East Asia amidst the popularity of South Korean top culture in Asia. *Cultural Studies, 25*(3), 383–404.

Connell, J. (2005). Toddlers, tourism, and Tobermory: Destination marketing issues and television-induced tourism. *Tourism Management, 26*(5), 763–776.

Connell, J. (2012). Film tourism: Evolution, progress and prospects. *Tourism Management, 33*(5), 1007–1029.

Couldry, N. (1998). The view from inside the 'simulacrum': Visitors' tales from the set of Coronation Street. *Leisure Studies, 17*, 94–107.

Croy, G., & Heitmann, S. (2011). Tourism and film. In P. Robinson, S. Heitmann, & P. U. C. Dieke (Eds.), *Research themes for tourism* (pp. 188–204). Oxon: CAB.

Dator, J., & Seo, Y. (2004). Korea as the wave of a future: The emerging dream society of icons and aesthetic experience. *Journal of Futures Studies, 9*(1), 31–44.

Dung, Y. A. O., & Reijnders, S. (2013). Paris offscreen: Chinese tourists in cinematic Paris. *Tourist Studies, 13*(3), 287–303.

Hallyu Future Strategy Forum. (2012). *Hallyu seeks sustainability*. Seoul: Hallyu Future Strategy Forum.

Hanaki, T., Singhal, A., Han, M., Kim, D., & Chitnis, K. (2007). Hanryu sweeps East Asia: How Winter Sonata is gripping Japan. *The International Communication Gazette, 69*(3), 281–294.

Herbert, D. (2001). Literary places, tourism and the heritage experience. *Annals of Tourism Research, 28*(2), 312–333.

Hong Kong Film Archive. (2011). Hong Kong Filmography. Retrieved August 10, 2016, from http://www.lcsd.gov.hk/CE/CulturalService/HKFA/documents/2005525/2007315/7-2-1.pdf

Huang, S. (2011). Nation-branding and transnational consumption: Japan-mania and the Korean wave in Taiwan. *Media, Culture and Society, 33*(1), 3–18.

Hui, D. (2006). *Study on the relationship between Hong Kong's cultural & creative industries and the Pearl River Delta*. Hong Kong: Centre for Cultural Policy Research, The University of Hong Kong.

Jang, K. (2011). A study of Korean wave's origin and usage. *Journal of Korean Contents Association, 11*(9), 166–173.

Johnston, J. (2006). Rosslyn invests in preparation for expected Da Vinci hordes. *The Sunday Herald* 16/05/2006: 18.

Joo, J. (2011). Transnationalization of Korean popular culture and the rise of "Pop Nationalism" in Korea. *The Journal of Popular Culture, 44*(3), 489–504.

Kachipande, S. (2013). Nollywood's impact on Tourism and 'Brand Nigeria'. *Consultancy Africa Intelligence*, http://www.consultancyafrica.com/. Accessed on 16 June 2013.

Kavoori, A. P. (Ed.). (2008). *Global Bollywood*. New York: NYU Press.

Kim, S. (2010). Extraordinary experience: Re-enacting and photographing at screen-tourism locations. *Tourism and Hospitality Planning & Development, 7*(1), 59–75.

Kim, S. (2012a). Audience involvement and film tourism experience: Emotional places, emotional experiences. *Tourism Management, 33*(2), 387–396.

Kim, S. (2012b). The relationships of on-site film-tourism experiences, satisfaction, and behavioural intentions: From the film-tourism perspective. *Journal of Travel & Tourism Marketing, 29*(5), 472–484.

Kim, J. O. (2015). Reshaped, reconnected and refined: Media portrayals of Korean pop idol fandom in Korea. *Journal of Fandom Studies, 3*(1), 79–93.

Kim, S., & Long, P. (2012). Touring TV soap operas: Genre in film tourism research. *Tourist Studies, 12*(2), 173–185.

Kim, S., & Nam, C. (2016). Hallyu revisited: Challenges and opportunities for the South Korean tourism. *Asia Pacific Journal of Tourism Research, 21*(5), 524–540.

Kim, S., & O'Connor, N. (2011). A cross-cultural study of screen-tourists' profiles. *Worldwide Hospitality and Tourism Themes, 3*(2), 141–158.

Kim, S. S., Argusa, J., Lee, H., & Chon, K. (2007). Effects of Korean television dramas on the flow of Japanese tourists. *Tourism Management, 28*(5), 1340–1353.

Kim, S., Long, P., & Robinson, M. (2009). Small screen, big tourism: The role of popular Korean television dramas in South Korean tourism. *Tourism Geographies, 11*(3), 308–333.

Kim, S. S., Lee, H., & Chon, K. S. (2010). Segmentation of different types of Hallyu tourists using a multinomial model and its marketing implications. *Journal of Hospitality and Tourism Research, 34*(3), 341–361.

KNTO [Korean National Tourism Organisation]. (2014). *An investigation on Hallyu tourism market*. Seoul: KNTO.

Lee, T. H., & Yoo, J. K. (2011). A study on flow experience structures: Enhancement or death, prospects for the Korean wave. *Journal of Travel & Tourism Marketing, 28*(4), 423–431.

Lewis, J., & Miller, T. (Eds.). (2003). *Critical cultural policy studies: A reader*. Oxford: Wiley-Blackwell Publishing.

Liu, Z. (2003). Sustainable tourism development: a critique. *Journal of Sustainable Tourism, 11*(6), 459–475.

Madrid-Morales, D., & Lovric, B. (2015). Transatlantic connection: K-pop and K-drama fandom in Spain and Latin America. *Journal of Fandom Studies, 3*(1), 23–41.

Martens, E. (2013). *Welcome to Paradise Island: the rise of Jamaica's cine-tourist image, 1891–1961* (Unpublished master dissertation). University of Amsterdam.

Matusitz, J., & Payano, P. (2012). Globalisation of popular culture: From Hollywood to Bollywood. *South Asia Research, 32*(2), 123–138.

McKercher, B., Wang, D., & Park, E. (2015). Social impacts as a function of place change. *Annals of Tourism Research, 50*, 52–66.

Mowbray, N. (2012). In search of an exotic isle: Beyond the eat, pray, love phenomenon in beautiful Bali. *Daily Mail Online*. Retrieved on 03 November 2012 from http://www.dailymail.co.uk/travel/article-2161186/In-search-exotic-isle-Beyond-Eat-Pray-Love-phenomenon-beautiful-Bali.html

Ng, B. W. (2008). Hong Kong young people and cultural pilgrimage to Japan: The role of Japanese popular culture in Asian tourism. In J. Cochrane (Ed.), *Asian tourism: Growth and change* (pp. 183–192). Oxford: Elsevier.

O'Connor, N., & Kim, S. (2014). Pictures and prose: Exploring the impact of literary and film tourism. *Journal of Tourism and Cultural Change, 12*(1), 1–17.

Oh, I. (2009). Hallyu: The rise of transnational cultural consumers in China and Japan. *Korea Observer, 40*(3), 425–459.

Okamoto, T. (2015). Otaku tourism and the anime pilgrimage phenomenon in Japan. *Japan Forum, 27*(1), 12–36.

Ooi, C. S. (2007). Creative industries and tourism in Singapore. In G. Richards & J. Wilson (Eds.), *Tourism, creativity and development* (pp. 240–251). London: Routledge.

Reijnders, S. (2011). *Places of the imagination: Media, tourism, culture*. Farnham: Ashgate Publishing.

Reijnders, S. (2016). Stories that move: Fiction, imagination, tourism. *European Journal of Cultural Studies, 19*(6), 672–689.

Riley, R., Baker, D., & Van Doren, C. (1998). Movie-induced tourism. *Annals of Tourism Research*, *25*(4), 919–935.

Roesch, S. (2009). *The experiences of film location tourists*. Bristol: Channel View Publication.

Ruhanen, L. (2013). Local government: Facilitator of inhibitor of sustainable tourism development? *Journal of Sustainable Tourism*, *21*(1), 80–98.

Ruoff, J. (Ed.). (2006). *Virtual voyages: Cinema and travel*. Durham: Duke UP.

Ryoo, W. (2009). Globalization, or the logic of cultural hybridization: The case of the Korean wave. *Asian Journal of Communication*, *19*(2), 137–151.

Seaton, A. V. (1998). The history of tourism in Scotland: Approaches, sources and issues. In R. MacLellan & R. Smith (Eds.), *Tourism in Scotland* (pp. 1–41). London: International Thomson Business Press.

Seaton, P. (2015). Taiga dramas and tourism: Historical contents as sustainable tourist resources. *Japan Forum*, *27*(1), 82–103.

Seaton, P., & Yamamura, T. (2015). Japanese popular culture and contents tourism – Introduction. *Japan Forum*, *27*(1), 1–11.

Seaton, P., Yamamura, T., Sugawa-Shimada, A., & Jang, K. (2017). *Contents tourism in Japan: Pilgrimages to "scared sites" of popular culture*. New York: Cambria Press.

Shim, D. (2006). Hybridity and the rise of Korean popular culture in Asia. *Media, Culture and Society*, *28*(1), 25–44.

Smith, M. (2009). *Issues in cultural tourism studies*. London: Routledge.

Su, H. J., Huang, Y. A., Brodowsky, G., & Kim, H. J. (2011). The impact of product placement on TV-induced tourism: Korean TV dramas and Taiwanese viewers. *Tourism Management*, *32*(4), 805–814.

Tuan, Y. (1974). *Topophilia: A study of environmental perception, attitudes and values*. Englewood Cliffs: Prentice-Hall.

Tzanelli, R. (2004). Constructing the 'cinematic tourist': The 'sign industry' of the Lord of the Rings. *Tourist Studies*, *4*(1), 21–42.

Tzanelli, R. (2013). *Heritage in the digital era: Cinematic tourism and the activist cause*. London: Routledge.

Urry, J. (2002). *The tourist gaze: Leisure and travel in contemporary societies*. London: Sage.

Van Es, & Reijnders, S. (2016). Making sense of capital crime cities: Getting underneath the urban façade on crime-detective fiction tours. *European Journal of Cultural Studies*, 1–19.

Watkins, H., & Herbert, D. (2003). Cultural policy and place promotion: Swansea and Dylan Thomas. *Geoforum*, *34*(2), 249–266.

Wattanacharoensil, W., & Schuckert, M. (2016). Reviewing Thailand's master plans and policies: Implications for creative tourism? *Current Issues in Tourism*, *19*(10), 1045–1070.

Waysdorff, A., & Reijnders, S. (in press). Destination: *Game of Thrones*. On the role of imagination in film tourism. *Participations*, *14*(1).

Weng, X. (2008). The decline of Hong Kong film industry. Retrieved on 12 July, 2016 from http://jmsc.hku.hk/hkstories/content/view/688/8530/1/0/

Wong, C., & McDonogh, G. (2001). Consuming cinema: Reflections on movies and marketplaces in contemporary Hong Kong. In G. Matthews & T. Lui (Eds.), *Consuming Hong Kong (pp. 81–116)*. Hong Kong University Press.

Yan, G., & Santos, C. A. (2009). 'China forever': Tourism discourse and self-orientalism. *Annals of Tourism Research*, *36*(2), 295–315.

Yen, C., & Croy, C. (2016). Film tourism: Celebrity involvement, celebrity worship and destination image. *Current Issues in Tourism*, *19*(10), 1027–1044.

Yoon, Y., Kim, S., & Kim, S. S. (2015). Successful and unsuccessful film tourism destinations: From the perspective of Korean local residents' perceptions of film tourism impacts. *Tourism Analysis*, *20*(3), 297–311.

Part I
Histories and Current Developments

Chapter 2
Imagining Tourism and Mobilities in Modern India Through Film

Jennifer Laing and Warwick Frost

Abstract Film allows an audience to imagine what travel and movement might potentially be like. This not only includes sights, attractions and experiences but extends to the possible impacts that travel might have on a person. This latter idea encompasses the concept of travel to a specific place being transformative. In the past, India was often represented in film in historical terms. However, in recent times, there has been a trend towards showing India and Indian culture in modern terms, characterised by the contrasts between the old and the new. Such changes also extend to cinematic representations of the mobility of the Indian diaspora. This chapter explores such issues through an analysis of recent films involving modern India. Three films are examined as case studies. The first two consider Westerners journeying to India. These are *The Darjeeling Limited* (2007) and *The Best Exotic Marigold Hotel* (2011). The third film, *UnIndian* (2015), considers mobilities and the Indian diaspora. All three films represent different images of modern India and have underlying themes of travel as transformative and life changing.

Keywords India • Film tourism • Transformation • Diaspora • Mobility

2.1 Introduction: From Colonial to Contemporary Representations of India

For most of the twentieth century, the image of India represented in cinema was historical. In the 1930s, Hollywood produced a number of highly successful 'Empire films', including *The Lives of a Bengal Lancer* (1935), *The Charge of the Light Brigade* (1936) and *Gunga Din* (1939). These films were popular in that they promoted pro-British sentiment as the political situation in Europe deteriorated and acted as surrogate 'Westerns' at a time when films about the American frontier were out of favour. Due to cost constraints, all were filmed around Lone Pine in California (Frost and Laing 2015; Richards 2001).

J. Laing (✉) • W. Frost
La Trobe University, Melbourne, VIC, Australia
e-mail: Jennifer.Laing@latrobe.edu.au; W.Frost@latrobe.edu.au

© Springer Nature Singapore Pte Ltd. 2018

S. Kim, S. Reijnders (eds.), *Film Tourism in Asia*, Perspectives on Asian Tourism, DOI 10.1007/978-981-10-5909-4_2

Hollywood returned to nineteenth-century India in the 1950s, as part of a trend towards bigger budget historical epics. Popular films included *Kim* (1950), *King of the Khyber Rifles* (1954) and *Bhowani Junction* (1956). Made after Indian independence in 1947, they depicted a world that no longer existed of the British Raj and an India of a century before. Similarly, another surge in the 1970s/1980s comprised historical films including *The Man Who Would Be King* (1975), *Gandhi* (1982) and *A Passage to India* (1984) (Richards 2001).

This focus on the past – to the virtual exclusion of the present – occurs throughout twentieth century Western cinematic representations of Asia. Whilst India is a major example of this phenomenon, it can also be seen with other Asian countries such as Thailand in *The King and I* (1956) and China in *55 Days at Peking* (1963). These two examples were filmed in Hollywood and Spain, respectively, and had Western actors made up to play the key Asian roles. Whilst we recognise that historical films are an important and fascinating genre and that they do influence travel, we argue that in constantly emphasising a romanticised imperial past, Western filmmakers ignored the economic and social changes leading up to the twenty-first century being dubbed the Asian Century.

It is only recently that the Western representation of Asia in film has changed. Most twenty-first century films about India are now set in modern times. Accordingly, they tend to explore the issues and paradoxes of modernising India, of economies, societies and customs in transition. In this chapter, our aim is to analyse three recent films and their representations of travel and modern India, particularly how the Western tourist experience and the mobility of the Indian diaspora are portrayed. The three films are the American *The Darjeeling Limited* (2007), the British *The Best Exotic Marigold Hotel* (2011) and the Australian/Indian co-produced *UnIndian* (2015). The three films were chosen as essentially Western productions, representing Western interaction with modern India and taking a largely comedic approach rather than that of a serious 'message' film.

2.2   The Influence of Film on Travel

Cinema is important in creating expectations about both destinations and the act of travelling. Reijnders argues that it leads to the construction of *places of imagination*, where 'in the head and heart of the fan or tourist ...the fascination begins which provides the motivation to visit the locations. That is precisely where the transitional moment takes place, the instant when the world of the imagination coincides with – or possibly contrasts with – physical reality' (Reijnders 2011, p. 234). Whilst Macionis and Sparks – and others – identified the prime motivation for film tourists was 'to see the scenery and landscape in real life' (2009, p. 97), there has been growing recognition that the story, characters, settings and atmosphere contribute profoundly to audience engagement and tourist motivation. Kim and Richardson found that 'the level of emphatic involvement with film characters can affect the perceptions viewers have of the place depicted' (2003, p. 222). Similarly, Beeton explained 'we view movies through ourselves in such a way to gain some personal meaning' and 'we put ourselves in the story, sights, sounds and emotions of the movie' (2005, p. 229). Frost went even further, arguing 'projecting striking visual images is rarely sufficient to carry a successful production … scenery is just a background'; instead the key appeal 'for the audience of potential tourists is these storylines present a "promise" of what might occur if they were to travel to the locations featured' (2010, p. 723).

Popularity and repetition also encourage this sense of connection between audiences and characters. In a study of Korean television drama, Kim found that many regular viewers developed a 'parasocial connection', whereby they began 'experiencing feelings of intimacy with the characters as if they were a close friend' (2012, p. 389). Similarly, Peters et al. (2011) found that there was a strong relationship between repeated watching of films – so that they became favourites of the individual viewer – and the decision to visit the destination featured.

The influence of film may be especially profound where a person has not travelled to that place, such that 'any images they have of it are inherently imagined' (Cherifi et al. 2014, p. 190). This may lead to *naïve images* that are less complex than those resulting from an actual visit and may be either romanticised or unduly harsh on a destination or its people (Cherifi et al. 2014). As di Cesare et al. (2009) found, films may create and confirm destination images and in some cases even completely change the image held by the viewer.

Mobility narratives in films allow audiences to imagine what travel and movement might potentially be like, through the sights, attractions and experiences depicted on screen, even where they don't involve tourism per se. Migrant mobilities are an example of non-tourist travel, resulting in diaspora communities that have been uprooted to new parts of the world and communities that may be constantly moving (Coles and Timothy 2004; Hall 2005). Increasingly, tourism is being understood 'within the framework of temporary mobility … [which] allows us to see tourism within a wider social context over the life span of individuals as well as to gain a greater appreciation of the constraints that prevent or limit mobility' (Hall 2005, p. 132).

The Indian diaspora around the globe, assessed at between 20–25 million and the third largest in the world (Bandyopadhyay 2008; Khorana 2014), offers film-makers a ready-made audience for stories that reflect their experiences, whether made by Bollywood (Bandyopadhyay 2008) or in the countries in which they have settled. For Western audiences, interactions with diaspora communities offer some knowledge and familiarity with exotic cultures. Indian migration, for example, has led to the spread of Indian cuisine around the globe, albeit sometimes modified for local Western tastes (Frost and Laing 2016). For tourists, food is a major part of the appeal of travel to India, though the reality is that a constant diet of Indian cuisine leads to nostalgic cravings to return to Western treats (Falconer 2013).

2.3   Film Tropes of Tourism and Mobility

The influence of film also extends to the possible impacts that the travel might have on a person. This encompasses the expectation that travel will be *transformative* (Frost 2010; Laing and Frost 2012, 2017). Research into the effects of tourism on individuals has included concepts as diverse as a rite of passage (Matthews 2014), a cross-cultural exchange (Dillette et al. 2016), a healing or therapeutical process (Higgins-Desbiolles 2003) or an opportunity for self-actualisation, even personal change (McGehee and Santos 2005; Noy 2004; Saunders et al. 2018). As personal transformation through travel is a common cinematic trope, this often engenders a belief amongst potential tourists that *their* travel will change *their* lives (Frost and Laing 2015; Frost and Laing 2018).

Another relevant common cinema trope is that of the traveller being a stranger in a strange land and accordingly having unsettling and dissonant experiences. For the viewer this affirms ideas that travel will be adventurous and stimulate personal development. Best (2009) notes this for films regarding Asian-Western encounters. In his study of Japanese travellers to Australia, there were 'narratives of dislocation, personal and physical, and of diverse desire set in iconic landscapes at once both alluring and alienating' (Best 2009, p. 129).

In regard to India, Lozanski (2013, p. 46) noted that 'much travel to India is informed by – if not directly overlapping with poverty tourism' and visitors expected to encounter beggars, a motif that is centre stage in many historical films as well as the Oscar winning film *Slumdog Millionaire* (2008). Films also often suggest that tourists have a much richer and interactive relationship with residents than might be ordinarily the case. In contrast, a study of travellers to India by Hottola (2014) found a lack of cross-cultural encounters, even amongst independent tourists. Instead, meaningful contact with locals was rare and was mainly confined to interactions with those employed in service roles in tourism, such as taxi drivers, souvenir sellers and accommodation staff. The recent rise of Bollywood films projects a different image of modern India, though it must be recognised that these are made primarily for viewing by the Indian domestic and diaspora markets (Bandyopadhyay 2008; Josiam et al. 2015).

2.4   Modern India and Indians on Film

In line with this literature, our aim is to explore how modern India is portrayed in films in terms of characters and experiences. Instead of iconic scenery, our interest is in the tensions of modernity and how they are projected as affecting travellers. The differences between India and the West are central to our study, and we seek to examine how the dissonance and disruption of travel and mobility are represented. The first two films we examine consider Westerners journeying to India. These are *The Darjeeling Limited* and *The Best Exotic Marigold Hotel*. The third film,

UnIndian, focuses on the Indian diaspora in Australia. For all three films, we undertake a *narrative analysis*, treating the films as texts and interpreting what they present about tourism and mobility, linked to other relevant sources and literature. All three films represent different images of modern India and Indians and have underlying themes of travel as transformative and life changing.

2.4.1 *The Darjeeling Limited (2007)*

Three American brothers, still mourning the death of their father, travel together through India. They board the Darjeeling Limited, a famed luxury tourist train – invented for the film – but inspired by similar tourist railways in India. The trip is arranged by the eldest, Francis (Owen Wilson), who has been in a motorcycle accident, and annoys the other two by wanting to make all the decisions. Unbeknown to the other two, he has organised for the brothers to visit their mother (Anjelica Huston), who is now a nun living in the Himalayas. The middle brother Peter (Adrien Brody) is at a crossroads of his life, unable to make a commitment to his girlfriend despite the impending birth of his first child, whilst the youngest brother, Jack (Jason Schwartzman), is an unsuccessful writer who has ended an unhappy relationship. The film is essentially a quest, with Francis pleading 'I want us to become brothers again like we used to be and for us to find ourselves and bond with each other. Can we agree to that? … I want us to make this trip a spiritual journey where each of us seek the unknown, and we learn about it. Can we agree to that?' In the end, this happens but quite differently than the brothers originally imagined.

On board the train, the brothers interact with two Indian railway employees: Rita the Steward (Amara Khan) and the Chief Steward (Waris Ahluwalia). This is suggestive of the contention of Hottola (2014) that most tourist encounters are with hospitality staff rather than ordinary locals. Whilst colonial era films might suggest to viewers that the Indian staff will be servile, even comical, that is not the case in this film. Both Rita and the Chief Steward come over as strong and intelligent, and the humour generated is at the expense of the Westerners. Jack has a quick fling with Rita, but when he seeks her out again – expecting that she will be available for him – she firmly tells him that she is no longer interested. When the brothers' behaviour becomes too excessive, the Chief Steward ejects them from the train. They offer him more money, but he refuses it. They are bewildered; as privileged Westerners they cannot believe that their money will not buy them whatever they want.

Money is no object to the brothers. They tote expensive Louis Vuitton luggage rather than backpacks, although they symbolically discard the bags at the end of the film when they run to catch the train. Jack has been living in a luxury Paris hotel, whilst Francis has the funds to pay for a personal assistant to come along on the trip and explains that he is 'gonna place an updated schedule under our doors every morning of all the spiritual places and temples that we need to see and expedite hotels and transportation and everything'. Eventually they are thrown off the train due to various misdemeanours such as an escaped snake and are left to their own devices when the PA leaves in a fit of pique. Leaving the train removes them from the protective bubble that they have built through their wealth and cultural background and leaves them exposed to life in the raw.

At this stage the film suddenly takes a serious turn, and India becomes real to the three hapless brothers. Wandering along, they come to the rescue of three young boys who have fallen into an irrigation ditch. Through selflessly diving in, two are rescued, but one boy drowns. The devastated brothers carry the body to the boy's father (Irrfan Khan) in a nearby village. There they are invited to attend his funeral, and unlike their father's funeral, which we do not see on screen and which they and their mother appear to have missed, the funeral ceremony in India is a visceral and heartbreaking ritual, where genuine emotions are expressed, and the body is unashamedly centre stage rather than hidden away. It is the funeral that their father should have had and they needed to experience and allows them to come to terms with their various life problems, including their relationship with their mother. With the death of the boy, the brothers experience tremendous guilt, even though they risked their lives to save him. Whereas up to this stage, India has been presented as quirky through a fictional train journey, the audience are now presented with both the reality of death and the abject poverty of the village.

Following this cathartic experience, the three brothers work together to put their lives in order. They do find their mother, but she once again abandons them. Nonetheless, they now function better and have clearer aims for when they return home. Furthermore – and importantly for viewers considering travel – they are all enchanted by India. As Peter summarises it 'I love the way this country smells. I'll never forget it. It's kind of spicy'. Before they return home, they decide to have another attempt at taking the famous tourist train journey through India. Symbolically, this time they throw away their expensive luggage in order to catch it.

It is notable that Howard's (2012) qualitative study of contemporary Himalayan travellers reveals that a number of the people he met were inspired to visit India through watching *The Darjeeling Limited*. One of his participants stated (p. 137): 'I saw this movie at the end of high school and ever since I wanted to go to India. I wanted to ride trains, end up in strange, random places and weird situations, wear the funky outfits and you know, have a spiritual adventure, just like in the film. The music, the colours, it all really captivated me at I guess an impressionable age'. For a Western film, it certainly provides a vision of India unlike anything seen previously.

2.4.2   *The Best Exotic Marigold Hotel (2011)*

A group of retired English people move to India to live permanently in the eponymous hotel. They are motivated by various reasons, including the cheap cost of living, particularly healthcare, a desire not to end their days in a retirement home and the attempt to find love. Sonny, the young hotel manager (Dev Patel), explains that his dream is to 'outsource old age! And it is not just for the British, there are many other countries where they don't like old people too!' The cast is full of established names from British theatre and film, including Dame Maggie Smith, Dame Judi Dench, Tom Wilkinson and Bill Nighy, and is designed to appeal to nostalgia, not just for colonial British India but for the various roles that these stars have had over the years. It is also part of a wave of British films aimed at the grey market (Dolan 2016), which depict older women as strong and resourceful rather than victims, including *Calendar Girls* (2003) and *The Love Punch* (2013). Interestingly, it spawned a television reality show, *The Real Marigold Hotel* (2016), where British celebrities, including former *Doctor Who* Sylvester McCoy and Miriam Margolyes, explore what it would be like to retire in India.

The Marigold Hotel is not, despite its advertising, particularly luxurious. This is a shock to the English at first, but gradually the delights of India take over, and the group of new residents mostly enjoy a sense of camaraderie with each other and the gracious hospitality of Sonny. Some like Evelyn (Judi Dench) are instantly prepared to be open to new experiences in India. As she observes: 'Initially you're overwhelmed. But gradually you realize it's like a wave. Resist, and you'll be knocked over. Dive into it, and you'll swim out the other side'. Others will never understand it, notably Jean (Penelope Wilton), who dislikes the food, endlessly complains and just wants to return home again, leading to her husband Douglas (Bill Nighy) engaging in an exasperated outburst: 'All you give out is this endless negativity, a refusal to see any kind of light and joy, even when it's staring you in the face'. In contrast to his wife, Douglas loves India, filling his days with excursions to temples and other historical sites. The expectation watching the film is that eventually India will bring them together again, but this is not the case, and they separate. In the closing scene, Douglas is portrayed as transformed. Finally abandoning wearing his European suits, he dresses casually and rides a motorbike around Jaipur, mimicking the look and behaviour of Sonny.

Graham (Tom Wilkinson) is the only one of the group to have visited India previously. Indeed he grew up there and becomes an unofficial mediator for the others. Gradually it is revealed that he was sent home to England as a teenager for having an affair with an Indian boy. He has returned to find his lost love and ask for forgiveness. He also has a terminal disease, and his death and funeral remind the others of their looming mortality. Muriel (Maggie Smith) is initially portrayed as a horrible racist, who has only come for a cheap operation. Whilst recuperating, she slowly changes, making friends with a cleaning woman who is an Untouchable. Through their hesitant encounters, we learn that Muriel was once a housekeeper, but she was fired for being old and now desperately needs meaning in her life. The film is thus a series of cameos showing different transformations, as people come out of their shells, face their fears and learn to cope with change and different environments. As such, it presents a positive message of old age and the continual ability of people to adapt, even in the twilight of their years. It also suggests a different attitude to ageing across cultures. Whereas Britain has largely wiped its hands of these people, India welcomes the elderly with respect.

A parallel plot involves Sonny and his struggles to achieve his ambitions and represents the tensions between the old and the new ways in India. His mother wants him to leave the hotel and focus on a high-status profession like his brothers.

Accordingly, she pushes to sell the hotel to developers. Sonny wants to prove himself by making the hotel a success. He also wants to marry Sunaina (Tena Desae), but they face opposition from both their families. His mother insists that she can arrange a much better marriage. The elderly Britons provide encouraging advice to Sonny – acting as surrogate uncles and aunts – and eventually Sonny wins through.

There is however a disturbing undertone in terms of the modern India represented in this film. It is curiously old-fashioned. India is a place for self-discovery and personal growth (mostly of outsiders), but it is also apparently a nation of people who *need help* and are endlessly obliging and grateful for the advice given to them by these English migrants (Lalwani 2012). When it appears that the hotel will fold, British ingenuity saves the day. Muriel examines the books and discovers that the hotel is solvent but just needs a practical co-manager to keep an eye on things. The film ends with the residents, except for Jean, agreeing to stay on and the business-like Muriel co-managing the hotel with the flamboyant Sonny, a post-colonial fantasy where the British return to India and save the day.

2.4.3 UnIndian (2015)

A co-production between Australia and India, funded in part by Tourism New South Wales, this film traded on the name of former Australian Test cricketer and fast bowler Brett Lee as the romantic male lead, as well as 'the recent emergence of Indians as an ethnic community of significance in contemporary multicultural Australia' (Khorana 2014, p. 254). Whilst cricket attracts a huge fan base in India and foreign cricketers are generally feted, Lee's fame was exceptional, even by Indian standards, and the deep connection he has with the country is acknowledged, as well as his blond good looks, broad smile and outgoing nature. Lee has multiple Indian sponsorships for products and a charitable foundation in India called Mewsic, which aims to get disadvantaged youth involved in music. In addition, Lee had written the lyrics for and recorded a song *You're the One for Me* in 2006 with an Indian female singer, which made number two on the Indian charts and appeared in the Bollywood movie *Victory* (2008).

Lee was thus an obvious choice for the lead in a film that was designed to appeal to both markets, capitalising on the parasocial relationship that his fans have with him through the media, creating feelings of intimacy (Kim 2012). As he wrote in his autobiography: 'India is a place where I feel different. In Australia people may recognise, idolise or hate me. They do in India as well, but the level of obsession and the sheer volume of people make it difficult to comprehend. It's in India I really feel like a superstar' (Lee 2011, p. 204). Even the film's director, Anupam Sharma, noted that Lee 'considers himself half Indian and always greets everyone with a namaste. He believes in a lot of Indian values, customs and traditions' (TNN 2016).

Whilst sport was used in *Bend it Like Beckham* (2002) to explore the tension experienced by Indian diaspora youth in engaging with the culture in their new countries, cricket is surprisingly pushed to the background in *UnIndian*. Instead, the plot revolves around the love story of two Sydneysiders – Will (Lee) an Australian teacher of English as a second language and Meera (Tannishtha Chatterjee), a single mother who says she is 'Not Australian enough for Australia yet. Not Indian enough for India anymore'. The plot is often clichéd, with Meera's mother in particular essentially a caricature, desperate for her to marry an Indian doctor and critical of her Western clothing. However, Meera's role is written as a strong-willed woman who balances bringing up her daughter with a career as Marketing Manager of Cochlear, the company that makes hearing implants (and an investor in the film).

Meera is initially wary of Will, having met him at a Holi celebration at Will's university, the famous festival of colours. She throws coloured powder over him and his white blazer, and he is entranced, both with the vibrancy of the traditional Indian celebration and Meera's vivacity. A series of chance encounters follow, intriguingly all built around Indian diaspora culture. This is in part explained by Will's best friend and housemate TK (Arka Das), an Indian who has lived in Sydney since he was a young boy. TK is thus the cultural mediator, drawing Will into this other culture. Apart from the Holi festival, TK involves Will and Meera in his online Indian cooking show. An additional cultural meeting place is the cricket club, where Meera's mother drags her daughter along to meet the Indian doctor.

Will teaches his students how to speak Aussie English ('Bloody oath mate', 'What a bloody ripper') but realises that he needs to learn how to woo an Indian woman. He asks TK 'Educate me. How do I pick up an Indian chick?' TK is incensed but gradually comes to understand that Will is sincere, whilst Meera is intrigued at his openness and uncomplicated nature. The film thus assists in a greater appreciation of the difficulties but also the enrichment that cross-cultural relationships bring and sends a message that modern young Indians are forging new paths and traditions in their new countries but not turning their backs on their heritage at the same time.

2.5 Discussion and Conclusion

In examining these films, four major themes are identified within these cinematic representations of modern India, Western travel within India and the mobility of the Indian diaspora. The first is that in these modern films, India and Indian culture are portrayed as attractive and accessible to Westerners. It is not surprising that both *The Best Exotic Marigold Hotel* and *The Darjeeling Limited* were set in Rajasthan, a region that already attracts Western tourists and is famous for its historic temples, palaces and towns. In utilising such a setting, the abject poverty and congestion associated with the major Indian cities are avoided. Similarly, *UnIndian* is not only set in Sydney but in the leafy green middle-class parts near the coast, rather than the poorer and more troubled inland Western Sydney. In this fantasy version of Sydney, little is said of racism, but rather the focus is on the struggles of the Indian migrants to fashion a new hybridised version of what it means to be Indian.

This positive portrayal of India extends beyond scenery to culture. Indian life is shown in all three films as vibrant and colourful. Indeed, in the two films regarding Western tourists, there is a deliberate contrast between sunny and colourful India and the cold and drabness of scenes in New York and England. Indian religion is depicted as attractive and welcoming, even in the funeral scenes in *The Best Exotic Marigold Hotel* and *The Darjeeling Limited*. In all three films, prominence is given to Indian cuisine and the importance of communal sharing of food.

The second theme involves the tensions arising from Indian modernisation. The clash between the old and the new is a feature in all three films. In *The Best Exotic Marigold Hotel*, references to work in call centres and clearing older areas for apartment development are balanced with plot points relating to the continuing custom of arranged marriages and the higher status attached to professional employment over commercial work. These last two elements of Indian society also feature strongly in *UnIndian*, and these are matched with Meera's desire to have a career and choose her own husband. In the quixotic *The Darjeeling Limited*, these issues are not so prominent, though instead a strong contrast is made between the modernising cities and the backwater village, seemingly unchanged for centuries. The hint is there that the small boys in the village will grow up to reject the struggle of village life and move to the city and a more Western lifestyle.

The third theme relates to the argument of Hottola (2014) that few tourists experience the real India, but rather their interactions are with service staff in hospitality and transport. This is certainly portrayed in *The Best Exotic Marigold Hotel* and *The Darjeeling Limited*. In the former the encounters are with the hotel staff and in the latter the train crew. However, as the Westerners stay longer, they start to have broader encounters, most noticeably when the brothers in *The Darjeeling Limited* visit the rural village. In *UnIndian*, cross-cultural encounters are quite different. In this film the focus is on meeting places and mediators, mixing the Indian diaspora and mainstream Australian society. Examples include the cricket club and the friendship between TK and Will that starts at primary school. This means that when Meera attends social events – even when they are primarily Indian as in the Holi festival – there are non-Indians present and participating with enthusiasm.

The fourth theme concerns transformation, and this brings us back to the literature on film and travel. As is commonly depicted in films, travel involves an emotional as well as a physical journey. The core characters start out discomfited and apprehensive. They are in a new cultural environment, and they need to step outside their protective bubble. In doing so they take risks, but the rewards – often unsought or unintended – involve change. Not everybody wants this, for example, Jean in *The Best Exotic Marigold Hotel* rejects India and returns home to England as soon as she can. Furthermore, the transformation may be dangerous, even involving death. Nonetheless, the great majority of travellers in these films are depicted as benefitting from their mobility. As distinct from twentieth century portrayals, modern India in these films is shown as an opportunity for personal transformation.

References

Bandyopadhyay, R. (2008). Nostalgia, identity and tourism: Bollywood in the Indian diaspora. *Journal of Tourism and Cultural Change, 6*(2), 79–100.

Beeton, S. (2005). *Film-induced tourism*. Clevedon: Channel View.

Best, G. (2009). Desire, incidental tourism and the other: Being Japanese in three Australian film landscapes. *Tourism Review International, 13*(2), 129–138.

Cherifi, B., Smith, A., Maitland, R., & Stevenson, N. (2014). Destination images of non-visitors. *Annals of Tourism Research, 49*, 190–202.

Coles, T., & Timothy, D. J. (Eds.). (2004). *Tourism, diasporas and space*. Routledge.

di Cesare, F., D'Angelo, L., & Rech, G. (2009). Films and tourism: Understanding the nature and intensity of their cause-effect relationship. *Tourism Review International, 13*, 103–112.

Dillette, A. K., Douglas, A. C., Martin, D. S., & O'Neill, M. (2016). Resident perceptions on cross-cultural understanding as an outcome of volunteer tourism programs: The Bahamian Family Island perspective. *Journal of Sustainable Tourism*, 1–18.

Dolan, J. (2016). 'Old Age' films: Golden retirement, dispossession and disturbance. *Journal of British Cinema and Television, 13*(4), 571–589.

Falconer, E. (2013). Transformations of the backpacking food tourist: Emotions and conflict. *Tourist Studies, 13*(1), 21–35.

Frost, W. (2010). Life-changing experiences: Film and tourists in the Australian outback. *Annals of Tourism Research, 37*(3), 707–726.

Frost, W., & Laing, J. (2015). *Imagining the American West through film and tourism*. London/New York: Routledge.

Frost, W., & Laing, J. (2016). Cuisine, migration, colonialism and diasporic identity. In D. Timothy (Ed.), *Heritage cuisines* (pp. 37–52). London/New York: Routledge.

Frost, W., & Laing, J. (2018). Long-distance walking in films: Promises of healing and redemption on the trail. In C. M. Hall, Y. Ram, & N. Shoval (Eds.), *The Routledge handbook of walking studies*. London: Routledge.

Hall, C. M. (2005). Reconsidering the geography of tourism and contemporary mobility. *Geographical Research, 43*(2), 125–139.

Higgins-Desbiolles, F. (2003). Reconciliation tourism: Tourism healing divided societies! *Tourism Recreation Research, 28*(3), 35–44.

Hottola, P. (2014). Somewhat empty meeting grounds: Travelers in South India. *Annals of Tourism Research, 44*, 270–282.

Howard, C. (2012). Horizons of possibilities: The telos of contemporary Himalayan travel. *Literature and Aesthetics, 22*(1), 131–155.

Josiam, B. M., Spears, D. L., Pookulangara, S., Dutta, K., Kinley, T. R., & Duncan, J. L. (2015). Using structural equation modeling to understand the impact of Bollywood movies on destination image, tourist activity, and purchasing behavior of Indians. *Journal of Vacation Marketing, 21*(3), 251–261.

Khorana, S. (2014). From 'de-wogged' migrants to 'rabble rousers': Mapping the Indian diaspora in Australia. *Journal of Intercultural Studies, 35*(3), 250–264.

Kim, S. (2012). Audience involvement and film tourism experiences: Emotional places, emotional experiences. *Tourism Management, 33*(2), 387–396.

Kim, H., & Richardson, S. (2003). Motion picture impacts on destination images. *Annals of Tourism Research, 30*(1), 216–237.

Laing, J., & Frost, W. (2012). *Books and travel: Inspiration, quests and transformation*. Bristol: Channel View.

Laing, J., & Frost, W. (2017). Nature and well-being: Explorer travel narratives of transformation. In J. Chen & N. Prebensen (Eds.), *Nature tourism: A global perspective* (pp. 11–22). London: Routledge.

Lalwani, N. (2012). The best exotic Marigold Hotel: An exercise in British wish-fulfilment. *The Guardian*. Retrieved February 28, 2017, from https://www.theguardian.com/commentisfree/2012/feb/27/best-exotic-marigold-hotel-compliance.

Lee, B. (2011). *Brett lee: My life*. Sydney: Ebury.

Lozanski, K. (2013). Encountering beggars: Disorienting travelers? *Annals of Tourism Research, 42*, 46–64.

Macionis, N., & Sparks, B. (2009). Film-induced tourism: An incidental experience. *Tourism Review International, 13*(2), 93–101.

Matthews, A. (2014). Young backpackers and the rite of passage of travel: Examining the transformative effects of liminality. In G. Lean, R. Staiff, & E. Waterton (Eds.), *Travel and transformation* (pp. 157–171). London/New York: Routledge.

McGehee, N. G., & Santos, C. A. (2005). Social change, discourse and volunteer tourism. *Annals of Tourism Research, 32*(3), 760–779.

Noy, C. (2004). This trip really changed me: Backpackers' narratives of self-change. *Annals of Tourism Research, 31*(1), 78–102.

Peters, M., Schukert, M., Chon, K., & Schatzmann, C. (2011). Empire and romance: Movie-induced tourism and the case of the Sisi movies. *Tourism Recreation Research, 36*(2), 169–180.

Reijnders, S. (2011). Stalking the count: Dracula, fandom and tourism. *Annals of Tourism Research, 38*(1), 231–248.

Richards, J. (2001). Imperial heroes for a post-imperial age: Films and the end of empire. In S. Ward (Ed.), *British culture and the end of empire* (pp. 128–144). Manchester/New York: Manchester University Press.

Saunders, R., Weiler, B., & Laing, J. (2018). Life-changing walks of mid-life adults. In C. M. Hall, Y. Ram, & N. Shoval (Eds.), *The Routledge handbook of walking studies*. London: Routledge.

TNN (2016, August 14). Brett Lee goes 'desi' for UnIndian. *The Times of India*. Retrieved December 24, 2016, from http://timesofindia.indiatimes.com/entertainment/hindi/bollywood/news/Brett-Lee-goes-desi-for-UnIndian/articleshow/53684806.cms

Chapter 3
Film Tourism in India: An Emergent Phenomenon

Joydeep Biswas and Glen Croy

Abstract India is the largest film producer in the world, annually producing more than 1800 films. Unsurprisingly, efforts to exploit film tourism have emerged at a national, state and business level. This chapter enhances the understanding of India's film tourism and efforts to establish a film tourism destination. These efforts included greater coordination between national and state governments to attract and facilitate film production. Added is a tourism strategy emphasis, in part, on film tourism, coupled with the added use of film in tourism promotions. Film tourism is an evident phenomenon around the country, though mostly at film studio locations. Other accounts provide limited support for an effect on tourist demand and lack of film-specific tourist attractions. However, the vast Indian film presence indicates subtle roles in tourism, establishing or reinforcing perceptions and stirring motivations to visit the range of pre-established attractions across the country. Future research on the subtle role of film on India's tourists and the filmic representations of the people is recommended. Overall, film tourism in India has much emerging potential.

Keywords Government • Indian cinema and film industry • Film parks • Film tourists • Slum tourism

J. Biswas (✉)
KIIT School of Management (KSOM), KIIT University, Bhubaneswar, India
e-mail: joydeep.biswas@ksom.ac.in

G. Croy
Department of Management, Monash Business School, Monash University,
Caulfield East, VIC 3145, Australia

Oxford School of Hospitality Management, Oxford Brookes University, Oxford, UK
e-mail: glen.croy@monash.edu

© Springer Nature Singapore Pte Ltd. 2018
S. Kim, S. Reijnders (eds.), *Film Tourism in Asia*, Perspectives on Asian
Tourism, DOI 10.1007/978-981-10-5909-4_3

3.1 Introduction

India is one of the largest national film producers in the world, with more than 1800 films produced annually (Central Board of Film Certification [CBFC] 2015). While to most outsiders, the Indian film industry is equivalent to Hindi films (colloquially known as Bollywood) and centered in Mumbai, actually, Indian films are produced and shot across the country. A key reason for the diversity of Indian films is the linguistically and culturally diverse Indian audiences. Prominent film studios like R K Studio, Film City, and Mehboob Studio are located in Mumbai. However, as films are shot across the country, there are many film studios outside Mumbai, for example, Ramoji Film City (Hyderabad), MGR Film City (Chennai), and Noida Film City (New Delhi) (India Marks 2016) (Fig. 3.1). To indicate scale, since 2005, Ramoji Film City, a 675-hectare studio, has been the largest in the world (Guinness World Records 2016). Unsurprisingly, regional film productions tend to shoot in their own states or regions due to audience connection and budgetary constraints. For example, Bengali films are often shot in West Bengal (Bengal Tourism 2016). As such, top film shooting locations are present all over the country, including Goa, Himachal Pradesh, Jammu and Kashmir, Tamil Nadu, West Bengal, Rajasthan, Uttar Pradesh, Punjab, and Kerala (Arora 2015; Bharti 2015; Bolly Locations 2016; Nandni 2014; Shoot Rajasthan 2016; Sudan 2015; Tripigator 2015). Moreover, main cities, including Kolkata and Delhi, have their own historical legacies and many films are based on characters from these cities (Singhania 2015).

Furthermore, there is an emerging use of India for internationally produced films. Some internationally high-profile films set in India include *Le Fleuve* (1951), *Gandhi* (1982), *Octopussy* (1983), *A Passage to India* (1984), *The Jungle Book* (1994), *The Bourne Supremacy* (2004), *Slumdog Millionaire* (2008), *Eat Pray Love* (2010), *The Best Exotic Marigold Hotel* (2011), *Life of Pi* (2012), *The Lovers* (2013), and *The Second Best Exotic Marigold Hotel* (2015). In addition to these, there are a number of films shot, though not set in India, including *A Mighty Heart* (2007), *The Dark Knight Rises* (2012), and *Zero Dark Thirty* (2012). The large number of films shot and being blessed with scenic locations, historic and cultural diversity, and unique flora and fauna has potential to make India a prominent film tourism destination, in addition to an international film production destination.

Efforts to exploit the potential of film tourism in India have emerged at a national, state, and business level. Nonetheless, while India is the largest producer of films in the world, there has been scant research on how this affects tourism to and in the country. Of the studies on India's film tourism, the focus has been on a depiction or meeting of "the other," generally privileged international tourists and poor slum-living Indians (Hottola 2002; Favero 2007; Diekmann and Hannam 2012; Privitera 2015). Other studied perspectives of Indian film tourism include the effect of Bollywood productions on the overseas travel of Indian travelers (Mohsin and Ryan 2007; Josiam et al. 2015), the role of films in domestic tourism (Chatterjee et al. 2008), and the use of video-film promotion (as compared to fictional film) by the National Tourism Ministry (Poonia and Chauhan 2015). Bharti (2015) has started

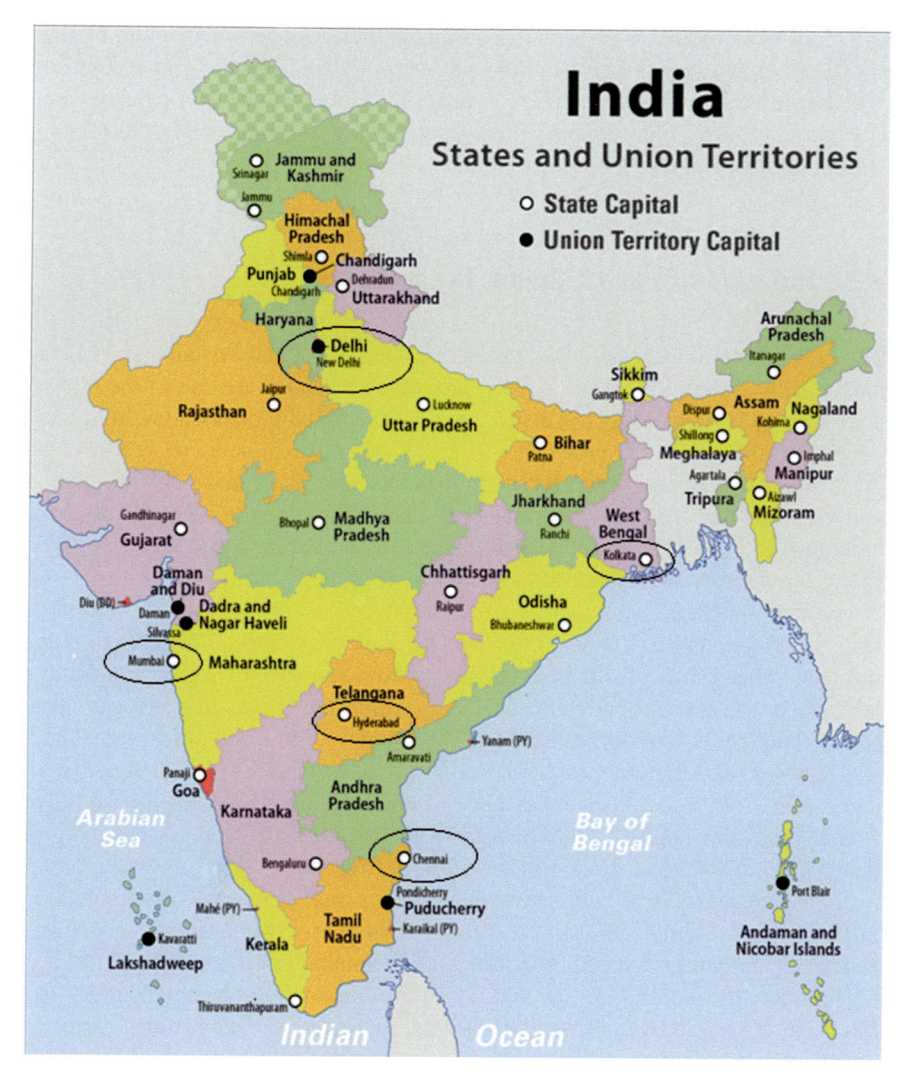

Fig. 3.1 Film locations across Indian States and Union Territories (Source: Wikipedia Creative Commons 2016)

the discussion on the future prospects of film tourism in India. However, it can be noted that there are very limited studies that have been conducted on film tourism related to Indian films. The chapter aims to fill this gap by generating an understanding of India's film tourism and identifying the efforts to improve India's position as a film tourism destination.

To fill the gap, the conceptual chapter will be presented in six parts. First, a background to India's film and cinema industry, and second, an overview of government support for filming in India is provided. Third, an overview of India's tourism trends and ministry initiatives is presented. Fourth, the Indian Government's film tourism efforts are highlighted. Fifth, the emergence of an Indian film tourism phenomenon is given with respect to film tourism destinations, film tourists, and a critique of the emerging outbound film tourism. Finally, suggestions for future research and conclusions are presented.

3.2   India's Film and Cinema Industries

The Indian film industry produces the largest number of films annually and has the most cinema admissions, and its gross box-office revenues are one of the highest across the globe. According to CBFC (2015), 1827 digital Indian feature films were issued certification in the year 2014–2015. In India, the policies related to films, press, broadcasting, and information are administered by Ministry of Information and Broadcasting (MI&B). The Ministry is also responsible for international cooperation in the field of mass media, films, and broadcasting and interacts with its foreign counterparts on behalf of Government of India.

As mentioned earlier, Indian films are produced across the country and in as many as 40 languages (CBFC 2015). This heterogeneity makes Indian film unique in many ways. Films of different languages cater to different regional audiences with distinct tastes and preferences. Hence, within the Indian film industry, each regional market is evolving differently. The diversity also leads to greater interaction between language markets in the form of remakes and talent exchanges. Hindi cinema, or Bollywood, contributes most to the overall Indian cinema in terms of revenue and thus holds an important position. In 2014–2015, Hindi cinema produced 297 of the total 1827 feature films (CBFC 2015). The other significant regional language films, with growing audiences and increasing film outputs, in 2014–2015 are Tamil (297 films), Telugu (284 films), Malayalam (195 films), Kannada (159 films), Bengali (154 films), and Marathi (127 films) (CBFC 2015).

Traditionally Indian film has had family-run production houses like Yash Raj Films, Dharma Productions, and RK Films. However, in recent times, with the advent of new film production houses like Anurag Kashyap Films, the filmmaking approach has become more corporate-like. Furthermore, India's foreign direct investment (FDI) regulations now permit 100% FDI under the film production automatic route (Ministry of Commerce and Industry [MC&I] 2000). This trend has bolstered overseas studios starting joint ventures with Indian producers. For example, Walt Disney has a controlling stake in UTV Software Communications (Walt Disney Studios 2012), Viacom has a joint venture with Network 18 (Viacom18 2016), and Fox Star has collaborated with Dharma Productions (Bhushan 2015; Deloitte 2016). These production houses are coproducing films with Indian producers and producing films on their own.

Much of the corporate transition and international investment is driven by the potential in Indian cinema. Indian cinemas sell approximately 2.5 billion tickets every year (McCarthy 2014; Statista 2015). This is the highest in the world followed by China, the United States of America (USA), and Mexico. However, due to lower ticket prices and screen penetration rates, the size of Indian film box-office revenue is considerably smaller than that of the USA and China (Cain 2015; Deloitte 2016; FICCI-KPMG 2015; KPMG-FICCI 2016; Kohli-Khandekar 2016). Specifically, in 2015 the domestic box-office revenue for Indian cinema was US$1.6 billion, which is nearly one-seventh that of highest grossing US box-office revenue of US$11.1 billion (Motion Picture Association of America 2015; Statista 2015). The total revenue for Indian film industry was slightly higher at US$2.2 billion, as domestic box-office revenues constitute only 74% of total revenues (Deloitte 2016). In addition to box-office takings, there has been growth in cable and satellite rights, merchandise and in-cinema advertising, mobile content (including music downloads), and music soundtrack rights (KPMG-FICCI 2016). Nevertheless, the Indian box office is expected to reach US$3.8 billion by 2020, growing at 10.5% per annum (Deloitte 2016; KPMG-FICCI 2016).

The continued revenue growth can be attributed to a range of factors. These factors include increasing per capita income and a growing middle class, aggressive promotion by production houses, saturation cinema film releases (e.g., *Bajrangi Bhaijaan* (2015) was simultaneously released in 4200 cinemas (KPMG-FICCI 2016)), overseas releases, new differentiated content in local languages, foreign-made films (e.g., in 2014–2015 289 foreign feature films were certified, including 255 from the USA (CBFC 2015)), and ancillary revenues like in-cinema advertising (Deloitte 2016; KPMG-FICCI 2016). The Indian film and cinema sectors have also benefited from a rise in the number of multiplex screens across the country. The increase in multiplexes has had a multiplicative effect by being coupled with rising ticket prices. Multiplexes accounted for approximately 26% of total screens in 2015. However, India still has a low screen density of nearly six screens per million as compared to 126 per million in the USA (KPMG-FICCI 2016). The density of multiplex screens is highly varied across the country. On one hand, metropolitan cities seem to be nearing saturation, where, on the other hand, Tier-II and Tier-III cities have a lot of untapped potential (Deloitte 2016). Therefore, in the short term, growth in box-office sales is anticipated to slow due to infrastructure bottlenecks. In part to overcome resource challenges and exploit the opportunities, there is some consolidation among cinema owners with Inox Leisure Limited acquiring Calcutta Cine Private Limited in 2007, Fame India Limited in 2013, and Satyam Cineplexes Limited in 2014 (INOX Leisure Limited 2016). Similarly PVR Limited also acquired Cinemax India Limited in 2012 and DT Cinemas in 2016 (PVR Cinemas 2016).

3.3 Government Support for Filming in India

As indicated earlier, the majority of filming in India is completed by and for the domestic film industry. In addition, given the scale of the sector, there have been many benefits including employment creation, increased tax collection, and infrastructure investment (Bharti 2015; EY and LA India Film Council 2014). Hence, it is not surprising that the Indian Government has taken various steps to further the domestic film industry and attract more international film production. The added advantages of collaborative international production are technological and cultural exchanges. Some of the steps taken by MI&B are coproduction treaties (India Film Commission [IFC] 2016), allowing 100% foreign direct investment (FDI) for films (MC&I 2000), financial incentives such as tax breaks (EY and LA India Film Council 2014; Natarajan and Kadhane 2015) and encouraging state governments to be "film friendly" (MI&B 2016a, n.p.).

India now has coproduction agreement treaties with 11 countries: Brazil, Canada, China, France, Germany, Italy, New Zealand, Poland, South Korea, Spain, and the UK (IFC 2016). Some of the mutual benefits of these treaties are allowing film units of a country temporary residence, importing technical equipment free of import duties and taxes, tax incentives, and joint entries to international film festivals. These benefits are also provided to international films if they meet certain conditions including minimum spending in India and showing India in an "appropriate" light. The combination of 100% FDI and treaties actually appears to have enhanced joint-production arrangements (MC&I 2000), no doubt partially to use local knowledge in overcoming burdensome approval and access processes (elaborated below). The greater collaboration with international filmmakers has resulted in Indian film producers being exposed to global technology and processes of filmmaking, thereby enhancing the domestic industry further. It also means increased investments for the Indian film industry from many global partners (Deloitte 2016; FICCI-KPMG 2014).

The governments, at national and state level, are incentivizing film production through grants, rebates, tax credits, and tax holidays, usually with conditions (EY and LA India Film Council 2014; Natarajan and Kadhane 2015). Some prominent examples of state government incentives to promote international film shooting are:

- Rajasthan: Films that are 75% shot in Rajasthan and given U certificates receive 100% exemption from the domestic entertainment tax for one year.
- Jammu and Kashmir: Waiver of taxes for filmmakers while they shoot in the state.
- Himachal Pradesh: 100% exemption from the domestic entertainment tax to filmmakers shooting in the state.

To further encourage state governments to be film friendly, the MI&B has recently instituted the "Most Film Friendly State" award as part of the National Film Awards. "The award aims to sensitize the Indian states towards film tourism, advantages of bringing in foreign filmmakers to shoot in their state, promote India as a preferred filming destination as well as encourage the growth of the film industry" (MI&B 2016a, n.p.). Criteria for the award include development of skills and capabilities, state and national government coordination, and reducing the film production and administrative bottlenecks (MI&B 2016b).

Nonetheless, even with the recent policy changes and incentives offered, as indicated above, India still presents many challenges for film production, largely encap-

Table 3.1 Trend of foreign tourist arrivals and foreign exchange earnings

Year	Foreign tourist arrivals (in millions)	Foreign exchange earnings (million US$)
2010	5.77	$14,193[P]
2011	6.31	$16,564[P]
2012	6.58	$17,737[P]
2013	6.97	$18,445[PR]
2014	7.67	$20,236[PR]
2015	8.03	$21,071[PR]

Source: Ministry of Tourism (2016)
[P] provisional, [PR] provisionally revised estimate

sulated by not having a National Film Commission to facilitate film production. Furthermore, a National Film Commission would also work to attract more film production to the country (EY, FICCI, Film Television Producers Guild of India, and LA India Film Council 2015; EY and LA India Film Council 2014). Unfortunately, the lack of a National Commission has resulted in regulatory and administrative bottlenecks, including the need for numerous approvals from various agencies and limited informational and operational assistance available during film production process. As such, the National Government took note and, in November 2015, the MI&B set up the Film Facilitation Office (Ramachandran 2015), to facilitate a single-window clearance for filmmakers and promoting film production in India. The Film Facilitation Office was proposed to assist film producers in getting required approvals, provide them with information on available shooting locations, and assist access to film facilities at all stages of production (Film Facilitation Office 2015; MI&B 2016c). In November 2016, it was also announced that the Film Facilitation Office film shooting permissions process was to be moved online (Lal 2016).

3.4 Indian Tourism Trends and Ministry Initiatives

The tourism sector is reportedly one of India's largest employment generators (Ministry of Tourism [MoT] 2016). There has been an increase in international as well as domestic tourists in recent years. The number of foreign tourists arriving in India in 2015 was 8.03 million, which was a growth of 4.7% over the previous year (MoT 2016). The estimate of domestic tourism was close to 1290 million tourists in 2014 registering a growth of 13% over 2013 (MoT 2016). Recent international tourist arrivals and foreign exchange earnings trends are depicted in Table 3.1, with growing arrivals and overall spending.

The MoT is the National Government agency to formulate policies and programs for development and promotion of tourism in India. The aim of these policies is to boost tourism around the country and make tourism an engine for inclusive economic growth. To achieve these aims, the Ministry collaborates with other stakeholders in the sector including various central ministries, agencies, the state governments, union territory administrations, and representatives of the private sector. The Director General of Tourism, under the MoT, has 20 domestic field offices and 14 overseas offices to promote India in international tourism markets. The overseas destinations where Indian tourism has offices include the USA, Australia, Singapore, Japan, China, Europe, West Asia, and South Africa (MoT 2016).

India's strategy is to promote India as a year-round destination, attracting tourists with all types of interests, and ensure repeat visitation. This is being implemented through ten tourism experience domains for development and promotion (MoT 2016). These ten tourism domains are cruise tourism, adventure tourism, medical tourism, wellness tourism, golf tourism, polo tourism, meetings, incentives, conferences and exhibitions (MICE), ecotourism, film tourism, and sustainable tourism. The MoT has supported these domains through the creation of task forces, committees, boards, and funding. Noticeably, one of these domains is film tourism, which will be the focus of the rest of the chapter.

3.5   Government Initiatives for Film Tourism

As part of the initiatives, the MoT has issued guidelines to state governments and union territory administrations for extending financial support to promote film tourism. According to the guidelines, the MoT supports up to five films in a given state or union territory with US$3000 based upon the films' exposure and potential to promote tourism (MoT 2012). All the same, for those films seen to gain even higher exposure, further investment is made. For example, the Oscar-winning film *Life of Pi* was partly shot in India, mainly in Puducherry and Munnar. In this case, the MoT and Puducherry State Government launched a "Land of Pi" campaign to promote Puducherry and Munnar as tourist destinations (MoT 2013). The campaign included "Land of Pi" posters at India's international tourism offices, it was featured on the "Incredible India" and Puducherry and Kerala tourism websites, Puducherry and Kerala tourist buses were "Land of Pi" branded, and short promotional films were uploaded to social media networks.

Furthermore, in an endeavor to establish India as a preferred filming destination, the MoT and MI&B signed a Memorandum of Understanding in 2012 to promote "Cinemas of India" as a sub-brand of "Incredible India" (MI&B 2012, 2013). The collaborative sub-brand "Cinemas of India" has been promoted at various international film festivals including the International Film Festival of India (Goa), European Film Market (Berlin), and the Cannes Film Festival (MoT 2016). The collaboration is aimed at developing synergy between tourism and the film industries and providing a platform for partnerships between Indian and international filmmakers.

3.6 Emergence of an Indian Film Tourism Phenomenon

As noted in the introduction, film production is widespread across India. With the numerous film locations and population of India, it may be anticipated that there are many film tourism destinations. However, beside the film parks, such as Ramoji Film City, there are not many specific film tourism destinations.

Nonetheless, there have been instances where Indian film shooting locations have seen an increase of tourists visiting them. An example of a location that has seen increased tourist visitation after being featured in a film is Pangong Lake, Ladakh (a contested region in north India bordering China). The lake was shown in climax scene of Hindi film *Three Idiots* (2009). In the *region*, there was a 194% increase in tourist arrivals between 2009 (79,087) and 2011 (179,491) (Angmo and Dolma 2015). Nevertheless, no dedicated film tourism activities are conducted at the lake, and it must be noted that tourist arrivals vary with incursions and natural events like floods. Another example of a location reportedly benefitting from film is Goa. The Chairperson of the Goa Chamber of Commerce and Industry stated that the joint promotion of Goa with the film *Dil Chahta Hai* (2001) boosted tourism (*Deccan Herald* 2010). Again, no specific film tourism activities are conducted at some of the well-known *Dil Chahta Hai* shooting locations, like Chapora Fort. Tessitore et al. (2014) also observed a positive impact on travel intentions to India after being shown prominently in reality television shows, though in their experimental design could not demonstrate changes in behavior. Instead of location based, India's film tourism appears to be largely studio based.

From an international tourist perspective, Mumbai provides India's film tours, though these are small in number (TripAdvisor 2016a). All of these appear to be day tours, indicating a supplementary activity to visiting the city and country. As part of these tours, tourists are taken to shooting studios and often provided an experience of live filming (Bollywood Tours 2016a; Mumbai Film City Tours 2016; World of Bollywood Tours and Travels 2016). The activities also include the history of Bollywood, access to makeup rooms and behind-the-scene technical areas, performing in a studio, dubbing voices over film scenes, and buying memorabilia (Bollywood Tours 2016a; Mumbai Film City Tours 2016; SJ Studios 2016). As previously indicated, similar tours are also conducted at other film studios like Ramoji Film City (Hyderabad) (Ramoji Film City 2016).

Many of the other filmed sites around India appear to be used in films due to their preexisting recognition and fame, such as palaces, forts, and temples (Bharti 2015; Shoot Rajasthan 2016). For instance, the twelfth-century fort city of Jaisalmer, Rajasthan, attracted further attention after prominently featuring in *Sonar Kella* (1974, released under the English title *The Golden Fort*) and reportedly attracted Bengali tourists (the film's language and main audience) (Shackley 1996, in error referred to *The Golden City*). However, she also notes that most tourists to the area were "exclusively motivated by the opportunity to take a camel safari" (p. 215). Nonetheless, many cities and regions in the country are promoted by explicit mention of films, such as West Bengal and Goa (Bengal Tourism 2016; Tripigator 2015).

Additionally, in the international context, other media audiences are introduced to India through film (e.g., *Eat Pray Love*: Kerr 2010; Moore 2010).

Another example of the mediated introduction to the destination is depicted in slums (Diekmann and Hannam 2012; Privitera 2015). *City of Joy* (1992, Kolkata) and *Slumdog Millionaire* (2008, Mumbai) have been especially noted for their influential portrayal of Indian poverty (Hutnyk 1996; Mendes 2010; Diekmann and Hannam 2012). Consequently, many western tourists have a desire to gaze on poverty (Lisle 2004), resulting in slum tourism. Tour operators have responded by designing slum tours (Diekmann and Hannam 2012; Reality Tours and Travel 2016). There is a lot of similarity between the way slum tours are conducted and the way these slums are portrayed in films (Diekmann and Hannam 2012). So much so that some film tour operators have also started combining slum and film tours (Bollywood Tours 2016b).

Overall, there do not appear to be many film destinations in India. Anecdotally, it is reported that domestic tourists visit *some* prominent locations after films' release. However, there are no film tourist activities being conducted at these sites. Presently, there is limited or no research establishing a causal relationship between increased visitation to these sites and depiction in films. All the same, it can be argued that at least some international tourists pursue activities in India based on images created by films (Favero 2007; Mendes 2010; Diekmann and Hannam 2012). Additionally, as demonstrated in Bandyopadhyay and Morais' (2005) study of American representations of India in tourism media, these images may well boost Indian tourism, though they also bolster the stereotypes of India as a land of spirituality, royalty, and poverty (also see Bandyopadhyay 2012).

As indicated by the limited number of film destinations and even tours, there are very limited indications of purposeful international film tourists in India. Those tourists that do participate in tours and visit the film parks, based upon Croy and Heitmann's (2011) film tourist typology, are indicatively casual film tourist. For these casual tourists, film appears to have played a role in the decision, though they are having a relatively shallow film experience (TripAdvisor 2016a, b). The user reviews, however, largely by domestic tourists, do not indicate the activities and tours influenced the decision to visit the destination, rather it appeared the film tour activities were a secondary attraction (Leiper 1990). Unsurprisingly, the research literature on purposeful film tourists in India is very limited (Bharti 2015).

Chatterjee et al. (2008) are an exception and noted that while films, along with other popular cultural resources, have an impact on choice of destination for urban Bengali domestic travelers, they are not prominent. Chatterjee et al. (2008) further reported that it is the culturally preferred exotic places, depicted in films, which can influence visitation interest. Essentially, as is being more argued in the wider film tourism literature (e.g., see Croy 2011; Kim and Kim online), India's films appear to have a broader spectrum of influence on images and motivations than a direct effect on behavior. Indian films are raising awareness, and reengaging audiences with India's attractions (Chatterjee et al. 2008; Angmo and Dolma 2015), including nostalgic colonialist populations (Bandyopadhyay 2012). Indeed, slum tourism effects of *City of Joy* and *Slumdog Millionaire* demonstrate the intimately interconnected nature of film and tourism in India that makes it difficult to discern specific influences (Privitera 2015).

Increasingly, though small in number, Indian films are being shot overseas and in a greater diversity of countries (Lewis 2009; Mohsin and Ryan 2007). Given the unique nature of Indian films, where drama is interwoven with song and dance sequences, it is mainly the song and dance sequences that are shot in foreign locations. Josiam et al. (2015) investigated the influence of these films on international destination images for Indian travelers, their proposed activities, and their purchasing behaviors. The study indicated that the films did affect Indians' overseas travel decisions; however clarified, this appeared to be largely due to greater levels of film engagement leading to greater destination awareness. Hence, while not a primary motivator, film played an important role in adding potential destinations to the awareness set, reflecting the argument above.

Some instances of increased Indian travel to international destinations have been reported. For example, the impact of Yash Chopra's Hindi films on Indian tourism to Switzerland is a common example (Stephens 2012). Chopra's impact on Swiss tourism has been recognized with a statue erected in his honor at Interlaken, as well as by naming a train and hotel suite after him (Chandrasekhar 2016). Between 2006 and 2015, Indian tourist nights in Switzerland increased from about 300,000 to 600,000 (Federal Statistical Office 2016), indicating some influence on tourist demand. Another example, this time a specific film, is *Krrish* (2006), which was largely shot in Singapore, taking advantage of that country's film production subsidies (EY and LA India Film Council 2014). Lewis (2009) and EY and LA India Film Council (2014) then reported that Indian visitation rose 1 million, from 6 million to 7 million, immediately after its release. However, this was a vast overstating of the change in visitation. Indian visitation to Singapore increased 13.6% in 2007 (the largest of a big market in that year), though only to 748,728 tourists (Singapore Tourism Board 2014). Between 2007 and 2015, the increase in 2007 was the largest from India (besides the 2010 post-financial crisis recovery). By the end of 2015, Indian visitation to Singapore in 2015 was 1.01 m (Singapore Tourism Board 2016). Indicatively, *Krrish* may have influenced Indian visitation to Singapore, though how the film influenced decisions is unknown.

Overall, film tourists in India appear to be small in number, and where they exist, not strongly motivated by film. All the same, films shot in India and Indian films shot overseas appear to be widening perceptions of internationally available destinations and, through this, influencing potential travel decisions.

3.7 Future Research and Conclusions

There is an emerging body of research on Indian film tourism, though India is vastly underrepresented in relation to the number of films and the size of the audience. This chapter has provided an insight into the Indian film and tourism sectors and efforts to exploit the film tourism opportunities. Nonetheless, many other areas of future research are needed. Three key research areas are prominent after undertaking this review. First, understanding the effects of Indian films on audiences' tourism image formation, motivations, decisions, and behaviors (see also Chapter 15 in this volume). Particularly, do Indian films just raise awareness of locations to visit and become a secondary attraction, or, are there other roles they play for potential travelers? Second, critical research is needed on the representation of India and Indians in particular through international films, and the potential of unrepresentative stereotypes, and consequences this may have for the people, place, and tourists. The third prominent area of future research, in terms of policy and challenges, is that of film, tourism and government collaboration, coordination, and administration. Of particular interest would also be the coordination between national, state, and regional levels of government and industry.

In conclusion, India is one of the largest film nations in the world and would therefore be expected to be one of the largest film tourism destinations. In this context, the objective of this chapter was to generate an understanding of India's film tourism and efforts undertaken to exploit these opportunities. The film industry is large and diverse, geographically and linguistically. The film sector is also growing, particularly with domestic consolidation of cinemas and on the production side with recently facilitated domestic-international partnerships. Furthermore, state and regional support and incentives are assisting filming around the country. Coupled with the growing film sector, domestic and international tourism demand and revenue are growing. Seeing the potential of these two sectors, the government has initiated film tourism efforts. These are beginning to be realized through greater levels of national and state government collaboration and recognition. However, it was highlighted that there are still limited film-specific tourism attractions in India and unsurprisingly limited evidence of film-specific tourists. All the same, small numbers of film attractions and tourists likely underplay the role that India-based films have on tourism. This was revealed in the outbound influences of overseas-shot Indian films and indicative effect on tourists' decisions. Overall, the changes to coordination between national and state-level governments through the Film Facilitation Office should enable greater realization of international film opportunities and international exposure. Joined with the growing domestic film sector, coordination with the MoT, and growing economic prosperity, there is great potential for emerging Indian film tourism opportunities.

References

Angmo, T., & Dolma, K. (2015). Mass media and film induced tourism in Leh District, Jammu and Kashmir, India. *International Journal of Science and Research, 4*(9), 301–305.

Arora, G. (2015). 13 locations in India made famous by Bollywood movies. *Scoop Whoop.* Retrieved November 20, 2016, from https://www.scoopwhoop.com/entertainment/locations-made-famous-bollywood-movies/#.fujfxlozh

Bandyopadhyay, R. (2012). 'Raj Revival' tourism. *Annals of Tourism Research, 39*(3), 1718–1722.

Bandyopadhyay, R., & Morais, D. (2005). Representative dissonance. *Annals of Tourism Research, 32*(4), 1006–1021.

Bengal Tourism. (2016). *Film shooting location & spots in West Bengal, India with Bengal Tourism*. Bengal Tourism. Retrieved November 29, 2016, from http://www.bengaltourism.in/film-cinema/shooting-spots-location.html

Bharti, P. (2015). Films and destination promotion: An exploratory study. *International Journal of Travel and Tourism, 8*(1/2), 50–61.

Bhushan, N. (2015). Fox's Star India and Bollywood studio Dharma productions announce 9 film deal. *The Hollywood Reporter*. Retrieved November 16, 2016, from http://www.hollywoodreporter.com/news/fox-s-star-india-bollywood-800028

Bolly Locations. (2016). Bollywood movies shot in India. *Bolly Locations*. Retrieved November 20, 2016, from http://www.bollylocations.com/countries/India

Bollywood Tours. (2016a). Zee green studio private tour. *Bollywood Tours*. Retrieved December 5, 2016, from http://www.bollywoodtours.in/packages/zee-green-studio-private-tour/

Bollywood Tours. (2016b). Bollywood with slum tour. *Bollywood Tours*. Retrieved December 29, 2016, from http://www.bollywoodtours.in/packages/bollywood-with-slum-tour/

Cain, R. (2015). India's film industry: A $10 billion business trapped in a $2 billion body. *Forbes*. Retrieved December 11, 2016, from https://www.forbes.com/sites/robcain/2015/10/23/indias-film-industry-a-10-billion-business-trapped-in-a-2-billion-body/#52f0df2c70d2

Central Board of Film Certification [CBFC]. (2015). *Annual Report from April 2014 to March 2015*. Retrieved November 15, 2016, from http://cbfcindia.gov.in/html/uniquepage.aspx?unique_page_id=30

Chandrasekhar, A. (2016). Swiss honour Indian filmmaker Yash Chopra with statue. *Swissinfo*. Retrieved December 11, 2016, from http://www.swissinfo.ch/eng/tourism-ambassador_swiss-honour-indian-filmmaker-yash-chopra-with-statue/42128072

Chatterjee, D., Das, A., Ganguli, F., & Dey, L. (2008). Domestic tourism of the urban Bengalis: A shared observation of the culture. *Tourism, 56*(1), 75–91.

Croy, G., & Heitmann, S. (2011). Tourism and film. In P. Robinson, S. Heitmann, & P. U. C. Dieke (Eds.), *Research themes for tourism* (pp. 188–204). Oxon: CABI.

Croy, W. G. (2011). Film tourism: Sustained economic contributions to destinations. *Worldwide Hospitality and Tourism Themes, 3*(2), 159–164.

Deccan Herald. (2010). 'Dil Chahta Hai' saved Goa tourism post 9/11 gloom. *Deccan Herald*. Retrieved December 29, 2016, from http://www.deccanherald.com/content/105091/dil-chahta-hai-saved-goa.html

Deloitte. (2016). *Indywood the Indian Film Industry*. Retrieved November 11, 2016, from https://www2.deloitte.com/content/dam/Deloitte/in/Documents/technology-media-telecommunications/in-tmt-indywood-film-festival-noexp.pdf

Diekmann, A., & Hannam, K. (2012). Touristic mobilities in India's slum spaces. *Annals of Tourism Research, 39*(3), 1315–1336.

EY and LA India Film Council. (2014). *Made in India: Attracting and incentivizing film productions*. Retrieved November 18, 2016, from http://www.mpaa-india.org/og-content/uploads/documents/1423834141made_in_india_final.pdf

EY, FICCI, Film Television Producers Guild of India and LA India Film Council. (2015). Unleashing the power of film tourism: The First step. *Film Television Producers Guild*. Retrieved November 29, 2016, from http://filmtvguildindia.org/pdf/Unleashing%20the%20Power%20of%20Film%20Tourism_the%20first%20step.pdf

Favero, P. (2007). 'What a wonderful world!': On the 'touristic ways of seeing', the knowledge and the politics of the 'culture industries of otherness. *Tourist Studies, 7*(1), 51–81.

Federal Statistical Office. (2016). *Swiss tourism statistics 2015*. Switzerland: Federal Statistical Office. Retrieved December 29, 2016, from https://www.bfs.admin.ch/bfs/en/home/statistics/tourism.assetdetail.1347712.html

FICCI-KPMG. (2014). *The stage is set*. Indian Media and Entertainment Industry Report 2014. Retrieved December 11, 2016, from https://assets.kpmg.com/content/dam/kpmg/pdf/2014/03/FICCI-Frames-2014-The-stage-is-set-Report-2014.pdf

FICCI-KPMG. (2015). #shootingforthestars. *Indian Media and Entertainment Industry Report 2015*. Retrieved December 11, 2016, from https://assets.kpmg.com/content/dam/kpmg/pdf/2015/03/FICCI-KPMG_2015.pdf

Film Facilitation Office. (2015). *Shooting of Feature Films, Reality TV Show and or Commercial TV Serials by Foreign Film Makers in India*. Retrieved November 11, 2016, from http://mib.nic.in/writereaddata/documents/Film_In_India_-_Step-by-Step_Guide.pdf

Guinness World Records. (2016). Largest film studio. *Guinness World Records*. Retrieved November 22, 2016, from http://www.guinnessworldrecords.com/world-records/largest-film-studio

Hottola, P. (2002). Touristic encounters with the exotic west: Blondes on the screens and streets of India. *Tourism Recreation Research, 27*(1), 83–89.

Hutnyk, J. (1996). *The rumour of Calcutta*. London: Zed Books.

India Film Commission [IFC]. (2016). Film treaties. *India Film Commission*. Retrieved November 18, 2016, from http://indiafilm.org/policies/film-treaties/

India Marks (2016). Indian film cities. *India Marks*. Retrieved November 22, 2016, from http://www.indiamarks.com/indian-film-cities/

INOX Leisure Limited. (2016). INOX Leisure limited is the diversification venture of the INOX Group into entertainment. *INOX Leisure Limited*. Retrieved November 11, 2016, from https://www.inoxmovies.com/Corporate.aspx?Section=1

Josiam, B. M., Spears, D. L., Pookulangara, S., Dutta, K., Kinley, T. R., & Duncan, J. L. (2015). Using structural equation modeling to understand the impact of Bollywood movies on destination image, tourist activity, and purchasing behavior of Indians. *Journal of Vacation Marketing, 21*(3), 251–261.

Kerr, F. (2010). *'Eat, Pray, Love': Now try the holiday*. Condé Nast Traveller. Retrieved December 29, 2016, from http://www.cntraveller.com/recommended/honeymoons-romantic-breaks/eat-pray-and-love/viewall

Kim, S., & Kim, S. (online). Segmentation of potential film tourists by film nostalgia and preferred film tourism program. *Journal of Travel & Tourism Marketing*, pp. 1–21.

Kohli-Khandekar, V. (2016). India's box office growth runs into a screen problem. *Business Standard*. Retrieved December 11, 2016, from http://www.business-standard.com/article/companies/india-s-box-office-growth-runs-into-a-screen-problem-116011801209_1.html

KPMG-FICCI. (2016). *The future: Now streaming*. Indian Media and Entertainment Industry Report 2016. Retrieved November 11, 2016, from http://aibmda.in/FICCI-KPMG-M&E-Report-2016.pdf

Lal, N. (2016). Foreign film permissions to go online. *The Times of India*. Retrieved November 11, 2016, from http://timesofindia.indiatimes.com/entertainment/hindi/bollywood/news/Foreign-film-permissions-to-go-online/articleshow/55580598.cms

Leiper, N. (1990). Tourist attraction systems. *Annals of Tourism Research, 17*(3), 367–384.

Lewis, D. (2009). The location power of Bollywood. *The Location Guide*. Retrieved December 11, 2016, from http://www.thelocationguide.com/blog/2009/11/the-location-power-of-bollywood/

Lisle, D. (2004). Gazing at ground zero: Tourism, voyeurism and spectacle. *Journal for Cultural Research, 8*(1), 3–21.

McCarthy, N. (2014). Bollywood: India's film industry by the numbers. *Forbes*. Retrieved November 11, 2016, from http://www.forbes.com/sites/niallmccarthy/2014/09/03/bollywood-indias-film-industry-by-the-numbers-infographic/#2960cb357bf0

Mendes, A. (2010). Showcasing India unshining: Film tourism in Danny Boyle's 'Slumdog Millionaire'. *Third Text, 24*(4), 471–479.

Ministry of Commerce and Industry [MC&I]. (2000). *Expansion of list of industries/activities eligible for automatic route for Foreign Direct Investment (FDI), Non Resident Indian (NRI) and Overseas Corporate Body (OCB) investment*. Ministry of Commerce and Industry, Department of Industrial Policy and Promotion, Government of India. Retrieved November 11, 2016, from http://dipp.nic.in/English/policy/changes/press2_00.htm

Ministry of Information and Broadcasting [MI&B]. (2012). Incredible India campaign to be promoted through cinemas of India Ministry of I&B and Tourism sign memorandum of understanding (MoU) MoU to promote "India as Filming Destination". Ministry of Information and Broadcasting, Government of India. Retrieved November 11, 2016, from http://pib.nic.in/newsite/erelease.aspx?relid=91510

Ministry of Information and Broadcasting [MI&B]. (2013). *Annual report*. Ministry of Information and Broadcasting, Government of India. Retrieved November 11, 2016, from http://mib.nic.in/writereaddata/documents/annualreport2012-13-english.pdf

Ministry of Information and Broadcasting [MI&B]. (2016a). *Minister inaugurates India pavilion at Cannes Film Festival*. Ministry of Information and Broadcasting. Retrieved November 11, 2016, from http://pib.nic.in/newsite/PrintRelease.aspx?relid=145335

Ministry of Information and Broadcasting [MI&B]. (2016b). *New category award to be conferred at the 63rd National Film Awards in May*. Ministry of Information and Broadcasting, Government of India. Retrieved November 11, 2016, from http://pib.nic.in/newsite/PrintRelease.aspx?relid=134573

Ministry of Information and Broadcasting [MI&B]. (2016c). *Film facilitation office an important step to promote India as filming destination*. Ministry of Information and Broadcasting, Government of India. Retrieved November 11, 2016, from http://pib.nic.in/newsite/PrintRelease.aspx?relid=145335

Ministry of Tourism [MoT]. (2012). *Guidelines for extending financial support to State Governments/Union Territory Administrations for promotion of film tourism*. Ministry of Tourism, Government of India. Retrieved November 11, 2016, from http://tourism.gov.in/sites/default/files/080320121058581_0.pdf

Ministry of Tourism [MoT]. (2013). *Chiranjeevi announces campaign "Land of Pi"*. Ministry of Tourism, Government of India. Retrieved November 11, 2016, from http://pib.nic.in/newsite/erelease.aspx?relid=91510

Ministry of Tourism [MoT]. (2016), *Tourism annual report*. Ministry of Tourism, Government of India. Retrieved November 11, 2016, from http://tourism.gov.in/sites/default/files/Annual%20Rreport%202015-16.pdf

Mohsin, A., & Ryan, C. (2007). Exploring attitudes of Indian students toward holidaying in New Zealand using the Leisure motivation scale. *Asia Pacific Journal of Tourism Research, 12*(1), 1–18.

Moore, M. (2010). In 'Eat Pray Love', Julia Roberts misses the true soul of India. *The Washington Post*. Retrieved December 29, 2016, from http://www.washingtonpost.com/wp-dyn/content/article/2010/08/12/AR2010081203593.html

Motion Picture Association of America. (2015). *Theatrical market statistics*. Retrieved November 11, 2016, from http://www.mpaa.org/wp-content/uploads/2016/04/MPAA-Theatrical-Market-Statistics-2015_Final.pdf

Mumbai Film City Tours. (2016). Dream tour. *Mumbai film city tours*. Retrieved December 9, 2016, from http://mumbaifilmcitytours.com/Details.aspx?ID=108&SID=390

Nandni. (2014). Ten most popular shooting locations of Bollywood. *Maps of India*. Retrieved November 20, 2016, from http://www.mapsofindia.com/my-india/travel/ten-most-popular-shooting-locations-of-bollywood

Natarajan, P., & Kadhane, S. (2015). Tax solace for promoting film tourism: Indian and global perspectives. *Paripex: Indian Journal of Research, 4*(1), 161–164.

Poonia, A. K., & Chauhan, G. S. (2015). A multimodal discourse analysis of select tourism video commercials of incredible India campaign. *International Journal of Tourism and Travel, 8*(1–2), 1–12.

Privitera, D. (2015). Film and the representation of the poverty: Touristic mobilities in developing countries. *Journal of Tourism, Culture and Territorial Development, 6*(4), 269–281.

PVR Cinemas. (2016). The journey so far. *PVR Cinemas*. Retrieved November 11, 2016, from http://www.pvrcinemas.com/aboutus

Ramachandran, N. (2015). India's NFDC to launch film facilitation office. *Variety*. RetrievedNovember 18, 2016, from http://variety.com/2015/film/asia/india-nfdc-to-launch-film-facilitation-office-1201644054/

Ramoji Film City. (2016). Film city tour. *Ramoji Film City*. Retrieved December 9, 2016, from http://www.ramojifilmcity.com/daytour/film-city-tour

Reality Tours and Travel. (2016). Slum tours. *Reality Tours and Travel*. Retrieved December 11, 2016, from http://realitytoursandtravel.com/slum-tour.php

Shackley, M. (1996). Community impact of the camel safari industry in Jaisalmar, Rajasthan. *Tourism Management, 17*(3), 213–218.

Shoot Rajasthan. (2016). *Film locations in Rajasthan, India*. Shoot Rajasthan. Retrieved November 22, 2016, from http://www.shootrajasthan.com/film-shooting-locations-rajasthan.html

Singapore Tourism Board. (2014). International visitor arrivals: Visitor arrivals (2007). *Singapore Tourism Board*. Retrieved December 30, 2016, from https://www.stb.gov.sg/(X(1) S(mwulpkglvgzeozcoxra14bhv))/statistics-and-market-insights/Pages/statistics-Visitor-Arrivals.aspx?AspxAutoDetectCookieSupport=1

Singapore Tourism Board. (2016). International visitor arrivals: Visitor arrivals (2015). *Singapore Tourism Board*. Retrieved December 30, 2016, from https://www.stb.gov.sg/(X(1) S(mwulpkglvgzeozcoxra14bhv))/statistics-and-market-insights/Pages/statistics-Visitor-Arrivals.aspx?AspxAutoDetectCookieSupport=1

Singhania, D. (2015). 19 Bollywood movies that capture India in an amazing way! *Holidify*. Retrieved November 29, 2016, from http://www.holidify.com/blog/bollywood-movies-that-show-india-in-an-amazing-way/

SJ Studios. (2016). Evening surprise Bollywood tour. *SJ Studios*. Retrieved December 9, 2016, from https://www.sjstudiobollywoodtour.com/evening-surprise-bollywood-tour/

Statista. (2015). Leading film markets worldwide in 2015, by number of tickets sold (in millions). *Statista*. Retrieved November 11, 2016, from https://www.statista.com/statistics/252729/leading-film-markets-worldwide-by-number-of-tickets-sold/

Stephens, T. (2012). Giving Swiss film locations some direction. *Swissinfo*. Retrieved December 11, 2016, from http://www.swissinfo.ch/eng/giving-swiss-film-locations-some-direction-/32071506

Sudan, T. (2015). Top 10 filming locations in India. *WIWIGO Blog*. Retrieved November 11, 2016, from https://www.wiwigo.com/blog/top-10-filming-locations-in-india/

Tessitore, T., Pandelaere, M., & Kerckhove, A. (2014). The Amazing Race to India: Prominence in reality television affects destination image and travel intentions. *Tourism Management, 42*, 3–12.

TripAdvisor. (2016a). Movie & TV tours in India. *TripAdvisor*. Retrieved December 29, 2016, from https://www.tripadvisor.com/Attractions-g293860-Activities-c42-t232-India.html

TripAdvisor. (2016b). Ramoji Film City. *TripAdvisor*. Retrieved December 29, 2016, from https://www.tripadvisor.com/Attraction_Review-g297586-d636879-Reviews-Ramoji_Film_City-Hyderabad_Telangana.html

Tripigator. (2015). 9 Favourite Bollywood destinations in Goa you have to visit! *Tripigator*. Retrieved November 20, 2016, from https://www.tripigator.com/blog/9-favourite-bollywood-destinations-in-goa/

Viacom18. (2016). About. *Viacom18*. Retrieved November 16, 2016, from http://www.viacom18.com/about/

Walt Disney Studios. (2012). Disney to acquire controlling interest in UTV software communications limited (UTV) in India. *Walt Disney Studios*. Retrieved November11, 2016, from http://waltdisneystudios.com/disney-to-acquire-controlling-interest-in-utv-software-communications-limited-utv-in-india/

Wikipedia Creative Commons. (2016). India administrative map. *Wikipedia*. Retrieved December 29, 2016, from https://en.wikipedia.org/wiki/File:India_-_administrative_map.png

World of Bollywood Tours and Travels. (2016). Tours and prices. *World of Bollywood Tours and Travels*. Retrieved December 9, 2016, from http://www.wobtat.parichaytheatre.com/tours.html

Chapter 4
Grand View Garden and a History of Chinese Film Tourism

Xiaoyu (Nancy) Zhang and Chris Ryan

Abstract This study presents a general background to film tourism in China. Film tourism is the inevitable result of socio-economic development, especially when consistent with state policies and the development of a consumer-led economy. Based on a representative case study, that of Grand View Garden, we aim to reflect on the development of Chinese film tourism within the past 30 years. Films not only move audiences but can motivate them to see and experience the relevant sites. Additionally, in the Chinese context, film tourism has come to require both local administrations and film industries to make popular films and TV series that can serve as an effective marketing tool to promote destinations in ways consistent with local and national policies.

Keywords Literary tourism • Chinese film tourism • TV series • Grand View Garden

4.1 Introduction

It has been said that film tourism has its roots in literature (Busby and Klug 2001; Iwashita 2003, 2006; Heitmann 2010) and that both films and books can influence tourist behavior (Busby and Klug 2001; O'Connor and Kim 2014). However, tourism studies about the relationship between film tourism and the phenomenon of literary tourism with reference to China still remain relatively scarce (Hao and Ryan 2013). Prior to film and television gaining popularity, mass media was dominated by books, magazines, and newspapers. For example, in the nineteenth century, famous British authors, such as Charles Dickens, would read their novels aloud to

X. Zhang (✉)
Tourism College, Beijing Union University, Beijing, China
e-mail: zhangxiaoyu51@126.com

C. Ryan
The China-New Zealand Tourism Research Unit, Waitako Management School, University of Waikato, Hamilton, New Zealand
e-mail: caryan@waikato.ac.nz

© Springer Nature Singapore Pte Ltd. 2018
S. Kim, S. Reijnders (eds.), *Film Tourism in Asia*, Perspectives on Asian Tourism, DOI 10.1007/978-981-10-5909-4_4

audiences as a form of entertainment, thus acquiring a celebrity status. In that pre-television period, tourists already traveled to the destinations described in books (Beeton 2005), and the Victorian poet, William Wordsworth, was as well known for his books on hiking in the Lake District as for his poetry. Literary works are therefore often a precursor for subsequent film production (Roesch 2009). As an example, a study of 36 popular films found that 42% were adaptations of much-loved novels such as *Harry Potter* and *The Lord of the Rings* (Roesch 2009). Iwashita (2006) also found that prior knowledge of a film's literary precursors was also likely to motivate tourists to visit film-related destinations.

Similar linkages between literature and tourism can be found in China. China has a long history, and literary tourism has existed from at least 207 BC when the Qin Dynasty first unified China. Hu (2016) notes that one of China's oldest books *The Classic of Mountains and Seas* not only recorded Chinese geography, history, animals, plants, minerals, medicine, culture, etc. but also induced people to travel to the destinations described in the book. That work, as a collection of stories and observations on China from about 250 BC to 200 AD, retained an influence even on Chinese feudal society, and its development of its road and canal networks was partly shaped by tourism as people traveled to view the ancient sites. During the Qin and following Han dynasties, land transport was built, extending in all directions, and this provided a convenient way for people to travel. For example, during the Western Han Dynasty (206 BC to 9 AD), the historian, Sima Qian, traveled the whole country, visiting historical sites and collecting legends. He then completed his historical work, *The Records of the Grand Historian (Shiji)* (thought to have been completed about 91 BC), that recorded early Chinese history (Yan 2002). These books guided the later generations to travel, just as did the books of Wordsworth some 1900 years later. Also, as an important foreign policy initiative in this period of the Western Han Dynasty, Zhang Qian's diplomatic mission to Xiyu (the Western Regions) developed the "Silk Road" and accelerated the sharing of food cultures between the Midland and Xiyu (Airey and Chong 2011). After that, many Chinese businessmen exchanged or sold silk and other goods with the West through the Silk Road. Today the Silk Road is one of Xi Jinping's major policy initiatives and is built around the many traditional tourism destinations located on the route such as Xi'an.

During the Tang (618 to 907 AD) and Song Dynasties (960 to 1279 AD), many bureaucrats and scholars, who felt frustrated in their careers or were motivated by religious thought, traveled into the mountain forests to escape and avoid society. Among these were the writers and poets such as Li Bai, Du Fu, Lu You, Liu Zongyuan, Su Shi, etc. (Airey and Chong 2011). For example, Li Bai's travel experiences inspired him to write many famous poems about Chinese mountains and rivers. One of Li Bai's more famous poems is "Climbing Yellow Crane Tower," and the Yellow Crane Tower in Wuhan remains a well-known tourism destination in China, although the current version of the Tower dates from 1981. Thus, many tourist destinations are known because of traditional poems, one example being the leisure experiences represented by early medieval Chinese literati at the Orchid Pavilion in Shanyin, Zhejiang province (Lavallee and Yan 2011).

The purpose of this chapter is to provide a better understanding of Chinese film tourism. The chapter will first provide a brief historical overview of literary and film tourism evolution in China, followed by a representative case study of Grand View Garden. The research site is not only a film set where the famous television series *The Dream of the Red Mansions* (an adaptation of the much-loved Chinese novel of the same name) was shot, but it is also a site with profound cultural and heritage significance due to the care with which the site was constructed. It will then discuss the current and future state of film tourism in China.

4.2 The Historical Background of Development of Film and Tourism Industries in China

In 2004, the Chinese scholars, Liu and Liu (2004), divided the history of Chinese film tourism into three stages: the first stage was from 1896 to 1986, the second phase covered the intervening period from 1986 to the earlier years of the twenty-first century, and the third stage represented the future. For the purpose of this chapter, an amendment is suggested, namely, the first two stages of Liu and Liu (2004) are combined, with the second stage being from 1986 to 2000, and the third stage covering the early years of the twenty-first century until now. Each will now be described in turn.

4.2.1 The First Stage (1896–1986)

In the August of 1896, the first film show in China occurred in Shanghai and was based on imported films. In 1906, the first Chinese film "Dingjunshan" (shot at Beijing Fengtai Photo studio) was shown to an enthusiastic audience, and this event marked the beginning of the Chinese film industry. However, the period from the late Qing Dynasty (the last feudal dynasty of China) to the founding of People's Republic of China in 1949 was a period that included foreign invasions and civil war, and Chinese filmmakers moved to cities such as Hong Kong, while a rump of the industry remained in areas such as Chingqing and Shanghai, with propaganda material being commissioned at times. Later, the years of famine associated with the Great Leap Forward and a minimizing of contacts with the Western world, especially after Mao's dispute with Khrushchev, meant Chinese tourism did not develop during this period (Li 2009). Thus, in the absence of accessible tourism and the hardships being faced by families, there was little linkage between film and tourism until much later in the century.

As an aside, regarding tourism, since the founding of the People's Republic of China in 1949, tourism might also have experienced three eras: that of Mao Zedong (1949–1978), Deng Xiaoping's era (1978–1997), and the Collective Leadership era

(1997 to now). It is only latterly that tourism became an important part of state activities, political life, and national development (Airey and Chong 2011), and combined with the resurgence of Chinese cinema, it might be stated that only in the last two decades has film tourism become an entity in China.

In the first 30 years after the founding of the People's Republic of China, tourism primarily served the needs of political policies and diplomacy (Li 2009). In late 1949, the Overseas Chinese Travel Agency was developed in Xiamen, Fujian province. This was responsible for overseeing Chinese travel to see relatives and go sightseeing (Li and Cao 2006). In 1952, the Asia Pacific Peace Conference was held in China, and after that, more foreigners visited China, and the China International Travel Agency was established in 1954. However, in the 1960s, tourism was paralyzed by the "Cultural Revolution." Even though the tourism service department was developed to provide travel, accommodation, and airline services for foreigners during this period, no one in China called this a "tourism industry." In other words, the travel department was responsible for civic reception but not business or leisure travel. Tourism was not seen as an independent entity, and there was no national tourism policy during this time.

The period of the Deng Xiaoping era from 1978 marks the beginning of the modern Chinese tourism industry due to the implementation of economic reform and an open-door policy (Qu and Tsang 2000). Deng Xiaoping played a pivotal role in national policy making and tourism development, and he believed that the development of international tourism could contribute to foreign exchange earnings. He established a series of economic-oriented policies in place so as to modernize Chinese society and the economy and realized that tourism had a role to play in such policies. Equally, by opening China to foreign visitors, the policy brought China more into the mainstream of international policy making after the years of Mao's isolationist policies.

Nonetheless, while the term "film tourism" would have little meaning to the majority of Chinese in this period, there were films produced that, among other aims, did have the objective of introducing China to a wider audience. Thus, during the latter years of the Maoist period, a number of notable Chinese films were produced and released, such as *Five Golden Flowers* (1959), *Liu Sanjie* (1960), *Ashima* (1964), *Shaolin Temple* (1982), *Romance on Lushan Mountain* (1980), etc. These films referenced the Chinese landscape and culture to advertise the country when shown overseas while confirming a sense of what it is to be Chinese for the domestic audience even as they escaped the still relatively harsh condition of daily life prevalent at that time.

While, by the standards of the early twenty-first century, initial international audiences were relatively small, many offshore visitors came to know Chinese culture and tourism destinations as a result of these films. For example, the first music and landscape story film was created in 1960 in Guilin Guangxi province. Entitled *Liu Sanjie*, the film was based on the personal history of the female singer, Liu Sanjie, who was famous for her good voice and songs (Hou et al. 2010). The songs were of the genre known as *Songs of the Hillsides*, being based on the songs of shepherds and famers and a tradition of song competitions that involved sequential singing and word play. The film is still easily accessible on YouTube.com. As any viewer can see, it features Guilin's beautiful mountains and river landscapes and traditional and ethnic culture. Guilin was one of the earliest cities to develop tourism after the reform and opening up, and Liu Sanjie culture was (at that time) among the first cultural assets to be developed as a specific Guilin-based attraction (Li 2015). Until now, both the film *Liu Sanjie* and the recent large-scale landscape-based production, *Impression of Liu Sanjie* night show on the banks of the Li River, have attracted scores of both national and international visitors to Guilin (Luo et al. 2011).

In the late 2009, The State Council of China issued the "Several opinions on further promotion of both the economic and social development of Guangxi province" and followed this by issuing the "Development planning outline for the construction of Guilin international tourism destination" that was approved by the National Development and Reform Commission in November of 2012 (National Development and Reform Commission 2017). This period of planning has focused on the development and protection of the local culture like *Liu Sanjie* and natural resources, as well as the improvement of basic facilities such as adding more flights and new routes to meet the demands, especially for the ASEAN countries and other main tourist cities at home and abroad (Development planning outline for the construction of Guilin international tourism destination 2017). As a result, over the years, Guilin has become a favorite destination for both Chinese inbound and domestic tourism despite its relatively remote location. Today airlines such as Delta and KLM fly directly to Guilin Liangjiang International Airport.

Another film from this period, *Shaolin Temple*, not only attracted large numbers of tourists at home and abroad but also promoted Kung Fu. Directed by Hsin-yan Chang, it took 2 years to make but sustained a sense of authenticity in the action sequences due to its use of Kung Fu artists rather than actors. It was also Jet Li's first film and has retained a cult following due to that reason. It also attracted more attention when the Russian President Vladimir Putin visited the monastery and was introduced to the monk who allegedly taught his daughter Wushu (Wu 2011). Today Shaolin Temple is a major tourist destination, and many come to study Wushu there, including many foreigners (Cynarski 2012). There is little doubt that the film and the commercial activities of the monastery have attracted and continue to attract tourists. For example, Shaolin Temple developed a large-scale landscape performance "Zen Music Shaolin Grand Ceremony" based on the Chinese traditional culture and Shaolin culture. From the first productions undertaken in 2007–2008, the show attracted about 170,000 national and international visitors (Chen et al. 2008). In a survey-based study of 392 international visitors, Chen et al. (2008) found most visitors were satisfied with the performance, stating they had experienced and learnt about Chinese traditional culture, as well as taking a close look at the martial arts they had seen on the films. The "Story of Kung Fu" has also, for several years, proven to be a popular show for tourists at the Red Theatre, Beijing, and has had over 3000 performances.

The province of Yunnan has also achieved fame through, in part, two classical films, *Five Golden Flowers* and *Ashima*, shot in the 1960s (Wu 2011). The former, directed by Wang Jiayi, takes full advantage of Yunnan's ethnic minorities but fits the *Weltzeitgeist* of the time as the lead character marries a Commune Director to the choral music *Under the Butterfly Spring*. The film title, *Ashima*, refers to the rock of that name in Stone National Forest, a UNESCO World Heritage Site now annually attracting thousands of visitors. In November of 2010, the "Films influence Chinese cultural tourism Awards" were given at the first Chinese international cultural tourism festival. Organized by both the China Tourism Association and Chinese Culture Promotion Society, the top three films were "Shaolin Temple," "Romance on Lushan Mountain," and "Five Golden Flowers," partly selected because of their broad international appeal (China Culture Promotion Society 2017).

These films had different influences on national and international visitors. There is little doubt that one motive for the making of films such as those noted above was to promote a new image of China to an international audience. China was and continues to be aware of the soft power of its culture and its tourism appeal (Li 2009; Dai et al. 2017). On the other hand, the economic shortages of the period from the 1960s to the late 1980s limited the ability of the domestic Chinese population to afford either time or finances for holiday taking, but nonetheless these films provided for many Chinese their first glimpses of Shaolin Kung Fu, Guilin's mountain and river, and Yunnan's minority cultures. The popularity of the films has also meant that they are repeated on television and today are easily accessible over the Internet, and thus their popularity has endured long after they were first produced and continues to attract Chinese tourists to the sites portrayed on the cinema screen. For example, the *Romance on Lushan Mountain* has been shown daily four times a day at the cinema since the film released at 1980 (Romance on Lushan Mountain 2017). Thus, the film won the certificate of "the longest first run of a film in one cinema is the *Romance on Lushan Mountain*" by the Guinness World Records (Romance on Lushan Mountain 2017).

With the overthrow of the "Gang of Four," Chinese government started to recognize tourism as a means to economic development and modernization. The China National Tourism Administration was initially formed in 1949, but especially since the late 1970s has developed policies that relate to enhancement of the natural and cultural resources of a destination while growing in importance as a state administrative body (China Tourism Academy 2009). However, while films prior to 1986 were being used to generate interest by tourists in a location, generally the aims tended to the political and the economic and the concepts of film tourism as understood in the West were not well appreciated in China. This slowly changed as the twentieth century grew to a close.

4.2.2 The Second Stage (1986–2000)

The period around 1986 represented an interesting period in the Chinese film industry for several reasons. That year marks the beginning of a transition, both economically and politically. Politically, the year was notable as the period of reform began to attract increasing conservative opposition in a process that was to lead to the events of June 1989 (Hao and Ryan 2013). Economically, from 1986 to 1991, tourism was increasingly refocused as an "economic industry" and began to establish a status within Chinese state planning for the economic advantages it could generate. First, tourism was incorporated into "The Seventh Five-Year State Plan for the National Economy and Social Development" in 1986; second, The State Council was asked to "vigorously develop tourism"; third, in 1991, "The Ten-Year Plan for National Economic and Social Development of China" and "The Eighth Five-Year State Plan for the National Economy and Social Development" clearly identified the character of tourism as an industry and listed the tourism industry as an important activity needing accelerated development within the tertiary sector (Li 2009).

The National Tourism Administration invested in a number of target areas that included Xi'an, Guilin, Suhang, Guangzhou, Beijing, and Shanghai among other cities. From the late 1980s to the early 1990s, an increasing number of tourist attractions and theme parks were established as a result of supportive national policies and market demands (China Tourism Academy 2009; see also Chap. 16 in this Volume). Many theme parks and film sets were constructed in the late 1980s, such as the Grand View Garden, Hibiscus Town, and Wuxi Film Studio (Liu and Liu 2004; Hao and Ryan 2013). The possible reasons for these developments include not only supportive national policies but also the rapid evolution of the Chinese film and television series of that period. For example, *Hibiscus Town* (芙蓉镇, Fúróngzhèn) filmed at a village named "Hongcun" was released at 1986. In Hao and Ryan's (2013) study, they describe how the village of Hong officially changed its name to Hibiscus Town (芙蓉镇, Fúróngzhèn) in 1997.

What is of interest for this chapter is that the community specifically changed its own structure and architecture to reflect the town as shown in the film, purposively seeking to represent the landscape and film language of the original film, even to the point of establishing rice tofu stalls to duplicate scenes from the movie. In order to evoke tourists' emotional connections with a film or television series and enhance their entertainment experiences, Kim (2010) suggested that destinations use symbolically and emotionally meaningful icons and special souvenirs to satisfy tourists, and it can be noted that many of these may references popular movies at film tourism sites.

In 1987, the earliest nationally developed and constructed film studio, Wuxi Movie and TV Base, marked the beginning of Chinese film tourism (Liu and Liu 2004; Chen et al. 2013). After that date, many famous television series like *Emperor Tang (1993)*, *Wu Zetian (1995)*, *The Romance of the Three Kingdoms (1994)*, and *Water Margin (1998)* were filmed at Wuxi Movie and TV Base and triggered a surge of film and TV tourism in China. During the 1980s and early 1990s, Wuxi Movie and TV Base itself attracted more than three million tourists every year (Liu and Liu 2004). After the success of the Wuxi Studios, other film studios or towns were constructed, such as the CCTV Nanhai Movie and TV Town, the Hebei Zhouzhou Movie and TV Town, the Hengdian World Studios, the Zhenbeibao Movie and TV Town, Tieling Longquan Resort, and so on (Liu and Liu 2004).

The Hengdian World Studios is the most popular and is even classified as a 5A national tourism area. Here, it should be noticed that the quality grade of Chinese tourism attractions is divided into five levels: 5A, 4A, 3A, 2A, and 1A. Thus "5A" is a normative and standardized quality rating system that represents the highest level of accreditation of tourism attractions in China. Chen et al. (2013) also pointed out that, in the late 1980s, the Chinese film and television industry was in its early stages of development, and film sets and studios became very popular attractions because of public interest in the movies and their stars, and thus film sites and studios came to the attention of the CNTA in rewarding such classification awards. Additionally, during this period, many film or TV series adapted famous literary works, such as *The Romance of the Three Kingdoms*, *The Dream of the Red Mansions*, and *Water Margin*.

4.2.3 The Third Stage (2000 to Now)

Entering the twenty-first century, with the rapid development of new media and patterns of information dissemination, tourists are able to earlier obtain tourism-related information in order to design their travel routes and choose activities directly or indirectly. Recently, Mafengwo, China's largest travel information-sharing website, released a report named "Report on the research of the travel styles by the post-90s generation" (Report on the study of the travel styles by the post-90s generation 2017). This report found that most people prefer to read books or watch films and TV series in order to understand the destinations before traveling. The more interesting finding is that the primary motivator to induce travel for the post-1990s generation is popular culture, including movies. The report showed 42% of the post-1990s generation visited sites or destinations as a result of the place being featured in their favorite films, TV series, cartoon, and variety shows, popular destinations such as Hokkaido (the film *Letters*), Sri Lanka (the cartoon *Spirited Away*), and Tokyo (the film *Your Name*).

It is undeniable that, in China, many places have become "hot spots" as a result of the destinations serving as settings for popular television series or film productions. Both the government and destinations have come to recognize the significant impact of film tourism.

As mentioned before, Chinese domestic tourism has a close relationship with films such as *Liu Sanjie* and *Raise the Red Lantern*. *Raise the Red Lantern* was shot at a historical house, that of the "Qiao Family" in Shanxi province. That film also aroused some foreign interest in the family life of the rich and the lives of oppressed daughters-in-law in Chinese feudal society. In 2006, another TV series *Qiao Family* was also filmed at Qiao Family house, and research undertaken by Wu et al. (2007) found that the number of visitors surged after the TV series were released. In 2005, the total revenue from film tourism was 24.064 million RMB, while it had increased to 56.776 million RMB after the broadcast of the TV series in 2006 (Wu et al. 2007).

Today destinations actively collaborate with the filmmaking companies. In March 2000, China's biggest movie theme park, Hengdian World Studios, began to provide its sets for free to film companies (Liu and Liu 2004). Since then, Hengdian has attracted many film companies to shoot productions at its various locations, and the subsequent popularity of its films attracted many visitors so that there were 1.23 million visitors by 2002 (Liu and Liu 2004). The huge number of visitors also promoted the rapid development of local economy including the real estate, construction, and financial industries. Since then, Hengdian World Studios has become the most famous and biggest active film theme park in China (see also Chap. 11 in this Volume). Another example is provided by the film *Riding Alone for Thousand Miles* (千里走单骑), filmed in Lijiang, Yunnan province, in 2005. The director, Zhang Yimou, and the Lijiang government asked a popular Japanese movie actor, Ken Takakura, to star in the movie to help increase visitation to Lijiang, an already well-known tourist location (Li and Beeton 2011). As a result destinations are increasingly adding other facilities to support a film theme, and they pay significant attention to local features and services such as restaurants and the development of souvenirs.

The case study noted below, that of Grand View Garden in Beijing, has similarly engaged in such policies, and today it runs a series of events and theatrical performances based not only on the novel but other aspects of eighteenth- and nineteenth-century Chinese history during the summer and public holiday periods to take advantage of its literary associations to attract higher numbers of visitors and additional revenue.

Some cities have taken to promote their attractions through product placement in films or television series. The romantic film "If You Are the One II" was shot at Yalong Bay Earthly Paradise Bird's Nest Resort (Sanya, Hainan) and released in 2010. Before the film was released, both the destination and resort were not well known in China. Now this place is a popular tourism site, and in the resort, the room used for the film commands a rate of 8800RMB (about 1300 US dollars) per night and is very difficult to book. Xixi Wetland is another site in this film. Hangzhou Xixi Wetland is well known in China due to this film, although there was only a small film clip shot there. "Xixi, please stay," a line in the film "If You Are The One," can be said to have contributed to increases in the surrounding real estate, while the sequel "If You Are The One II" contributed to yet more tourists traveling to Beijing and Hainan (Wu 2011).

In 2012, a popular film, "Tai Jiong," earned more than US$1.2 billion in China, which not only made it a "box office success" but also attracted a huge number of Chinese tourists to the filmed locations in Thailand (Wen 2010). Before the release of the film, many Chinese associated Thailand solely with sea and beach locations, but this film showed another side of Thailand, including the culture, the food, and the local life. After the release of the film, many Chinese tourism companies provided special "film ("Tai Jiong") tourism packages" to Chiang Mai (the location of the film), with a consequent threat to the site's carrying capacity (Wen 2013).

The China Tourism Administration has come to recognize the importance of film tourism. It reported that in the first half of 2015, a historical TV series named *The*

Ordinary World, adapted from Luyao's 1991 novel of the same name, proved a popular hit, and tens of thousands of visitors daily came to the film sites at Suide City, Shanxi, and numbers of such tourists at locations like the "Shuangshui Village"exceeded those of many of the province's traditional tourist sites (The Ordinary World 2015). The costume TV series, *Nirvana in Fire*, gained high audience rating in 2015, and today Wuxi, Western Zhejiang grasslands, and Hengdian Word Studios compete to attract audiences and fans (Nirvana in Fire 2015). A 2015 TV series *The Grave Robbers' Chronicles* (again based on Chinese literature) has also induced large numbers of fans of the novel to visit Changbai Mountains, and again the carrying capacity has been exceeded on some days (The Grave Robbers' Chronicles 2016). With seven more seasons planned, it would seem the Changbai Mountain area will attract visitors for many years to come. However, given the size of China's domestic tourism (some 4 billion visits in 2015), film tourism promotion for many existing tourist locations represents "the icing on the cake," and questions may be asked about the longevity of some film-based destinations.

4.3   The Example of Grand View Garden

In 1983, the China TV drama production center planned to choose a location in Beijing to produce a television series based on the classical novel, *The Dream of the Red Mansions*, with the same name. *The Dream of the Red Mansions* (Simplified Chinese: 红楼梦; Pinyin: *Hongloumeng*) is considered one of China's four greatest novels (along with *The Romance of the Three Kingdoms*, *Journey to the West*, and *Water Margin*) and is a masterpiece of Chinese literature. It is generally regarded as probably the most romantic novel in the history of Chinese literature with its love lost heroine committing suicide.

In order to collect the data about the developing history of the Garden, qualitative research methods were employed. The second author has visited the site many times, while the first author experienced the Garden as a visitor over an eight-month period, attended special events based on the novel or television series that are frequently held at the Garden, and thereby shared in the emotions felt by stakeholders, namely, visitors, residents, and employees. Documents played a major role in informing the authors about the Garden's development history and to permit comparisons over time. The documents obtained include secondary data such as financial statements, previous existing photography, events recording publicly available introductions to each garden, the researcher's diary notes about the places researched, etc.

Furthermore, this study employed face-to-face semi-structured interviews to investigate the management staff's attitudes about Grand View Garden. For the interviews, a total number of ten senior officials were selected to evaluate the Garden's past history, present situation or problems, and future plans. Each interview lasted approximately 40 minutes, and some of the more prominent officials were interviewed two or three times. For the data recording, both the use of a voice recorder and making notes were found to be useful ways for the researcher to record, check, and confirm the respondents' opinions.

At that time, the China TV drama production center suggested replicating international practice and the construction of a "film set" that could become a tourism destination after production had finished. In 1983 the production center signed an agreement with Xuanwuqu Construction Commission to build a garden named the Grand View Garden in Xuanwuqu District, Beijing. The China TV drama production center invested 750,000 yuan (about 110,000 US dollars), and Xuanwuqu government invested 2.5 million yuan (about 370,000 US dollars) to build the garden and copies of Qing Dynasty palaces. Through many government meetings and related experts' advice, the location known as the South Vegetable Garden (Pinyin: *Nancaiyuan*) was chosen as the site to build the film set. During the Ming and Qing dynasties, the garden was used as a vegetable farm for the royal family (Beijing Grand View Garden 2016). At that time, the site was just a simple garden with no featured architecture, meaning it was effectively a green field site suitable for the building of Grand View Garden based on the novel's description of the palace and its grounds. Figures 4.1 and 4.2 provide an indication of the visitor experience and the nature of the site.

In January of 1984, CCTV News first broadcast the news about the construction of Grand View Garden. The district government held the opening ceremony of the Garden's construction in April 1984. They instructed all parties involved "to be faithful to the original novel, respect the experts, use real materials, and construct real scenery and buildings." The garden was well laid out and artistically designed according to the traditional Chinese art of gardening. It was filled with oriental pavilions, crisscrossed with flowers and plants, and replicated the grounds that delighted the Chinese nobles of the period of the novel.

Before starting to build the garden, the district government signed a contract with a well-established construction company specializing in reproduction architecture and also employed many consultants, including horticulturists, architects, archeologists, folklorists, and experts on the history of the novel. Many meetings subsequently occurred to reach a consensus. Further, in order to suit contemporary needs, these experts also paid attention to the Garden's structure (including the layout of the architecture, scale, the width of paths, and functions) during the design process. The Beijing government and the State Administration of Radio, Film, and Television all took the project very seriously and discussed the design of the Garden with the relevant experts more than a hundred times. Before construction, the design drawing of the Garden was amended seven times. The actual construction of the Grand View Garden experienced three stages: the first phase of construction was mainly used to produce the TV series; the second phase added some attractions and supporting buildings; the third phase saw the completion of the Garden.

Fig. 4.1 Mansion and Garden

4.3.1 Stage One of Grand View Garden

Hudson and Ritchie (2006a, b) suggested that film tourism destinations could be divided into four steps: before production, during production, before release, and after release. They indicate that, during the production stage, the destination marketing organizations should work with the producer's publicists to ensure consistent messaging about the filmed locations, as well as building the first linkages between the film or television series and the location (Hudson and Ritchie 2006a). However, during the television series' production in Grand View Garden, the Chinese media industry was undeveloped, and most families had no television at that time. Unexpectedly, the *Dream of the Red Mansions* (Red) television series adopted from the great novel still attracted huge attention from the masses. The amount of popular attention and energy that people spent in covering the production was definitely a surprise to the production team, and as the section chief Li said:

> ...we did not expect that Grand View Garden could be so popular during the production of the Red television series... at that time, many people asked that the Garden be opened to the public, and who even waited at the gate and wanted to pay to visit the Garden...we were very embarrassed as too many tourists visiting the Garden should affect the filming. This issue also attracted the then government's attention, the mayor discussed the problem with the Administration and suggested opening to the public and charged a very high ticket price of 1 RMB as we thought there would be just a few people wanting to buy such an expensive ticket to visit...maybe you don't know, the ticket price of The Palace Museum was just 0.5 RMB at that time.... (Pers.comm)

Fig. 4.2 Visitor is taken in a sedan chair dressed in period style

The Garden was very profitable in the first phase after its opening. After the television series was released in 1987, the Garden received more than 3 million tourists and total tourism revenue of 4.53 million RMB, even though the ticket price was 2 yuan (an expensive price at that time). Visitors expected to experience the traditional and cultural Garden and to see and explore whether the landscape matched the novel's description or location as depicted in the TV series, as well as learn about Chinese historical culture (Zhang et al. 2016). At this stage, the roles of the Garden were "movie set" and "Red theme park," and the famous Garden not only cooperated with companies to develop Red-themed souvenirs but also attracted many business investments.

Grand View Garden has received high praise from state leaders and different social sectors, as well as being welcomed by the broad masses. In the years after the Garden's opening, thousands of tourists have visited it, with up to 20,000 a day. For several years after opening, many political leaders and high-ranking officials from China's central government and foreign-distinguished guests visited the garden. Furthermore, many famous "redologists" (enthusiasts and students of the novel) and experts also made visits, providing specific guidance to the development of the Garden. Hou Renzhi, a professor of Peking University, said "the Grand View Garden is helpful in reviving Liao Jin culture, protecting the moat around the south of the city, as well as benefiting urban afforestation and beautification."

The Grand View Garden successfully transferred a fictional world described in the *Red* novel to a real garden and has won many awards. The garden is the first "Garden of a Literary Masterpiece" in China, and among the awards it is "Beijing

New 16 Scenery," "Top 10 buildings of 80s in Beijing," "Forty Top tourism destination in China," etc. Grand View Garden has great significance in many different industries, including redologists who dubbed it as another dream out of *The Dream of the Red Mansions*, the construction sector that sought to retain the essence of "Red" culture, the horticultural industry and the heritage sector that pointed out that the garden is an important cultural heritage site, and the literary and art circles who praised a new style that combined film with landscape architecture (Beijing Grand View Garden 2016).

4.3.2 Stage Two of Grand View Garden

The second stage (1996–2005) is a period of decline as interest in the Garden was greatly diminished, and both the visitor numbers and tourism revenues decreased. The Garden was once an attractive destination but gradually faded from people's memories. The possible reasons are, in the 1980s, the underdevelopment of media (television series), for there were few television series or films produced and broadcasted at that time in China. As the 1990s dawned, television ownership expanded, and more television series slowly emerged. These included *Journey to the West*, and simultaneously film sets or theme parks (e.g., *Journey to the West Theme Park*) appeared. Therefore, while the original *Red* series was repeated on television several times, the Garden faced increasing competition and many challenges. The Chinese-planned market economy officially ended in 1992 and then entered the era of the "socialist market economy with Chinese characteristics." Thus, the tourism industry changed to being a market-driven activity and generally fitted well with the new market economy orthodoxy as a demand-driven sector. After 1990, Chinese tourism achieved a higher rate of development and emerged as a sunrise industry.

4.3.3 Stage Three of Grand View Garden: 2000 to Now

Grand View Garden experienced a rapid growth in visitor numbers from 2005 to 2006. The Garden entered the Beijing Annual Ticket Program, cooperated with Beijing TV to produce a major talent show named "Human in Dream of Red Mansions" in order to select suitable actors for the remaking of the Red television series directed by Li Shao-hong, and played an important role in providing activities and spreading Chinese classical culture during the 2008 Olympic Games.

Further, the Garden developed and promoted many kinds of tourism activities, especially during public holidays. *Temple Fair* is the first and the largest performance and is always held from the first to the fifth day of Chinese New Year. The Red-themed Temple Fair is very popular in Beijing and attracts many visitors, and visiting *Grand View Garden Temple Fair* is an important part of many locals' Spring Festival Holiday.

Since 2000 two major problems have become increasingly evident, namely, a lack of financial support and a poorly educated staff approaching retirement age. As a governmental public institution with its own revenue and expenditure (事业单位 自收自支), the Garden could maintain professional services and facilities during the first stage of its history as a result of the huge number of visitors that created profits and attracted business investments. However, throughout the second stage, tourism revenue gradually became harder to sustain, meaning a degradation of the previously high quality of service due to a decline of popularity in the market place. In the third phase, the number of visitors has increased because of the annual ticket program, but the Garden not only profits less from the annual ticket holders but also has to spend more time and money to maintain the facilities than before. Unfortunately, due to its legal status, it was unable to obtain continuous government funding to support the park.

Another problem is that many staff is of retirement age and possesses poor educational qualifications, a factor mentioned by the manager and section chiefs during interviews in 2016. Many staff have worked at the Garden for more than 20 years, and the Garden has recruited few new employees since 2000. In the light of the Garden's current situation and difficulties, the Garden plans to recruit professional and highly qualified staff and to develop or enrich the cultural and recreational attractions, as well as build a new creative platform. It also plans to change its legal status to that of a corporate entity.

However, there have been growing numbers of tourists until about 2014, when visitation to Beijing stalled, partly because of publicity over poor air quality. But general economic growth has brought opportunities and problems. In the National Day Holiday in 1999, Chinese scenic sites first faced "the blowout" of visitors (Zhang and Liu 2008), when the numbers of the public traveling exceeded the capability of the transport sector to cope with the demand. While not attaining the numbers of the distant past, the Garden has been recently able to attract higher visitation during the Golden Weeks with it hosting the special events, performance, and firework displays noted above.

4.4   Conclusions

This chapter began with a description of the history of Chinese film tourism. Initially, while films were a favorite entertainment medium for those who could access them, often the location was not explicit as a result of the then political and economic backgrounds. At the first stage of Chinese film tourism, the tourism industry lacked a consciousness that film could induce tourism. Nonetheless some filmed destinations and cities became popular as a result of some films released around the 1960s, such as Guilin (*Liu Sanjie*). In the second stage since 1986, Chinese film tourism entered a period of rapid development. From approximately the 1980s, with the development of economy, the location became almost unwittingly more popular as more people had access to the cinema and television and films became more an entertainment medium as distinct from being a vehicle for overt propaganda. One such example was Grand View Garden, albeit many implicit political messages are still discernable within the series – messages that reinforced notions of Chinese culture, its role as a distinguishing feature of being Chinese, and the implicit Confucian and Buddhist adherence to reciprocal hierarchical values. In the third stage when entering the twenty-first century, filmmaking came to collaborate more closely with the location, and destination marketing authorities came to recognize the importance of filmmaking in attracting visitation to any given location. Both the government and industries began to realize the effect of film tourism, and some local governments took the initiative to achieve a travel effect through collaboration with film companies.

In China, film tourism is an exciting new form of tourism but not as developed as in the West. According to the latest statistics, since the first film tourism studio Wuxi Movie and TV City were built in 1987, about 1000 studios have since been established in the past 25 years. Of these, 80% of them are thought to be losing money, 15% earned barely enough money to survive, and only 5% of the studios are profitable (China Economic Net 2013). It is estimated that the total investment of the whole Chinese film studios has reached about 50 billion RMB. Though most studios are losing money, there remain many companies seeking to invest large sums to build new studios, which have caused the supply of film studios to significantly exceed demand (China Economic Net 2013). The president of Peking University Cultural Industry Academy, Chen Shaofeng has noted that in 2008, except for Hengdian and a few other film studios, most Chinese film studios and sets are unsuccessful and fail to be attractive film tourism or cultural sites (Cultural industry 2008). In 2016 though the era of joint Chinese-American film production has emerged, and that may stimulate further international interest, one example being the use of the movie *The Great Wall* to engender interest. Additionally, Chinese finance is becoming international as evidenced by the 2017 film, *Ghost in the Shell*, a US-China-Canada coproduction with significant input from Weka Studios in Wellington, New Zealand.

In short, China is increasingly taking advantage of cinematic links as is undertaken in the West, but there are least two caveats to this process. First, the artistic and creative processes have to appeal to the public. While Peter Jackson successfully relocated New Zealand into Tolkien's novels of "Middle Earth," the film *Australia* was less successful in its promotion of Australia. Second, the cinema is increasingly no longer the only way of viewing films, and campaigns associated with cinema going must now consider social media, the viewing of films through smart television, and the disaggregation of not only movie audiences but also the very experiences of film viewing. However, Chinese cinema audiences are increasing as the quality and quantity of theaters grow in China, thereby creating opportunities for film-based tourism.

References

Airey, D. W., & Chong, K. (2011). *Tourism in China: Policy and development since 1949*. New York: Routledge.

Beeton, S. (2005). *Film-induced tourism*. Clevedon: Channel View Publications.

Beijing Grand View Garden. (2016). Retrieved on November 27, 2016 from http://www.bjdgy.com/yshg.htm

Busby, G., & Klug, J. (2001). Movie-induced tourism: The challenge of measurement and other issues. *Journal of Vacation Marketing, 7*(4), 316–332.

Chen, N., Bai, K., Qiao, G. H., & Piao, G. X. (2008). 入境游客对中国传统文化旅游产品满意度的实证研究以禅宗少林音乐大典为例 [A demonstrative study on inbound tourists' satisfaction with Chinese traditional cultural tourism product]. 旅游学刊 *[Tourism Tribune], 6*(23), 24–29.

Chen, S. F., Huang, J. Z., & Li, X. W. (2013). Discussions on the relationships between movie & TV bases and the real estate. *Tourism Planning & Design, 9*, 122–127.

China Culture Promotion Society. (2017). Chronicle of events in 2010.Retrieved from http://www.ccps.com.cn/File/News/20131031/2013103108060585.html

China Economic Net. (2013).Retrieved on February 2, 2017 from http://www.ce.cn/

China Tourism Academy. (2009). *Development of China Tourism Research 1978–2008*. Beijing: China Travel & Tourism Press.

Chinese cultural tourism contribution award. (2010). Retrieved on February 5, 2017 from http://www.chinanews.com/cul/2010/10-24/2608351.shtml

Cultural Industry. (2008). *People*. Retrieved from http://cpc.people.com.cn/GB/66888/66889/7092535.html

Cynarski, W. J. (2012). Travel for the study of martial arts. *Journal of Martial Arts Anthropology, 12*(1), 11–19.

Dai, B., Jiang, Y., Yang, L., & Ma, Y. (2017). China's outbound tourism: Stages, policies and choice. *Tourism Management, 58*, 253–258.

Development planning outline for the construction of Guilin international tourism destination. (2017). Retrieved from http://bgt.ndrc.gov.cn/zcfb/201211/W020121129607681571253.pdf

Hao, X. F., & Ryan, C. (2013). Interpretation, film language and tourist destinations: A case study of hibiscus town, China. *Annuals of Tourism Research, 42*, 334–358.

Heitmann, S. (2010). Film tourism planning and development-questioning the role of stakeholders and sustainability. *Journal of Tourism and Hospitality Planning & Development, 7*(1), 31–46.

Hou, J. N., Yang, H. H., & Li, X. D. (2010). 旅游演艺产品中地域文化元素开发的思考-以《印象刘三姐》为例 [Thoughts on the exploration of regional culture elements in the tourism performing arts- a case study of Impression the Liu Sanjie]. 旅游论坛 *[Tourism Forum], 3*(3), 284–287.

Hu, X. (2016). 生命意识视角下的《山海经》文化旅游资源开发 [Cultural tourism development based on <<The Classic of Mountains and Seas>>]. 旅游纵览 *[Tourism Overview], 7*, 273–274.

Hudson, S., & Ritchie, J. R. B. (2006a). Film tourism and destination marketing: The case of caption Corelli's Mandolin. *Journal of Vacation Marketing, 12*(3), 256–268.

Hudson, S., & Ritchie, J. R. B. (2006b). Promoting destinations via film tourism: An empirical identification of supporting marketing initiatives. *Journal of Travel Research, 44*(4), 387–396.

Iwashita, C. (2003). Media construction of Britain as a destination for Japanese tourists: Social constructionism and tourism. *Journal of Tourism and Hospitality Research, 4*(4), 331–340.

Iwashita, C. (2006). Media representation of the UK as a destination for Japanese tourists: Popular culture and tourism. *Journal of Tourist Studies, 6*(1), 59–77.

Kim, S. (2010). Extraordinary experience: Re-enacting and photographing at screen tourism locations. *Tourism and Hospitality Planning & Development, 7*(1), 59–75.

Lavallee, T. M., & Yan, L. (2011). Galloping our minds beyond the boundaries: Exploring leisure in the poetry of the Orchid Pavilion gathering. In H. Xiao (Ed.), *Contemporary perspectives on China tourism* (pp. 47–65). London: Taylor & Francis Ltd.

Li, T. Y. (2009). *Lv You XueGaiLun* (6th ed.). Tianjin: Nankai University Press.

Li, W. (2015). 刘三姐文化旅游开发研究综述 [the review of the tourism development of Liu Sanjie culture]. 创新 *[Innovation], 4*(9), 59–65.

Li, Y., & Beeton, S. (2011). Is film tourism all the same? Exploring Zhang Yimou's films' potential influence on tourism in China. *Tourism Review International, 15*, 293–296.

Li, Y. R., & Cao, H. S. (2006). *Tourism.* Beijing: Qinghua University Press.

Liu, B. Y., & Liu, Q. (2004). On the present situation and trend of the development of China's movie and TV tourism. *Journal of Tourism Tribune, 6*(19), 77–81.

Luo, S. F., Huang, Y. L., Cheng, D. P., & Ding, P. Y. (2011). 情感因素对游客体验与满意度的影响研究——以桂林山 水实景演出"印象·刘三姐"为例 [Study on the effect of affective factors on tourist experience and satisfaction]. 旅游学刊 *[Tourism Tribune], 1,* 51–58.

National Development and Reform Commission.(2017). "Development planning for the construction of Guilin international tourism destination" approved by the National Development and Reform Commission. Retrieved from http://bgt.ndrc.gov.cn/zcfb/201211/t20121129_516519.html

Nirvana in Fire.(2015). *People.* Retrieved from http://media.people.com.cn/n/2015/1117/c40606-27824125.html

O'Connor, N., & Kim, S. (2014). Pictures and prose: exploring the impact of literary and film tourism. *Journal of Tourism & Cultural Change, 12*(1), 1–17.

Qu, H., & Tsang, N. (2000). Service quality in China's hotel industry: A perspective from tourists and hotel manager. *International Journal of Contemporary Hospitality Management, 12*(5), 316–326.

Report on the research of the travel styles by the post-90s generation. (2017). Retrieved from http://www.mafengwo.cn/

Roesch, S. (2009). *The experiences of film location tourists.* Clevedon: Channel View Publications.

Romance in Lushan. (2017). *China Lushan.* Retrieved from http://www.china-lushan.com/lushan-lian/index.php

The Graver Robbers' Chronicles.(2016). *China National Tourism Administration.* Retrieved from http://www.cnta.gov.cn/xxfb/xxfb_dfxw/jl/201608/t20160819_781193.shtml

The Ordinary World.(2015).*China National Tourism Administration.*Retrieved on Janurary 7, 2017 from http://www.cnta.gov.cn/xxfb/hydt/201506/t20150627_717056.shtml

Wen, F. (2013). 从《泰囧》谈旅游产业中的电影营销 [Thoughts on the film tourism marketing in the tourism industry from Taijiong]. 中国商论 *[China Journal of Commerce], 6,* 93–97.

Wu, J. (2011). Analysis and strategic suggestions for China's film and TV tourism. In G. Zhang, R. Song, & D. Liu (Eds.), *Green book of China's tourism* (pp. 185–198). China Outbound Tourism Research Institute: Heide.

Wu, P., Ge, Q. S., Xi, J. C., & Liu, H. L. (2007). A study on the formation and developing machanism of movie-induced tourism. *Journal of Tourism Tribune, 7*(22), 52–57.

Yan, W. S. (2002). *Chinese history and culture.* Beijing: Tsinghua University Press.

Zhang, G. R., & Liu, D. Q. (2008). *China's tourism development: Analysis and forecast.* Beijing: Social Sciences Academic Press.

Zhang, X. Y., Ryan, C., & Cave, J. (2016). Residents, their use of a tourist facility and contribution to tourist ambience: Narratives from a film tourism site in Beijing. *Tourism Management, 52,* 416–429.

Part II
The Impact of Film Tourism

Chapter 5
Drama Off-Screen: A Multi-stakeholder Perspective on Film Tourism in Relation to the Japanese Morning Drama (*Asadora*)

Elisabeth Scherer and Timo Thelen

Abstract This chapter is dedicated to tourism induced by the Japanese morning drama (*asadora*), a very popular genre since the early 1960s. Based on a review of Western and Japanese theories of audience participation and film tourism as well as on field research on the filming location of one recent *asadora*, we investigate the phenomenon of film tourism from a multi-stakeholder perspective, thereby considering the following participants: the fans as active audience, the media producers and their marketing strategies and the local communities which provide the filming locations and implement strategies for the development of film tourism. For the latter, we suggest to differentiate more clearly between the distinct parties involved. Through this more nuanced view, it becomes clear why the planning and organisation of film tourism can become a double-edged sword. General insights on the opportunities and risks of film tourism make this case study relevant also beyond the Japanese context.

Keywords Japan • Drama series • Audience participation • Local communities • Rural revitalisation • Asadora

5.1 Introduction

> Now, let's set out on the journey, without fear,
> Even if these are only small steps.
> The places you're meant to see,
> The people you're meant to meet
> Are waiting for you.
>
> (*Marezora*, opening song of the morning drama *Mare*, 2015)

The Japanese morning drama (*renzoku terebi shōsetsu*, short: *asadora*) is an enormously successful product: it has been attracting people of all ages since the

E. Scherer (✉) • T. Thelen
University of Dusseldorf, Dusseldorf, Germany
e-mail: scherer@phil.hhu.de; tthelen@phil.hhu.de

© Springer Nature Singapore Pte Ltd. 2018
S. Kim, S. Reijnders (eds.), *Film Tourism in Asia*, Perspectives on Asian Tourism, DOI 10.1007/978-981-10-5909-4_5

beginning of the 1960s and today still reaches the highest audience ratings on Japanese television. For many people, the *asadora* has become a habitual element of daily life; shown during breakfast, they offer a topic of discussion throughout the rest of the day. Although this series format has long been of relevance to tourism, very little attention has been paid to it in the English language research on film tourism, whereas anime tourism in Japan has been treated in various studies (e.g. Okamoto 2015; Suzuki 2011; Yamamura 2015). Seaton (2015) has done research on the so-called *Taiga dorama*, a very popular historical series format, and notes that it is "routinely assumed that Taiga dramas will induce tourism booms" (p. 83). The same holds true for the *asadora* format: due to its great presence in everyday life and the character of its content, it is very suitable for stimulating viewers to travel.

The *asadora*, produced like the *Taiga dorama* by the state-run broadcaster NHK, usually tells the life story of a female protagonist over 6 months and is being broadcast from Monday to Saturday from 8:00 to 8:15 a.m. The *asadora* has long been regarded as a typical "housewife" TV format, but the audience has recently become more diverse, with the highest audience ratings for women over 50 and men over 60 (Hoshi et al. 2017, p. 90). On average, audience ratings of *asadora* nowadays are around 20%, which is very high compared to other TV shows in Japan. Recent studies show that watching *asadora* has become habitualised to such a degree that many people even watch it if they do not particularly like the story (Nihei and Sekiguchi 2016). This does not mean that the audience does not care about the content, on the contrary: the interaction of the audience with the series has increased through social media, and it has become more important than ever for NHK to take audience activity into account.

While the *Taiga dorama* is usually shot at historical sites such as battlefields, castles, etc., which are often already oriented towards tourists, *asadora* producers regularly choose rural regions as locations. This carries a special potential to make rather remote areas attractive for tourism and to contribute to regional revitalisation. Because of this potential, the Japanese government has actively promoted film tourism since the late 2000s, using the keyword "contents tourism" (*kontentsu tsūrisumu*) (see also Chap. 16 in this volume). These promotional activities in Japan were inspired by the huge boom in tourism induced by Korean TV series from 2000 onwards, which has attracted both the attention of policy-makers and researchers (Kim et al. 2007; Kim 2012).

Yamamura (2015, p. 77) considers a triangular network of fans, copyright holders and local communities as crucial for film tourism in Japan. Successful negotiations between these three parties are expected to lead to mutual benefits. We adopt Yamamura's model in our chapter and examine the case of fan activities and film tourism related to *asadora* from a multi-stakeholder perspective—an approach that is still rare in film tourism research. First, we deal with the role of fans as "active audience"; second, we discuss the position of the copyright holders and media producers; and third, we investigate the role of local communities at the filming locations. Although we deal with them in separate chapters, the activities of these three actors are indeed closely linked and interdependent. Since we argue that film tourism can only become prosperous if it is firmly rooted in fan culture, we make the audience's perspective our starting point. While the first two sections treat the series format in general, the third is based on field research conducted by Timo Thelen at the locations of the *asadora Mare* (2015). We consider this particular case as a "failure story", which can provide valuable lessons on the opportunities and risks of film tourism.

5.2 *Asadora* and the Active Audience

Enthusiastic *asadora* spectators certainly cannot be compared to Star Trek fans, whom Henry Jenkins used in his classic *Textual Poachers* (Jenkins 1992) as an example of the great productive power of fandom. With their relatively short time span, and sequels being the exception, Japanese series have less potential for long-term loyalty. However, the success of *asadora* cannot be reduced to the effects of short-term commercial strategies alone, but it is also rooted in the practices of the audience. Audience ratings are an important indicator for the success of a series; however, according to Takō, they alone do not indicate how popular an *asadora* really is. For example, the series *Chiritotechin* (2007/08), with its below average audience ratings of 15.9%, has produced particularly passionate fans, and a Rakugo boom occurred because of how the protagonist of the series practices this traditional humorous storytelling art.

A classic example of the power of *asadora* to stimulate audience participation is the series *Oshin* (1983/84), which reached record audience ratings of 52.6% on average and spawned the buzzword "oshindrome", which described the enthusiasm for this media product. The series tells the story of a poor peasant girl, who experiences World War II and the harsh reality of the post-war era, until she finally becomes the owner of a supermarket chain. The heroine Oshin became a role model for many people, as well as a symbol of the development of the Japanese nation in the twentieth century. Nationwide, people exchanged ideas about *Oshin* in fan meetings and created fan magazines, and NHK received a large quantity of fan mail. The series, however, was also controversial: In September 1983, there was a discussion meeting of women in Kyōto, who were annoyed by *Oshin*'s ideal image of the all-enduring woman ("Zakkichō" 1983).

Talking about the *asadora* and other small performative acts in everyday life—that is, acts designated by Fiske (1992, p. 37–39) as the "enunciative productivity" of fans—is still quite common in the context of *asadora*: According to a survey on *Amachan* (2013) conducted by the NHK Broadcasting Culture Research Institute (Nihei and Sekiguchi 2014, p. 18), 39% of the audience talk about the series with their families, and 30% exchange their ideas about it with friends and acquaintances. Another popular activity is the repetition of words and slogans from the series (11%), and 2% said they had visited the region in which the series is set. This kind of performative participation was also crucial for the enjoyment of *Oshin*: for instance, during the broadcasting of the series, eating rice with radish (*daikonmeshi*) became a popular custom among families. This dish expresses the poverty of

Oshin's family in the series and stands for a simple but honourable life. Shefner-Rogers et al. (1998) state that *Oshin's* success is rooted in its power to induce a particularly high degree of such audience interaction.

As Kelly (2004) points out, an important part of being a fan is the desire for intimacy with the object of interest. Because of their daily presence and their function as a relaxed, ritualised start to everyday life, *asadora* offer an excellent framework for the development of intimacy with the figures and content of the series. *Asadora* producer Yaguchi even declares: "If things go well, audience and programme can become completely one" (Takō 2012, p. 290). Such an intensive reception is also referred to as "para-social interaction", which means that the viewer feels a seemingly immediate relationship to the fictional characters, "as if they were in the circle of one's peers" (Horton and Wohl 1956, p. 215). In many cases, the fictional counterpart is perceived and treated like a "real" person—usually only playfully, in a "willing suspension of disbelief" but sometimes also with bizarre consequences: Yūko Tanaka, for example, the actress who played Oshin, received parcels with rice from many viewers, because Oshin was so poor in the series (Shefner-Rogers et al. 1998, p. 10).

What also contributes to the success of the *asadora* is that by experiencing the stories simultaneously, the viewers feel connected in a kind of (national) "imagined community" (Anderson 2006). Hansen (2016) regards the NHK morning programme as a "secular morning ritual", a "repeated activity that defines them and sustains them as we, Japanese" (p. 15). Due to the digitisation and diversification of the programme, this feeling might have become weaker over the last few years, but at the same time, the Internet and social media offer countless new possibilities for the audience to participate. The NHK study on *Amachan* (Nihei and Sekiguchi 2014) also clearly confirms the significance of the Internet for the reception of a series. A small, but extremely committed part of the *asadora* audience shows an increased presence on the Internet, exchanges opinions, publishes fan works, and thereby influences the public's perception of the series. Twitter is especially important: during the broadcast of *Amachan*, over 6 million tweets were posted under the hashtag #Amachan (Nihei and Sekiguchi 2014, p. 24), ranging from simple comments to elaborate drawings by professional illustrators. This type of audience participation "calls for no fan-communal setting" (Hills 2013, p. 138), and each individual is able to participate spontaneously. Fan activities, however, do not unfold in a completely free and independent space; they are also linked to economic interests. For example, some illustrators use fan art as a catalyst for their business, and for NHK, the world of the series is expanding through social media, creating new market potentials.

For the development of film tourism, audience activities online is also of great relevance: Twitter posts often refer to the locations of the *asadora*. Users share their own photos of the filming locations, declare their interest in local food and comment on dialect terms. In the case of *Mare* (2015), fans posted pictures of the morning market of Wajima, the local town hall and of various souvenirs. Even a member of the popular idol group NMB48 shared photos of herself on a salt field in Noto, on which she pretends to work there (Naiki Kokoro 2015). As Kim (2010) explains, tourists often re-enact certain scenes from a series for such photos, thus intensifying the experience of intimacy with the world of the series. Such pictures often encourage other fans to travel, since "the replication of images of actual pilgrimage sites on the web reinforces precisely their original significance" (Couldry 2003, p. 93). The Twitter activities also show that for audiences, a sense of authenticity is an important factor: people often complain online if the representation of a certain region in a series does not match the local conditions, thus presenting producers with the challenge to pay closer attention to detail.

5.3 Interweaving Place and Story in the Production and Marketing of *Asadora*

Media producers have long realised that they have to take the interests and activities of the audience into account for the purpose of creating a loyal fanbase and new economic resources. Already in the case of *Oshin* (1983/84), producers catered to fan desires on a grand scale: music, merchandise, stage plays as well as book and magazine publications related to the series were marketed. Even *Oshin* toilet paper was available, and *Oshin* merchandise for children was promoted in newspapers using the slogan "Experience the excitement beyond television" ("Terebi ijō" 1984). The *asadora* thus clearly is an example of a comprehensive media mix strategy, which Steinberg (2012) describes for the Japanese anime sector. This strategy creates a material presence for the fictional characters in everyday life and satisfies the viewers' desire to participate in the world of the series: "The character good functions as a monad or medium through which the consumer can pass into the character's world" (p. 188).

Tourism was also part of this media mix strategy, especially in the Yamagata Prefecture, where the protagonist grows up in the series. For instance, a large ad in the daily newspaper Yomiuri Shinbun, promoted a tour to "Oshin's home", including visits of Sakata City and a hot spring as well as a cherry harvest experience ("'Oshin' no furusato" 1983). Such packaged *Oshin* tours were offered by the leading Japanese tourism agencies, which also became beneficiaries of the boom. The city of Sakata, on the other hand, made sure that fans could find fragments of *Oshin*'s world on location and provided for a wide range of different souvenirs. *Asadora* tourism was thus highly professionalised at the time but not an entirely new phenomenon. For instance, after the *asadora Tamayura* (1965/66), wedding trips to Miyazaki Prefecture became fashionable ("Terebi shōsetsu" 1977), and fans of the series *Ohanahan* (1966/67) were enthusiastic about the Meiji-period charms of Ōzu city in Ehime Prefecture ("Meiji būmu" 1966). Initially, this kind of tourism was more an unintended side effect, but local actors soon became aware of its potential and began to actively stimulate it. When local authorities of Tendō learned about NHK's plans to shoot the series *Ichiban boshi* (1977) in their city, for example, they prepared themselves with PR measures on a large scale ("Terebi shōsetsu" 1977).

Therefore, *asadora* tourism is a phenomenon that first emerged from audience activity and still only works if producers and local stakeholders succeed in stimulating the imagination of the audience. The fans' decision to travel is sparked by their desire for interaction, their longing to have a share in the world of the series. Riley and van Doren (1992) emphasise that a film can create a convincing tourist experience through the "contextual package" (p. 269) of the story. In addition to the visual appeal of a landscape and the connection with popular actors, for example, the "romantic ethos common in film scripts" can be significant. Kim (2012) also notes that an emotional attachment to the content and the (nostalgic) values conveyed in the series may become a very important motivation for film tourism. As Urry and Larsen (2011) point out, the feelings and expectations induced by films or series have a great influence on the general perception of a place so that "film landscapes identify with and represent actual landscapes" and "tourism destinations in part become fantasylands or Mediaworlds" (p. 113). However, this does not mean that film tourists no longer distinguish between the media world and the actual situation on site: Reijnders (2011) stresses that the popularity of media tourism is precisely the result of the tourists' recreation of the "symbolic contrast between imagination and reality" (p. 17). At the filming locations, the fans are thus looking for references and material anchor points for the world of their imagination in order to fill the "geographical blanks" that arise during that process.

In order to make tourism a promising part of a media mix strategy, producers have to stimulate the imagination of the audience and their desire to search for the reference points of their imaginary world. When producing *asadora*, a crucial point is usually a coherent representation of rural Japan; this representation is linked to nostalgia, tradition and Japanese national identity through the story (see also Chap. 9 in this volume). This kind of portrayal of the countryside is connected to the "hometown" (*furusato*) discourse, a concept which conveys similar connotations to the German word Heimat ("native place"). Since the 1970s, this trope of "hometown" has become a dominant and stable representation of an idealised rural lifestyle in Japan, which frequently appears in consumer culture and tourism (Creighton 1997). In the production of *asadora*, therefore, a whole arsenal of popular stereotypes may be used, which are associated with certain emotions and longings.

NHK combines beautiful shots of landscapes with the presentation of local handicraft and traditions, e.g. the production of lacquerware and local festivals in *Mare*. A voice-over narrator occasionally comments on such sequences, which is reminiscent of tourism videos. Local landmarks, such as bridges, prominent buildings or rocks, which have the potential to become the anchor points of the fans' imagination on site, are regularly shown throughout the whole series. In addition, local food or dishes can play an important role in *asadora*. In Japan, "local food" has been associated with "nostalgia, nature, sustainable agriculture" (Rath 2015, p. 146) since the 1970s and is marketed as a delicacy. In the series, the characters regularly consume such specialities, like a handmade sea salt in *Mare* or a stew dish (*mamebujiru*) in *Amachan*; this provides tourists the opportunity of a culinary interaction if they visit the region. The regional identity is also present in *asadora* through the local dialect, which is presented in a simplified form, so that the national audience can understand it. Since the mid-1970s, NHK has engaged dialect consultants for *asadora* production (Tanaka 2014, p. 24–25), a fact that is regularly mentioned in *asadora* paratexts such as documentaries and contributes to an overall impression of authenticity. Local artisans and farmers also regularly act as consultants, and classical media such as breakfast television, daily newspapers or magazines are used to give the region more visibility in connection with the series.

Recently, the Internet is increasingly used for a successful interweaving of story and place. NHK not only conducts extensive research on the *asadora*'s impact on social media but also wants to influence the development of online discussions, gain presence for their content on a wide range of platforms, and to utilise user-generated content to expand the narrative universe of the series. For instance, NHK creates special websites with information on the *asadora* filming locations. The series *Hiyokko* (2017), which is partly set in Ibaraki Prefecture, features a website with Ibaraki news, an Ibaraki blog and messages from the actors. The main actress Kasumi Arimura enthuses about the landscape, the friendliness of the people and the food: "When, after a long time, I was standing there, in a place where you have nothing in mind but nature, my heart has really opened up" (NHK 2017). The main actresses also have their own blogs, Twitter and Instagram accounts, which contribute to the expansion of the *asadora* universe and make the actress and the main character more tangible for the fans. Here, idyllic photos and descriptions of the locations also spark the audience's interest to travel. The popular stars as "influencers" guarantee a particularly great response: A photo of Kasumi Arimura in a rural setting in Ibaraki with an enthusiastic comment about her grandpa from the series, gained almost 114,000 likes and over 360 comments on Twitter (Arimura 2017).

5.4 Local Communities in the Context of *Asadora* Tourism

The third party related to film tourism is the local community that provides the filming location. Frost (2006) argues: "It is important to understand that film-induced tourism rarely just happens. Rather it needs to be developed, promoted and managed if it is to have any long-term impact" (p. 77). The starting points are often bottom-up movements initiated by the desires of fans which then lead to planning concepts by local communities in collaboration with the media producers and copyright holders (Yamamura 2015). Beeton (2005) also emphasises the important role of local communities in the planning of film tourism instead of top-down approaches. Our previously mentioned examples of early film tourism related to *asadora* in Japan, such as in the case of *Oshin*, were also initiated by fan activities and then recognised by local stakeholders for local planning. However, since film tourism has become a popular subject in regional development, national or local governments have become involved in the strategic planning of fan pilgrimage. In Japan, the governmental attention for film tourism can be regarded as part of a general offensive in inbound tourism and the international promotion of "Cool Japan" soft power (Seaton and Yamamura 2015, p. 6). Furthermore, as a means to revitalise the highly over-aged and depopulated countryside of Japan, regional planners and pol-icy-makers also regard film tourism as a new economic resource for structurally weak regions.

A prominent case of regional revitalisation is the *asadora Amachan* (2013), set in Iwate Prefecture, where the March 2011 tsunami devastated its coastal areas. At the first presentation of *Amachan* in June 2012, NHK's scriptwriter Kankurō Kudō expressed the hope that this *asadora* might help to revitalise the region and to restore its public image (NHK 2012). Due to the popularity of *Amachan*, the number of visitors to Iwate Prefecture saw a dramatic increase of 86% in 2013, a number which remained rather stable throughout 2014 (Tajima 2015, p. 25). Furthermore, with the intention to continue this positive legacy of the *asadora*, many projects such as street art and concerts related to *Amachan* were held locally. However, investigating the case of *Amachan*, Tajima (2015) expresses his doubts regarding the sustainability of the inflow of tourists over the next decade—a fundamental issue of film tourism. In addition, he states that not all locals were happy about the sudden influx of tourists and the reidentification of their hometown, newly per-ceived as only the home of *Amachan*. Jang (2016) mentions that even in the 1970s, when film tourism was yet a minor phenomenon in Japan, tensions between local communities and visiting fans have occurred (p. 86).

Such a phenomenon raises the question: who exactly are the so-called local com-munities that negotiate film tourism activities? We believe that a further separation of the term is necessary. For the case of the *asadora Mare*, which we have investi-gated during fieldwork stays from 2015 to 2017, we propose to split up four levels of the so-called local community that became involved in film tourism and should be considered in the analysis: (1) the Prefectural Office, (2) the Mare Promotion Council (Mare suishin kyōgi kai), (3) the Wajima City Tourist Office and Tourist Association (Wajima-shi kankōka/kankō kyōkai) and (4) local people. Although there are complex interrelations between these four levels, which are difficult to investigate in detail, there is a clear hierarchy of power and a general tendency of top-down decision-making.

5.4.1   The Prefectural Office

The *asadora Mare* is set in Ishikawa Prefecture located in the central part of Japan's main island Honshū on the coast of the Sea of Japan. Most of the filming took place in locations belonging to Wajima City (ca. 27,000 inhabitants), an over-aged and depopulated municipality on the Noto Peninsula. The Prefectural Office expected an increased inflow of tourists during the broadcast of *Mare* due to the great atten-tion that a new *asadora* generally receives. Instead of bottom-up movements initi-ated by fans, the planning of film tourism appears as part of the prefecture's general strategy for tourism development. This is evidenced by the fact that *Mare*'s broad-cast started just 2 weeks after the opening of a new bullet train (Hokuriku Shinkansen) track from Tōkyō to Kanazawa City, the prefecture's capital and economic centre.

Fig. 5.1 *Mare* melody road sign on display at a parking area (Source: Authors 2017)

Most tourists must first transfer to Kanazawa City in order to reach the filming locations in Wajima City (the small airport of Wajima with only two flight connections per day is only a minor option). Most tourists go from Kanazawa City by highway bus or (rental) car to Wajima City; the trip takes about 2 h.

Arguably the best-known project of the Prefectural Office in regards to promoting tourism through *Mare* can be seen just prior to arriving in Wajima City. The last section of the highway was rebuilt into a melody road (the longest in Japan at 1.2 km in length), in which the depth and spacing of the grooves combine to play *Mare*'s opening theme song as they are driven over (Fig. 5.1). Melody roads (also known as musical or singing roads) are a rather new phenomenon in Japan, with the first one being established in 2004 (Yoshino et al. 2008). There are also melody roads in other countries such as China, Mexico or Denmark; but in Japan, they are probably most prominent with around 30 melody roads all over the country playing melodies ranging from local folksongs to theme songs of anime movies. In case of Noto, the construction costs were officially also declared as a measure for accident prevention and infrastructure improvements; however, many of the local people we interviewed expressed doubt regarding the necessity of this prestigious project (locals rumour that the construction costs were around 42 million Yen / 350,000 Euro). Augé (1995) defined highways as non-places without story; however, by transforming this highway section into a melody road, it became a place related to the fictive universe of the *asadora*. The visitors do not merely drive into Wajima City anymore; they are unavoidably reminded that they are entering the imaginative world of *Mare*.

5.4.2 *Mare Promotion Council*

In the Noto Peninsula, the Mare Promotion Council was in charge of the touristic activities for *asadora* fans. As a working group established by several local municipalities and the related chamber of commerce, it was a short-lived initiative limited to the fiscal year 2015, when *Mare* was aired; their homepage—as well as NHK's official homepage on *Mare*—disappeared shortly after. A film tourism consultant of the Japan Travel Bureau (Japan's largest and formerly government owned travel agency) served as professional advisor for the council. Financially supported by the Prefectural Office, the council was meant to use the *Mare* content for the promotion of tourism in the Noto region. Such working groups are a common phenomenon in Japan; for example, there was a similar unit established in the case of *Amachan* that even travelled to Kishiwada City in Ōsaka to learn from the local experience of film tourism related to the *asadora Carnation* of 2011 (Tajima 2015, p. 21). Based in Kishiwada City, the Asadora Location Network (Asadora butaichi nettowāku) is a project that aims for a mutual support and learning process for the filming locations of *asadora*. In early 2017, eight municipalities which appeared in six *asadora* participated in this network project (Asadora Location Network 2017).

The Mare Promotion Council created an alternative version of the official *Mare* logo, which was permitted by NHK for promotional items such as flags (Fig. 5.2) or posters. Yamamura (2015) argues that copyright issues are crucial in film tourism. Depending on the media producers/copyright holders' will to collaborate with local governments or initiatives, media content related goods and activities can become overwhelming or rather limited in number, and in some cases, generally forbidden. Couldry (2003) mentions the important aspect that media institutions are usually located at the centre, i.e. in metropolitan areas and therefore distant from the marginal communities that become mediatised (p. 81). Thus, it is no surprise that NHK has its own related company that produces most goods exclusively, and that the broadcaster seems rather unwilling to license products made by other (e.g. rural-based) companies. The difficult issue of copyright becomes even more apparent when looking on the package of official NHK souvenirs such as sweets. Instead of a photo of the *Mare* actress, the package only shows a female shadow or a comic

Fig. 5.2 *Mare* flag with the logo of the Mare Promotion Council in Wajima City and the NHK official logo at a souvenir shop in Kanazawa City (Source: Authors 2015)

figure in allusion of the *asadora* heroine to avoid licence payments to the actress and her agency. In the end, most copyright holders such as NHK prioritise their own business and have no particular agenda towards supporting local communities in their development of film tourism projects.

Besides promotional items and a homepage with a large focus on local information, the Mare Promotion Council organised a stamp and a twitter photo rally. For the stamp rally, fans were meant to visit three places in Noto where they could stamp a postcard which should be sent back in exchange for a gift. Such stamp rallies are a common practice at tourist destinations and also appear in the domain of film tourism (e.g. Yamamura 2015, p. 68). In case of the twitter photo rally, fans were encouraged to take pictures of five filming locations with an integrated *Mare* sticker. These photos were then posted on twitter using a special hashtag (#notosutanpurarī; written in Japanese), and the best one hundred of which were promised a gift. However, it appears that only 11 individuals participated in this one-year-long event. This case demonstrates the extent in which regional planner's expectations differ from actual audience engagement in promotional activities.

5.4.3 Wajima City Tourist Office and Tourist Association

The Wajima City Tourist Office belongs to the Wajima City Office, i.e. the local government, while the Wajima Tourist Association is a private organisation primarily focused on local hot spring tourism. However, both institutions appear to be connected in their activities, following similar goals such as an increase of tourists including *Mare* fans. From April to December 2015, the Tourist Association organised a three times daily minibus tour from Wajima City to a filming location in the city's outskirts that served as *Mare*'s village, during which local volunteers offered visitors 30-minute guided tours to well-known places from the production. Following the cessation of this tour programme, the Tourist Association has offered maps of the filming locations and model courses on their homepage. The Tourism Office also prints maps for fan pilgrimage (Fig. 5.3), which are available at the Tourist Guide Centre at the former Wajima station. As the local public transport is limited, a car is necessary to visit most spots outside of the city's centre. The narrative of the *asadora* created a misleading fictional landscape, where all iconic spots seem rather nearby. Looking on the real map, however, there are distances of more than 60 km; a phenomenon that Frost (2006) named "local dissonance" (p. 71). Baudrillard (1988) argues that once territory preceded maps but that in the postmodern age maps precede the territory and its landscape (p. 166). In case of film tourism, media producers rearrange features of an existing landscape into a fictional map, which fans are then supposed to recreate through their travels. Within the fans' reproduction of these maps of "places of the imagination" (Reijnders 2011), the boundaries between the fictional world of the media content and the existing landscape seem to vanish into what Urry and Larsen (2011) call the "mediatised gaze" (p. 115). By posting their tourist experiences on social media, the fans' pilgrimage photos might coincidently become evidence for the authenticity of the local places appearing in a film production.

In contrast to the Prefectural Office and the short-lived Mare Promotion Council, the Wajima Tourist Office is the most important actor that still aims to continue the *asadora*'s legacy to attract fans. In June 2016, the Wajima Drama Memorial House (Wajima dorama kinenkan) was established. It contains original interiors of the film set (Fig. 5.4) and a place where visitors can buy a small selection of souvenirs, some of which are licensed NHK goods, (e.g. key holders, cups, spoons etc.) but most are locally produced foods with only a loose relation to *Mare*'s world. Located next to Wajima's morning market, the arguably most famous tourist attraction, one might expect that many visitors of the Drama Memorial House do not come particularly as *Mare* fans but rather as regular visitors. A basic problem of the data associated with film tourism is that it is ambiguous; one particular media content and its active fandom cannot be considered as the sole causal mechanism for the inflow of tourists, a plethora of other factors could also be influential. Likewise, in the case of *Mare*, it is difficult to say whether the increased number of visitors to Wajima City in 2015 (plus ca. 30%; Wajima 2017) is a result of the *asadora*'s broadcast or rather the impact of a greater regional tourism strategy such as the new bullet train track and its promotion in national mass media, for example.

Fig. 5.3 *Mare* location map of the Wajima Tourist Office (Source: Authors 2017)

Fig. 5.4 Inside the Wajima Drama Memorial House (Source: Authors 2017)

5.4.4 Local People

The locals of Wajima City were involved in the production of the *asadora* from the beginning; some handicraft men served as experts and dozens of residents participated as extras during the filming of local festivals (see also Chap.11 in this volume). The careful integration and consideration of the local identity guaranteed their collaboration and positive feedback:

> "They filmed parts of *Mare* inside my family's house. The filming crew were very friendly.
> It was great fun for us." (Female, 18, high school student, interviewed in April 2015)

Many small shops in Wajima City began to display *Mare* posters in their windows, even if they were not selling related souvenirs. The national attention of the *asadora* and the region had a feel good effect on many locals who were proud of their apparently authentic representation on national television. For instance, the annual abalone festival 2015 (a commercial event of the local fishermen union) used the *Mare* opening song in an endless loop as background music.

However, as the *asadora*'s broadcast succeeded, a rather conservative and old-fashioned gender ideal became more obvious in the narrative. The heroine Mare gives up her ambitious dream of an international career as pastry chef for devoting her life to her husband and fulfilling the social expectations of being housewife and mother. This development not only irritated parts of the audience but also locals in Wajima City:

"Normally, *asadora* show modern and progressive types of women. *Mare*, however, was different, and that's the reason why many people don't like it anymore." (Male, 58, farmer, interviewed in October 2016)

According to a survey of NHK (Nihei and Sekiguchi 2016), many viewers state that they felt attracted by the series' representation of the rural landscape, the local dialect and handicraft (37%) as well as the filming locations (36%), while they complained about the flow of the narrative (26%), the script (23%) and the heroine's character (16%) (p. 34). If the audience does not enjoy the story, then the often mentioned short lifespan of film tourism becomes inevitably even shorter. This may explain why the legacy of *Oshin* and *Amachan*, for example, seems rather long-lasting, while *Mare*'s traces were rapidly disappearing:

"Everybody has already forgotten about *Mare*; it's normal when the next *asadora* starts, the craze is over." (Male, 60, journalist and consultant, interviewed in March 2017)

Despite this supposed normative phenomenon of forgetting one *asadora* for the next, *Mare* reappeared in the news headlines in August 2016. One of the main actors, whose character was well received by the viewers, was accused of rape. Not only did this scandal eliminate plans for a future television rerun of the *asadora* and the sale of its DVD/Blu-ray stock, its cultural legacy has now taken on a negative outlook:

"You had better to stop talking to local people about *Mare*, that's embarrassing for them [because of the scandal]." (Female, 26, PhD student and local researcher, interviewed in October 2016)

This quote exemplifies how, for the local community, *Mare*'s legacy has become detrimental. Some policy-makers such as the governor of Ishikawa Prefecture, who mentioned *Mare* as great success for the prefecture at a public speech in October 2016, try to keep the positive image alive; yet it is undeniable that this scandal has had a negative impact for film tourism in Wajima City:

"When the Drama Memorial House was opened in summer 2016, about 700 people per day visited this place on weekends or holidays. Recently, there are not more than 150 visitors on such days. Although the winter season is less attractive for tourists, that scandal is probably also an important reason." (Female, 40, staff of the Wajima Drama Memorial House, interviewed in March 2017)

The Drama Memorial House, along with the melody road, remains as inevitable *lieux de mémoire* (Nora 1989) of an *asadora* that left an ambiguous legacy for the locals of Wajima City. Hence, through the case study of *Mare*, this analysis illustrates the limitations of using film tourism as a predictable measure for rural revitalisation.

5.5   Conclusion

The aim of this study was to reconsider the multi-stakeholder perspective in film tourism. As the case study of *Mare* illustrates, the triangular network of participants in the phenomenon of film tourism as described by Yamamura has to be further investigated. What is called "local community" actually includes various parties with differing interests, such as the local government, film tourism working groups, tourist offices and associations and local people. Although these parties vary in many aspects, e.g. in their influence, approach and means, they are following the common belief that film tourism can contribute to the economic revitalisation of their region. In case of Japan, the interrelations between them are difficult to investigate, as they represent different levels of power, and types of institutions or organisation; however, one can expect that there is a general tendency to top-down decision-making as most projects depend on the support of the local governments. The disparity of financial power between the different parties is evident: the local government can rebuild a highway section, while the local tourist association recently only provides maps of the filming locations. Furthermore, local working groups in charge of film tourism, such as the Mare Promotion Council, are increasingly reliant upon various translocal connections (with tourist advisors in the capital Tōkyō, or networks of film tourism communities as seen in the case of Kishiwada City, for example). Thus, the network and actions of stakeholders categorised as local communities are indeed very complex and deserve more attention in the study of film tourism.

Carefully implemented bottom-up oriented measures and activities appear to have a more valuable outcome than top-down prestige projects. In fact, the mere interpretation of film tourism as a strategic planning option for local governments bears many risks, in particular for the local community. Although increases of tourist visits to filming locations appears to be a quasi-automatic effect of popular mass media content such as *asadora*, there are developments and events that might endanger this economic resource, such as an unpopular progression of the storyline or scandals related to the production or cast of the series. Previous studies have shown that the film tourism rush often remains rather short-lived in Japan, thus limiting the efficiency of film tourism for sustainable long-term regional development (Seaton 2015; Suzuki 2011). Additionally, for the local communities, possible negative outcomes of film tourism are frequently discussed in research, such as pollution, heavy traffic, or even increased crime rates due to unregulated tourists' activities (Riley and Van Doren 1992; Beeton 2005; Yoon et al. 2015).

In the case of *Mare*, the final blow given by the rape scandal was unpredictable for all parties, but it was clear before the scandal that the various interest groups had already failed in making Noto a "place of imagination": the orientation towards tourism was partly too obvious in the series, the characters apparently induced little desire for intimacy or interaction, and the "tourist experience" offered on location was rather limited. Therefore, we conclude that any projects aiming at promoting film tourism have to take fan activity and the audience's desire for stimulating content seriously. Only if the imagination is inspired to go on a journey, will fans set out to explore the world of a series on location. It is only if they are able to discover fragments of their imaginary worlds that the fan experience will spread across the digital landscape to become a widely shared passion and a benefit for all parties.

References

Anderson, B. (2006). *Imagined communities: Reflections on the origin and spread of nationalism* (Rev ed.). London: Verso.

Arimura, K. [kasumi_arimura.official]. (2017, March 21). Message posted on Instagram, https://www.instagram.com/p/BR5kTXmB9l_/?hl=ja

Asadora Location Network. (2017). Asadora butai-chi nettowāku kyōgikai. Retrieved April 11, 2017, from http://www.asadora.jp

Augé, M. (1995). *Non-places: An introduction to supermodernity*. London/New York: Verso.

Baudrillard, J. (1988). Simulacra and simulations. In M. Poster (Ed.), *Jean Baudrillard. Selected writings* (pp. 166–184). Cambridge: Polity Press.

Beeton, S. (2005). *Film-induced tourism*. Clevedon: Channel View Publications.

Couldry, N. (2003). *Media rituals. A critical approach*. London: Routledge.

Creighton, M. (1997). Consuming rural Japan: The marketing of tradition and nostalgia in the Japanese travel industry. *Ethnology, 36*(3), 239–254.

Fiske, J. (1992). The cultural economy of fandom. In L. A. Lewis (Ed.), *The adoring audience: Fan culture and popular media* (pp. 30–49). New York: Routledge.

Frost, W. (2006). From backlot to runaway production: Exploring location and authenticity in film-induced tourism. In S. Beeton, G. Croy, & W. Forst (Eds.), *International tourism and media conference proceedings 2006* (pp. 70–78). Melbourne: Tourism Research Unit, Monash University.

Hansen, W. (2016). Creating modern Japanese subjects: Morning rituals from Norito to news and weather. *Religions* [online], 7(3). Retrieved from http://www.mdpi.com/2077-1444/7/3/28

Hills, M. (2013). Fiske's 'textual productivity' and digital fandom: Web 2.0 democratization versus fan distinction? *Participations, 10*(1), 130–153.

Horton, D., & Wohl, R. R. (1956). Mass communication and para-social interaction: Observations on intimacy at a distance. *Psychiatry, 19*, 215–229.

Hoshi, A., Hayashida, M., & Arie, K. (2017). Terebi rajio shichō no genkyō. *Hōsō kenkyū to chōsa (The NHK Monthly Report on Broadcast Research), 67*(3), 88–99.

Jang, K. (2016). Kontentsu ga tsukuru 'keishiki'. In T. Yamamura, P. Seaton, K. Jang, T. Hirai, & Y. Kouta (Eds.), *The scope of contents tourism studies* (pp. 83–97). Sapporo: Hokkaido University.

Jenkins, H. (1992). *Textual poachers: Television fans and participatory culture*. London: Routledge.

Kelly, W. W. (2004). Introduction. Locating the fans. In W. W. Kelly (Ed.), *Fanning the flames. Fans and consumer culture in contemporary Japan* (pp. 1–16). Albany: State University of New York Press.

Kim, S. (2010). Extraordinary experience: Re-enacting and photographing at screen tourism locations. *Tourism and Hospitality Planning & Development, 7*(1), 59–75.

Kim, S. (2012). Audience involvement and film tourism experiences: Emotional places, emotional experiences. *Tourism Management, 33*, 387–396.

Kim, S. S., Agrusa, J., Lee, H., & Chon, K. (2007). Effects of Korean television dramas on the flow of Japanese tourists. *Tourism Management, 28*(5), 1340–1353.

Meiji būmu de roke daihanjō. Aichi-ken Ōzu no shimin wa bikkuri. (1966, July 12). *Yomiuri Shinbun* (evening edition), p. 10.

Naiki Kokoro [@naiki_cocoro]. (2015, September 22, 14:34). Message posted on Twitter, https://twitter.com/naiki_cocoro/status/646437460889612288

NHK. (2012). Kankuro Kudo-san ga kataru! 'Ama-chan' wa konna dorama. Retrieved April 11, 2017, from https://www.nhk.or.jp/dramatopics-blog/100000/122888.html

NHK. (2017, February 27). Shutsuensha messēji. No. 1 hiroin Arimura Kasumi. Retrieved from http://www.nhk.or.jp/mito/hiyokko/message/01.html

Nihei, W., & Sekiguchi, S. (2014). Sōsharu' ga umu terebi shichōnetsu!? Amachan genshō ga nagekaketa mono. *Hōsō kenkyū to chōsa (The NHK Monthly Report on Broadcast Research), 64*(6), 2–17.

Nihei, W., & Sekiguchi, S. (2016). Saikin kōchōna 'asadora' o, shichōsha wa dono yō ni mite iru ka. *Hōsō kenkyū to chōsa (The NHK Monthly Report on Broadcast Research), 66*(3), 14–42.

Nora, P. (1989). Between memory and history: Les lieux de mémoire. *Representations, 26,* 7–24.

Okamoto, T. (2015). Otaku tourism and the anime pilgrimage phenomenon in Japan. *Japan Forum, 27*(1), 12–36.

'Oshin' no furusato Sakata, Ginzan onsen to sakuranbo-gari [advertisement]. (1983, May 31). *Yomiuri Shinbun* (evening edition), p. 7.

Rath, E. C. (2015). The invention of local food. In J. Farrer (Ed.), *The globalization of Asian cuisines. Transnational networks and culinary contact zones* (pp. 145–164). New York: Palgrave Macmillan.

Reijnders, S. (2011). *Places of the imagination: Media, tourism, culture.* Farnham: Ashgate Publishing.

Riley, R. W., & Van Doren, C. S. (1992). Movies as tourism promotion. A 'pull' factor in a 'push' location. *Tourism Management, 13*(3), 267–274.

Seaton, P. (2015). Taiga dramas and tourism: Historical contents as sustainable tourist resources. *Japan Forum, 27*(1), 82–103.

Seaton, P., & Yamamura, T. (2015). Japanese popular culture and contents tourism – Introduction. *Japan Forum, 27*(1), 1–11.

Shefner-Rogers, C. L., Rogers, E. M., & Singhal, A. (1998). Parasocial interaction with the television soap operas 'Simplemente Maria' and 'Oshin'. *Keio Communication Review, 20,* 3–18.

Steinberg, M. (2012). *Anime's media mix: Franchising toys and characters in Japan.* Minneapolis: University of Minnesota Press.

Suzuki, K. (2011). Some overlooked drawbacks of Japanese media-induced tourism: A critical reinvestigation. *Ritsumeikan Chirigaku, 23,* 11–25.

Tajima, Y. (2015). NHK Asa no renzoku terebi shōsetsu 'Amachan' no Kuji-shi ni okeru juyō. *Doshisha University Social Science Review, 116,* 15–40.

Takō, W. (2012). *Taisetsu na koto wa minna asadora ga oshiete kureta.* Tōkyō: Ōta shuppan.

Tanaka, Y. (2014). 'Amachan' ga hiraita atarashii tobira. 'Hōgen kosuperedorama' ga dekiru made. In S. Kinsui, Y. Tanaka, & M. Okamuro (Eds.), *Dorama to hōgen no atarashii kankei* (pp. 22–43). Kasama Shoin: Tōkyō.

Terebi ijō no kandō o ajiwatte kudasai [advertisement]. (1984, March 14). Asahi Shinbun (morning edition), p. 18.

Terebi shōsetsu to gotōchi no munazanyō. (1977, February 13). *Yomiuri Shinbun* (morning edition), p. 23.

Urry, J., & Larsen, J. (2011). *The tourist gaze 3.0* (2nd ed.). Los Angeles: Sage.

Wajima City. (2017). Kankō dēta. Retrieved April 11, 2017, from http://wajimanavi.lg.jp/www/data/

Yamamura, T. (2015). Contents tourism and local community response: Lucky star and collaborative anime-induced tourism in Washimiya. *Japan Forum, 27*(1), 59–81.

Yoon, Y., et al. (2015). Successful and unsuccessful film tourism destinations: From the perspective of Korean local residents' perceptions of film tourism impacts. *Tourism Analysis, 20*(3), 297–311.

Yoshino, M., et al. (2008). Evaluation of musical pavement in Kawade-cho, Toyota. *Journal of National Institute of Technology, Toyota College, 41,* 95–100.

Zakkichō. (1983, September 18). *Mainichi Shinbun,* p. 23.

Chapter 6
The Beach Goes Full Circle: The Case of Koh Phi Phi, Thailand

Faye Taylor

Abstract Arguably, one of the most significant factors influencing the development of tourism on Phi Phi Island, Thailand, was the filming of *The Beach* in 1998. *The Beach*, based upon the novel by Alex Garland in 1996, describes a backpacker's quest for an island utopia. Ironically, the novel was not intended to celebrate backpacker culture but to criticise it. On Phi Phi, the primary filming location, both the book and the subsequent film opened the floodgates to millions more backpackers to join the multitude already making their way along the well-trodden tourist trail. In the period prior to and during the filming, the controversy surrounding *The Beach* was tremendous amongst environmental activists and the media. This chapter explores the debates and controversies surrounding the impact of Fox's decision to film *The Beach* on Phi Phi and draws upon longitudinal field research to map the nature of tourism development from the point of filming to the present day. Has *The Beach* gone full circle?

Keywords *The Beach* • Phi Phi • Film tourism • Fox • Stakeholders • Impacts

6.1 Introduction

An increasing volume of researchers have explored the phenomenon of film tourism. This has been undertaken from a range of differing perspectives, for example, the impact that filming in a particular location can have upon destination image (Heitmann 2010; Young and Young 2008; Hahm and Wang 2011; Yoon et al. 2015), the motivations and experiences of film tourists (Macionis and Sparks 2009) and, most widely, the impact upon inducing tourism demand (Hudson and Ritchie 2006; Heitmann 2010; Riley et al. 1998; Young and Young 2008). There is a wide consensus that selecting a destination as a filming location for a television programme or movie will bring about an increase in volume of tourists (Beeton 2010) on account of a desire to see the filming location (Hudson and Ritchie 2006; Beeton 2010;

F. Taylor (✉)
Nottingham Trent University, Nottingham, UK
e-mail: faye.taylor@ntu.ac.uk

Riley et al. 1998), and this will in turn generate positive economic consequences for the destination's stakeholders (Hudson and Ritchie 2006; Beeton 2010; Croy 2011; Yoon et al. 2015) and in some cases positive sociocultural consequences (Dyer et al. 2003). Some researchers have taken a film (or destination specific) approach (Grihault 2003) through which to analyse the above research themes, for example, Hudson and Ritchie (2006) in the case of Cephalonia and *Captain Corelli's Mandolin*, Connell (2005) in the case of the Isle of Mull and *Balamory* and Busby and Klug (2001) in the case of *Notting Hill*.

One such destination that has been the target of academic attention since 1998, when Fox productions selected it as the filming location for the motion picture *The Beach*, starring Leonardo Di Caprio, is that of Maya Bay, located on the island of Koh Phi Phi Leh, in the Krabi province of the Thai Andaman (Taylor 2012; Law et al. 2007; Cohen 2005). Studies of the political economy of tourism development (Cohen 2005; Taylor 2012) within this region have noted stakeholder conflict in respect of access, management and governance of *The Beach* (Maya Bay), concerns regarding the neo-liberalism of nature (Law et al. 2007) and, in some cases, researchers have suggested (Cohen 2005) that the actual filming in this location has catalysed the same effect (described within Alex Garland's novel) on Phi Phi itself.

This chapter will consider the case of *The Beach's* filming on Phi Phi. Given that the message in Alex Garland's novel (1996), which inspired the film, is about rampant tourism destroying a destination, the author will draw upon the various debates and discussions surrounding *The Beach* and Koh Phi Phi, in addition to her own longitudinal research fieldwork on the islands (between 2000 and 2015), to consider what the long-term impact of the film has been. Moreover, to what extent has the filming catalysed a form of environmental decay as described by Garland?

Fox's motion picture *The Beach* follows the story of Richard, a backpacker in Thailand on a quest to find an island utopia. Richard's quest is eased when he meets Daffy, a suicidal drifter who shares knowledge of a secret beach, on a paradise island, that is free from the parasites and destruction of civilisation. The film was actually based upon the novel by Alex Garland. Ironically, the novel was not intended to celebrate backpacker culture but to criticise it. The story tracks the development of the community on *The Beach* to the point that their fierce desire for secrecy and isolation erodes the values that drove its establishment. The book and the subsequent film opened the floodgates to millions more backpackers to join the multitude already making their way along the well-trodden tourist trail. This chapter will consider the issues and debates surrounding the impact of film tourism, using the case of *The Beach* and the Phi Phi Island archipelago. The decision by Fox and the Thai Royal Forestry's decision to use Phi Phi Le's Maya Bay as the prime filming location was shrouded in controversy from the outset yet remains one of the most important factors in influencing the tourism development of the Phi Phi Islands. Whether this is a good thing or not will be called into question within this chapter. We will consider, has the message of Alex Garland's novel *The Beach (1996)*, through the film, been realised?? (Shelby-Biggs 2000).

6.2 Methodology

This chapter is constructed in light of longitudinal research fieldwork and observations on the Phi Phi Islands from 2000 until the present day. The goal of the research was to assess the influence of political economy and interpretations of sustainability, over the post-tsunami tourism redevelopment of the Phi Phi Islands. However, throughout the research, the impact of *The Beach* upon Phi Phi's tourism development was a dominant theme, as well as being a powerful indicator of the political economy and development ideology surrounding tourism development in Thailand. The chapter is therefore formed through both familiarity with the literature base and debate surrounding *The Beach*, but a personal mapping, via fieldwork and primary data collection, of the tourism development has occurred on the Phi Phi islands following on from the filming of *The Beach* in Maya Bay.

Over the period of longitudinal study, frequent visits were made to the islands, with a concentration of visits made during 2005–2006 (on account of living in Phuket at that time) in order to collect data. Several return visits were made to Phi Phi, by the author, in 2011, 2012 and 2015 for a number of reasons. Firstly, to add a sense of completeness to the study of a longitudinal nature and secondly, to add credence and further evidence that the conclusions and recommendations are indeed accurate and realistic.

A multi-strategy research approach was employed with a plurality of stakeholder groups who have a vested interest in tourism development. They include Thai and non-Thai residents of Phi Phi, government representatives, tourists, academics and activists and the tourism industry.

These stakeholders were structured via a theoretical sampling strategy and recruited purposively via personal communication or visits. Snowball sampling was also employed as additional respondents were suggested during the fieldwork. In total, 29 in-depth semi-structured interviews were conducted. Interview respondents were questioned on their nature of familiarity with the island and their opinions on the circumstances that led to the island's record on sustainable development. They were also questioned on whether there was a consistent and explicit philosophy underpinning the island redevelopment and of how the concept of sustainable development was being used by stakeholders within the discourse surrounding the planning and redevelopment of the island. Subsequently a questionnaire was administered to 38 Thai residents with questions relating to the themes of their opinions on the advantages and disadvantages of tourism, their hopes and vision for the future of the island, barriers in achieving what they desire for the future and finally, their conceptualisation of sustainability.

The fieldwork occurred in three phases. Phase one, 2005–2006, consisted of exploration and piloting. Phase two, 2006–2008, when primary data was collected via in-depth interview, personal observations were undertaken and visual data was collected. Phase three, 2011–2015, when follow-up observations and visual data were collected.

6.3   A Geographical Overview of the Phi Phi Islands

Phi Phi Don and Phi Phi Le are, to many, the epitome of a paradise island location. Incorporated into the Hat Noppharat Thara National Marine Park in 1983, the island group is located within the Ao Nang sub-district of the Krabi Province of southern Thailand as illustrated by the maps below, 42 kilometres from the holiday mecca of Phuket and 38 kilometres from the provincial capital, Krabi Town (www. phi-phi.com). They represent another addition to the great number of island and beach destinations in southern Thailand, which include Koh Samui, Koh Phuket, Koh Phan Ngan and Koh Tao, which developed beginning in the 1980s to support tourism activities. Phi Phi is within easy travelling distance (by boat) of both Phuket and Krabi, the journey taking approximately 90 min. Despite being more accessible in recent times, the islands bear similarities to Cohen's (1983) description of Koh Samui in the 1980s: they are little incorporated into the national society and only superficially controlled by the national civil administration and police (Fig. 6.1).

Figure 6.2 illustrates the two main islands within the group: Phi Phi Don, the largest inhabited island (8 km long by 2 km wide), and Phi Phi Le (3.5 km long and 1 km wide), which is uninhabited on account of its National Park status. This is of notable importance in the controversy surrounding *The Beach*. Whilst Phi Phi Le was the chosen filming location for Fox's motion picture, the development of tourism occurred where development was permissible, on the larger island, Phi Phi Don, and most specifically the central Tonsai/Ao lo Dalaam area (familiarly termed the "apple core"). It is widely deemed that *The Beach* is accountable for the extent of development that has occurred on Phi Phi Don.

The distinctive nature of the islands when they were in the initial stages of tourism development (early 1980s) was made clear by travel writer, Joe Cummings (2005b:2): *"the green-tipped limestone peaks rising above the still sea … the impossible beautiful crescent of turquoise-rimmed sand, offered a single set of simple thatched-roof bungalows"*. At that time the islands could only be reached by a 4-hour long tail boat trip from the port of Krabi Town. The tourism infrastructure was limited for those who were searching for something different and to escape from the hordes that frequented the normal tourist trail, likened to Cohen's "drifters" and somewhat similar to Richard's desires in *The Beach*. The Phi Phi islands and the Krabi region in its entirety are characterised by limestone cliffs coated with a thick layer of jungle, as depicted in Fig. 6.3. The nature of these limestone cliffs make logging and access difficult, and therefore these areas are home to diverse ecosystems (Fahn 2008). The limestone itself is of archaeological significance, and the "karst" structure and chemical components result in cave formations, home to fragile ecosystems (Fahn 2008). Human action and interference can cause severe effects for these ecosystems.

Fig. 6.1 Map to illustrate the location of the Phi Phi islands within the Krabi Province (Source: http://aiat.in.th/ejc2017/front/show/about-krabi. Accessed 27.02.2017)

Fig. 6.2 Phi Phi Don (Source: http://www.ko-phiphi.com/maps/. Accessed 24.11.2016)

6.4 Significance and Development of Tourism on Phi Phi

Tourism to Thailand currently contributes THB 1037.3 billion (approximately US$ 29 million) towards gross domestic product, comprising 8.6% of GDP and generating 2.2 million jobs directly, comprising 5.8% of total employment. The contribution of tourism to the Thai economy is expected to grow 8.2% per annum to 7.9% of GDP and account for 2.99 million jobs by 2021. Dodds (2010) recognises the support that is afforded to the tourism industry in Thailand as a means for economic development, which reflects modernist principles. However, she cautions that the costs of such development are often not considered as readily as the financial gains. This is something that rings true in the case of Phi Phi. The effects of mass tourism

Fig. 6.3 Tonsai Bay (*left*) and Ao Lo Dalaam bay (*right*) with the central apple core area, Phi Phi Don Island (Author's own, Taken 28.3.2006)

are noted within her study, in the poor quality of marine water and death of the coral reef, effects which mirror those of other Thai beach resorts like Patong Beach in Phuket, southern Thailand (Dodds 2010).

On the Phi Phi Islands, the infrastructure on the flat, sandy isthmus of land between the bays of Ao Tonsai and Ao Lo Dalaam on Phi Phi Don has developed since the 1980s to support increasing numbers of tourists and is described as "packed with multi-storey concrete hotels, pizza parlours, dive shops, and souvenir stands – behind which stood rotting piles of garbage" (Cummings 2005a:1). However, despite these apparent environmental consequences of tourism development, the islands' popularity continued to increase, and development continued to take place with a lack of planning that has resulted in encroachment onto the Hat Noppharat Thara National Marine Park (Cummings 2005a, b). Dodds et al. (2010) highlight the similarities between Phi Phi and Gili Trawangan in Indonesia through their empirical research on both islands in respect of the development challenges posed by a burgeoning tourism industry constrained to a small area within a national marine park. They note how an increase in tourism infrastructure has led to environmental degradation through unchecked development (Dodds et al. 2010; Dodds 2010).

Prior to the tsunami of December 2004, visitor numbers to Phi Phi had reached approximately 1.2 million annually (Dodds 2010; Brix et al. 2007, 2011), up from 150,000 immediately following the filming of *The Beach* in 2000. This then reduced to 500,000 following the tsunami (ibid. 2010). The bulk of visitors are in fact day-trippers from Phuket and Krabi, totalling at times 5000 per day prior to the tsunami (Dodds 2010). An accurate picture of visitor numbers to the islands is difficult to ascertain, however, as there is no formal registration for arrivals (personal communication, November 2006). A method of registering arrivals was only introduced following the reconstruction of a deepwater pier in Tonsai in 2009 and subsequent implementation of a 20 baht arrival fee in 2010, although the extent to which arrivals are logged and reported is still yet to be seen. Additionally, as most day-trippers arrive by speedboat to the shores of Tonsai, bypassing the pier, they also bypass the 20 baht arrival fee. Additionally, resorts on the north-eastern beaches may offer their own private transfers via catamaran from Phuket's Rassada Pier, which again bypasses registration at the pier on Phi Phi (http://www.hospitalitynet.org/news/4020701.html). This makes quantifying visitor numbers to the islands accurately, rather difficult, although currentfigures are estimated at 1.4 million per annum, reaching 10,000 per day in peak tourist season.

Figure 6.4 below provides a summary of the key milestones in Phi Phi's social and tourist-related development. One must note, however, that data on tourist arriv-

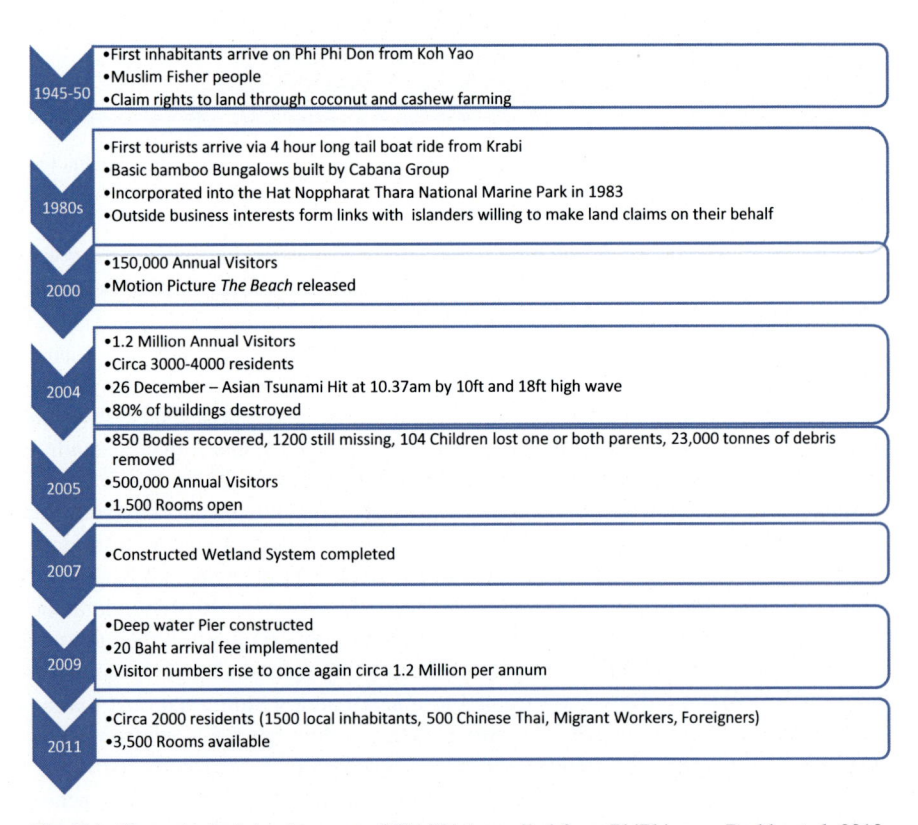

Fig. 6.4 Chronological development of Phi Phi (compiled from PhiPhi.com; Dodds et al. 2010; Cohen 1983)

als to the island are limited as a result of a lack of a reliable method of registering arrivals, until the inception of the 20 baht registration fee in 2009 (Dodds 2010).

6.5 The Controversies of *The Beach*

It is clear that the development of tourism on Phi Phi Don (where development is permissible) has been catalysed by the recognition afforded to Maya Bay through the filming of *The Beach* in 1998. This can be seen in the surge in visitor numbers from 150,000 annual visitors in 2000 (at the point of the film's release) to 1.2 million annual visitors pre-tsunami in 2004. *The Beach* presented as one of the most dominant themes within the qualitative data collection amongst the "tourist" stakeholder group. As one respondent stated, *"I came here to see the place where The Beach was filmed, to watch the film in one of the many restaurants around the island and to be photographed in the 'perfect' beach resort"*. It was clear that *The Beach* represented an important element of the tourist gaze for Phi Phi, as Law et al. (2007) also found, and this fuelled a rapid growth in demand for travel to the islands. However, this growth has not come without controversy.

Certainly, in the period prior to and during the filming, the controversy surrounding *The Beach* was tremendous amongst environmental activists and the media (e.g. Ekachai 1998; Fuengprichavai 1998; Ing 1998; Laopaisarntaksin 1998; Noikorn 1998; Puthipucha 1998;). There was extensive press coverage in Thai-based English language dailies such as the Bangkok Post and The Nation, not to mention other international press to document that permission had been granted by the Thai Royal Forestry Department to film on National Park Land (Bangkok Post, 6/11/98; 29/10/98; 30/10/98; 12/11/98; The Nation, 13/11/98; 15/11/98; 21/11/98. These are only a small sample of articles that overwhelmed the press at that time). These articles, led by Thai-based environmentalists and academics, voiced sincere opposition to the actions of both the Thai Royal Forestry Department and 20th Century Fox, with key arguments associated with permission being granted in the first place and the restructuring of Maya Bay. It was claimed by these opponents that in exchange for a cash contribution of 4 million baht (approx. US$ 114,000), a "permanent damage deposit" of 5 million baht (approx. US$ 143,000) (The Nation, 3/11/98) and the promise of increased tourism receipts of 300 million baht (Bangkok Post, 30/10/98), the production team were permitted not only to remove native plants such as giant milkweed, sea pandanus and spider lily that support the sand dunes and prevent erosion but to plant coconut trees (Bangkok Post, 29/10/98) to more accurately mirror "paradise" (Bangkok Post, 30/10/98). Opponents were outraged not only that restructuring was permitted, in violation of the 1992 Environmental Protection Act and the 1961 National Park Act (The Nation, 11/11/98), but that this case was another "vulgar sell-out" by the country's policymakers in the name of the tourist dollar (The Nation, 4/11/98).

Many of the accusations made against 20th Century Fox during filming are centred around the alleged "environmental restructuring" of Maya Bay in order to more closely mirror their perception of paradise, which was perceived to include swaying palm trees, not naturally occurring in this particular location. Law et al. (2007) recognise the role that this environmental "staging" held in line with the tourist "gaze". It is argued that authorities permitted reconstruction of Maya Bay in order to satisfy Hollywood's stereotype of an exotic beach (Bangkok Post, 30/10/98). Why had Phi Phi Le been selected as the location for filming "paradise" if paradise requires cosmetic upgrading? The restructuring included uprooting native plants and planting over a hundred coconut palms. A concern voiced by islanders and environmental activists alike is that removing native shrubs can lead to topsoil eroding and being washed into the sea during the monsoon, choking the coral in Maya Bay. In fact, further criticism has been made of those officials who considered these coconut palms should remain after filming in order to justify the label of "paradise" (The Nation, 3.11.98). Further "restructuring" to accommodate the needs of visitors post filming (like toilet facilities) caused controversy then and are still the cause of much dissatisfaction now (Thamrongnawasat 2016). Islanders also noted their lack of power to leverage change. As one landowner said in a face to face interview back in 2006:

> the Royal Forestry Department ... are so powerful then [sic], they have a powerful voice, more powerful than the locals. So they now start to build up a toilet on the island [sic], and there is supposed to be no building but now there is some kind of construction so now we have a toilet and a small office for the officer who takes care of Maya to stay overnight.

This view of discontentment with, firstly the granting of permission to film and secondly the way in which May Bay was being exploited, was shared by other stakeholders:

> One thing that everyone seems to have missed is that Phi Phi was, and still is, a National Park. By Thai law no permanent structures are allowed on National Park [land]. That means that many tsunami victims were residing in illegally built lodging. I don't know why a good lawyer hasn't picked up on this.

Not only did the case of *The Beach* illustrate a neglect for the environment alleged by environmentalists, academics and the media alike, it also exposed wider concern regarding the political agenda of the Royal Forestry Department, which is responsible for the administration of Thai National Parks. Maya Bay is part of the Hat Noppharat Thara National Marine Park, and therefore development or restructuring is prohibited; and yet the Royal Forestry Department agreed to the filming based upon the "donation" of 4 million baht (approx. US$ 114,000) plus a 5 million baht (approx. US$ 143,000) "environmental bond" (Bangkok Post, 25/10/98). Environmentalists and academics allege that, despite being protected by National Park status and with Phi Phi Le being also a conservation area under the protection of the Environmental Act of BE2535 (Ing 1998) and alterations being prohibited under Article 16 of the National Park Laws, the Royal Forestry Department approved the filming in exchange for a 5 million baht damage guarantee, 4 million baht contribution in order to establish a Forestry Protection Unit (The Nation, 3/11/98) and an estimated 300 million baht (approx. US$ 8.6 million) in projected tourism revenue, to "nourish" the money-craving nation (Bangkok Post, 30/10/98).

It was voiced by some commentators that the "sell-out" of Thailand's environmental resources was no different to the sale of bodies in the sex districts of Patpong, Bangkok, claiming that anything can be sold to titillate the desires of the tourist (Puthipucha 1998). Despite various demonstrations, campaigns, the submission of a petition against the filming and a subsequent enquiry conducted by a panel of environmentalists, headed by Surapol Surada of Chulalongkorn University (The Nation, 4/12/98), filming was be permitted, despite the sentiment that the panel was not neutral, being set up by the Royal Forestry Department (The Nation, 5/12/98, Bangkok Post, 5/12/98). These events illustrated the willingness of policy-makers to be influenced in the name of economic gain, a lack of environmental pre- and post-impact assessment and inadequate consultation with all stakeholders. There was also much publicity at the time of threats being made against the lives of key activists in the campaign against filming (The Nation, 4/12/98; The Nation, 1/12/98).

This case points to the wider concern for the fate of Thailand's National Parks, voiced in an article of The Nation on 2nd December 1998 where it was argued that

> "places like Phi Phi Don will suffer under the weight of environmental decay like Pattaya … but the Phi Phi islands were not supposed to follow either of these routes. Like other increasingly popular spots such as Koh Samet and Koh Chang, the area is supposed to be a National Park … National Parks are the one place where the rules of the marketplace are not supposed to reign".

The dynamics and nature of the struggle between the Thai government and other actors were viewed by Cohen (2005) through a political economy lens, who concluded that Maya Beach was a "paragon of absurdity" after evaluating the critical discourses surrounding the filming presented by different stakeholder groups. Another critical observer of the case of Phi Phi and *The Beach* (Forsyth 2002) counters that certain stakeholders (environmental activists) had in fact overstated the film's environmental impact to "empower criticisms of the state".

6.6 The Impacts of *The Beach*

Despite this controversy, visiting Phi Phi both pre- and post-tsunami, it would appear that local businesses consider *The Beach* to be the core of Phi Phi's tourist product, recognising and capitalising upon the economic benefits associated with fulfilling the desire to visit and be photographed in the same location as Leonardo Di Caprio, which is saddening when the islands have so much else to offer. On visiting Phi Phi Don, almost every boat trip available from or to Phi Phi includes within its itinerary "Maya Bay – home of *The Beach*", and almost every restaurant within its daily schedule plays *The Beach* on DVD for crowds of travellers (personal observations throughout 2002–2012).

Whilst the filming of *The Beach* has undoubtedly created awareness of the Phi Phi islands, a "driver" of tourism development, it is undeniable that the beauty of the islands and profusion of underwater and land-based attractions meant that they had already been gathering momentum as tourist destinations prior to this. Following the release of this motion picture and subsequent increase in demand, the island infrastructure was adapted hastily and without any apparent consideration for planning (Fahn 2008), a response mirroring that observed by Beeton (2016) in the wake of the filming of *Sea Change* in Barwon Heads, Australia. Stakeholders noted the environmental impact that an increase in tour boats (to see Maya Bay) had brought about:

> and the fuel, if you see the ferry [sic] that arrive in the morning and the long tail boat, sometimes you can see the oil on the water on the surface but the oil never leave[s]. We have a tide, high tide, low tide, but at the pier if you look down at the bottom you see a residue, a brown residue on the bottom. The cause is also from the fuel from the ferries and long tail boats. (Landowner on Phi Phi, via interview, 2005)

This rapid expansion in demand is documented by The Nation (1/12/98), who claim that unless arriving on the island before 12 noon, there is no accommodation to be found. They also record a steep rise in the price of food and accommodation due to this excess demand, a similar finding to that of Riley et al. (1998) in other film locations. It is therefore no wonder that *The Beach* acted as a catalyst for a building boom, regardless of planning considerations or safety. Ironically, the same mismatch in terms of supply and demand was described by tour agencies when the author visited Phi Phi Don again in December 2011. Once again, visitors are advised to take the morning boat to Phi Phi on account of a lack of accommodation (personal communication with tour agencies on Phi Phi, December 2011). Similar drawbacks were observed in other film tourism locations, for example, the impact upon the "quiet moorland community" of Goathland following the filming of *Heartbeat*. Tooke and Baker (1996) similarly observed this impact upon carry capacity in their study of the UK film industry.

In an attempt to manage visitor flows to Maya Bay, a National Park entrance fee of 400 baht (for international tourists) was levied in 2007; however, this has done little to stem the volume of tourists wishing to step foot on Leo's beach, and those that do not wish to pay the fee can still enter the bay, generating environmental concerns in respect of water and noise pollution as well as overcrowding and the impact upon the spirit of the place. Current researchers and environmental activists in this field are calling into question the administration of these fees (Thamrongnawasat 2016) and demanding a closure to Maya Bay, to permit regeneration of bleached coral and other marine life (Phuket Gazette 16/05/16).

Additionally, there is ongoing conflict between boat tour operators and the Royal Forestry Department concerning the fee, which threatens to undermine the administration and governance of the fee system (Bangkok Post 22/02/17). Boat operators claim that the fee levy influences tourism demand but this is countered by the Royal Forestry Department, who claims that numbers are still on the increase, citing 212, 299 foreign visitors in 2015 and 1.3 million in 2016, with a yield of 600 million baht (approx. US$ 17 million) (Bangkok Post 22/02/17). Nevertheless, such a sharp increase (fivefold) within 1 year may be deemed both questionable and alarming, on account of discrepancies in reported figures. No wonder activists continue to lobby against visitation outright to Maya Bay, deeming it an environmental disaster (Bangkok Post 07/07/16).

6.7 *The Beach* Today

So, 16 years on, what is the collective legacy of the Thai Royal Forestry Department and Fox's decision to use Maya Bay as the filming location of *The Beach?*

Whilst it would be unjust to attribute all of Phi Phi's problems to *The Beach*, as Busby and Klug (2001) caution in their research regarding the challenges of measuring film tourism in London's Notting Hill, the film undoubtedly catalysed the growth in tourism, as a form of organic image (Gunn 1988) to Maya Bay. The impacts of tourism growth being felt not only on Maya Bay itself but to a greater extent on Koh Phi Phi Don, whereby a lack of clarity concerning National Park boundaries made infrastructure development possible. The problem is that the pace and scale of growth was, and still is, untenable, in a destination which lacks capacity to accommodate tourist volumes of this extent and also lacks robust infrastructure to support the resource demands of such high volumes of tourists (Taylor 2012; Thamrongnawasat 2016). The detrimental societal and environmental problems are notable and were widely cited within the data collection, for example, one island resident noted through an interview in 2006, the implications of a shift away from drifter style backpacker tourism towards mass tourism, indicating also their own progression along Doxey's index of irritation:

> A long time ago it was backpackers, people who wanted to do something a little bit different. Now we are getting our 'Magaluf' types. I hate it and the drinking, this is a Muslim island and it is a National Park. It is horrible, the people [tourists] are so wasted on Sangsom (Thai Rum), and they are walking around the streets completely pissed up.

This chimes with the findings of Beeton (2001) who observed that film tourism has the ability to commodify and alter the mix of tourists to an area, impacting upon the traditional holiday market (in Phi Phi's case backpackers), irritating the locals (Beeton 2016) and introducing a new, intrusive style of tourism. Like with the findings of Heitmann's (2010) research, through the case of *The Beach* and Koh Phi Phi, one can question the viability of film tourism for sustainable tourism development.

What is interesting is that even after such time has elapsed, *The Beach* still forms a powerful component of the destination brand for the Phi Phi Islands and particularly Maya Bay, being regarded as synonymous with *The Beach*. This extends Riley et al.'s (1998) earlier work which found that visitation increases generally for a period of 4 years after filming. The effect on Phi Phi is much longer. In fact, the islands are still promoted by the Tourism Authority of Thailand on the basis of *The Beach* as below:

> Phi Phi Ley was featured in the Hollywood blockbuster movie The Beach, a story about the ultimate secluded island beach. Maya Bay was a suitable choice as it epitomizes the stunning beauty of these islands: a bay of pellucid aquamarine water surrounded by towering limestone cliffs that harbours an arcing, white sand beach. (http://uk.tourismthailand.org/About-Thailand/Destination/Ko-Phi-Phi)

In the author's latest visit in 2015, the ferry taken with Andaman Wavemaster from Phuket's Rassada Pier was full to capacity: all interior seats were filled and no deck space was available as the deck was packed with groups of travellers of mixed ages sunbathing and drinking. These were travellers with technology: expensive cameras and laptops were clearly on display, the epitome of a post-modern flash packer (Paris and Teye 2010; Paris 2012; Hannam and Diekmann 2010; Cohen 2010) or, as Paris and Teye (2010) term them, "the digital nomads", members of a new global elite that symbolise an ongoing convergence in society of technology, mobility and daily life. Phi Phi is still appealing and a popular choice for tourists seeking a beach-based experience in the south of Thailand. Informal conversations on this visit indicated a perception of the island as a place to party and to tan, comparable with Koh Phan Ngan, renowned for monthly full moon parties. It seemed that the party started the moment these larger groups stepped on the boat. This was the basis of the island's appeal back in 2006 when data was collected from visitors to the island; when asked why they came to the island, motivation was based upon, *"the beaches, aesthetic beauty, diving, nightlife and the 'laid back' atmosphere"*. In the case of Phi Phi, as Macionis and Sparks (2009) also found, *The Beach* does not appear to be a primary motivator, most visitors are "incidental" film tourists, which has a tendency to bring about unsustainable forms or organic growth.

The author's travel party had reserved accommodation in which she had stayed many times before during the field study. Upon arrival at the bungalows, the author and accompanying travel party were greatly disappointed at the state of disrepair the resort had fallen into and the presence of a large block of rooms that had been constructed by the owner, which impeded the once-pleasing views from the hillside bungalows. This served to illustrate the pressure in the central part of the island: increasing demand for bed space coupled with a lack of capacity and multiple landowners in a small area, all wishing to capitalise on their assets (there is no need to point out the short-sightedness of this approach). It was clear that sustainability has not been, and will not be, on the agenda of the majority of the landowners and business owners in the central part of the island. As an early interview respondent (an Ecotourism Operator) had suggested in 2006, the island is being *"raped"*.

The image below depicts how precious an asset land in the central area of Phi Phi is perceived as and how tightly packed the constructions are. Again, this is the same form of construction used prior to the tsunami, which heightened vulnerability, exacerbated the number of casualties and caused great destruction in human, infrastructure and economic terms (Ingram et al. 2006). Members of the travel party were overwhelmed by how claustrophobic the central part of the island felt. Buildings are crammed into a very small area and in fact now represent a further hazard in terms of fire evacuation. Waste was either overflowing from bins or strewn on the ground beside footpaths and the smell from the waste was pungent. The author recalled a comment made by one of her interview respondents, an island resident, many years earlier in 2007: *"Tourists have eyes and they have noses, they can smell the shit"* (Fig. 6.5).

This served as a vivid reminder that the present needs of the island are not being met, and the island is essentially in survival mode. This situation does not seem to have abated since the main phase of data collection in 2005–2008. At that time, one tour operator offered the opinion that:

Fig. 6.5 View from the Tropical Garden Bungalows (Author 2015)

The infrastructure is not robust enough to support the growing number of accommodation and businesses growing on the island. One example [that] may be cited is the filthy and unhygienic flooding that seems to be a regular event on one of the main roads.

In the intervening years, a new deepwater pier has been constructed, but the benefit here is limited to facilitating greater volume of tourist traffic. The wastewater treatment and wetlands system were constructed, but these benefits are only key players in the central part of the island, who are attached to the system, and it functions improperly, as will be discussed below. A resolution surrounding other utilities is still yet to be reached (Fig. 6.6).

One of the main sustainability initiatives (Dodds 2010; Brix et al. 2007, 2011), the wastewater treatment and wetlands system in the centre of the island, was, in 2007, hailed to be a rehabilitation project which would "secure sustainability by

Fig. 6.6 Constructed Wetlands (Author's own 2008)

applying low-cost, robust, ease of operation and appropriate technologies" (Brix et al. 2007, p. 2). Sadly, the system was already limited in its potential benefit to islanders as it only served the main business and hotel area (Brix et al. 2007). However, not only are there limitations in its functioning, as observed by Brix et al. (2011), visually the area is unappealing. Many of the plants in the wetlands had died, and there is an extremely strong and unpleasant smell in the area (it is known colloquially as the "poo garden", as below), and a "clogging" (Brix et al. 2011) of the system results in constant flooding of the footpaths adjacent to the wetlands with grey water:

> the reservoir is a bone of contention on the island. Germans came in and built the water treatment plant, reservoirs and holding tanks and I don't think it even ran for a day before it got broken and then the locals didn't know how to run it. People do these things and then they leave and there is no continuation.

The final image below was taken on Maya Beach, Phi Phi Le, on New Year's Eve 2015. It reveals the real irony of Alex Garland's (1997) novel *The Beach*. Intended as a critique of backpacker culture, and designed to show how each person's quest for utopia may eventually cause the decay of a destination, this longitudinal research on Phi Phi has demonstrated Garland's (1997) message entirely. Selected in the late 1990s as a filming location for the film *The Beach* due to the Royal Forestry Department being willing to permit filming and environmental restructuring in this National Park, the subsequent fame of Phi Phi caused a boom in the already bur-

Fig. 6.7   *The Beach* revisited (Source: Author 2015)

geoning tourism industry in a very limited space. The image below shows a very large group of tourists today mimicking the photograph taken by the character played by Leonardo Di Caprio and his fellow travellers, showing that the story is still very much alive in the minds of visitors to the islands. The immense pressure of this demand upon an infrastructure and space that is demonstrably fragile, and thus from the images of decay above, one can see that Garland's (1997) message has been realised:

> *Therein lies perhaps the greatest irony of* The Beach*: the movie itself is about rampant tourism destroying the environment. Or perhaps there's no mistake about it: the studio proved its point before the movie even brought the message home to the people.* (Shelby-Biggs 2000, p. 2)

As Cohen (2005, p. 15) accords, Maya Beach is a *"paragon of absurdity"*, primarily as the film's producers sought to adapt the pristine beach to the stereo type of a paradisiac island beach, in order to suit the shooting of a film about an idyllic pristine beach" (Fig. 6.7).

6.8 Conclusion

Fox's motion picture *The Beach* tells a story designed to prompt reflection on our contemporary mode of tourism consumption. However, ironically, both at the time of filming and ever since, the use of Maya Bay on Phi Phi Le Island, Thailand, has been shrouded in controversy. At the time of filming, this took the form of criticism for the environmental restructuring of Maya Bay, to satisfy the Western viewers' interpretation of paradise. Since, this takes the form of environmental pressure placed on Maya Bay on account of the volume of trip boats and tourists wishing to see "Leo's Beach". This has had a knock on effect on the form and nature of tourism development on Phi Phi Le's sister island, Phi Phi Don, where development is permissible.

It is undeniable however that *The Beach's* legacy is a long lasting one, which exceeds that observed in previous studies. On balance, it is debatable whether the legacy is a positive one. Despite the marked impact upon destination image, flow of visitors and subsequent economic prosperity and infrastructure development, this needs to be balanced against accession of carrying capacity (on both islands), environmental degradation (again on both islands) and negative societal impacts (on Phi Phi Don).

The extent to which the benefits from tourism to see Maya Bay reach the community on Phi Phi Don is also questionable and has been explored at length in other studies of the political economy of tourism development on the Phi Phi Islands (Taylor 2012). This leaves very much a situation whereby there is continued lack of consensus between relevant stakeholders. The threat to the Phi Phi islands, and particularly Maya Bay on Phi Phi Le, is again high on the agenda of environmental activists; with the case for "closing" the beach entirely for a defined period to permit regeneration being championed by academic Dr. Thon Thamrongnawasawat.

So, has the film *The Beach* gone full circle in the case of the Phi Phi Islands? Both the author's own fieldwork and wide range of other studies since suggest that it has. *The Beach* has ironically catalysed a form of tourism development that the novel warned about; destructive. Some say that the tsunami of 2004 offered a "clean slate" opportunity to replan and rezone the islands along more sustainable lines. However, as the fieldwork demonstrated, the philosophy underpinning the island's development was and is still economic. As one commentator stated:

> the economic drive that predominates the mentality is greed. Get as much out of the tourist for as little as you can. Do nothing to attract the tourist, leave piles of rubbish lying around so that someone else will lift it, display rudeness and generally take the money. Future development is built around this philosophy and shows no signs of abating.

Any prospect of sustainability continues to be undermined by a range of barriers and conflicts. These conflicts arise from powerful stakeholders pursuing their own interests and desired outcomes, in order to suit their own needs rather than those of the community as a whole. The historic pursuit of volume to the neglect of the natural resources upon which demand to the islands is based in unviable. Control of the island's resources is maintained through "status" rather than a sense of "togetherness". This, coupled with land scarcity, creates an environment whereby each landowner and business owner looks out for their own interests. Sadly, the situation on Phi Phi represents a Tragedy of the Commons. However, whilst actors do have an incentive to avoid over-exploitation of common pool resources to ensure the longevity of the tourism industry and their own livelihoods, they do not appear to recognise this.

References

Beeton, S. (2001). Smiling for the camera: The influence of film audiences on a budget tourism destination. *Tourism Culture and Communication, 3*(1), 15–25.

Beeton, S. (2010). The advance of film tourism. *Tourism and Hospitality Planning & Development, 7*(1), 1–6.

Beeton, S. (2016). *Film-induced tourism*. Clevedon: Channel View Publications.

Brix, H., Koottatep, T., & Laugesen, C. H. (2007). Wastewater treatment in tsunami affected areas of Thailand by constructed wetlands. *Water Science and Technology, 56*(3), 69–74.

Brix, H., Koottatep, T., Fryd, O., & Laugesen, C. H. (2011). The flower and the butterfly constructed wetland system at Koh Phi Phi—System design and lessons learned during implementation and operation. *Ecological Engineering, 37*(5), 729–735.

Busby, G., & Klug, J. (2001). Movie-induced tourism: The challenge of measurement and other issues. *Journal of Vacation Marketing, 7*(4), 316–332.

Cohen, E. (1983). Insiders and outsiders: The dynamics of development of bungalow tourism on the islands of Southern Thailand. *Human Organization, 42*(2), 158–162.

Cohen, E. (2005). The beach of 'The Beach'—The politics of environmental damage in Thailand. *Tourism Recreation Research, 30*(1), 1–17.

Cohen, S. (2010). Re-conceptualising lifestyle travellers: Contemporary 'drifters'. In K. Hannam & A. Diekmann (Eds.), *Beyond backpacker tourism: Mobilities and experiences* (pp. 64–84). Clevedon: Channel View Publications.

Connell, J. (2005). Toddlers, tourism and Tobermory: Destination marketing issues and television-induced tourism. *Tourism Management, 26*(5), 763–776.

Croy, G. (2011). Film tourism: Sustained economic contributions to destinations. *Worldwide Hospitality and Tourism Themes, 3*(2), 159–164.

Cummings, J. (2005a). 'Post-Tsunami visit to the Phi Phi Archipelago', *Chiang Mai News*, 26 February.

Cummings, J. (2005b). 'Andaman Coast Post-Tsunami Landscape: Island Recovery', *TAT Governor Corner*, 28 February.

Dodds, R. (2010). Koh Phi Phi: Moving towards or away from sustainability? *Asia Pacific Journal of Tourism Research, 15*(3), 251–265.

Dodds, R., Graci, S. R., & Holmes, M. (2010). Does the tourist care? A comparison of tourists in Koh Phi Phi, Thailand and Gili Trawangan, Indonesia. *Journal of Sustainable Tourism, 18*(2), 207–222.

Dyer, P., Aberdeen, L., & Schuler, S. (2003). Tourism impacts on an Australian indigenous community: A Djabugay case study. *Tourism Management, 24*(1), 83–95.

Ekachai, S. (1998). What it all boils down to is greed, *Bangkok Post*, 12 November.

Fahn, J. (2008). *A land on fire: The environmental consequences of the Southeast Asian boom*. New York: Basic Books.

Forsyth, T. (2002). What happened on "The Beach"? Social movements and governance of tourism in Thailand. *International Journal of Sustainable Development, 5*(3), 326–337.

Fuengprichavai, R. (1998). At the movies or at the beach, where were you?, *The Nation*, 17 November.

Garland, A. (1997). *The beach*. London: Penguin Books Ltd.

Grihault, N. I. C. K. I. (2003). Film tourism-the global picture. *Travel and Tourism Analyst, 5*, 1–22.

Gunn, C. A. (1988). *Vacationscape: Designing tourist regions*. Van Nostrand Reinhold.

Hahm, J., & Wang, Y. (2011). Film-induced tourism as a vehicle for destination marketing: Is it worth the efforts? *Journal of Travel & Tourism Marketing, 28*(2), 165–179.

Hannam, K., & Diekmann, A. (Eds.). (2010). *Beyond backpacker tourism: Mobilities and experiences* (Vol. 21). Clevedon: Channel View Publications.

Heitmann, S. (2010). Film tourism planning and development—Questioning the role of stakeholders and sustainability. *Tourism and Hospitality Planning & Development, 7*(1), 31–46.

Hudson, S., & Ritchie, J. B. (2006). Film tourism and destination marketing: The case of captain Corelli's mandolin. *Journal of Vacation Marketing, 12*(3), 256–268.

Ing, K. (1998). Examining roles and policies of film board and RFD, *The Nation*, 13 November.

Ingram, J. C., Franco, G., Rumbaitis-del Rio, C., & Khazai, B. (2006). Post-disaster recovery dilemmas: Challenges in balancing short-term and long-term needs for vulnerability reduction. *Environmental Science & Policy, 9*(7), 607–613.

Laopaisarntaksin, S. (1998). Filming of the beach cleared, *Bangkok Post*, 6 November.

Law, L., Bunnell, T., & Ong, C. E. (2007). The beach, the gaze and film tourism. *Tourist Studies, 7*(2), 141–164.

Macionis, N., & Sparks, B. (2009). Film-induced tourism: An incidental experience. *Tourism Review International, 13*(2), 93–101.

Noikorn, U. (1998). Green protest at film slammed *Bangkok Post*, 12 November.

Paris, C. M. (2012). Flashpackers: An emerging subculture? *Annals of Tourism Research, 39*(2), 1094–1115.

Paris, C. M., & Teye, V. (2010). Backpacker motivations: A travel career approach. *Journal of Hospitality Marketing & Management, 19*(3), 244–259.

Puthipucha, V. (1998). Phi Phi vandalism the latest vulgar sell-out *The Nation*, 4 November.

Riley, R., Baker, D., & Van Doren, C. S. (1998). Movie induced tourism. *Annals of Tourism Research, 25*(4), 919–935.

Shelby-Biggs, B. (2000). The two faces of Leo, *The Envirolink Network*, 4 February.

Taylor, F. (2012). *Post disaster tourism development of Phi Phi Island: Political economy and interpretations of sustainability*.

Thamrongnawasat, T. (2016, July 7). Phi Phi's Maya Bay: Overcrowding an environmental disaster, *The Bangkok Post*, Retrieved from http://www.bangkokpost.com/learning/advanced/1029745/phi-phis-maya-bay-overcrowding-an-environmental-disaster

Tooke, N., & Baker, M. (1996). Seeing is believing: The effect of film on visitor numbers to screened locations. *Tourism Management, 17*(2), 87–94.

Yoon, Y., Kim, S., & Kim, S. S. (2015). Successful and unsuccessful film tourism destinations: From the perspective of Korean local residents' perceptions of film tourism impacts. *Tourism Analysis, 20*(3), 297–311.

Young, A. F., & Young, R. (2008). Measuring the effects of film and television on tourism to screen locations: A theoretical and empirical perspective. *Journal of Travel & Tourism Marketing, 24*(2–3), 195–212.

Chapter 7
The Impacts of Film Tourism on Place Change and Tourist Experience: A Lesson from *Eat Pray Love* in Bali, Indonesia

Eerang Park

Abstract This chapter aims to analyse and discuss how the tourist experience has been transformed over time in Ubud, Bali, in part by the impacts of the Hollywood film *Eat Pray Love* (*EPL*). A sudden influx of *EPL*-motivated tourists has resulted in dramatic and long-lasting changes to the existing tourism products and activities offered *in loco*. A subsequent change in the role and function of places to facilitate these new tourism products and activities is noticeable, changes that have also altered the experiences of tourists. The most significant changes that have taken place as a result of the impacts of the film *EPL* are twofold: the commodification of agricultural places and the commodification of social practices and sacred rituals. During this process, new hybrid forms of tourism experiences have been created, which have in turn led to the enrichment of the tourism experiences on offer in Ubud. A longitudinal autoethnographic approach was employed using direct observations and experiences, informal conversations with locals and other tourists, photographs and field accounts of the tours in June 2010, July 2013 and April 2016.

Keywords Place change • Landscape • Social practice • Autoethnography • Bali

7.1 Introduction

Place is an integral part of the human experience, offering meaning and relationships. People often develop emotional ties to places as well as a strong sense of place; thus, insiders and outsiders are not defined by their physical or cognitive relationship with a place, but rather by their emotional attachment to it (Tuan 1975). The concept of 'insideness' is explained by people's identity of place, which differentiates it from other places. There are three essential components that explain

E. Park (✉)
School of Management, Victoria University of Wellington, PO Box 600,
Wellington 6140, New Zealand
e-mail: eerang.park@vuw.ac.nz

© Springer Nature Singapore Pte Ltd. 2018
S. Kim, S. Reijnders (eds.), *Film Tourism in Asia*, Perspectives on Asian Tourism, DOI 10.1007/978-981-10-5909-4_7

place identity: the physical setting, the activities, situations and events associated with a particular place, and the meanings developed by one's experiences of a place (Relph 1976). These three components are particularly important in the context of film tourism, for the film tourist experience is inherently linked to the personal consumption of media representations of a place, representations that are influenced by various media content or production values, including scenery, characters, storylines, and settings (Frost and Laing 2015; Kim 2012b). During this process, audience members typically develop a positive affective bond between themselves and the filmed locations by means of the contextualised symbolic and embedded meanings behind the screen (Couldry 1998; Kim 2010, 2012b; Reijnders 2011).

The emotional and symbolic dimensions of the touristic experience are therefore significant for film tourists who can go beyond the tangible cognitive dimension of the filmed locations in search of an existential authentic place experience that relies upon the events and situations that unfold in the film (Couldry 1998). This in turn leads to the creation of new touristic spaces and the contextualization of anticipated touristic experiences at film locations. Here there is a possible, and perhaps inevitable, conflict between insiders (i.e. local residents) and outsiders (i.e. film tourists), as the subjective and symbolic meanings that film tourists have of filmed locations are often (very) different to those held by local residents, depending on the media representation and imagery created by the film or TV drama (see also Chaps. 6 and 8 in this Volume).

Therefore, places that appear as backdrops in film and TV programmes often undergo unexpected changes or transformations in their roles and functions. The impacts of the Yorkshire TV series *Heartbeat* on cultural and spatial conflicts between tourists and local residents exemplify this. Mordue's (2001) study examined how the role and function of the aesthetics of idyllic rural life and its significance for the residents of Goathland, UK, were adversely disrupted and radically changed by the sudden and continuing influx of *Heartbeat* tourists, who were motivated to experience the dramatised and romanticised rural life and its mythos. Such changes in places are largely due to the different ways that film tourists, in this case, consume places in search of memorable authentic film tourism experiences, while the same places have different meanings from a local perspective.

According to McKercher et al. (2015), there are three types of places in a destination: (1) *tourism places* where tourists are welcome to occupy and consume the facilities and services of the destination, (2) *shared places* where tourists and locals coexist and share the functions of the destination, and (3) *non-tourism places*, which are exclusive for local residents. This typology of places is in line with the dichotomy of the front and back stages of the authentic tourist experience (Cohen 1979; MacCannell 1973). The above case of *Heartbeat* shows the transformation of a non-tourism rural place into a shared place, and that transformed place is located between the front and back stages. In this context, the influx of film tourism is an important agent of such changes. These changes are collectively referred to as film tourism impacts and inevitably result in continuous changes to tourists' experiences.

Despite the close relationship between place change and the transformation of the tourist experience in the context of film tourism, research on film tourism experiences has largely focused on the pre-stage of the travel experience, in particular tourist motivation and the destination selection process (Brenda 2007; Hudson et al. 2011), as well as actual on-site experiences (Buchmann et al. 2010; Carl et al. 2007; Kim 2010, 2012a, b). Most research on this subject is limited to the contexts of the one-off approach, which means that there is a paucity of a processual approach to understanding how tourist experiences change over time alongside changes in the roles and functions of filmed locations. Also, the impacts of film tourism have mostly been researched from the perspectives of local communities and residents, in terms of their perceptions of the impacts of film tourism, and thus their attitudes towards film tourism (Beeton 2005; Connell 2005a, b; Yoon et al. 2015). Yet, research from the tourist perspective remains limited in terms of how film tourism impacts play a crucial role in changing the role and function of filmed places and thus altering or transforming tourist experiences over time.

Having acknowledged the above research gaps, this chapter aims to explore how tourism products and activities, and subsequent tourist experiences, have been influenced and transformed over time in Ubud, Bali, where the Hollywood film *Eat Pray Love* (*EPL*) was shot in 2009 and which has subsequently experienced an influx of film tourists, since the film's release in 2010 (see also Chap. 8 in this Volume). A longitudinal autoethnographic approach was employed, and the author undertook three field trips to Ubud and its surrounding areas, in 2010, 2013, and 2016, respectively. An in-depth discussion of the perceived changes to landscape, tourism products, and activities, which have been influenced by the increasing popularity of *EPL*-related tourism, is provided, while the author's personal reflection and analysis of the lived experiences of being a tourist in Ubud provides further insights into the transformation of the tourist experience in Ubud.

7.2   Research Methods

The current study adopts an autoethnographic approach that allows the use of personal experiences, views, narratives, thoughts, and observations to understand the lived experiences of the film tourist. The process of reflective writing and the organising of sources of evidence can also be used to question and discover the meanings and relations of the film's impacts on the tourist experience within the specific context of the destination in question. Autoethnography provides 'a critical and reflexive way of inquiry' (Noy 2008, p. 143) based on the description and analysis of personal experiences (Ellis et al. 2011). The method involves the researcher being an active participant, which is particularly relevant for a tourism researcher (Frost and Laing 2015).

Although there is growing recognition and appreciation of the appropriateness and usefulness of the autoethnography approach in the field of tourism studies, its limited use as a tourism research method has been pointed out (Frost and Laing 2015; Komppula and Gartner 2013). This is largely because the exclusive use of the personal story has been criticised as problematic in terms of its legitimacy within the canonical scholarly environment (Holt 2003). However, Noy (2008) asserted that the autoethnography is an emerging innovative qualitative research method that allows researchers to explore their voices, emotions, and personal and sometimes intimate moments embodied with both sense and knowledge. This is particularly relevant to the film tourism context, in which serious film tourists are motivated and immersed in retracing every step taken by the characters from their beloved films, as if the characters belonged only to them (Kim 2012b; Reijnders 2010, 2011); this is described as media pilgrimage in ritual places (Couldry 1998).

Film tourism researchers have found that different groups of film tourists, such as specific/purposeful, incidental, casual, or serendipitous film tourists, have different sets of motivations, interests, and expectations, which affect the experiences that they seek (Croy and Heitmann 2011). With this in mind, I consider myself to be a casual film tourist, and thus, my lived film tourism experiences were less proactive and personalised than those of purposeful or serious film tourists. In addition, a cognitive distance between myself and the destination was somehow maintained for the purpose of observing and analysing the destination experiences. This allowed me to look at this studied phenomenon from both the insider and outsider perspective, which tends to be more mutual. The three trips to Ubud in Bali were undertaken in June 2010, July 2013, and April 2016. On every visit, I hired a local taxi driver who simultaneously acted as a tour guide and toured the island with me for 2–3 days. Data for the current study is drawn from my direct observations and experiences, informal conversations with locals and other tourists, photographs, and field accounts of the tours.

7.3 Research Context: From a Cultural Tourism Destination to a Film Tourism Destination

Bali, often called the 'Island of the Gods', attracts international tourists due to its strong and rich culture, the thousands of local Hindu temples, and the beautiful scenery and beaches. Tourists to Bali are lured by ritual dance and performances, local music, and skilled handicrafts, including the traditional textiles made using a special dyeing technique, known as Batik. The government's strategic development of tourism in Bali has distinguished the target markets of each region by different types and levels of accommodation and resort development, tourism products, and local amenities. Ubud has been known as the Balinese centre of tradition, culture, and arts with its local markets, historic places, museums, artist studios, and galleries. Located on the central island, Ubud is one of the most accessible mountain villages, while the Monkey Forest, Tegallalang Rice Terraces, and dance performances steeped in mythology are the must-see local attractions, with tourists visiting to buy local paintings and sculptures.

In contrast to the luxury resort development on the island's beaches, such as Nusa Dua, small-scale hotels and homestays have been developed in the central

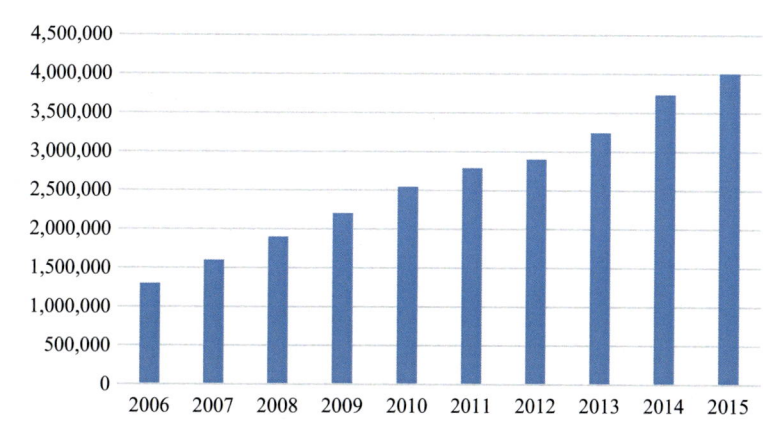

Fig. 7.1 International tourist arrivals in Bali (Source: Data & Information Centre of Indonesian Tourism Ministry and Indonesian Central Statistical Bureau)

mountain village in Ubud, which are more independent and attract budget tourists. Similar to Kuta, which attracts surfers and independent tourists by offering non-rated, low-price lodging rooms, thus causing the area to become commercialised and developed in an unplanned manner, Ubud has recently undergone a rapid tourism development in a small-scale local entrepreneurial manner. After the film *EPL* was released, many of the unknown and sometimes unremarkable locations shown in the film have suddenly become crowded with tourists. Many *EPL* tour packages have been offered and actively promoted by the Bali Tourism Board since the film premiered, thus boosting the image of Bali as a spiritual tourist destination (Erviani 2010). Similar packages have mushroomed from both local and international tour operators (O'Connor and Kim 2014). Such packages include a session with Ketut Liyer, a local healer in Ubud who the main character of the film met during her journey, tours of the locations used in the film, and even visits to sacred sites (usually temples) that encourage meditation and self-reflection.

O'Connor and Kim (2014) reported the impact of *EPL* in terms of visitor arrivals in Bali, numbers which had fallen since the 2002 Bali bombings, but have been rapidly recovering since the *EPL* book was published in 2006. This growth has continued, reaching 22 million arrivals in 2009, when *EPL* was filmed in Ubud; since the release of the *EPL* film in 2010, the number of arrivals has continued to increase, as shown in Fig. 7.1.

The impact of *EPL* is more prominent in Ubud, which forms the main backdrop of the film where the main character, played by Julia Roberts, visits and stays. Ubud currently presents a hybrid style of tourism, embracing both backpackers and young, well-heeled independent tourists. Once renowned as a centre of artistic tradition, Ubud has recently seen the growth of numerous high-end boutique hotels overlooking the rice fields, alongside densely populated backpackers' lodges, Western-style shops, restaurants and cafés, convenience stores, and money exchange shops on the main streets.

From the opening scene of the film, in which Bali's picturesque rice terraces are depicted, with Julia Roberts' character riding her bicycle between the rice paddies, the attention of a global audience is captured. The unique Balinese architectural style and Hindu temples are presented as even more beautiful and exotic in the film. Staying in a villa in the farming village of Ubud, with its wooden Balinese architecture, agricultural landscape, fishponds, and meditation temple, Julia Roberts regularly practises meditation while facing the tranquil rice fields, rides her bicycle through the village, and visits the traditional healer and medicine man from whom she learns the Balinese philosophy of the balance of life, as do the locals in Ubud; this stands in stark contrast to her life back home. The less civilised but more spiritually enriched lifestyle portrayed in the film is alluring for audiences, particularly those who are mostly settled in Westernised, urban surroundings; they can readily empathise with the character, the filmed location, and the life and culture of the people that live there.

During my third visit, various types of accommodation had already been established alongside the rice fields in Ubud and more were under construction. *EPL* influences often appeared in street shops that promoted items and locations under the theme of 'love', while interest in the rice terraces was clear from the new types of activities that were appearing nearby, such as cafés in rice fields and the strolling through rice terraces. The following sections will analyse these observations and experiences in detail.

7.4 Transformed Place, Transformed Tourist Experience

Over the past 6 years, each visit has confirmed for me how fast Bali is changing, from the airport to the rural agricultural village. Bali was already a mature holiday destination when I first visited in 2010. My first impression of the rural landscape and chaotic streets, with its less well-developed infrastructure, has remained the authentic image of Ubud. This was at the beginning of the promotion of *EPL* tourism, when most tourists still visited the island seeking natural and cultural experiences. The holy temples were still only open to local Hindus, and the landscape was less actively engaged in promoting (film) tourism products; instead, most landscapes were consumed and experienced through observation.

On my second visit in 2013, when the *EPL* impacts on tourism were becoming more visible, tourists were seeking the locations depicted in the film. A formerly unknown local area, Padang Padang Beach, was crowded with most international tourists and tour guides, while *EPL*-themed tour packages were common products promoted and sold by local travel agencies. Women travelling – some alone and some with friends – were encountered more often at such attractions, with many looking for the local markets and villa where Julia Roberts' character had visited and lived. Nevertheless, the tourists still appreciated the rural landscapes that could be viewed at lookouts or viewpoints, and the agricultural land was still available for farming.

By the time of my most recent visit in 2016, Ubud had undergone a huge transformation and several local places, such as rice fields and holy temples, were open to visiting foreign tourists. It seems, however, that the direct impacts of *EPL* had decreased as there were fewer *EPL* tour programmes. While there continued to be interest in the local healer and palm reader, these impacts seemed to have expanded to the wider region and to other local areas. Accordingly, the destination experience had become richer and more diverse as new types of tourism experiences were provided by local communities. Tourists were becoming more immersed in the local community by engaging with farmers through a stroll or tour in the rice terraces and by learning about Balinese philosophy and culture through taking part in local cookery classes, participating in meditation and religious rituals in temples, listening to palm readers, and receiving healing from the traditional healer. Adopting the typology of places developed by McKercher et al. (2015) – i.e. non-tourism, tourism, and shared place – it can be said that many of the previously non-tourism places in Ubud were now shared places. The role and impacts of the film *EPL* have been considerable in creating new demand for and interest in these non-tourism places, such as the houses of the medicine men and healers, where only locals used to go.

Of these many changes, I found that the most fundamental difference between Ubud in 2010 and 2016 was the substantial change in the landscape as a result of infrastructure developments such as roads and a new bridge, a more well-organised rural landscape, the many commercial signs for love – and in particular *EPL*-themed products and package tours – which gave an impression of the island as being more associated with *love* rather than its historic and cultural image as the Balinese centre of tradition, culture, and arts. Such changes have consequently appeared to change the tourist experience. I found that the most obvious change in the tourist experience in Ubud and its vicinity, as a result of the aforementioned changes in the landscape, was related to the change in the original role and function of the physical setting of agricultural and social spaces, a change that has influenced the place identity of those places.

Indeed, the marked changes were particularly obvious in agricultural spaces and locals' social spaces (e.g. medicine men and traditional healers), which were often used as settings or backdrops for tranquil and spiritual scenes in *EPL*. These daily spaces, predominantly used by local people as *non-tourism places*, have been transformed into tourists' purposeful spaces, as either *shared places* or *tourism places*; accordingly, such a transformation of destination experience is related to the original meanings of those places, as the place identity has evolved in terms of its authenticity and due to the process of commodification.

Authenticity and commodification are essential concepts that explain the tourist experience (Cohen 1988; MacCannell 1973). Tourists seek authentic experiences that are often seen as the possessions of local people, untouched by outsiders or commercialisation. As such, the commodification of tourist objects and places is inevitably associated with the fluid notion of the authentic experience, which is felt and addressed according to different preferences, influences, and perspectives on the travel experience (Cohen 1988). In the context of film tourism, the role and function of a backdrop, that is, a very common place from the perspective of locals, becomes a significant part of the tourist experience; thus, the impacts of film tourism on a destination are highlighted in the process of commodification of that common place from a local perspective (Riley et al. 1998), which often used to be a *non-tourism place*.

The commodification of a place refers to the superficial consumption of staged characteristics of that place, which is often mentioned as staged authenticity in terms of the tourist experience (MacCannell 1973). A location's characteristics are derived from various agents, such as the physical setting, culture, people, customs, and more. A sense of place and place identity is created by those agents, as local residents foster an emotional attachment to that place; for tourists, however, the influence of the consumable attributes of that place on the authenticity of their experience is stronger. Consequently, while locals and tourists coexist in a destination, place changes can mean different things and have different purposes depending on one's stance. Tourists, as outsiders, seem to be goal-oriented users of a place who generate impacts, but tourist demand creates social practices that form a new shared place and/or tourism place (Framke 2002). In a similar vein, a film's influence on changing demand and indeed the transformation of a place is evident in Ubud, due to its association with *EPL*.

While it is understood that commodification has led to changes in Ubud over the past 6 years, this does not necessarily mean the destruction or change of the authentic experience that Ubud has to offer to tourists. Rather, the film's impacts, including the commodification of Ubud, should be understood in a different way. In the following section, it will be analysed in the two forms of commodification of place related to the tourist experience in Ubud, which are the commodification of the agricultural landscape and the commodification of social practices and sacred rituals.

7.4.1 Romanticised Rice Fields: From Farmers' Production Space to Tourists' Consumption Place

A primary reason for the transformed tourist experiences in Ubud was the place changes of the rice fields through the commodification of the agricultural landscape in imitation of scenes shown in the film. Interestingly, there was no stereotypical association between the environmental condition and the activities in the transformed place and the experiences of that place; rather, the overall atmosphere and aura used to experience the activities seen in the film are more engaged and diverted. The rice fields exemplify this phenomenon. It was evident from the newly developed boutique accommodations in the middle of rice fields as well as local cafes that boasted spectacular views of rice fields as a foreground, scenes that were similarly consumed through the screen.

Tourism in Ubud currently makes full use of the rice fields to create new tourism products and experiences; this commodification of the agricultural landscape of

Ubud appears to be partially driven by increased demand due to impact of *EPL*. On my first visit, in the year the film was released, I found that many holidaymakers still preferred to stay in beach or oceanside resorts in Denpasar and would visit Ubud to watch a dance performance, visit artist galleries and shops, and for sightseeing in the Monkey Forest. Overall, the landscape of Ubud was a mixture of chaotic narrow roads, market streets, and rural farmland, with backpackers, day tour visitors, and local residents and farmers remaining distinct in their respective precincts; farmland and rice paddies signalled the agricultural economic life of the rural community that was far from the world of tourism. Moreover, the Tegallalang Rice Terraces, which is a must-see attraction, was more picturesque. There were no outsiders in the green fields apart from a few farmers; the scenery was therefore seen as peaceful and natural, and exclusively for the use of the rural Balinese community as part of their mundane or daily social, economic, and cultural activities.

However, the rice fields in 2016 were occupied by construction workers building hotels and other types of boutique accommodation; otherwise, these tranquil rice fields appeared pleasantly harmonious with beautiful villas set in the middle of green farms. The tourists' gaze – influenced and romanticised by *EPL* – is not limited to the mere expectation of an exotic agricultural landscape but has been expanded to include engaging with insiders in the agrarian community and consuming the agricultural landscape, while continuing to stay in luxury accommodation, which we call 'tourism paradox'. Local investors and entrepreneurs have immediately responded to this kind of increased demand by developing a large number of boutique hotels that match and thus satisfy tourists' expectations.

The hotel I stayed in Ubud also promoted the tranquil rural agricultural landscape (i.e. rice fields) as a benefit of staying there, but when I checked in, I was met with an apology about the ongoing construction of an extension to the hotel and that of another hotel that was being developed right next to the building I was staying in. The benefit of the view of the rice fields, as promised when I booked the trip, was not experienced during my field visit; instead, I was visiting at a very significant moment in the transformation of the place from a rice field into tourist facilities (see Fig. 7.2). Accordingly, my expectation of feeling that I was part of the 'exotic' agrarian community whose language, foods, and other cultural aspects were different from my own was not achieved; rather, my position as an outsider utilising a purpose-built tourism facility was confirmed.

When I moved to a more remote rural area, it was easier to find small-scale accommodation equipped with a separate meditation temple (see Fig. 7.3). I was thus able to rethink the meaning and type of the authentic experience of Ubud, regardless of my eagerness to pretend to be – or at least have a taste of being – an insider like the main character in the film. In terms of style and location, the newly developed accommodation in Ubud constitutes a new tourism product that is recognised as offering a very unique Balinese-style stay in Ubud, despite it not being related to farm tourism or agritourism.

The film tourists' fantasy of the rice fields in Ubud seems to reflect a desire to experience a magical place, such as Walt Disney World theme park, where anything magical can happen (see also Chap. 16 in this Volume). This is significant for film

Fig. 7.2 Hotels under construction in rice fields, Ubud (Source: Author)

Fig. 7.3 A meditation temple in the rice fields, Ubud (Source: Author)

tourists as it provides an emotional landscape rather than a cognitive landscape of Ubud. Tourists staying in hotels located in the middle of rice fields can walk around the farm in their yoga suit and take part in local yoga classes. Hotels also run regular yoga classes and meditation sessions against the backdrop of the rice fields, so that anyone can put themselves in the shoes of Julia Roberts' character and live as though they were the main characters of the film. Tourists can walk along the path between the rice paddies, ride bicycles, and relax in the rice fields.

Fig. 7.4 A local café with the rice field view in Ubud (Source: Author)

As such, the very landscape of green rice fields is being widely promoted and sold across Ubud, for example, in the case of a small local café that has a banner that says 'enjoy delicious food with a spectacular view'. Regardless of the quality and taste of their food, such businesses have been thriving with Western tourists eating pasta and sandwiches next to the rice paddies; even this scene, for me, was seen as an authentic experience in Ubud (see Fig. 7.4).

Ironically, the place of agriculture, which is regarded as the symbolic place of dignified hard labour in the agrarian society, simultaneously signals the very location of a relaxing holiday, and this new role and function of the agricultural place in Ubud that is uniquely transforming a non-tourism place into a shared place. Consequently, the change and transformation of a production place into a place of consumption has created new tourism activities and experiences themed around the rice fields; this is very similar to the udon noodle tourism phenomenon in Japan (Kim and Ellis 2015).

The biggest surprise during my last visit to Bali in 2016 was the changes to the Tegallalang Rice Terraces. These once exclusive agricultural farms now receive tourists while local farmers generate extra income by opening their rice paddies to tourists and acting as tour guides. As such, one of the most dramatic landscapes of green, cascading rice farms sprawling across the valley in Ubud is no longer available, yet there are always people enjoying the view of and walking in the Tegallalang Rice Terraces (see Fig. 7.5). Unlike tourists in the past, who enjoyed the vista at the viewpoints or hillside cafés, tourists today go along the steep footpath down to the paddy, followed by local children begging for money.

A new product has also been developed by the local people. They have set up a crude photo stage with the rice terraces in the background, which they use as another income source (see Fig. 7.6). The price list shows that it costs IDR 50,000

Fig. 7.5 Tourists in the walking tour at the Tegallalang Rice Terraces (Source: Author)

Fig. 7.6 A photogenic spot at the Tegallalang Rice (Source: Author)

(approximately US$4) for one professional photo including a frame, or IDR 10,000 for a selfie with one's own cell phone. But the price ranges vary and are negotiable, depending on the entrance level, while a local tour guide and professional local photographer can be hired, according to a local farmer. He stated that the entrance fees are managed by the village and are shared among the villagers and rice field owners, with a small percentage going to the government.

As mentioned earlier, place changes, including new buildings and tourists occupying non-tourism places differently, seem to be the obvious reason for the changes in touristic experiences, but I would argue that it is not simply the place and its rice fields, but rather the landscape of the rice fields that is now the ultimate product that has been commodified and sold in Ubud since the filming of *EPL*. Tourists' special attachment to the rice fields can be explained by Tuan's (1977) social meaning of place based on the continuing relationship between humans and place. After watching the film and seeing the beauty of the rice fields, fans of *EPL* (and thus potential tourists in Ubud) have been developing special meanings of these rice fields as places of holiday activities through their cognitive and emotional connection to this imagined agricultural space.

7.4.2 Sacred or Seductive Ritual Practice?

EPL produced two Balinese celebrities in Ubud; Ketut Liyer, a medicine man from whom Julia Roberts' character learnt about Balinese philosophy, and Wayan Nuriasih, a spiritual healer who cured her wounds and maintained a friendship with her. It was not difficult to find out about the lives and businesses of both celebrities after the release of the film, both from Internet travel news and social networking sites. On my first and second visits, no local tour guides suggested that I visit a local astrologer or traditional healer as a Balinese cultural tourism activity, but on my third visit, I saw many lone female tourists visiting these two celebrities, escorted by tour guides.

An online search for Ketut's place of residence revealed that Ketut is not a proper noun indicating the person I was looking for. Rather, there were various businesses, including a B&B, café, and travel services named after Ketut. I approached the concierge service at the hotel in which I was staying and learned that Ketut Liyer had been famous in Ubud long before *EPL*, and that the concierge staff also used to visit him. It was then mentioned that many locals, including himself, no longer visit Ketut Liyer the medicine man, as his place is no longer for the local community. I was told two interesting stories. First, the name Ketut means the fourth child in a family in the Balinese naming system, which has four common names based on birth order. This is why there are many businesses with the name Ketut; they are named after their owners' name, in this case, Ketut, if the owner is the fourth child in his family. Second, medicine men are very common in Bali and do not run their businesses like modern, profit-oriented businesses. They essentially exist as a community service. With a unique gift for palm reading, fortune telling, healing, and meditation, medicine men offer a service to local community members who need spiritual healing hands. They do not charge for their service, but local people sometimes bring small amounts of money, fruit, food or other gifts as a token of their gratitude. The medicine man shown in the film has now become extremely busy, with a constant queue of tourists waiting with number tags, making his services very expensive for local people (see also Chap. 8 in this Volume).

The original Ketut was too old to accept visitors (and he passed away after my visit in 2016); instead, his son has continued the business servicing tourists. When I visited Ketut's residence, the words of the concierge staff rang true. The house was being expanded and they were even providing services such as B&B, painting, palm reading, meditation and so forth, which are all attractive to tourists. This business and the way that the younger Ketut spoke to his guests seemed to accurately mirror the scene from the film, such that one had the illusion of being in the film; his gestures, words, and smiles were identical to those from the film, even though the stories of the individual visitors could not be same as that of Julia Roberts' character.

It was a perfectly staged authentic experience (MacCannell 1973) and a re-enactment of a scene from *EPL* (Kim 2010); if I was a serious film tourist, the very moment in which I was spatially, temporally, and corporeally there would be more than enough to create an emotional engagement. However, I questioned whether I had had a spiritual experience at all. From the objective authenticity perspective, staged authenticity based on a film's narrative still gives the value of truth; yet I could not stop asking myself whether I had received the real 'spiritual' help that local Balinese people seek from this medicine man, or even if I had received a taste of local Balinese life and culture.

In contrast to Ketut's ongoing popularity, Wayan's business was doing relatively poorly. When I entered her place of business, there were no visitors and she recommended that I make a booking if I needed treatment. The healing shop was decorated with a copy of her presentation on the media in relation to *EPL*. She promoted herself to me, showing countless 'thank you' messages from international tourists whose health problems and symptoms were alleviated by her treatment. As with Ketut Liyer, Wayan had become a local entrepreneur, and now their talents are no longer sacred for local communities but are mainly used by tourists and are seen as seductive ritual practices available in Ubud.

7.5 Conclusion

The impacts of film tourism on local communities and residents have been well documented. However, there has been a lacuna in our understanding of how tourism experiences have been transformed over time due to the impacts of film tourism and the subsequent changes in the roles and functions of places where tourist experiences are staged and performed. To fill this research gap, the current study adopted a longitudinal autoethnography approach to analyse and discuss the transformation of tourism products and activities as a result of a film's impacts on a destination. The geographical focus was Ubud in Bali, which recently experienced a sudden influx of film tourists associated with the Hollywood film *Eat Pray Love* (2010). In 2009, *EPL* was filmed in five of the main villages in Ubud, namely, Pengosekan, Nyuh Kuning, Padang Tegal, Peliatan, and Ubud central village, and was released in 2010. Since then, both local and international tourism businesses have attempted to capitalise on the significance and popularity of the new *EPL* tourism patterns and trends by developing and offering a variety of tour and accommodation packages tailored to include the main *EPL* experiences portrayed in the film.

Tourists' experiences of Ubud in Bali have been evolving from conventional cultural tourism to more complex or indeed hybrid types of cultural experiences; the role of film in this transformation of tourists' experiences is apparent. The change in the role and function of place, namely, *place change* as discussed in this chapter, due to the film *EPL*, is the most significant and dominant factor that has changed tourists' experiences. The place change in Ubud has been twofold: the commodification of the agricultural place and the commodification of social practices and sacred rituals. The former refers to the constant transformation of rice fields from the symbolic agricultural production place of dignified hard labour in an agrarian society to the very consumption location of a relaxing holiday. This new role and function of the agricultural place that was dramatised and romanticised in the film *EPL* has successfully led to the transformation of a traditionally *non-tourism place* into a *shared place* or even *tourism place*, with a symbolically strong pulling power. This was confirmed by the newly developed small-scale boutique accommodation located in the middle of rice fields, as well as the local cafés that boasted spectacular views of rice fields as both a foreground and as their selling point. These businesses were then able to provide theatrical stages for visitors to re-enact scenes that were consumed through the screen, repeating the experience of consuming the landscape through watching the film.

The latter is related to the process of commodification of the places of medicine men and spiritual healers. The very place of social, cultural, and ritual practice among the locals of Ubud and the unique talent of the medicine men and spiritual headers that originally existed as a community service have become a profit-oriented business and a tradable or consumable product for tourists. This is further evidence of the impacts of film tourism on place change and the transformation of the tourist experience.

As such, the phenomenon of film tourism in Ubud shows the significant role of film backdrops and their meanings in adding a new experiential layer to existing tourism products and activities in places such as the rice fields and local spiritual places of Ubud. To some extent, tourists' cultural experiences of Ubud have been extended and diversified by the injection of these new types of tourist experiences created by the *place change*.

The current film tourism literature argues that personal meaning is often more important than the visual images shown in film in generating film tourism and that such meanings come from the audiences' engagement with storylines, mediafigures, sights, and more (Beeton 2005; Frost 2010; Kim 2012b). In this sense, Frost (2010) argued that the visual image of scenery shown in the film is not what the destination is offering audiences but is just a background for the events that will likely happen when audiences travel to the destination. Similarly, Reijnders (2011, 2016) emphasises that audiences' emotional longing for visiting film locations is because they are seeking events that take place in their imagination, while the destination that they visit is a physical reference to those events that can actually take place.

However, in the case of Ubud in relation to *EPL*'s impacts, the close relationship between place change and tourist experience transformation go beyond the above domain of film tourists' emotional and symbolic attachment to the filmed locations. It also goes beyond the dichotomy of positive and negative impacts of film tourism on tourists and local residents. While locals and tourists may coexist in a destination, place changes can have different meaning and have different purposes depending on one's stance. Thus, the case of Bali demonstrates that new places being created as a single purpose place (i.e. either *tourism place* or *non-tourism place*) are transformed into multifunctional places that are shared between tourists and locals, where authentic Balinese travel experiences are formed and shared by more than simply film tourists. By reporting on this transformed backdrop through which the tourist experience transforms and evolves in the context of film tourism, this chapter enhances our knowledge of film tourism in Asia and beyond.

References

Beeton, S. (2005). *Film-induced tourism*. Clevedon: Channel View.

Brenda, C. (2007). Film-induced tourism in Asia: A case study of Korean television drama and female viewers' motivation to visit Korea. *Tourism Culture and Communication, 7*(3), 207–224.

Buchmann, A., Moore, K., & Fisher, D. (2010). Experiencing film tourism: Authenticity and fellowship. *Annals of Tourism Research, 37*(1), 229–248.

Carl, D., Kindon, S., & Smith, K. (2007). Tourists' experiences of film locations: New Zealand as 'Middle Earth'. *Tourism Geographies, 9*(1), 49–63.

Cohen, E. (1979). A phenomenology of tourist experiences. *Sociology, 13*, 179–201.

Cohen, E. (1988). Authenticity and commoditization in tourism. *Annals of Tourism Research, 15*(3), 371–386.

Connell, J. (2005a). Toddlers, tourism and Tobermory: Destination marketing issues and TV-induced tourism. *Tourism Management, 26*, 763–776.

Connell, J. (2005b). What's the story in Balamory?: The impacts of a children's TV programme on small tourism enterprises on the Isle of Mull, Scotland. *Journal of Sustainable Tourism, 13*, 228–255.

Couldry, N. (1998). The view from inside the 'simulacrum': Visitors' tales from the set of Coronation Street. *Leisure Studies, 17*, 94–107.

Croy, G., & Heitmann, S. (2011). Tourism and film. In P. Robinson, S. Heitmann, & P. U. C. Dieke (Eds.), *Research themes for tourism* (pp. 188–204). Oxon: CABI.

Ellis, C., Adams, T. E., & Bochner, P. (2011). Autoethnography: An overview. *Historical Social Research, 36*(4), 273–290.

Erviani, N. K. (2010, August 18). Bali offers tourists 'Eat, Pray, Love' package, *The Jakarta Post*, Retrieved from http://cbe.thejakartapost.com/news/2010/08/18/bali-offers-tourists-%E2%80%98eat-pray-love%E2%80%99-package.html-0

Framke, W. (2002). The destination as a concept: A discussion of the business-related perspective versus the socio-cultural approach in tourism theory. *Scandinavian Journal of Hospitality and Tourism, 2*(2), 92–108.

Frost, W. (2010). Life-changing experiences: Film and tourists in the Australian outback. *Annals of Tourism Research, 37*(3), 707–726.

Frost, W., & Laing, J. (2015). On the trail of Errol Flynn: Explorations in autoethnography. *Tourism Analysis, 20*(3), 283–296.

Holt, N. L. (2003). Presentation, legitimation, and autoethnography: An autoethnographic writing story. *International Journal of Qualitative Methods, 2*(1), 18–28.

Hudson, S., Wang, Y., & Gil, S. M. (2011). The influence of a film on destination image and the desire to travel: A cross-cultural comparison. *International Journal of Tourism Research, 13*(2), 177–190.

Kim, S. (2010). Extraordinary experience: Re-enacting and photographing at screen tourism locations. *Tourism and Hospitality Planning & Development, 7*(1), 59–75.

Kim, S. (2012a). The relationships of on-site film-tourism experiences, satisfaction, and behavioural intentions: The case of Asian audience's responses to a Korean historical TV drama. *Journal of Travel & Tourism Marketing, 29*(5), 472–484.

Kim, S. (2012b). Audience involvement and film tourism experiences: Emotional places, emotional experiences. *Tourism Management, 33*(2), 387–396.

Kim, S., & Ellis, A. (2015). Noodle production and consumption: From agriculture to food tourism in Japan. *Tourism Geographies, 17*(1), 151–167.

Komppula, R., & Gartner, W. C. (2013). Hunting as a travel experience: An autoethnographic study of hunting tourism. *Tourism Management, 35*, 168–180.

MacCannell, D. (1973). Staged authenticity: Arrangements of social space in tourist settings. *American Journal of Sociology, 79*, 589–603.

McKercher, B., Wang, D., & Park, E. (2015). Social impacts as a function of place change. *Annals of Tourism Research, 50*, 52–66.

Mordue, T. (2001). Performing and directing resident/tourist cultures in heartbeat country. *Tourist Studies, 1*, 233–252.

Noy, C. (2008). The poetics of tourist experience: An autoethnography of a family trip to Eilat. *Journal of Tourism and Cultural Change, 5*(3), 141–157.

O'Connor, N., & Kim, S. (2014). Pictures and prose: Exploring the impact of literary and film tourism. *Journal of Tourism and Cultural Change, 12*(1), 1–17.

Reijnders, S. (2010). On the Trail of 007: Media Pilgrimages into the World of James Bond. *Area, 42*(3), 369–377.

Reijnders, S. (2011). *Places of the imagination: Media, tourism, culture*. Farnham: Ashgate.

Reijnders, S. (2016). Stories that move: Fiction, imagination, tourism. *European Journal of Cultural Studies, 19*(6), 672–689.

Relph, E. (1976). *Place and placelessness*. London: Pion Books.

Riley, R., Baker, D., & van Doren, C. (1998). Movie-induced tourism. *Annals of Tourism Research, 25*(4), 919–935.

Tuan, Y.-F. (1975). Place: An experiential perspective. *Geographical Review, 65*(2), 151–165.

Tuan, Y.-F. (1977). *Space and place*. Minneapolis: University of Minnesota Press.

Yoon, Y., Kim, S., & Kim, S. (2015). Successful and unsuccessful film tourism destinations: From the perspective of Korean local residents' perceptions of film tourism impacts. *Tourism Analysis, 20*(3), 297–311.

Chapter 8
Changes in Local Residents' Perceptions and Attitudes Towards the Impact of Film Tourism: The Case of *Eat Pray Love* (*EPL*) Film Tourism in Ubud, Bali

Sangkyun Kim, Gregorius Suri, and Eerang Park

Abstract Despite the growth of film tourism studies, there has been a paucity of academic attention given to the impacts of film tourism on local communities and residents at film tourism destinations. This chapter adopts a longitudinal approach and aims to examine and discuss how, and the extent to which, local residents' perceptions and attitudes towards the impacts of film tourism at a film tourism destination have changed, been transformed and/or adjusted over time. The findings suggest that during the film production stage, the local communities generally had positive perceptions and attitudes towards the impacts of film tourism and anticipated further positive indirect effects of the film's production in the future. However, their generally positive perceptions and attitudes gradually began to change during the post-production effects (PPEFs) phase, leaving them with mixed perceptions and attitudes.

Keywords Perceived impacts • Film production • Community • Longitudinal approach • *Eat Pray Love*

S. Kim (✉)
School of Business and Law, Edith Cowan University, 270 Joondalup Drive,
Joondalup, WA 6027, Australia
e-mail: s.kim@ecu.edu.au

G. Suri
Tourism Department, Government of Belu Regency, East Nusa Tenggara, Indonesia
e-mail: goriz.suri@gmail.com

E. Park
School of Management, Victoria University of Wellington, PO Box 600, Wellington 6140,
New Zealand
e-mail: eerang.park@vuw.ac.nz

© Springer Nature Singapore Pte Ltd. 2018
S. Kim, S. Reijnders (eds.), *Film Tourism in Asia*, Perspectives on Asian
Tourism, DOI 10.1007/978-981-10-5909-4_8

8.1   Introduction

Residents' perceptions and attitudes towards the impact of tourism (Easterling 2004; Garcia et al. 2015; McKercher et al. 2015; Nunkoo et al. 2013) as well as the film tourism phenomenon (Beeton 2010; Connell 2012; Croy and Heitmann 2011) have each been widely acknowledged over recent decades. A proliferation of empirical and theoretical approaches to the former confirms that it is one of the most extensively researched areas of tourism (Garcia et al. 2015; McGehee and Andereck 2004; Nunkoo et al. 2013). The nature and magnitude of the impacts of film tourism has also been anecdotally evidenced from international case studies, most notably from the UK, US, Australia, New Zealand, Ireland, and South Korea (Connell 2012). However, there has been a paucity of academic attention given to the impacts of film tourism on local communities and residents at film tourism destinations (Yoon et al. 2015).

The dearth of research on this particular topic is ironic, given the crucial importance of residents' involvement and collaboration for sustainable tourism development (Beeton 2008; Heitmann 2010; Mordue 2001) and for tourism to be a 'community industry' (Nunkoo et al. 2013, p. 6). In the context of film tourism in particular, local residents 'have a limited control over the imageries and representations of their residential areas created by film or TV production' (Yoon et al. 2015, p. 298) and therefore '…have to live the consequences of what image has been portrayed' (Heitmann 2010, p. 39). For example, in the case of *Snowtown* in South Australia, in which the film of the same name portrayed the infamous *Snowtown* murders and the dark past of the town, residents who still held strong emotional and sentimental attachments to the town expressed strong resentment and resistance against the film's production and its subsequent film tourism development (Kim and Butler 2015).

The case of *The Beach* in Thailand is another example. Koh Phi Phi Island, Thailand's sun, surf, and snorkel haven, suddenly became an ideal 'Edenic destination' for young Western tourists searching for clubbing, drugs, and the sex trade. The spin-off effect of film tourism associated with *The Beach* had various detrimental impacts on local communities, such as increases in crime and prostitution, which resulted in massive protests by local and regional organisations and communities (Tzanelli 2006; see also Chap. 6 in this volume). Mordue's study (2001) on *Heartbeat*, an English TV series set in Goathland, in the county of Yorkshire, England, addressed the cultural and spatial conflicts between tourists and local residents due to the dramatised and romanticised idyllic rural life and myth created through its film imageries. For further details, Yoon et al. (2015) summarised the issues and impacts of film tourism that have emerged from previous studies.

Despite the above efforts, the status of research on residents' perceptions and attitudes towards film tourism (development) and its perceived impacts on communities and residents has been unsystematic and atheoretical and has been characterised by site-specific anecdotal evidence and subsequent discussions over time. Much of the research is descriptive and involves one-off cases, which means that longitudinal studies are still limited. Thus, changes in the way that impacts are perceived by local residents, particularly during different phases of the film production process, for example, during the production and post-production effects (PPEFs) phases, have been under-researched. Given these research gaps, the current chapter adopts a longitudinal approach and aims to examine and discuss how, and the extent to which, local residents' perceptions and attitudes towards the impacts of film tourism at a film tourism destination have changed, been transformed, and/or adjusted over time. The findings from this study raise issues about the role of government and self-efficacy in place identity in the Indonesian context.

8.2 Research Context and Geographical Location

The geographical focus of this chapter is Ubud in Bali in the Indonesian archipelago, a district in the Gianyar Regency. Tourism in Bali began in 1920 when the Royal Dutch Travel Company added the island to its itinerary, and these days Bali attracts over 2.5 million tourists every year. Ubud is approximately 42.38 km^2 in size with a total population in 2011 of 70,408 people (Gianyar Statistic Bureau 2012). The area consists of six traditional villages, including the Ubud District, and is located 20 km north-east of Denpasar, the capital city of Bali Province (Bali Tourism Board 2016).

Since the eighth century, Ubud has been the centre of Balinese culture (e.g. natural medicine and healing), religious practices and rituals, and art (e.g. dancing, drama, temples, monasteries, and architectural remains) in part because of the influence of the various dynasties that have ruled Bali for many years. The name Ubud originates from 'Ubad', the word for 'medicine' in the ancient Balinese language (Ubud Writer Festival 2013). Ubud is considered to be 'the most chic bohemian destination in the world' (James 1999, p.29). It gained prominence after many foreign artists were invited to visit the island, which stimulated the greatest art works in the area. Ubud has also emerged as a high-profile international destination, whilst still maintaining its integrity as the centre of Balinese art and culture.

As noted by O'Connor and Kim (2014), Ubud in Bali recently experienced a sudden influx of niche or special interest tourists, namely, film tourists associated with the Hollywood film *Eat Pray Love* (2010) that was filmed in Ubud in 2009 and released in 2010. Both local and international tourism businesses attempted to capitalise on the significance and popularity of the new *Eat Pray Love*-related (hereafter *EPL*) tourism patterns and trends by offering a variety of tour and accommodation packages tailored to include the main *EPL* experiences portrayed in the film (Gillies 2013; see also Chap. 7 in this volume).

This significant increase in the number of tourists visiting Ubud has also been confirmed in a report from the Tourism Department of Gianyar Regency (2013), which demonstrated that there was a significant increase in inbound tourism (international and domestic tourists) following the film's release in 2010, from 725,165 tourists in 2010 to 1,445,959 tourists in 2012 (Gianyar Tourism Department 2013).

The Indonesian Tourism and Creative Economy Ministry and the Balinese tourism industry considered this unprecedented effect of *EPL* to be a new tourism phenomenon and welcomed its largely positive effect on the Balinese economy, which was traumatised by terrorist bombings in 2002 and 2005 (O'Connor and Kim 2014).

Furthermore, the location of Ubud is unique as a research area for those studying the impact of film tourism on residents as it was already a famous tourist destination in Bali long before the *EPL* film phenomenon; studies of the impact of film tourism tend to take place in rural settings where there was little tourism prior to the sudden influx of film tourists (Riley et al. 1998; Mordue 2001; Roesch 2009). As already mentioned, Ubud experienced a sudden surge of different yet somewhat over-commercialised tourism patterns and products specifically targeted at *EPL* film tourists, which resulted in the transformation of existing cultural tourism market segments, either being partially replaced by or coexisting with the new developments. Such a complex and multilayered research context is expected to provide a unique contribution to the existing film tourism literature and thus enhance our understanding of local residents' perceptions and attitudes towards the impact of film tourism during different phases of a film's production.

8.3   Data Collection and Research Participants' Profiles

For this chapter, a qualitative approach with in-depth interviews with local residents was executed in five of the main villages in Ubud, namely, Pengosekan, Nyuh Kuning, Padang Tegal, Peliatan, and Ubud Central, where the *EPL* film was mostly set. The data collection was undertaken in mid-June to July 2014. With a convenient sampling method, around 80 potential respondents were randomly approached on the street and were given a series of screening questions to establish whether they perceived particular impacts of the *EPL* film phenomenon during its filming and after it was released and whether they were willing to share their experiences, viewpoints, and opinions. Of these, 22 respondents were recruited, consisting of six females and 16 males. The interviews were all conducted in the respondents' homes or workplaces, wherever they felt most comfortable sharing their opinions and experiences. Each interview lasted between 30 and 50 minutes. The participating local community members were coded LC1 to LC22.

The majority of the respondents were high-school graduates aged between 22 and 56 years old, inclusively. The majority of the respondents worked in tourism-related businesses, or at least had a family member who worked either part-time or full-time in the tourism industry. Their occupations included farmer, photographer, travel agent, librarian, NGO officer, spiritualist, doctor, shopkeeper, money exchange agent, *warung* (local snack bar) owner, taxi driver, restaurant manager, government officer, kiosk owner, massage shop owner, and art shop owner. The length of their residency in Ubud was between 16 and 46 years, with 32 years of residency being the mean.

8.4   FINDINGS: The Community's Perceptions and Attitudes Towards the *EPL* Film During Filming

The local residents experienced both immediate material and non-material impacts of the *EPL* film (tourism). Whilst traffic congestion (e.g. LC10, LC13, LC14) and conflicts between community members due to the uneven distribution of monetary compensation during the film production (e.g. LC4, LC8) were perceived somewhat negatively, the overall perceived impacts at this stage led to the formation of positive and supportive perceptions and attitudes towards the community impacts of *EPL* film tourism.

The material impacts perceived were mainly related to the direct monetary benefits injected into the local community, which can be categorised as follows:

1. Extra job opportunities through individual participation in the film's production, for example, as supporting actors or extras, site managers, or film crew assistants
2. Lending out of shops, land (e.g. rice fields), properties, or other facilities (e.g. parking) for the film's production
3. Financial compensation for the blocking off of some roads and neighbourhoods for filming
4. A sudden increase in food and beverage sales for local vendors and *warungs* to accommodate film crews and the domestic visitors who came to Ubud to directly experience the production of a Hollywood film and to glimpse at movie stars such as Julia Roberts

The above material gains during the film production stage were rather temporary but mostly welcomed, given that they generated improvements in the financial circumstances of ordinary Balinese households, which were particularly welcome given the region's persistently high unemployment rate and low and unstable incomes (Bell 2015). The direct monetary benefits received by some residents from the production of the film were considered a once-in-a-lifetime windfall and were thought to be exceptionally generous by local standards. Indeed, it was reported that the *EPL* film contributed to around 300 new jobs in local communities, generating USD 12.5 million for the local economy during the course of the film's production (Will 2011); this was most certainly welcomed by the local people.

The non-material benefits and costs (both individual and collective) include (1) new once-in-a-lifetime experiences and self-esteem, (2) personal growth and learning opportunities, (3) enhanced local community pride and increased concern about the future over-commercialisation of their cultural and ritual values and meanings, and (4) despondency and fear of a return to pre-*EPL* life.

The fact that this was the first Hollywood film to be shot in Ubud meant that having first-hand experience of the process of Hollywood film production and being able to watch global movie stars act and perform provided the local community members with authentic and unforgettable 'new once-in-a-lifetime experiences'. Those who directly participated in the film's production even witnessed another dimension of extraordinary once-in-a-lifetime experiences related to their own personal narratives during the production process. This led to increased self-esteem and pride, which then helped in the development of strong place attachments to Ubud. Not only would these personal experiences and stories be remembered, but they could also form a reservoir of collected personal stories that would unfold and be shared with others during their lifetime. For example, LC22 and LC7 enthusiastically stated:

> … I [will] urge all of my relatives and my daughters' friends to watch the movie … and everyone [will] knows that I am a Hollywood actress even if I am only an extras and appear for a couple seconds (laughing)…I am very proud of myself….(LC22)

> … For ordinary people like us, it's an amazing and interesting experience to know how a professional film shooting looks like and also know a film star from abroad … also unforgettable to directly witness the film activity and atmosphere of film shooting ….(LC7)

Furthermore, personal growth and learning opportunities were also positive experiences that came from direct exposure to the film production process, especially in terms of the film crew's punctuality and professionalism. Some respondents (e.g. LC2) considered this to be 'real life or philosophical lessons and practices' that they could personally relate to and could learn from, thus becoming better or more competent people.

Along with these individual non-material benefits, the local community also collectively experienced enhanced local community pride during the film production phase. A sense of community pride or belonging to Ubud, where Hindu religious and cultural practices have been deeply embedded into everyday life for decades as an expression of local and cultural identities, was strongly felt as film crews and even internationally famous movie stars sincerely followed every step of the rituals and traditional ceremonies prior to the film's shooting. This allowed the local community to not only appreciate these outsiders' respect for their culture and traditions but also to showcase it to the rest of the world, as demonstrated below.

> I was with the movie stars and [film] crews since the beginning, and it was quite fascinating to see that they were willing to follow all the rituals and traditional ceremony prior to the shooting seriously, which might be different from what they have been through in their other projects … I think it was a good way of introducing our culture and tradition, wishing for blessing from our late ancestors before starting a big event ….(LC2)

However, some of the respondents (e.g. LC6, LC17) saw this negatively as a form of commodification of their cultural and ritual practices and values. Particular concern was expressed about the role played by the medicine man Ketut Liyer in the film, as some felt that the mission of the medicine man is to communicate with the ancestors, not to participate in films. This attitude was not held by everyone, however, especially those who work in the tourism industry or who see the direct economic benefit of the film and who acknowledge the importance of the film in sharing their rituals and traditional ceremonies with outsiders who, in return, assist them in gaining a strong sense of pride and place attachment. In addition, curiosity about their way of life may increase and attract additional tourists to Ubud.

However, some locals – particularly casual part-time employees such as shop-keepers – expressed fear and despondency at the prospect of returning to their everyday routines and statuses following the personal economic benefits gained from the film's production. For these local people, film production had allowed them to earn a higher wage than usual by doing relatively little, e.g. as film extras walking around. These easy, decent economic gains were something like a dream for them, but were destined to only last for a short period of time. Although the dangerous nature of such temporary and unstable economic gains has been addressed (Beeton 2001; Croy 2011; see also Chap. 11 in this volume), the unavoidable return from such a 'dream' to the 'reality' of on-going financial hardship and disappointment led to a state of despondency and gloom.

8.5 Residents' Perceptions and Attitudes During the Post-production Effects (PPEFs) Phase

Residents' perceptions and attitudes towards the impact of *EPL* film tourism during the post-production stage are deemed to be more complex, vivid, realistic, and dynamic. They can be summarised by the following: (1) new entrepreneurial opportunities and economic benefits for certain groups, (2) enhanced self-pride and local community pride, (3) the preservation and commodification of cultural identity and value, and (4) congestion and overcrowding.

8.5.1 New Entrepreneurial Opportunities and Economic Benefits for Certain Groups

The emergence of new small- and medium-sized enterprises (SMEs), and increased incomes from such new businesses, can clearly be seen. Newly opened bicycle-hire companies, car-hire freelancers, and travel agents mushroomed immediately after the film's production. This is due to the increased demand for *EPL*-themed tourism products such as biking, traditional massage, traditional medicine, food and drinks, yoga, and medicine man services.

Local people saw this as an immediate and opportunistic response to the sudden influx of *EPL* film tourist market, who often have a particular desire to experience Julia Roberts' opening scene in the film, in which she is cycling through the rice paddies and other idyllic green and natural areas in Ubud (O'Connor and Kim 2014). Figure 8.1 shows a local bicycle-hire shop and tourists cycling in Ubud.

A series of tour packages to Ketut Liyer's house, such as 'Ketut Liyer Journeys', were also developed to meet the demand for conversations with him and tours of his house (see Fig. 8.2), as portrayed in the film. Local printing companies also took advantage of this by producing brochures and leaflets of the *EPL* tourism packages,

Fig. 8.1 Local bicycle-hire shop and tourists biking in Ubud (Source: Authors 2014)

Fig. 8.2 Ketut Liyer journey package (Source: Authors 2014)

Fig. 8.3 Ketut Liyer's Newly Expanded House (Source: Authors 2017)

which were very popular until 2013. As having a tourism-related job is empirically proven to be a determinant of residents' perceptions of the impact of tourism (Easterling 2004; Gu and Ryan 2008), those employed in the tourism industry were more aware of such tourism market changes and newly emerging market segments associated with *EPL* film tourism. For local travel agents and car-hire companies, the tour of Ketut Liyer's house is described as a newly emerging pilgrimage or as a must-do tourist activity, as can be seen below:

> There were quite busy on the early years after the film was released … until now we still pick up guests from airport and hotels, and deliver them to Ketut Liyer's house which I can say because of the film …it's like a must to do for those *EPL* tourists…. (LC12)

Despite the aforementioned economic benefits gained during the PPEFs phase, some of the respondents did not personally perceive any economic benefits from the film and subsequent film tourism boom, even after the film was released. They pointed out that it had only benefitted those groups of people who were directly involved in the film's production or were in the tourism industry. The figure who was most often cited as the one who had received the greatest economic benefits was Ketut Liyer, a medicine man featured in the *EPL* film who became an overnight celebrity. Others, however, such as local travel agents, have also directly or indirectly benefitted from Ketut's celebrity status, as has the film tourism industry in Ubud more generally.

As shown in Fig. 8.3, it is still true because Ketut's house has been recently fully expanded and now provides new services such as B&B, hair salon, and painting, as of May 2017 (see also Chap. 7 in this Volume).

8.5.2   Enhanced Self-Pride and Local Community Pride

Much like during the film production stage, the respondents saw self-pride and local community pride as one of the most positive non-material impacts of *EPL* film tourism experienced during the PPEFs stage. They all commented on how proud they were as local residents of Ubud to host an international event (i.e. *EPL* film shooting) in their area. Some of the quotations below demonstrate local people's enthusiasm for self-pride and local community pride:

> …when the film was released it was a boom here. The response was really fantastic…It's such a must-watch film for the people here…everyone was really proud and had a high appreciation of the film…. (LC10)

> … After the release of the film I feel more proud to be an Ubud person. I think it is the most beautiful place in Bali … Ubud is different …. (LC18)

8.5.3   The Preservation and Commodification of Cultural Identity and Value

Local people posited that their enhanced appreciation of the importance of sustaining and retaining their traditions and culture embedded in their cultural identity and values was another important intangible benefit of *EPL* film tourism. The influx of film tourists during this phase allowed local people to observe and (re)confirm that *EPL* film tourists were motivated to experience local culture, ritual ceremonies, and the traditional way of life in Ubud, as depicted in the film. This was even extended to their immediate environment, where cultural identities and values unfold and are practised, as local people were driven to take greater care of their land and the surrounding environment.

Thus, local people acknowledged that the *EPL* film tourism phenomenon gave them an invaluable opportunity to rethink their cultural identities and values as tourism assets, and to preserve their traditional arts, rituals, traditions, as well as other forms of cultural artefacts and elements, not only as being central to their lives but also as the centrepiece of Ubud. As a result, local people developed inner appreciation and a greater willingness to sustain and retain their traditions for future generations. This finding is in line with Durham's (2008) suggestion from an empirical study on three contemporary films, namely, Lasse Hallström's *Chocolat*, Jean-Pierre Jeunet's *Le Fabuleux Destin d'Amélie Poulain*, and James Ivory's *Le Divorce*. She suggests that films can strengthen the cultural identity of a country depending on how it is depicted. Her study also suggests that tourism can help keep local cultures alive, maintain cultural identities, and pass on cultural beliefs and rituals to future generations.

However, the respondents also suggested that Ketut Liyer and his family's practice may lead to the demoralising and materialising of their cultural identities, values, and meanings, arguing that they were already over-commodified and contrary to Hindu beliefs and teachings. This negative attitude, caused by the inevitable commodification of cultural identities and values, was also found during the film production stage. Below is the perspective of one local person on the commodification issue associated with Ketut, who also commodified himself following the unprecedented rise in his popularity:

> A medicine man is a gifted man, he has the innate power ... they don't ask for money when helping people. In old days if you come to them, you just give them what you have. It could be food, fruit, or money but according to your ability. If they start to ask for money, then they will lose their power ... I have a pity on Ketut because I think he's getting old and senile and many people commoditise him .... (LC22)

8.5.4   Congestion and Overcrowding

Traffic congestion and overcrowding in places shared by local people, as part of their daily social, cultural, and economic practices, and tourists were complained about by local people. This is not a new phenomenon as it has also been observed in similar studies of Koh Phi Phi Island in Thailand following the release of *The Beach* (Tzanelli 2006; see also Chap. 6 in this volume) and the Isle of Mull in Scotland which is associated with the children's television programme *Balamory* (Connell 2005). In the case of *EPL* film tourism, Ubud is known as a densely packed area with a relatively poor road system compared to Denpasar and Nusa Dua in Bali. As a result, the rapid changes caused by the sudden influx of *EPL* film tourists have certainly created a need for extra facilities and expanded infrastructure, such as an improved road system especially in the Ubud central area.

However, it seems that local authorities do not have sound film tourism planning or development programmes with short- or long-term implementation plans. Thus, local people have criticised local authorities' failure to monitor and control the congestion and overcrowding issue in a more effective way. To some extent, this is understandable as many of the negative impacts generated by film tourism for host communities are due to unplanned and sudden inflows of tourists to incidental and unprepared tourism destinations (Connell 2012; Mordue 2001; Yoon et al. 2015). This can mean that generally positive initial attitudes may deteriorate over time (McKercher et al. 2015). The criticism and resentment felt by local people is presented below:

> The most frustrating thing is the traffic congestion, especially in the morning and in the afternoon ... mostly caused by tourists, big buses, and private taxi ... I think the authorities should limit the number of vehicles to enter this area .... (LC11)

> ... too many big buses enters this area and make the traffic even worse ... many lands has turning into buildings and makes it really crowded, which is not really good for long term tourism in Ubud .... (LC10)

8.6 Conclusion

Significant literature exists on the impacts of tourism on local communities as well as on the phenomenon of film tourism. When these two fields are combined, however, there is a paucity of academic attention paid to the impacts of film tourism on local communities and residents of film tourism destinations. A longitudinal approach seems to be the scarcest in this context. This chapter aimed to present and discuss the issues identified with reference to the perceived impacts of film tourism on the local residents of Ubud in Bali, where the Hollywood film *Eat Pray Love* (*EPL*) was shot in 2009, and which has subsequently experienced a sudden influx of this emerging tourism market segment, namely, film tourism, since the film's release in 2010.

The changes in local residents' perceptions and attitudes towards the impact of film tourism generated by *EPL* were examined. The findings in this chapter were based on research data collected from mid-June to July 2014. In-depth interviews with 22 local residents from Pengosekan, Nyuh Kuning, Padang Tegal, Peliatan, and Ubud Central villages, where *EPL* was mostly set, were the foundation of this study.

During the film production stage, the vast majority of respondents perceived immediate positive impacts generated by direct and indirect economic development and benefits, as well as non-material or nonmonetary benefits such as new life-changing experiences, improved self-esteem, personal growth, learning opportunities, and enhanced collective local community pride. Although some negative aspects such as traffic congestion, uneven economic gain, and despondency were experienced, these were at marginal levels so that local people's positive perceptions outweighed the identified adverse effects of film tourism. In general, the local communities had positive perceptions and attitudes towards the impacts of film tourism and anticipated further positive indirect effects of the film's production in the future.

However, the respondents' general positive perceptions and attitudes during the film production stage gradually began to change during the post-production effects (PPEFs) phase, leaving them with mixed perceptions and attitudes. It was evident that local people perceived continuing positive benefits of film tourism in relation to new entrepreneurial opportunities and economic benefits, enhanced self-pride and local community pride, and enhanced recognition of the importance of preserving cultural identity and values. At the same time, they stressed the perceived negative impacts of film tourism, namely, their concern that the vibrant religious and ritualistic communities of Ubud, and their distinctive way of life, with its strong ties to the beliefs and teachings of Hinduism, could be in danger of being gradually lost through the commodification of cultural identity and values.

Furthermore, local people were resentful that certain groups had received most of the economic gains associated with film tourism. In particular, they mentioned Ketut Liyer, the medicine man featured in *EPL* who became an overnight celebrity. Their criticism of the over-commercialised economic activity of his family harmed their desire for community harmony in Ubud. Congestion and overcrowding during the PPEFs stage were also perceived negatively as local people experienced rapid changes that caused multiple issues related to their daily social, cultural, and economic activities in public places, which they now have to share with a substantially increased number of tourists.

In response to the above perceived costs of film tourism in Ubud, the central and local governments as well as the tourism authorities should establish stringent regulations and guidelines for all possible stakeholders including local communities to ensure that film tourism is effectively and sustainably developed and managed.

References

Bali Tourism Board. (2016). *Ubud.* Retrieved November 13, 2016, from http://www.balitourismboard.org/ubud.html

Beeton, S. (2001). Smiling for the camera: The influence of film audiences on a budget tourism destination. *Tourism, Culture and Communication, 3*(1), 15–26.

Beeton, S. (2008). Location, location, location: Film corporations' social responsibilities. *Journal of Travel & Tourism Marketing, 24*(2–3), 107–114.

Beeton, S. (2010). The advance of film tourism. *Tourism Planning and Development, 7*(1), 1–6.

Bell, C. (2015). Tourists infiltrating authentic domestic space at Balinese home cooking schools. *Tourist Studies, 15*(1), 86–100.

Connell, J. (2005). 'What's the story in Balamory?': The impacts of a children TV programme on small tourism enterprises on the Isle of Mull, Scotland. *Journal of Sustainable Tourism, 13*(3), 228–255.

Connell, J. (2012). Film tourism: Evolution, progress and prospects. *Tourism Management, 33*(5), 1007–1029.

Croy, W. G. (2011). Film tourism: Sustained economic contributions to destinations. *Worldwide Hospitality and Tourism Themes, 3*(2), 159–164.

Croy, C. W., & Heitmann, S. (2011). Tourism and film. In P. Robinson, S. Heitmann, & P. U. I. Dieke (Eds.), *Research themes for tourism.* Cambridge, MA: CAB International.

Durham, C. A. (2008). Finding France on film: Chocolat, Amélie and Le Divorce. *French Cultural Studies, 19*(2), 173–197.

Easterling, D. S. (2004). The residents' perspective in tourism research: A review and synthesis. *Journal of Travel & Tourism Marketing, 17*(4), 45–62.

Garcia, F. A., Vazquez, A. B., & Macias, R. C. (2015). Resident's attitudes towards the impacts of tourism. *Tourism Management Perspective, 13*, 33–40.

Gillies, E. (2013, April 29). *Getting away from the 'Eat, Pray, Love' Ubud.* Retrieved from http://www.jakpost.travel/news/getting-away-from-the-eat-pray-love-ubud-KlE3RWFNoXDg6hbC.html

Gianyar Statistic Bureau. (2012). *Gianyar in figures.* Retrieved October 15, 2013, from http://www.gianyarkab.go.id/

Gianyar Tourism Department. (2013). *Data of visitors number.* Gianyar: Bali.

Gu, H., & Ryan, C. (2008). Place attachment, identity and community impacts of tourism: The case of a Beijing hutong. *Tourism Management, 29*(4), 637–647.

Heitmann, S. (2010). Film tourism planning and development: Questioning the role of stakeholders and sustainability. *Tourism Planning and Development, 7*(1), 31–46.

James, J. (1999, August). Ubud, the heart of bali. *The Atlantic Monthly, 284*, 26–30. Retrieved from http://search.proquest.com/docview/223098713?accountid=10910

Kim, S., & Butler, G. (2015). Local community perspectives towards dark tourism development: The case of Snowtown, South Australia. *Journal of Tourism and Cultural Change, 13*(1), 78–89.

McGehee, N. G., & Andereck, K. L. (2004). Factors predicting rural residents' support of tourism. *Journal of Travel Research, 43*, 131–140.

McKercher, B., Wang, D., & Park, E. (2015). Social impacts as a function of place change. *Annals of Tourism Research, 50*, 52–66.

Mordue, T. (2001). Performing and directing resident/tourist cultures in heartbeat country. *Tourist Studies, 1*(3), 233–252.

Nunkoo, R., Smith, S. L. J., & Ramkissoon, H. (2013). Residents' attitudes to tourism: A longitudinal study of 140 articles from 1984 to 2010. *Journal of Sustainable Tourism, 21*(1), 5–25.

O'Connor, N., & Kim, S. (2014). Pictures and prose: Exploring the impact of literary and film tourism. *Journal of Tourism and Cultural Change, 12*(1), 1–17.

Riley, R., Baker, D., Van Doren, C., & S. (1998). Movie induced tourism. *Annals of Tourism Research, 25*(4), 919–935.

Roesch, S. (2009). *The experiences of film location tourists*. Bristol: Channel View Publication.

Tzanelli, R. (2006). Reel Western fantasies: Portrait of a tourist imagination in The Beach (2000). *Mobilities, 1*(1), 121–142.

Will, R. (2011, August). Eat pray film: After the success of eat pray love, the country is trying to attract new blockbusters to shoot in Indonesia. *Forbes Indonesia*, pp. 46–47. Retrieved August 25, 2014, from http://www.balifilm.com/news_archives/FORBES%20Indonesia_Aug2011.pdf

Yoon, Y., Kim, S., & Kim, S. (2015). Successful and unsuccessful film tourism destinations: From the perspective of Korean local residents' perceptions of film tourism impacts. *Tourism Analysis, 20*(3), 297–311.

Part III
The Film Tourist Experience

Chapter 9
Nostalgia and the Development of Film Tourism Products and Activities: The Case of Korean Audiences of Hong Kong Films

Sangkyun Kim and Seongseop (Sam) Kim

Abstract Nostalgia plays a crucial role not only in stimulating perceived familiarity with certain locations but also in motivating tourists to visit the locations and satisfying on-site experiences in the context of film tourism. However, the role of nostalgia has, until now, not been fully theorised and integrated in related theories on film tourism. This chapter aims to examine and identify the role of nostalgia in the development of future film tourism products and activities in Hong Kong, particularly those that target Korean audiences who enjoyed Hong Kong films produced from the 1970s to the late 1990s. The findings suggest that nostalgia formed by lasting memories of these Hong Kong films from the 'good old days' is represented and embodied by (1) memories of films' content and film stars, (2) memories of film backdrops, (3) reminiscence of mimicking, (4) envy of Hong Kong society and (5) memories of Hong Kong history and culture. Stronger feelings of nostalgia and sentimentality, particularly associated with film content and film stars, as well as film backdrops, are crucial to the support needed for the development of Hong Kong film tourism-related tour programmes.

Keywords Memory • Nostalgia • Product development • Hong Kong • Quantitative

9.1 Introduction

This chapter aims to examine the role of nostalgia in the development of potential film tourism products and activities in Hong Kong, particularly those that target Korean audiences that enjoyed Hong Kong films produced from the 1970s to the

S. Kim (✉)
School of Business and Law, Edith Cowan University, 270 Joondalup Drive,
Joondalup, WA 6027, Australia
e-mail: s.kim@ecu.edu.au

S. Kim
School of Hotel & Tourism Management, Hong Kong Polytechnic University,
17 Science Musuem Road, TST East, Kowloon, Hong Kong

© Springer Nature Singapore Pte Ltd. 2018
S. Kim, S. Reijnders (eds.), *Film Tourism in Asia*, Perspectives on Asian
Tourism, DOI 10.1007/978-981-10-5909-4_9

late 1990s. The results presented in this chapter are partially derived from a larger film tourism research project investigating the structural relationships between key concepts in film tourism, including nostalgia, cultural proximity, and involvement. The chapter primarily focuses on the results of nostalgia for about Hong Kong films among prospective Korean film tourists and the related film tourism products and activities. The results are presented in three main sections: (1) characteristics of the samples, (2) nostalgia about Hong Kong films among Korean audiences, and (3) support for Hong Kong film tourism product development and preferred film tourism activities. Given that the data were derived from a very particular setting, namely, Korean fans of Hong Kong films made in the 1970s to the late 1990s, the chapter commences with an introduction of the research locale.

9.2   The Popularity of Hong Kong Films in Korea

Hong Kong films gained unrivalled popularity as the hub of the Asian film industry prior to the new millennium (Wong and McDonogh 2001). Many film audiences in Asia grew up watching Hong Kong action movies featuring martial arts, gangsters, and crime stories, with some exceptions such as romance or comedy movies (Pan and Ryan 2013). In particular, Bruce Lee became an iconic star of Hong Kong films through his famous collection of martial arts films, including *The Big Boss* (1971), *Fist of Fury* (1972), *The Way of the Dragon* (1972), *Enter the Dragon* (1973), and *Game of Death* (1978). Lee was a legend in Asia, especially among young male audiences at that time. In the following decades, many of these audience members maintained fond memories of Lee's films, which they first saw at a time when other entertainment was very limited (Chosun Ilbo 2016). These audience members are now in their 40s or older, and for many of them, Bruce Lee's films still trigger memories and nostalgia for a cherished past. Consequently, middle-aged people often visit the Hong Kong Heritage Museum, which exhibits Bruce Lee memorabilia. Likewise, Lee's iconic statue on the *Avenue of Stars* in Hong Kong is a popular tourist destination, where middle-aged nostalgia-driven tourists go to reminisce about his films and re-live those poor but happy days, by re-enacting Lee's actions and even taking photographs of their re-enactments.

Though Hong Kong movies were popular throughout Asia, they struck a particular chord with Korean audiences. During their heyday, Hong Kong films influenced the worlds of fashion, design, lifestyle, personal values, food preferences, and the entertainment industries in Korea (Lee 2006). Watching Hong Kong films in the theatre or on an analogue television set with video cassettes hired from video rental shops was considered an enjoyable pastime among the Korean youth. Video rental shops mushroomed in the 1980s up until the 1990s, and Hong Kong films were always in high demand.

Thus, the popularity of Hong Kong films in Korea at that time led to a kind of generational hype as social phenomenon (Chosun Ilbo 2016). The phenomenon even provided a vehicle for some Hong Kong movie stars to appear in commercial advertisements on Korean television. For example, Chow Yun-fat appeared in a soft drink commercial (1989), while Leslie Cheung was in a chocolate bar advertisement (1989). These commercials were immediately and immensely helpful in boosting product sales. Popular journalism highlighted that Korean fans of Hong Kong movies often mimicked the actions of Hong Kongese actors and actresses by performing martial arts, wearing sunglasses, smoking cigarettes, posing like gangsters, wearing the same make-up, and/or imitating scenes word for word (Kim 2015; Lee 2006).

9.3 Literature Review

According to Howard (2012), nostalgia is defined as a longing for the past or a fondness for possessions and activities associated with days gone by. It can elicit a variety of emotional and affective responses by reflecting things associated with the past. The concept of nostalgia has been explored in a variety of disciplinary areas including gerontology (Synnes 2015), pathology (Dey 2016), advertising (Zhao et al. 2014), anthropology (Berliner 2012), consumer behaviour (Holbrook 1993), and media studies (Zaatari 2015). It has also begun to be applied to the identification of motivational factors or experiences of senior tourism (Hsu et al. 2007; Sellicka 2004), heritage tourism (Bartoletti 2010; Leong et al. 2015; Yeh et al. 2012), and sports tourism (Gordon 2013).

Furthermore, nostalgia plays a crucial role in the transformation of an ordinary location into a symbolically special place that inscribes identity, ideology, power, myth, history, culture, symbolism, freedom, romanticism, and philosophy (Chen et al. 2014; Leong et al. 2015; Sellicka 2004). Similarly, the troika of nostalgia, film, and audiences has been documented well within the context of film tourism. When media audiences such as film or TV audiences visit film locations, their personal attachment with the locations can partially be understood as symbolic memory or nostalgia (Kim 2012a; Roesch 2009; Reijnders 2016). This is because they are continuously psychologically and emotionally involved in the plots and stories, actors, backdrops, songs, and scenic backgrounds while watching their beloved media programmes (Buchmann et al. 2010; Couldry 1998; Pan and Ryan 2013; Roesch 2009). Film narratives in particular contribute to positive evaluations of film locations where the landscape, as either the front or back stage of the film, is associated with positively perceived values such as nostalgia, happiness, freedom, and imagination (Reijnders 2016).

Thus, a film's location forms a focal point as a prestigious performance stage upon which film tourists often re-enact or mimic their favourite scenes and narratives (Kim 2010; Reijnders 2016; Robinson 2015). They often become more sentimental when touching props, imitating the motions of actors, reciting actors' lines, and singing songs from the original soundtrack when visiting film tourism destinations and waiting for cast members and film makers at fan meetings (Kim 2012a). These are characteristics of specific or purposeful film tourists (Kim 2012a;

Macionis and Sparks 2009; Rittichainuwat and Rattanaphinanchai 2015). This emotional connection is linked to an interest in a "sense of place" or "place attachment" (Kim 2012b; Roesch 2009) or the identity of film locations (Couldry 1998). Likewise, film tourists are interested in experiencing locations from the perspective of the beloved character(s) (Buchmann et al. 2010; Reijnders 2016; Roesch 2009). As such, nostalgia plays a crucial role not only in stimulating perceived familiarity with film locations but also in motivating film tourists to visit locations and providing satisfying on-site experiences.

Despite the above effort of prior studies on film tourism, the role of nostalgia has, until now, not been fully theorised and integrated in related theories on film tourism. Rather, it has been documented based on the results of empirical inductive research and thus has been limited to empirical examinations and subsequent interpretive explanations of nostalgic sentiments or activities in a film tourism destination. An exception is the work of Kim (2012a) who posits that intimate, memory-related film tourist experiences are the main drivers in the creation of memorable tourism experiences. Emotional or affective involvement while watching a media programme (e.g. films and television dramas), albeit different genres (Connell 2012), contributes the most to film tourists' experiences of intimacy and memory (Kim 2012a; Kim and Assaker 2014). The memories of beloved stories performed by beloved actors are therefore central for film tourists as former audiences to develop symbolic connectedness to and increased familiarity with and nostalgia for film locations.

9.4   Research Methods

To develop items pertaining to nostalgia about Hong Kong films, an extensive review of journals, magazines, and books relevant to film critiques, social trends, culture and film, and the characteristics of Hong Kong films produced in the 1970s to the late 1990s was conducted (Lee 2006; Pan and Ryan 2013; Robinson 2015; Suni and Komppula 2012; Wong and McDonogh 2001). Previous studies of consumer behaviour were also reviewed (Holak 2013; Holbrook 1993; Marchegiani and Phau 2013).

A preliminary questionnaire was then developed, and its items were further discussed and clarified through in-depth interviews with a pool of 20 Korean residents who reported enjoying Hong Kong films from the relevant period. The topics covered during the interviews included the respondents' emotional and behavioural involvement, the effects of the films on the respondents and their lives, the films' social motifs, the circumstances of the domestic film industry, the respondents' intentions to engage in film tourism in Hong Kong, and their preferred activities and film tourism programmes.

Based on the above, the items chosen to identify and measure nostalgia after watching Hong Kong films included participants' memories of scenes or backdrops; images of Hong Kong that are featured in these films; the films' stories, feelings, music, and background images; the visual effects of Kung Fu films (e.g. flying in a

Kung Fu movie); re-enacting or discussing the film after having watched it; and interest in the culture, society, or history of Hong Kong. The items chosen to identify and measure participants' preferred film tourism activities (without any guide or tour) and products included film tourism tour programmes in loco, TV, or mobile programmes on film tourism activities and special event programmes themed around Hong Kong films and film stars. The items chosen to identify and measure their preferred film tourism activities included visiting film sites, fan meeting events, and tasting Cantonese food (e.g. visiting the restaurants or cafes featured in the films). The questions were then revised using a pilot study involving 50 Korean residents who were familiar with old Hong Kong films.

The main survey was conducted using an online survey tool, which was chosen for its advantages, such as the rapid collection of samples from the target population, the ability to control sample selection using planned quotas, and the user friendliness of the website (Grönlund and Strandberg 2014). Data were collected from October 1 to 15, 2015, using an online company with 1.12 million panellists. The selection of respondents was restricted to individuals who were 40 years of age or older, had not visited Hong Kong yet, had watched at least two Hong Kong films from a list of 30 released from the 1970s to the late 1990s, and recognised at least one film star from a list of 11 film stars from that time. Of the 620 questionnaires completed, 610 were used for further data analyses because of missing data accounting for more than 25% of total answered questions.

9.5 Results

9.5.1 Characteristics of the Sample

A frequency analysis of the respondents' demographic profiles showed that 51.3% were male, and 84.4% were married. The age group distribution is as follows: 34.9% of the sample were aged 40–49 years old, whereas 30.6% were in their early 50s, and 26.4% were 55 or older. With regard to occupation, 45.4% were company workers and 22.3% were housewives. From the sample, 62.8% lived in a metropolitan or large city and 32.3% lived in a medium-sized or small city.

Regarding their individual exposure to Hong Kong films released in the 1970s to the late 1990s, 21.8% of respondents reported having watched three films or less, 27.2% had watched four to six films, 16.4% had watched seven to nine films, and 34.6% had watched 10 films or more. In short, more than half of the respondents had watched at least seven Hong Kong films during this time. More than 81% of the respondents reported recognising at least ten Hong Kong movie stars from that time. Jackie Chan and Bruce Lee were the most recognised, with 99.5% and 99% recognising them, respectively. More than 90% of respondents also knew the following Hong Kong movie stars: Chow Yun-fat, Leslie Cheung, Sammo Hung, Andy Lau, and Wang Zuxian. About 26.5% reported that they still watched Hong Kong films.

The top three most watched Hong Kong films out of the 30 listed in the questionnaire were: *A Better Tomorrow* (1986), *Swordsman II* (1992), and *Police Story* (1985).

Concerning the Hong Kong film fandom during that period, 59.8% of the respondents agreed, whereas only 9.3% either disagreed or strongly disagreed that the label of fandom referred to them. Approximately 59% of the respondents had already experienced film tourism destinations or film shooting locations either domestically or in foreign countries. This 59% are therefore more likely to visit Hong Kong as a film tourism destination in the future, as those with previous film tourism experiences are more likely to visit film tourism locations again (Kim and O'Connor 2011; Macionis and Sparks 2009).

9.5.2 Factor Analyses and Reliability Tests

To identify the underlying dimensionality of the instruments used in this study (i.e. nostalgia for Hong Kong films, preferred nostalgia-driven film tourism products, preferred film tourism activities), exploratory factor analyses were conducted using principal component factoring and varimax rotation.

First, a nostalgia scale containing 26 items was factor analysed, which determined that a five-factor solution, in which each factor had an eigenvalue of over 1.0, was appropriate. An examination of a scree plot supported the factor solution. The five extracted domains explained 17.84, 12.26, 11.10, 9.58, and 6.90% of the variance, respectively. The value for the Kaiser-Meyer-Olkin (KMO) measure of sampling adequacy was .92, and the Bartlett's test for sphericity produced a value of 6578 ($p < 0.001$). These values validate the factor model and the existence of one or more factors in the factor solution. The factor loadings, which measure the correlation between the observed measurements and the factors, were located between .43 and .85, closer to and far exceeding the 0.45 threshold proposed by Comrey and Lee (1992), respectively. In terms of internal consistency for the items within each domain, the reliability alphas for the five factors ranged from .79 to .84. The reliability alphas for all five factors were in excess of the threshold (0.70) recommended by Nunnally (1978). Table 9.1 presents the results in full.

Second, the factor analysis of the preferred nostalgia-driven film tourism products generated a three-factor model with an eigenvalue greater than 1.0. The results from the examination of the scree plots confirmed the three-factor dimensionality structure. The three domains explained 31.5, 23.8, and 20.9% of the variance, respectively. The value for the KMO measure of sampling adequacy was .95, and the Bartlett's test for sphericity produced a value of 4872 ($p < 0.001$). Thus, the factor solution was valid and confirmed the existence of one or more factors in the factor model. The factor loadings ranged from .43 to .82. Regarding the measurement of internal consistency for the items within each domain, the reliability alphas for the three factors were .91, .84, and .80, respectively. The reliability alphas for all three factors far exceeded the threshold (0.70). The results are exhibited in Table 9.2.

Table 9.1 Factor analysis of nostalgia about Hong Kong films

Domains and items	Factor loading	Communality	Mean
Domain 1 (envy of Hong Kong society)			
(α = .84, eigenvalue = 4.64, explained variance = 17.84%, grand mean = 3.28)			
I believed Hong Kong's political and social system looked stable	.74	.63	2.85
I believed the industrial products featured in the films were technologically advanced	.74	.62	3.23
I believed Hong Kong's economic development was advanced	.72	.61	3.43
I envied Hong Kong society as shown in the films	.68	.53	3.00
I believed that Hong Kong society, as shown in the films, was vivid and dynamic	.65	.55	3.60
I felt that the society depicted in the Hong Kong films was free and not restricted	.55	.41	3.38
The Hong Kong food featured in the films looked tasty	.54	.46	3.43
Domain 2 (memory of films' content and film stars)			
(α = .79, eigenvalue = 3.19, explained variance = 12.26%; grand mean = 3.83)			
The fighting/martial arts scenes in the Hong Kong action movies were interesting	.78	.66	4.03
The storylines in the Hong Kong films were intriguing	.70	.56	3.94
The fight scenes featured in the films were memorable	.67	.58	3.94
The special effects in the films (e.g. flying in a kung fu movie) were wonderful	.65	.52	3.68
The fashion style of the Hong Kong film stars was stylish and beautiful	.53	.49	3.53
The Hong Kong film stars were attractive	.47	.42	3.85
Domain 3 (reminiscence of mimicking)			
(α = .82, eigenvalue = 2.89, explained variance = 11.10%, grand mean = 3.29)			
I repeated or followed the lines that the actors/actresses spoke	.79	.71	3.12
I mimicked the actions of the Hong Kong film actors/actresses such as performing martial arts, wearing sunglasses, smoking cigarettes, and putting on make-up	.76	.66	3.19
I wanted to learn the martial arts featured in the films	.71	.67	3.46
I wanted to have the brand products featured in the films	.61	.64	2.91
Hong Kong films were the topic of talk or gossiping among friends	.45	.65	3.77
Domain 4 (memory of film backdrops)			
(α = .79, eigenvalue = 2.49, explained variance = 9.58%, grand mean = 3.58)			
I liked the background music in the films	.58	.51	3.85
The alleys, traditional markets, restaurants, and buildings featured in the films were memorable	.54	.60	3.22
The scenes of streets at night featured in the films were shiny and vivid	.51	.57	3.59

(continued)

Table 9.1 (continued)

Domains and items	Factor loading	Communality	Mean
The background scenery featured in the Hong Kong films was beautiful	.44	.48	3.60
The scenes in the Hong Kong films showed us that Hong Kong was an international city	.43	.42	3.73
The Hong Kong harbour as featured in the films was fantastic	.43	.53	3.50
Domain 5 (memory of Hong Kong history and culture)			
(α = .74, eigenvalue = 1.79, explained variance = 6.90%, grand mean = 3.25)			
I could understand Hong Kong history through the historical stories shown in the films	.85	.78	3.08
I could understand the Hong Kong/Chinese customs and culture featured in the Hong Kong films	.81	.75	3.42

Note: Items were measured on a 5-point Likert scale [*"strongly disagree"* (1), *"neutral"* (3), *"strongly agree"* (5)]

Lastly, the factor analysis of the preferred film tourism activities driven by nostalgia produced a three-factor solution in which each factor had an eigenvalue exceeding 1.0. The three domains accounted for 28.78, 26.65, and 21.31% of the variance, respectively. The value for the KMO measure of sampling adequacy was .92, and the Bartlett's test for sphericity produced a value of 3958 ($p < 0.001$). This indicates that the factor model was valid and the number of extracted factors was one or more. The factor loadings were between .45 and .86. Regarding the internal consistency of the items within each domain, the reliability alphas for the three factors were .89, .76, and .82, respectively. The reliability alphas for all three factors surpassed the threshold (0.70). The results are presented in Table 9.3.

9.6 Nostalgia About Hong Kong Films Among Korean Audiences

Korean audiences of Hong Kong films rated their personal memories of the films' content (e.g. storyline) and movie stars as being the most important nostalgia domain when recalling old Hong Kong films that they had watched, with a grand mean score of 3.83. In particular, "martial arts scenes", "gangsters' fighting scenes", and "attractive stylish Hong Kong film stars" were rated highly when it came to triggering nostalgia about Hong Kong films. This suggests that a deep emotional connectedness between the audience and the film content – celebrities, characters, and story in particular – is a key factor in them becoming film tourists (Kim 2012a, b; Lee et al. 2008). The significance of celebrity involvement with film audiences has been also documented.

Table 9.2 Factor analysis of Korean audience's interest in Hong Kong film tourism product development

Domains and items	Factor loading	Communality	Mean
Domain 1 (development of film tourism tour programme)			
(α = .91, eigenvalue = 3.47, explained variance = 31.50%, grand mean = 3.34)			
During a visit to Hong Kong, a travel package that includes visits to Hong Kong film sets should be developed	.82	.83	3.33
During a visit to Hong Kong, a travel package that includes visits to the Hong Kong Film History Museum should be developed	.81	.84	3.29
Travel guidebooks that introduce Hong Kong film scenes and locations should be published	.79	.78	3.30
Travel packages that include visiting places featured in films should be developed	.70	.72	3.38
During a visit to Hong Kong, a tour programme that interprets the famous Hong Kong films that took place in the "good old days" should be developed	.57	.64	3.42
Domain 2 (development of TV or mobile programme)			
(α = .84, eigenvalue = 2.61, explained variance = 23.76%, grand mean = 3.07)			
Programmes that explain Hong Kong films should be developed by Korean TV networks	.79	.78	3.07
Internet portal sites where Hong Kong films are introduced should be developed	.75	.77	3.13
Mobile products featuring downloadable Korean translations for Hong Kong film star information, content, pictures, and text messages should be developed	.56	.81	3.02
Domain 3 (Development of Fan Meeting Event)			
(α = .80, eigenvalue = 2.30, explained variance = 20.88%, grand mean = 3.13)			
"Fan sign" events that Hong Kong film stars attend should be organised	.43	.75	3.06
Fashions or accessories that Hong Kong film stars wear should be developed as products for tourists	.78	.81	3.07
Music concerts that are themed with Hong Kong film original sound tracks (OSTs) or background music should be held	.60	.66	3.26

Note: Items were measured on a 5-point Likert scale ["*strongly disagree*" (1), "*neutral*" (3), "*strongly agree*" (5)]

The next important nostalgia domain was related to their memory of film backdrops, with the second highest grand mean score of 3.58. In this context, film backdrop includes "background music" and the "cityscape, streetscape, and landscape in Hong Kong" that have been used as backgrounds and foregrounds in film productions (e.g. alleys, traditional markets, restaurants, the skyscrapers that surround Victoria Peak, Hong Kong harbour). As such, the busy, chaotic streets and alleys of Hong Kong that are always featured in Hong Kong films, with their neon signs, teahouses, and food stalls open day and night, are atmospheric and are often

Table 9.3 Factor analysis of Korean audience's interest in film tourism activities

Domains and items	Factor loading	Communality	Mean
Domain 1 (visiting filmed locations)			
(α = .89, eigenvalue = 2.88, explained variance = 28.78%, grand mean = 3.27)			
I'd like to visit indoor/outdoor film sets	.79	.79	3.42
I'd like to visit the film studios that developed the films	.78	.79	3.16
I'd like to buy things that were shown in the films in the "good old days"	.75	.70	2.97
I'd like to visit alleys, traditional markets, buildings, and restaurants that were shown in the films in the "good old days"	.66	.72	3.46
I'd like to visit the Hong Kong film history Museum	.45	.66	3.33
Domain 2 (tasting film-featured food)			
(α = .76, eigenvalue = 2.67, explained variance = 26.65%, grand mean = 3.47)			
I'd like to taste the Hong Kong (Cantonese) food featured in the films in the "good old days"	.85	.81	3.50
I'd like to go to the restaurants that Hong Kong actors/actresses visited in the films and eat food	.83	.83	3.44
Domain 3 (meeting with Hong Kong film stars)			
(α = .82, eigenvalue = 2.13, explained variance = 21.31%, grand mean = 3.36)			
I'd like to meet the movie stars from the "good old days"	.86	.85	3.56
I'd like to take part in "fan sign" meetings with film stars from the "good old days"	.77	.80	3.16

Note: Items were measured on a 5-point Likert scale ["*strongly disagree*" (1), "*neutral*" (3), "*strongly agree*" (5)]

seen as a cliché or a staple of Hong Kong's traditional and unique culture and society. It is these film backdrops that Korean audiences immediately and strongly associate with Hong Kong films from days gone by. Background music also plays a crucial role in allowing the audience to recall film stories and backdrops, as music can add a powerful augmented means of expression to the existing visual images and imagery by particularising its affective resonance, thanks to its important ability to create atmosphere and underline the psychological states of the characters (Copland as cited in Carroll 1996, p. 139).

Although earlier studies on the role of music in film tourism and nostalgia are very limited, the role of music in creating personal and emotional memories and nostalgia for locations visited by global music fans, in the context of music tourism, has been documented (Bolderman and Reijnders 2016); this has been often conceptualised as a nostalgia industry (Gibson and Connell 2007). Also, Kim (2012c) highlights that background music as a non-visual sense supports and enhances the overall memorable viewing experiences of films. Background music associated with particular memorable scenes can be therefore very emotionally resonant; this is closely related to our memory and nostalgia, whether the scenes are exhilarating or poignant. In this regard, Roesch (2009) showed a picture of a *Star Wars* fan watching the horizon in contemplation while listening to the sound track on his earphones.

It is suggested, for example, that Korean audiences who vividly remember *Chungking Express* (1994), which portrayed the light and dark of Hong Kong society, immediately associate the film with some of its greatest background OSTs (Original Sound Tracks), namely, *Dreams* originally sung by The Cranberries and *California Dreaming* by Mamas & Papas. This is similar to *Only You* from *Fallen Angels* (1995) and the Cantonese remake of the 1980s classic *Take My Breath Away* from *As Tears Go By* (1988).This is again about music as a tool for reminiscence as mentioned earlier; it has a close relationship with emotional and affective aspect of film tourist experiences.

By comparison, cognitive information about the social, cultural, and historical backgrounds of the country in which a film is set, which are unfolded and represented in the film's storyline, was the least important stimulus of nostalgia. The "envy of Hong Kong society" and "memory of Hong Kong history and culture" domains of nostalgia were given grand mean scores of 3.28 and 3.25, respectively. Although Korean audiences agreed that the item entitled "Hong Kong films were the topic of talk or gossiping among friends" as a collective social memory-related nostalgia item (3.77) was an important trigger for their nostalgia about Hong Kong films, they did not strongly believe that the domain of the reminiscence of mimicking, with a grand mean score of 3.29, was as important as their memories of film content, movie stars, and film backdrops.

9.7   Support for Hong Kong Film Tourism Product Development and Preferred Film Tourism Activities

Korean audiences of Hong Kong films produced from the 1970s to the late 1990s generally expect to experience a tailored film tourism destination product when visiting Hong Kong as a nostalgia film tourism destination, with a grand mean score of 3.34. They wanted the tour programme, if developed, to include visits to Hong Kong film sets, places, and locations featured in films, as well as the Hong Kong Film History Museum. It is interesting to note that they rated a special interpretation tour programme of famous Hong Kong films from the 1970s to 1990s with the highest mean score of 3.42. They also more or less welcomed the introduction of a travel guidebook specialising in the scenes and locations of Hong Kong films, with a mean score of 3.30. This finding is contrasted with an early study of Reijnders (2010) in which the fans of *James Bond* movies were found to be more individualistic and independent as travellers, tailoring their own itineraries, whereas it is consistent with the findings of Buchmann et al. (2010), who suggest that the majority of the *Lord of the Rings* fans who participate in dedicated film location tours do so in order to encounter the fellowship of other enthusiastic fans. While this mixed narrative cannot be interpreted using the Western and non-Western (i.e. Asian) dichotomy, this is an interesting area that needs to be further explored in a wider context.

Although they support the development of a Hong Kong film stars' fan meeting event (with a grand mean score of 3.13) and TV or mobile programmes about Hong Kong films and film stars (with 3.07), they seemed less interested in film tourism products associated with Hong Kong films that do not involve actual corporeal mobility and visits to locations and places featured in the films they enjoyed watching in days gone by. One interpretation is the importance of physical presence and embodied interactions with film locations and places from a film tourist perspective (Buchmann et al. 2010; Couldry 1998; Kim 2012a), given that film tourists often want to confirm "iconic parts or everything of what was depicted on the screen through their eyes and camera lenses" (Kim 2012a, p. 394). It is noteworthy that they were, however, more interested in Hong Kong film-themed music concerts, with a mean score of 3.26. One implication, therefore, is that background film music and OSTs are, at least for Korean audiences, strongly associated with their nostalgia for Hong Kong films and the pastime of watching them on VHS, which confirms the role of music in creating powerful augmented affective resonance and nostalgia.

Regarding film tourism-related activities, Korean audiences rated tasting film-related food, such as the Cantonese cuisine featured in these films, and eating in restaurants featured in these films as being the most preferred tourism activity, with a grand mean score of 3.47, followed by meeting Hong Kong film stars (3.36) and visiting film locations (3.27).

9.8 Conclusion

To some extent films can stimulate nostalgia when they tell stories of the "good old days" or when they are analogous to one's own story or that of one's community in this case, the Korean audiences that enjoyed Hong Kong films produced from the 1970s to the late 1990s. The content and storylines of old films stored in an individual's memory can often serve as nostalgic vestiges of times past and can encourage an individual viewer to form an emotional and symbolic connection with particular stories or scenes. Locations used in the making of films or TV dramas, whether as backgrounds or foregrounds, can then become nostalgia-stimulating spaces for some audiences, whose memories and reminiscences are evoked by the stories and events associated with the shooting locations. Therefore, one's memories of a film's location can be a crucial guide to his or her selection of a tourism destination, given that nostalgia-creating films present positively familiar and important images of such locations in the minds of audience members (Kim 2012a; Kim and Assaker 2014; Robinson 2015; Suni and Komppula 2012).

Despite the above significance of nostalgia in such a context, few studies have explored the potential for preferred film tourism products and activities. In this chapter, the potential described above was theoretically discussed and empirically tested and confirmed. For Korean audiences of Hong Kong films produced from the

1970s to the late 1990s, nostalgia formed by lasting memories of these films from the "good old days" is represented and embodied by (1) memories of films' content and film stars, (2) memories of film backdrops, (3) reminiscence of mimicking, (4) envy of Hong Kong society, and (5) memories of Hong Kong history and culture. Stronger feelings of nostalgia and sentimentality, particularly associated with film content and film stars, as well as film backdrops, are crucial to the support needed for the development of Hong Kong film tourism-related tour programmes.

Viewers rather marginally agreed that they would be interested in tasting film-related food, meeting their favourite Hong Kong film stars, and visiting film locations from their favourite Hong Kong films, if they were to visit Hong Kong as a film tourism destination. This might be interpreted that the Korean audiences of Hong Kong films were not actively engaged with the questions about their support for Hong Kong film tourism product development and preferred film tourism activities, given that these questions were not personal.

Although the Hong Kong government has developed film tourism-related attractions such as the *Avenue of Stars* and the restoration of Bruce Lee's old residence, these efforts have been made with little research examining the role of nostalgia in film tourists' preferences for products and activities related to those destinations. Thus, the findings presented in this chapter can be used in the future development of film tourism products and activities, given that the memory-related experiences of film tourists play a crucial role in the creation of memorable tourism experiences, influencing their intentions to visit or revisit a location (Kim 2012a, b), which can include intimate, nostalgic, and sentimental tourist experiences at film tourism destinations that are closely tied to audiences' motivations to become film tourists (Kim 2012a; Macionis and Sparks 2009).

While the findings of this chapter contributed to closing the identified research gaps and thus enriching the film tourism literature, there is still a need for future research on the role of nostalgia in film tourism in a wider context, for example, in relation to gender, class, and ethnicity. Furthermore, international comparative research on this subject comparing the similarities and differences of different cultures would be welcomed.

References

Bartoletti, R. (2010). 'Memory tourism' and the commodification of nostalgia. In P. Burns, C. Palmer, & J. A. Lester (Eds.), *Tourism and visual culture* (pp. 23–42). Wallingford: CABI.

Berliner, D. (2012). Multiple nostalgias: The fabric of heritage in Luang Prabang (Lao PDR). *Journal of the Royal Anthropological Institute, 18*(4), 769–786.

Bolderman, S. L., & Reijnders, S. L. (2016). Have you found what you're looking for? Analysing tourist experiences of Wagner's Bayreuth, ABBA's Stockholm and U2's Dublin. *Tourist Studies, 16*(3), 234–252.

Buchmann, A., Moore, K., & Fisher, D. (2010). Experiencing film tourism: Authenticity and fellowship. *Annals of Tourism Research, 37*(1), 229–248.

Carroll, N. (1996). *Theorizing the moving image.* Cambridge: Cambridge University Press.

Chen, H., Yeh, S., & Huan, T. (2014). Nostalgic emotion, experiential value, brand image, and consumption intentions of customers of nostalgic-themed restaurants. *Journal of Business Research, 67*(3), 354–360.

Chosun Ilbo. (2016). Repairing of "A better tomorrow" in theatres in celebration of 30 year anniversary. *Chosun Ilbo*. January 29, 2016. Available at http://news.chosun.com/site/data/html_dir/2016/01/29/2016012900051.html

Connell, J. (2012). Film tourism-evolution, progress and prospects. *Tourism Management, 33*(5), 1007–1029.

Comrey, A., & Lee, H. (1992). *A first course in factor analysis* (2nd ed.). Hillsdale: Lawrence Erlbaum.

Couldry, N. (1998). The view from inside the 'simulacrum': Visitors' tales from the set of Coronation Street. *Leisure Studies, 17*, 94–107.

Dey, D. (2016). The nostalgia of values: Popular depictions of care crisis towards ageing parents in India. *Journal of Human Value, 22*(1), 26–38.

Gibson, C., & Connell, J. (2007). Music, tourism and the transformation of Memphis. *Tourism Geographies, 9*(2), 160–190.

Gordon, K. O. (2013). Emotion and memory in nostalgia sport tourism: Examining the attraction to postmodern ballparks through an interdisciplinary lens. *Journal of Sport and Tourism, 18*(3), 217–239.

Grönlund, K., & Strandberg, K. (2014). Online panels and validity: Representativeness and attrition in the Finnish eOpinion panel. In M. Callegaro, R. Baker, J. Bethlehem, A. S. Göritz, J. A. Krosnick, & P. J. Lavrakas (Eds.), *Online panel research: A data quality perspective* (pp. 86–103). New York: Wiley.

Holak, S. L. (2013). From Brighton beach to blogs: Exploring food-related nostalgia in the Russian diaspora. *Consumption, Markets and Culture, 17*(2), 185–207.

Holbrook, M. B. (1993). Nostalgia and consumption preferences: Some emerging patterns of consumer tastes. *Journal of Consumer Research, 20*(2), 245–256.

Howard, S. A. (2012). Nostalgia. *Analysis, 72*(4), 641–650.

Hsu, C. H. C., Cai, L. A., & Wong, K. K. F. (2007). A model of senior tourism motivations: Anecdotes from Beijing and Shanghai. *Tourism Management, 28*(5), 1262–1273.

Kim, S. (2010). Extraordinary experience: Re-enacting and photographing at screen- tourism locations. *Tourism and Hospitality Planning & Development, 7*(1), 59–75.

Kim, S. (2012a). Audience involvement and film tourism experiences: Emotional places, emotional experiences. *Tourism Management, 33*(2), 387–396.

Kim, S. (2012b). The relationships of on-site film-tourism experiences, satisfaction, and behavioral intentions: The case of Asian audience's responses to a Korean historical TV drama. *Journal of Travel & Tourism Marketing, 29*(5), 472–484.

Kim, S. (2012c). The impact of TV drama attributes on touristic experiences at film tourism destinations. *Tourism Analysis, 17*(5), 573–585.

Kim, S. J. (2015. July 23). Movie diary. *Kyungnam Ilbo*. http://www.knnews.co.kr/news/articleView.php?idxno=1154269

Kim, S., & Assaker, G. (2014). An empirical examination of the antecedents of film tourism experience: A structural model approach. *Journal of Travel & Tourism Marketing, 31*(2), 251–268.

Kim, S., & O'Connor, N. (2011). A cross-cultural study of screen-tourists' profiles. *Worldwide Hospitality and Tourism Themes, 3*(2), 141–158.

Lee, H. (2006). Peripherals encounter: The Hong Kong film syndrome in South Korea. *Discourse, 28*(2/3), 98–113.

Lee, S., Scott, D., & Kim, H. (2008). Celebrity fan involvement and destination perceptions. *Annals of Tourism Research, 35*(3), 809–832.

Leong, A. M. W., Yeh, S., Hsiao, Y., & Huan, T. (2015). Nostalgia as travel motivation and its impact on tourists' loyalty. *Journal of Business Research, 68*(1), 81–86.

Macionis, N., & Sparks, B. (2009). Film-induced tourism: An incidental experience. *Tourism Review International, 13*(2), 93–101.

Marchegiani, C., & Phau, I. (2013). Development and validation of the personal nostalgia scale. *Journal of Marketing Communications, 19*(1), 22–43.

Nunnally, J. (1978). *Psychometric theory* (2nd ed.). New York: McGraw Hill.

Pan, S., & Ryan, C. (2013). Film-induced heritage site conservation: The case of Echoes of the Rainbow. *Journal of Hospitality and Tourism Research, 37*(1), 125–150.

Reijnders, S. (2010). On the trail of 007: Media pilgrimages into the world of James bond. *Area, 42*(3), 369–377.

Reijnders, S. (2016). Stories that move: Fiction, imagination, tourism. *European Journal of Cultural Studies, 19*(6), 672–689.

Rittichainuwat, B., & Rattanaphinanchai, S. (2015). Applying a mixed method of quantitative and qualitative design in explaining the travel motivation of film tourists in visiting a film-shooting destination. *Tourism Management, 46*, 136–147.

Robinson, P. (2015). I remember it well: Epiphanies, nostalgia, and urban exploration as mediators of tourist memory. *Tourism, Culture and Communication, 15*, 87–101.

Roesch, S. (2009). *The experiences of film location tourists*. Bristol: Channel View Publications.

Sellicka, M. C. (2004). Discovery, Connection, Nostalgia. *Journal of Travel & Tourism Marketing, 17*(1), 55–71.

Suni, J., & Komppula, R. (2012). SF-filmvillage as a movie tourism destination: A case study of movie tourist push motivations. *Journal of Travel & Tourism Marketing, 29*, 460–471.

Synnes, O. (2015). Narratives of nostalgia in the face of death: The importance of lighter stories of the past in palliative care. *Journal of Aging Studies, 34*(August), 169–176.

Wong, C., & McDonogh, G. (2001). Consuming cinema: Reflections on movies and marketplaces in contemporary Hong Kong. In G. Mattews & T. Lui (Eds.), *Consuming Hong Kong* (pp. 81–116). Hong Kong: Hong Kong University Press.

Yeh, S., Chen, C., & Liu, Y. (2012). Nostalgic emotion, experiential value, destination image, and place attachment of cultural tourists. *Advances in Hospitality and Leisure, 8*, 167–187.

Zaatari, Z. (2015). Desirable masculinity/femininity and nostalgia of the "anti-modern": Bab el-Hara television series as a site of production. *Sexuality and Culture, 19*(1), 16–36.

Zhao, G., Muehling, D. D., & Kareklas, I. (2014). Remembering the good old days: The moderating role of consumer affective state on the effectiveness of nostalgic advertising. *Journal of Advertising, 43*(3), 244–255.

Chapter 10
Factors Hindering the Intention of Tourists to Visit Film Tourism Locations: The Case of the Korean TV Drama *Descendants of the Sun* (DOTS)

Aaron Tham and Sangkyun Kim

Abstract While the film tourism phenomenon has been welcomed by both practitioners and scholars, there remains a critical gap in our current understanding as to the determinants that hinder tourist intentions to visit film tourism locations. This chapter aims to elucidate some of these factors using the case of the Korean TV drama series *Descendants of the Sun* (DOTS). This successful Korean TV series was filmed across several locations in Korea and Greece. The research found that three important mitigating factors affected the propensity of the audience to visit Greece. They include safety, affordability and accessibility and familiarity. These hindering factors were dramatically diminished when participants assessed Korea as a potential film tourism destination associated with DOTS, showing how participants cognitively appraised destinations that were concurrently featured in media programme(s). Knowing more about these hindering factors will lead to better informed theory and practice of destinations seeking to take advantage of the potential of film tourism demand.

Keywords Greece • Hindering factors • Intention • Safety • Affordability • Cultural proximity

A. Tham (✉)
School of Business, University of the Sunshine Coast, Sippy Downs, QLD, Australia
e-mail: mtham@usc.edu.au

S. Kim
School of Business and Law, Edith Cowan University,
270 Joondalup Drive, Joondalup, WA 6027, Australia
e-mail: s.kim@ecu.edu.au

© Springer Nature Singapore Pte Ltd. 2018
S. Kim, S. Reijnders (eds.), *Film Tourism in Asia*, Perspectives on Asian
Tourism, DOI 10.1007/978-981-10-5909-4_10

10.1 Introduction

The close relationship between popular media and tourism in general, and film tourism in particular, is not a new research area; research has been conducted in this area since the late 1990s. Previous studies of film tourism have mainly dealt with the economic impacts of film tourism in relation to destination image enhancement, destination marketing and increases in tourism demand (Croy 2010; Hudson and Ritchie 2006; Hudson and Tung 2010; Hudson et al. 2011; Riley et al. 1998), as well as destination choice (Bolan et al. 2011; Iwashita 2006), host communities (Beeton 2008; Mordue 2001; Yoon et al. 2015), motivations behind film tourism (Macionis and Sparks 2009) and film tourists' experiences (Buchmann et al. 2010; Carl et al. 2007; Kim 2010, 2012a).

Among the above themes, destination image management has been one of the most heavily researched areas in the context of film tourism (Connell 2012). This is largely because destination image is a prime component of potential tourists' decision-making (and subsequent destination choice) and sustainable destination management (Croy 2010). Thus, previous studies have attempted to theoretically and empirically support the causal relationship between potential tourists' perceptions of the locations depicted in films or TV dramas and their subsequent behavioural intention in the context of film tourism (Lee et al. 2008; Wong and Lai 2015; Yen and Croy 2016; Yen and Teng 2015).

Previous studies collectively confirm that a positively perceived destination image arising from the development of an emotional bond or affective connectedness between the audience and media characters and contents is an immediate antecedent of behavioural intention. In this regard, Kim (2012a) and Reijnders (2010) demonstrate that the affective component of audience involvement plays a crucial role in forming personalised memories and symbolic meanings, which are then of paramount importance when audiences come to the end of the decision-making process. Such a sense of connectedness and emotional attachment becomes a primary motivator (Connell 2012; Couldry 1998; Kim 2012a), at least for purposeful film tourists who "actively seek out places portrayed on TV [and film] as well as their personalised and symbolised meanings and values (Kim 2012a, p. 394–5)".

As such, film commissions and destination marketing organisations (DMOs) worldwide are increasingly becoming involved in active engagement and collaboration with various film production stakeholders, in the quest for positive economic gains (Hudson and Tung 2010). Research has even shown that cooperative and collaborative campaigns between film and tourism stakeholders are a strong way to induce film tourists (Croy 2010; Hudson and Ritchie 2006).

However, the relevant literature suggests that destination image and/or the imagery generated by popular media, such as film and TV dramas, as an autonomous agent (Gartner 1994), is generally complex and multifaceted (Croy 2010), and filmed locations or areas often have limited control over the imagery created and portrayed by film or TV production companies. DMOs are rarely able to select the films being produced (Hudson and Tung 2010). Also, the promotional ability and pulling power of each film are not the same, and thus some films and TV series have little impact, whereas others may be very powerful in inducing film tourism. In a similar vein, not every individual audience member becomes a film tourist, given that film tourism often occurs as an incidental part of general leisure tourism (Di Cesare et al. 2009; Macionis and Sparks 2009).

Having acknowledged the nature of film tourism, it is interesting to note that there is a paucity of research that aims to understand the determinants *hindering* the intentions of media audiences to visit film tourism locations, although some have attempted to understand the characteristics of actual film tourists in terms of sociodemographic characteristics, travel patterns, media product preferences and motivations (see also Chap. 11 in this Volume). A critical prerequisite for the formulation of effective destination marketing strategies remains incomplete as long as insufficient attention is given to examining the underlying characteristics of media audiences who have little or no intention of visiting certain film tourism locations. Thus, this chapter aims to examine the hindering factors that affect the intentions of potential film tourists to visit film tourism destinations.

10.2 Korean TV Drama *Descendants of the Sun* (*DOTS*): Research Context

The chapter is built around a research project associated with one of the more successful recent South Korean TV drama series, *Descendants of the Sun* (*DOTS*). The 16 episodes of *DOTS* were aired on Korean Broadcasting System 2 (KBS 2) every week between February and April 2016 and achieved an average audience rating of 27% (with 36% for the last episode) and subsequently topping the TV audience ratings across many Asian countries. For instance, Ng (2016) reported that more than 60% of viewers in Singapore and Hong Kong have watched *DOTS* using the Viu app. Viu (https://web.viu.com/en/) is a subscription-based web application that is available in several Asian countries, allowing users to stream their favourite drama series on their technological devices, such as mobile phones or tablets (Tung 2016).

DOTS featured prominent Korean celebrities including Hye-Kyo Song, a leading actress with a successful career in Korean TV dramas (Jang 2012; Kim 2007). The script is based on a romantic love story between the leading actor Joong-Ki Song (who plays an army captain named Si-jin) and Hye-Kyo Song (playing a doctor named Mo-yeon), set in a fictional war zone. While the main shooting locations were in Korea, some episodes were filmed overseas, across several locations in Greece (i.e. Zakynthos, Lemnos and Arahova), which featured a storyline in which Si-jin receives military orders to lead his soldiers on a peacekeeping mission in the fictional country of Urk.

The success of *DOTS* polarised opinions among the countries in which it was broadcast. Thailand, for instance, invited the cast of *DOTS* to publicise the value of military regimes in keeping law and order (Bahk 2016). In comparison, the Chinese government warned its citizens of the harm of watching excessive Korean TV dramas such as *DOTS*, arguing that they may be detrimental to one's personal health (Tan 2016). Notwithstanding these opinions, its popularity and success have resulted in more than 2 billion views in China, and the series will soon be exported to at least a further 30 countries globally (Bonquin 2016). These will include India, the UK, Russia, Saudi Arabia, Hong Kong, the Philippines, Cambodia and Singapore (Woo 2016).

The focus of this chapter is the filmed locations of *DOTS* in Greece, for the following important reasons. First, film tourism in Korea has been well documented as an inbound tourism drawcard among international audiences of popular Korean media programmes (Kim et al. 2009; Kim and Wang 2012; Lin and Huang 2008). However, little is understood of the outbound film tourism phenomenon from the perspective of international audiences of Korean TV dramas, especially when overseas film locations are used in the production of TV dramas or films (Liou 2010; Yamamura 2015). Second is that few studies have researched the shooting locations of film or TV productions that are used in an unfamiliar cultural context to the main target audience (Corbin 2014) or that differ from the country of origin of the film producers (Glover 2012).

Regarding the filmed locations of *DOTS* in Greece, Hernandez (2016) reported that some tour operators in Korea and Singapore have already begun advertising tours to the shooting locations, including Zakynthos, Lemnos and Arahova. It is also noteworthy that these places in Greece have previously been studied in relation to the environmental impacts of existing tourism activities, as some of the locations feature remote islands and are thereby more susceptible to environmental damage when exposed to seasonal tourism demand patterns (Dodouras 2013; Marinos 1983; Prunier et al. 1993). The environmental and ecological issues are of particular importance for Zakynthos, which is classified as a marine park as it is a natural nesting environment for turtles (Katselidis et al. 2013; Spiropoulou et al. 2015). Other earlier studies have considered the sociocultural impacts of tourism development in these Greek locations (Dimitriadis 2013; Vakoufaris et al. 2007).

10.3 Research Methods

As an exploratory case study, semi-structured qualitative in-depth interviews with *DOTS*' audiences/fans who had already watched the series were conducted. Expressions of interest were placed on several online forums and social media platforms between November and December 2016, to invite individuals to participate in this research project. The online search for relevant sites was undertaken using keywords such as *DOTS* on Google and Yahoo search engines, as well as *DOTS*-related sites on Facebook. This led the researcher to a few forums that are dedicated to ongoing discussions of *DOTS*, such as Soompi (https://www.soompi.com/) and Facebook sites (https://www.facebook.com/groups/1097754136949817/?ref=br_rs).

Most of the individuals that went on to participate in the research responded to the expression of interest within the first week of the message being posted.

The selection of respondents was restricted to individuals who had watched *DOTS*, were over 18 years of age, were conversant in English and had not visited Greece. No restrictions were placed, however, on the participants' nationalities. All of the 20 individuals who expressed an interest in being part of the research were contacted via email to schedule an online interview, subject to their availability and access to videoconferencing software such as Skype. Of the 20, 15 were found through Facebook, while the remaining five were found through Soompi forums. A total of 13 interviews (nine from Facebook and four from Soompi) were conducted between 16 November and 16 December 2016, and each interview was on average 45 minutes in duration. The remaining seven who had expressed an interest were not interviewed as they were either not contactable or could not agree on a mutually convenient time. Nevertheless, 13 participants took part in a semi-structured interview designed along the following sections: (1) exposure to *DOTS* and influence on their interest in visiting Greece, (2) constraints/barriers as to visit intentions and (3) demographic information as to engagement with *DOTS*.

The interview data were transcribed and analysed with the assistance of NVivo. To assist with the systematic analysis of the data, the researchers followed Miles and Huberman's (1984) three-stage process of data reduction, data display and conclusion drawing and verification. This process enabled the copious amounts of interview transcripts to be coded into themes. As no new themes had emerged after these 13 interviews were completed, it was deemed that theoretical saturation had occurred (Bowen 2008; Guest et al. 2006).

A brief description of the participants' profiles is presented in Table 10.1. It provides some interesting insights into potential film tourists among the audiences of *DOTS*. Only one of the participants was male, while the great majority of the participants possessed at least university qualifications and were from the Southeast Asia region, including Singapore, the Philippines and Cambodia. The predominant age group was between 18 and 34 years old. Despite the small sample size, the above demographic patterns are similar to earlier film tourism studies that use Korean TV dramas as case studies (Chan 2007; Kim 2012a, b; Yang 2012).

10.4 Findings

The great majority stated that they had not had any strong motivations to visit Greece before watching *DOTS*. However, *DOTS* had, for some, inspired and, for others, reinforced interest in visiting Greece. They were fully aware that settings in *DOTS* were fictitious locations and researched the shooting locations online to discover their real names. Their awareness of some of the filmed locations, such as Zakynthos, Lemnos and Arahova, is noteworthy as these destinations were not widely known among Asian audiences prior to the screening of *DOTS*. In this regard, Participant 10 commented:

Table 10.1 Participants' profiles

Participant	Gender	Age group	Highest educational qualifications	Occupation type	Annual income	Country of residence
1	Female	18–34	Postgraduate	Professional/ self-employed	US$30,000-$45,000	Singapore
2	Female	18–34	Postgraduate	Professional/ self-employed	US$30,000-$45,000	Singapore
3	Female	18–34	Postgraduate	Professional/ self-employed	US$30,000-$45,000	Singapore
4	Female	35–50	Postgraduate	Professional/ self-employed	US$60,001 and above	Singapore
5	Female	35–50	Undergraduate	Professional/ self-employed	US$60,001 and above	Singapore
6	Female	18–34	Postgraduate	Professional/ self-employed	Under US$30,000	Philippines
7	Female	18–34	Postgraduate	Professional/ self-employed	Under US$30,000	Peru
8	Female	35–50	High school and under	Professional/ self-employed	Under US$30,000	Singapore
9	Female	18–34	Postgraduate	Not disclosed	Under US$30,000	Philippines
10	Female	18–34	Postgraduate	Professional/ self-employed	Under US$30,000	Singapore
11	Female	18–34	High school and under	Student	Under US$30,000	Singapore
12	Female	18–34	Postgraduate	Professional/ self-employed	Under US$30,000	Cambodia
13	Male	18–34	Postgraduate	Professional/ self-employed	Under US$30,000	Philippines

[I didn't know where the shooting locations were, but] I really love to visit the beach where the lead actor and actress were dating…what a beautiful place I want see that place!

As such, audiences create associations with the production values or media content of a particular media programme and its characters, stories and locations (Kim 2012b, Croy 2010). These associations often become strong emotional and affective bonds between the audience and their beloved media programme, which inspire them to visit the filmed locations in order to reinterpret and re-experience the dramatised events (e.g. dating while on a peacekeeping mission in the fictional country of Urk) and the lives of those depicted on screen. According to Croy (2010, p. 24), this personalised association is a powerful tool to "enhance the awareness of the destination, reducing barriers to travel, whilst at the same time creating incentives".

Despite the reinforced interest and motivation to visit film tourism locations in Greece, it is noteworthy that only a handful of the participants felt that *DOTS* increased their intentions to visit Greece. For those whose intentions were not enhanced, even after continuous exposure to *DOTS*, the identified determinants hindering their intention to visit Greece include dispersed film locations, safety, language barriers, affordability and accessibility, lack of travelling companions and familiarity. This chapter focuses on safety, affordability and accessibility and familiarity, as they were the determinants mentioned most often by the participants.

10.4.1 Safety Considerations

Safety was mentioned by almost all of the participants as a hindering factor in determining their likelihood of visiting Greece after watching *DOTS*. Participant 3 highlighted that safety was an overriding consideration in her travel decisions:

> Wherever I go, I think about whether it is safe to go there. The world has seen several cases of terrorist attacks, political turmoil, war etc. in the last few years, and for me, some places are a no go – including Greece.

Furthermore, other participants suggested that safety became of greater concern after watching particular scenes in *DOTS* featuring exchanges of gunfire between peacekeepers and gun smugglers. Participant 12 stated that "The fighting and guns in *DOTS* was so real...made me wonder if Greece was also like that...an unsafe destination". This comment shows how TV dramas and other fictional media have the potential to portray a destination in an unfavourable light, despite the aesthetic beauty depicted in other scenes in *DOTS*.

Generally speaking, the discussion surrounding the safety issue supports the existing literature in that decision-makers often perceive the destination image and then use safety considerations as a proxy in moderating their choices (George and Booyens 2014). Given that there are likely to be alternative destinations that would meet their desired tourism needs, it is evident that, for these risk-averse participants, safety considerations would result in the elimination of potential destinations, in this case, Greece.

There were some exceptions to the concerns regarding safety illuminated in the discussion thus far. Only a few participants were willing to take the risk to visit Greece, with the aim of helping the country overcome its problems. This view would perhaps only be held by a small segment of potential *DOTS* tourists to Greece. For instance, Participant 13 mentioned that:

> I wouldn't think Greece is unsafe, though it had gone through some economic and political strife in recent times. In fact, I would consider that they would be more likely to welcome tourists to help in addressing some of the problems in Greece, such as recession and unemployment issues...I think I will go in the near future to also support the country in these areas through tourism.

10.4.2 Affordability and Accessibility

Affordability was another frequently mentioned hindering factor for *DOTS* audiences. At least nine of the participants spoke at length about the costs of visiting Greece, though they did have an enhanced awareness and interest in Greece as a potential film tourism destination. Such views are best encapsulated by Participant 2: "Oh, wish I could go and view this lovely country Greece…but my finances forbid me". For some participants, *DOTS* prompted them to research the costs associated with visiting Greece, but many baulked once they discovered the costs of airfares, accommodation and other associated expenses related to getting to the filmed locations of *DOTS*.

As such, affordability became a determinant hindering their likelihood of visiting Greece, with most stating that they were more likely to consider saving up to visit Greece within the next two to 5 years. However, the participants did compare the costs of visiting Greece with that of South Korea, where *DOTS* was also filmed. It is noteworthy that most of the participants stated that they would be more prepared to visit South Korea, because it was perceived to be more affordable and accessible. Participant 1 elaborated upon this:

> From Singapore and other Asian countries, there are several flights to get to Korea, and so there is price competitiveness of airlines one can choose from. Moreover, Korea is not an expensive destination in terms of accommodation, food and getting around as compared to Greece. That is why I am more likely to go to South Korea.

As Korea is an air hub in Asia, the proliferation of airlines means there is greater consumer choice, which reduces the perceived costs of visiting the country. Moreover, some of the participants commented that they had heard more about, or had personally visited, Korea and concluded that it was a destination that did not appear to be an expensive destination. For this reason, their preference was to visit the filmed locations of *DOTS* in Korea rather than those in Greece, if they were to engage in film tourism related to this TV drama.

This finding suggests that when a film or TV series is filmed in two or more locations in different countries, audiences are likely to consider the affordability of getting to the different filmed locations. This is similar to what Hooper (2015) postulates as the *distance decay* effect, which characterises the less appealing nature of destinations that are located far away from the home environment and are therefore perceived to be less price competitive. This outcome validates the work of Lee et al. (2012) on examining the distance decay effects of tourism demand, which can be extended to the likes of media-induced tourism preferences.

10.4.3 Familiarity

The *DOTS* audience also highlighted their levels of familiarity with the culture and society of the countries in which filming took place as a hindering factor for visiting Greece. In the case of *DOTS*, this relates to the increased knowledge about a destination that participants have that inform their tourism decisions. When probed, the participants stated that they had a more realistic destination image of Korea and thus a greater level of familiarity with the filmed locations in Korea compared to those in Greece. This was due to their familiarity with the Korean language and culture and its different attributes:

> I have watched numerous Korean [TV] dramas that were filmed in the country, and also follow some of the *DOTS* celebrities on social media, so I already know much about the destination (Participant 4).

> There is such a strong Korean presence in Singapore – food, movies, music, mobile phones and even a Korean Tourism Board branch office...My family, friends and I are well acquainted with their culture (laughs) (Participant 5).

> I have been to Korea several times both for leisure and work, so it is not too unfamiliar for me. Getting to the [TV] drama locations (e.g., *DOTS*) would be easier (Participant 9).

The comments above are indicative of how greater familiarity with Korea has resulted in the forming of a more realistic and familiar destination image that is advantageous, at least for these DOTS' fans or followers, when stimulating film tourism demand. Similarly, the concept of *cultural proximity* (Straubhaar 1991) in explaining patterns of regional trade in programming and local audience's consumption of imported media programmes has been introduced to the field of film tourism studies (Su et al. 2011). Su et al. (2011) confirm that the stronger the cultural proximity that an audience feels towards a country portrayed in a film, the greater the likelihood of them evaluating the characters and landscapes associated with the filmed locations more positively.

This is also supported by Jung (2016), who suggests that exposure to Korean culture through various sources, including popular media, is highly influential on foreign tourists and their receptivity towards visiting the destination. Also, the above quotes support the view that familiarity may be a result of them knowing about other elements of Korea due to cultural diffusion within the Asian consumer markets, better known as the Korean wave or *Hallyu* phenomenon (Huang 2011; Kim and Nam 2016; Ryoo 2009). For this reason, the participants can more easily associate the *DOTS* celebrities with Korea rather than with Greece. As such, it appears that planning a visit to Korea on the back of *DOTS* is less complex, as potential audiences will likely exhibit greater familiarity with the destination. This then translates into stronger destination appeal, with TV drama series' such as *DOTS* elevating destination loyalty (Chiu et al. 2016).

10.5 Conclusion

Whilst *DOTS* has been instrumental in generating greater awareness of Greece among international audiences of the series, intention to travel to Greece remains ambivalent due to a combination of various hindering factors, including safety perceptions, affordability and accessibility and cultural proximity. Through the construction of place awareness, the availability and evaluation of potential film tourism destinations are indeed evoked as choices at the forefront of their minds, which is consistent with Croy (2010) who suggests that the key role of film tourism is to create images of places, awareness, motivations, expectations and familiarity.

However, Di Cesare et al. (2009) empirically suggested that although the audience has a stronger desire to visit filmed locations after following exposure to their beloved media programme, this psychological desire diminishes sharply as the decision-making process of the audience reaches the final stage of purchasing film tourism-related products and/or activities. To some extent, the findings in this chapter support the study of Di Cesare et al. (2009). In this context, the chapter makes its own contribution to enhancing our current limited knowledge of this matter by adding that the presence of mitigating agents or determinants hindering the intentions of *DOTS* fans was one reason that leads to a process of prioritisation, especially if more than one potential international destination is featured in the series. This is because destination choice warrants other considerations, such as safety, affordability, accessibility and familiarity or cultural proximity, each of which is important for tourists' final decisions. Yet it remains premature to make a conclusive comment, as the hindering factors mentioned above may also be core pulling factors in other contexts, for example, justice tourism in areas and/or situations of war or political conflicts and tensions such as Palestine (Issac 2010; Issac and Hodge 2011).

Hence, while Korean films or TV dramas will likely continue to draw large audiences throughout Asia, travel demand associated with film tourism destinations remains largely dedicated to inbound tourism in Korea. Nonetheless, it is still early days for Greece in terms of its role in *DOTS*, and so subsequent studies on this interesting phenomenon are needed.

This research lends further insight into the types of mitigating factors that result in destination preferences, an area that is largely omitted in the extant literature. The implications for Greece, therefore, are to address these mitigating factors by reinforcing its safe and picturesque scenery, taking advantage of new low-cost flight routes from Asia and thereby promoting value-for-money travel options and amplifying cultural affinity through food and other cues. Such efforts could then position Greece more favourably in the Asian tourism market and enhance its appeal as a TV drama-induced tourist destination.

The current research has some inherent limitations. It was conducted in English as a medium of communication and thereby excluded other potential audiences who speak other languages that *DOTS* has been translated into. Another limitation is that the participants were sharing their opinions and perceptions based on stated intentions, which does not always correspond to actual travel behaviour.

Future studies could conduct face-to-face interviews with actual film tourists on-site. Other studies could investigate the longitudinal effects of *DOTS* and viewers' propensity to travel. Such studies could examine whether viewers who have been more frequently exposed to the series are more likely to travel to Greece and other filmed locations, as well as whether they have different motivations or anticipate different experiences from visiting Greece. Finally, further studies could replicate this research in other languages in which *DOTS* has been translated. This would make a further contribution to our current knowledge in this field of study.

References

Bahk, E. (2016). *Thai PM calls on people to watch 'Descendants of the Sun'*. Retrieved March 16, 2017 from http://www.koreatimes.co.kr/www/news/culture/2016/03/386_200662.html

Beeton, S. (2008). Location, location, location: Film corporations' social responsibilities. *Journal of Travel & Tourism Marketing, 24*(2–3), 107–114.

Bolan, P., Boy, S., & Bell, J. (2011). We've seen it in the movies, let's see if it's true: Authenticity and displacement in film-induced tourism. *Worldwide Hospitality and Tourism Themes, 3*(2), 102–116.

Bonquin, L. (2016). *The final episode of 'Descendants of the Sun' is here; Millions are expected to stay glued on TV*. Retrieved March 16, 2017 from http://en.yibada.com/articles/116305/20160414/final-episode-of-descendant-sun-millions-expected-stay-glued-tv.htm

Bowen, G. (2008). Naturalistic inquiry and the saturation concept: A research note. *Qualitative Research, 8*(1), 137–152.

Buchmann, A., Moore, K., & Fisher, D. (2010). Experiencing film tourism: Authenticity and fellowship. *Annals of Tourism Research, 37*(1), 229–248.

Carl, D., Kindon, S., & Smith, K. (2007). Tourists' experiences of film locations: New Zealand as 'Middle-Earth'. *Tourism Geographies, 9*(1), 49–63.

Chan, B. (2007). Film-induced tourism in Asia: A case study of Korean television female viewers' motivation to visit Korea. *Tourism Culture and Communication, 7*(3), 207–224.

Chiu, W., Zeng, S., & Cheng, P. (2016). The influence of destination image and tourist satisfaction on tourist loyalty: A case study of Chinese tourists in Korea. *International Journal of Culture, Tourism and Hospitality Research, 10*(2), 223–234.

Connell, J. (2012). Film tourism: Evolution, progress and prospects. *Tourism Management, 33*(5), 1007–1029.

Corbin, A. (2014). Travelling through cinema space: The film spectator as tourist. *Journal of Media & Cultural Studies, 28*(3), 314–329.

Couldry, N. (1998). The view from inside the 'simulacrum': Visitors' tales from the set of Coronation Street. *Leisure Studies, 17*(2), 94–107.

Croy, G. (2010). Planning for film tourism: Active destination image management. *Tourism and Hospitality Planning & Development, 7*(1), 21–30.

Di Cesare, F., D'Angelo, L., & Rech, G. (2009). Films and tourism: Understanding the nature and intensity of their cause-effect relationship. *Tourism Review International, 13*(2), 103–111.

Dimitriadis, E. (2013). Attitudes towards tourism development: Residents' perceptions in the islands of Lemnos and Hydra. *Tourismos, 8*(1), 133–151.

Dodouras, S. (2013). Conservation and management of Greek landscapes: The case study of Lemnos Island. *Geopolitics, History, and International Relations, 2*, 145–158.

Gartner, W. (1994). Image formation process. *Journal of Travel & Tourism Marketing, 2*(2–3), 191–216.

George, R., & Booyens, I. (2014). Township tourism demand: Tourists' perceptions of safety and security. *Urban Forum, 25*(4), 449–467.

Glover, P. (2012). Michael Palin's *Himalaya*: Potential impact of television travel diaries on destination image. *Tourism Review International, 16*(2), 113–124.

Guest, G., Bunce, A., & Johnson, L. (2006). An experiment with data saturation and variability. *Field Methods, 18*(1), 59–82.

Hernandez, V. (2016). *'Descendants of the Sun' Tour Brings Fans to South Korea & Greece*. Retrieved March 16, 2017 from http://en.yibada.com/articles/118124/20160421/descendants-of-the-sun-tour-brings-fans-to-south-korea-greece.htm

Hooper, J. (2015). A destination too far? Modelling destination accessibility and distance decay in tourism. *GeoJournal, 80*(1), 33–46.

Huang, S. (2011). Nation-branding and transnational consumption: Japan-mania and the Korean wave in Taiwan. *Media, Culture and Society, 33*(1), 3–18.

Hudson, S., & Ritchie, J. (2006). Film tourism and destination marketing: The case of captain Corelli's Mandolin. *Journal of Vacation Marketing, 12*(3), 256–268.

Hudson, S., & Tung, V. (2010). Lights, camera, action...!: Marketing film locations to Hollywood. *Marketing Intelligence & Planning, 28*(2), 188–205.

Hudson, S., Wang, Y., & Gil, S. (2011). The influence of a film on destination image and the desire to travel: A cross-cultural comparison. *International Journal of Tourism Research, 13*(2), 177–190.

Issac, R. K. (2010). Alternative tourism: New forms of tourism in Bethlehem for the Palestinian tourism industry. *Current Issues in Tourism, 13*(1), 21–36.

Issac, R. K., & Hodge, D. (2011). An exploratory study: Justice tourism in controversial areas – The case of Palestine. *Tourism Planning and Development, 8*(1), 101–108.

Iwashita, C. (2006). Media representation of the UK as a destination for Japanese tourists. *Tourist Studies, 6*(1), 59–77.

Jang, S. (2012). The Korean wave and its implications for the Korea-China relationship. *Journal of International and Area Studies, 19*(2), 97–113.

Jung, Y. (2016). The effect of Korean culture familiarity of foreign tourists on the Korean consumer behaviour. *Journal of Digital Convergence, 14*(5), 197–205.

Katselidis, K., Schofield, G., Stamou, G., Dimopoulos, P., & Pantis, J. (2013). Evidence-based management to regulate the impact of tourism at a key marine turtle rookery on Zakynthos Island, Greece. *Oryx, 47*(4), 584–594.

Kim, J. (2007). Why does Hallyu matter? The significance of the Korean wave in South Korea. *Critical Studies in Television, 2*(2), 47–59.

Kim, S. (2010). Extraordinary experience: Re-enacting and photographing at screen-tourism locations. *Tourism and Hospitality Planning & Development, 7*(1), 59–75.

Kim, S. (2012a). Audience involvement and film tourism experience: Emotional places, emotional experiences. *Tourism Management, 33*(2), 387–396.

Kim, S. (2012b). The impact of TV drama attributes on touristic experiences at film tourism destinations. *Tourism Analysis, 17*(5), 573–585.

Kim, S., & Nam, C. (2016). Hallyu revisited: Challenges and opportunities for the south Korean tourism. *Asia Pacific Journal of Tourism Research, 21*(5), 524–540.

Kim, S., & Wang, H. (2012). From television to the film set: Korean drama *Daejanggeum* drives Chinese, Taiwanese, Japanese and Thai audiences to screen-tourism. *International Communication Gazette, 74*(5), 423–442.

Kim, S., Long, P., & Robinson, M. (2009). Small screen, big tourism: The role of popular Korean television dramas in south Korean tourism. *Tourism Geographies, 11*(3), 308–333.

Lee, S., Scott, D., & Kim, H. (2008). Celebrity fan involvement and destination perceptions. *Annals of Tourism Research, 35*(3), 809–832.

Lee, A., Guillet, B., Law, R., & Leung, R. (2012). Robustness of distance decay for international travellers: A longitudinal approach. *International Journal of Tourism Research, 14*(5), 409–420.

Lin, Y., & Huang, J. (2008). Analyzing the use of TV miniseries for Korea tourism marketing. *Journal of Travel & Tourism Marketing, 24*(2–3), 223–227.

Liou, D. (2010). Beyond Tokyo rainbow bridge: Destination images portrayed in Japanese drama affect Taiwanese tourists' perception. *Journal of Vacation Marketing, 16*(1), 5–15.

Macionis, N., & Sparks, B. (2009). Film-induced tourism: An incidental experience. *Tourism Review International, 3*(2), 93–101.

Marinos, P. (1983). Small island tourism: The case of Zakynthos, Greece. *Tourism Management, 4*(3), 212–215.

Miles, M., & Huberman, M. (1984). Drawing valid meaning from qualitative data: Toward a shared craft. *Educational Researcher, 13*(5), 20–30.

Mordue, T. (2001). Performing and directing resident/tourist cultures in heartbeat country. *Tourist Studies, 1*(3), 233–252.

Ng, G. (2016). *Descendants of the sun star Song Joong Ki: "It feels natural for me to be in a soldier's uniform"*. Retrieved March 16, 2017 from http://www.straitstimes.com/lifestyle/entertainment/descendants-of-the-sun-star-song-joong-ki-it-feels-natural-for-me-to-be-in-a

Prunier, E., Sweeney, A., & Geen, A. (1993). Tourism and the environment: The case of Zakynthos. *Tourism Management, 14*(2), 137–141.

Reijnders, S. (2010). Places of the imagination: An ethnography of the TV detective tour. *Cultural Geographies, 17*(1), 37–52.

Riley, R., Baker, D., & Van Doren, C. (1998). Movie induced tourism. *Annals of Tourism Research, 25*(4), 919–935.

Ryoo, W. (2009). Globalization, or the logic of cultural hybridization: The case of the Korean wave. *Asian Journal of Communication, 19*(2), 137–151.

Spiropoulou, I., Karamanis, D., & Kehayias, G. (2015). Offshore wind farms development in relation to environmental protected areas. *Sustainable Cities and Society, 14*(Feb), 305–312.

Straubhaar, J. (1991). Beyond media imperialism: Asymmetrical interdependence and cultural proximity. *Critical Studies in Mass Communication, 8*, 1–11.

Su, H. J., Huang, Y., Brodowsky, G., & Kim, H. J. (2011). The impact of product placement on TV-induced tourism: Korean TV dramas and Taiwanese viewers. *Tourism Management, 32*(4), 805–814.

Tan, H. (2016). *Descendants of the Sun smash hit prompts Beijing to warn on South Korean dramas*. Retrieved March 16, 2017 from http://www.cnbc.com/2016/03/16/descendants-of-the-sun-smash-hit-prompts-beijing-to-warn-on-south-korean-dramas.html

Tung, C. (2016). *Viu to offer Singaporeans head start on Korean dramas and variety shows*. Retrieved March 16, 2017 from https://e27.co/viu-offer-singaporeans-head-start-korean-dramas-variety-shows-20160111/

Vakoufaris, H., Kizos, T., Spilanis, I., Koulouri, M., & Zacharaki, A. (2007). Women's cooperatives and their contribution to the local development of the north Aegean region Greece. *Journal of Rural Cooperation, 35*(1), 19–41.

Wong, J., & Lai, T. (2015). Celebrity attachment and behavioural intentions: The mediating role of place attachment. *International Journal of Tourism Research, 17*(2), 161–170.

Woo, J. (2016). *Descendants of the Sun' to be exported to over 27 countries*. Retrieved March 16, 2017 from http://english.yonhapnews.co.kr/culturesports/2016/03/23/0701000000AEN20160323008100315.html?c49b0118

Yamamura, T. (2015). Contents tourism and local community response: *Lucky star* and collaborative anime-induced tourism in Washimiya. *Japan Forum, 27*(1), 59–81.

Yang, J. (2012). The Korean wave (Hallyu) in East Asia: A comparison of Chinese, Japanese, and Taiwanese audiences who watch Korean TV dramas. *Development and Society, 41*(1), 103–147.

Yen, C., & Croy, G. (2016). Film tourism: Celebrity involvement, celebrity worship and destination image. *Current Issues in Tourism, 19*(10), 1027–1044.

Yen, C., & Teng, H. (2015). Celebrity involvement, perceived value, and behavioural intentions in popular media-induced tourism. *Journal of Hospitality and Tourism Research, 39*(2), 225–244.

Yoon, Y., Kim, S., & Kim, S. (2015). Successful and unsuccessful film tourism destinations: From the perspective of Korean local residents' perceptions of film tourism impacts. *Tourism Analysis, 20*(3), 297–311.

Chapter 11
Inside the Chinese Film Industry: On the Motives and Experiences of Extras at Hengdian World Studios

Min Xu and Stijn Reijnders

Abstract Induced by the numerous popular films produced at Hengdian World Studios in China, many people move to Hengdian themselves to experience the filming and, where possible, to become part of the production team. Previous studies have examined the behaviour and experiences of tourists at film studios. However, little is known about the practices of those who immerse in these film tourism locations for a longer period of time, such as the extras. In order to understand their motivations and experiences, this study employs qualitative interviews with 15 extras at Hengdian. Results show that most extras undergo a similar process consisting of three steps: people enlist themselves as extras based on dreams and high ambitions; during their first months, these dreams and the 'magic' of filming are mostly demystified, especially when they are confronted with the multilayered hierarchy of the film industry; finally, those who stay learn to live within the hierarchy while making plans to move upwards. By shedding light on the meanings behind extras' experiences, this chapter offers an original perspective on both the symbolical and practical power structure of the Chinese film industry.

Keywords Extra • China's film/TV industry • Media participation • Media ritual • Symbolic power • Film studio

11.1 Introduction

The Chinese film and television industry is booming, and the group of extras is growing likewise. At China's Hengdian World Studios, the world's largest outdoor film studio, more than twenty thousand people have registered in the actors' union. Each day between two and three thousand extras participate in TV/film productions in the so-called Hollywood of the East (Ma 2015).

M. Xu (✉) • S. Reijnders
Erasmus University Rotterdam, Rotterdam, The Netherlands
e-mail: xu@eshcc.eur.nl

© Springer Nature Singapore Pte Ltd. 2018
S. Kim, S. Reijnders (eds.), *Film Tourism in Asia*, Perspectives on Asian Tourism, DOI 10.1007/978-981-10-5909-4_11

So far, extras have received little attention in academic literature, even though they have been a part of the film and television industry almost from its conception. Important work has been done on the experiences of film tourists, who travel to film studios and other film locations with the aim of 'getting closer to the media world' (e.g. Kim 2010, 2012; Kim and Wang 2012; Couldry 2003, 2005; Reijnders 2011). In most cases, this concerns *short-term* tourists, e.g. participating in a two-hour tour or visiting film locations individually as part of a day trip. However, very little is known about 'ordinary people' – like the extras from Hengdian – who immerse in film studios for a longer period. Their motives and experiences will most probably differ from those of day trippers and have the potential to deepen our understanding of the relation between film, experience and place. Indeed a closer look at the World Tourism Organization (1991) definition of tourism does not seem to exclude the experiences of most extras: 'Tourism comprises the activities of persons traveling to and staying in places outside their usual environment for not more than one consecutive year for leisure, business and other purposes' (as cited in Holden 2016, p. 4).

In this chapter, we take Nick Couldry's concept of media rituals as a point of departure. Couldry suggests that there is a distinction between anything 'in the media' and anything which is not. Being 'in' the media can empower people or objects and offer them a privileged status. As we argue in this chapter, most people become extras because they want to be 'in' the media, hoping to gain a deeper experience that goes beyond the superficial touristic practices. More in particular, this chapter will investigate the motives and experiences of 'Hengdian drifters' at China's Hengdian World Studios, revolving around the following questions: Why are people motivated to become extras in Hengdian? How do they experience being 'in' the media? What are the deeper, long-term meanings attached to their experiences? Finally, how do their motivations and experiences differ from *short-term* film tourists?

In order to answer these questions, we have conducted interviews with 15 respondents. However, before diving into an analysis of these interviews, we would first like to present the theoretical framework that has guided our research.

11.2   Theoretical Framework

When trying to explain and theorize the continuous attraction of being an extra, we need to rely on more general theory concerning media rituals, as we focus on extras' experiences 'in' the media rather than their performing experiences per se. Particularly interesting is the work of Nick Couldry (2003).

According to Couldry, media rituals are formalized 'actions organised around key media-related categories and boundaries' or patterns (2003, p. 2) and function as the crucial mechanism that reinforces assumed legitimacy of the media's social centrality (2003, p. 2). In media rituals, categories of thought are acted out, among which the most important category difference lies in between anything 'in the media' and anything which is not (Couldry 2003, p. 47). Couldry suggests that the distinction between 'media world' and 'ordinary world' is essential for naturalizing the media's concentration of symbolic power (2000, p. 15) and the underlying value that media 'stand in' for or represent the social world (2003, p. 27). People take it for granted that the 'media world' is special, somehow better than 'ordinary life', and that 'media people' are special (2000, p. 45).

Film tourists' experiences have been associated with the dichotomy between 'inside' and 'outside' the media. For example, Kim and Wang (2012) point out three dimensions of on-site film tourists' experiences: 'prestige and privilege'; 'beyond screen, sensory experience and re-enactment'; and 'intimacy and memory'. Tourists feel excited to be at the filmed locations in person, touch costumes and props from the drama and hear more cultural stories as well as behind the scenes stories about producing the drama, etc. (Ibid.). Understandably, the feeling of 'prestige and privilege' is connected with the presumption of entering 'the media world'. Another example is Reijnders's study of Bond pilgrimages, where he shows how the symbolic difference between 'inside' and 'outside' the media is intertwined with other power configurations such as – in this case – notions of masculinity (Reijnders 2010, 2011).

Yet, as we argue in this paper, extras immerse themselves in the 'media world' for a longer period, and thus they might have more intense experiences with this symbolic difference. In his study of visitors at the set of Coronation Street, Granada Studios Tour (2000), Couldry notices that a few people try to become extras and briefly discusses those who succeed in becoming extras and are 'playing with boundaries' (2000, p. 116–118). Couldry explains this desire to act and appear on television not only by the difference between acting and nine-to-five jobs but also by the symbolic difference between in and outside the media. Even the tiniest role and smallest appearance on television might be enough to become an 'ordinary' part of the media world.

Building on Couldry's theoretical insights, studies have been done to understand media participation of 'ordinary people' who are not media professionals, experts or newsworthy (e.g. Andrejevic 2004, p. 145; Aslama 2009). Referring to Couldry's 'myth of the media centre' (2003), Turner (2015, p. 113) demonstrates that ordinary celebrities acquire a different status as they succeed in moving from the non-media world into the 'social centre' of the media (Couldry 2003). Motives of ordinary people for media exposure are, however, more complicated than the desire for fame. For example, many media participants have the intention to gain a life-changing experience or impart information publicly, to feel important and special (Ibid.; Andrejevic 2004; Aslama 2009; Syvertsen 2001). What then does such a life-changing experience consist of?

To contribute to this body of knowledge, we investigate the whole process of extras' practices and the relation to the assumed media's social centrality.

11.3   Research Methods

Hengdian World Studios is located in Hengdian, a town of Dongyang in Zhejiang Province, a 5-hour drive southwest of Shanghai, China. With 165 thousand inhabitants (Chen 2015), the town consists of studios and busy streets. Tourists usually visit Hengdian for one or 2 days. During a three-day break in New Year, 119,500 tourists visited Hengdian World Studios, including its theme park (Zhao 2017; see also Chap. 4 in this Volume). Yet, mass tourism is only one part of the business strategy of Hengdian. On any given day during off-peak season, participants of media productions may outnumber visitors. Since 1996, crews from approximately 1800 film and TV productions have worked in Hengdian, with 285 productions in 2016 alone (Zeng 2016). The popularity of Hengdian World Studios is stimulated by the fact that since 2000, its outdoor scenery has been available to use for free by domestic and international crews. Media professionals are therefore attracted to Hengdian to shoot movies and TV dramas, greatly boosting the service sector in the town (Ying 2012).

This study aims to advance our understanding of people who make efforts to act and get 'in the media', offering a phenomenological perspective on their ambitions and experiences. For this case study, 15 semi-structured in-depth interviews were conducted.

The respondents were recruited in Hengdian and via extras' internal social networks. In total, 14 male respondents and one female respondent from various provinces around China have been interviewed. The gender ratio is reasonable, as Hengdian is abundant in filming locations for costume dramas, war films, and television series, and there is a much larger demand for male extras. The age difference was minimal, ranging from 23 to 32 years old.

The length of the interviews varied from 40 minutes up to one and a half hours. Key questions were determined in advance, with the goal to investigate motives for becoming extras, experiences of acting and getting 'in the media' and reflections after having been extras 'in the media' for some time. During the interviews, respondents were allowed to bring up their own discussion topics. The interviews were audio-recorded, transcribed, coded and thematically analysed (Bryman 2012).

Prior to the interviews, efforts were made to get acquainted with several extras and to get familiar with the extras' working and living environment, including the actors' union, main film studios and filming locations, surrounding streets and recruiting processes. This fieldwork in Hengdian took place in late December 2015. Since then, complementary to the interviews, we joined and paid attention to the social networks of the extras, especially images and thoughts they shared during and after participating in productions, most of which were updates of long working hours and exhaustion, selfies in costumes and sometimes with celebrities and spectacular moments during filming such as Kung Fu scenes and fire explosions. Being aware of extras' latest practices and becoming acquainted with their vocabulary and expressions were helpful in terms of generating trust during the interviews, asking specific questions and interpreting questions in the right way (Kvale and Brinkmann 2009).

The analysis in the following sections is based on a three-step process that emerged from most of the interviews. To begin with, Hengdian drifters expect to have a different lifestyle once they have become extras. They make a conscious decision to follow their dreams of acting. When they have immersed 'in' the media, however, most extras experience a process of demystification and obtain 'inside' knowledge that enables them to see the media world without rose-tinted glasses. Those who decide to stay longer strive to make progress within the hierarchy and recognize the effects of being an extra on their personalities.

11.4 A Once-in-a-Lifetime Experiment

Most extras in Hengdian, the so-called Hengdian drifters or *HengPiao*, are young people from other provinces, mostly in their twenties or thirties, often without any professional acting training. They move to Hengdian and rent a simple room close to the actors' union, which is one of the assembly points for the extras that have been selected for the productions. The extras compose a diverse community, and major differences can be noted in terms of appearance, stature, educational background, life and working experience.

During the peak season for filmmaking, extras work an average of 6 days a week, even in the middle of winter, before Chinese New Year. They have active social networks, where heads of extras publish the latest recruitment announcements with strict requirements, related to, e.g. age and height. Extras that have been selected for roles such as pedestrian, soldier, Qing dynasty guard or palace maid meet at the designated places around five o'clock in the morning for day scenes, take a bus to filming locations and work until the late afternoon. Alternatively, extras meet up late in the afternoon and work until early in the morning for night scenes.

When asked about their motivations to join this busy and somewhat insecure community of extras, most respondents explain that they wanted to explore what it is like to be an extra and to work in the film/TV industry:

> I am here to have fun, to explore a different lifestyle. I just wanted to go out, experience a little bit here and see what it is about and how it works. I will continue if I enjoy it, or find another lifestyle if I don't like this. (Yong, Shandong Province, 32 years old, 1 month in Hengdian)

> I came here because of the film 'I Am Somebody'. [...] Because I haven't worked in this industry, I was full of anticipation. (Litian, Guizhou Province, 32 years old, 1 month in Hengdian)

From these two quotes, it becomes clear that before arriving in Hengdian, Yong and Litian were curious about the film studio and expected this place to be different and enjoyable. Other respondents also use the words 'explore' and 'experience' to describe their early motivations, regarding the practice as a 'try', either trying out a job in the film/TV industry or trying a different lifestyle. Most of them know that extras' appearance on the television is fleeting and marginal, but they don't seem to care; their motivations do not necessarily derive from the wish to appear on the television. Putting the *experience* prior to the *visibility* is a finding which resonates with prior studies on media participation (e.g. Andrejevic 2004; Aslama 2009; Syvertsen 2001; Wei 2016).

As Dyer (1977) suggests, 'entertainment offers the image of 'something better' to escape into, or something we want deeply that our day-to-day lives don't provide'. For would-be extras, participating in film and TV productions contains the hope of getting closer to the media and entertainment world than by simply watching the television from home. What then is this 'something' extras seek and cannot find in daily life? What do extras talk about when they talk about such an exploration, experience or lifestyle?

> One seems to have a double life – we live in two worlds by performing different parts as an actor. What an actor plays can be quite different from the reality. (Peng, Henan Province, 23 years old, 3 months in Hengdian)

> Becoming an actress is my dream ever since I was a little girl. […] Acting allows me to explore what it is like to be another character and to explore different lives. In this way, I can enrich my own life. (Qiyue, female, Hubei Province, 27 years old, a week in Hengdian and 2 years in Huairou Film Base in Beijing previously)

The reason why this 'something' cannot be found in daily life is precisely because it is fundamentally 'different', as Peng sees it. Unlike audiences of film and TV productions who may seek the image to 'escape into', as Dyer suggests, extras embrace the chances to become part of a fictional world. Extras' participation leads them to have the impression that they possess the imaginative happenings at film studios in their own lives. In other words, not only the tasks extras carry out but also the roles they play in fictional settings become 'real' enough to be seen as part of their lives. Qiyue expresses similar motivations, and her standpoint as well as childhood dream are shared by many respondents. The idea of being other characters is what they like about acting as well as the 'something' attracting them. Becoming extras offers them opportunities for being various characters for a while, shifting roles and playing with their own identities.

This finding is consistent with existing studies on film tourism, which have found that some film tourists want to step into the shoes of their beloved characters by visiting locations associated with the stories (Reijnders 2016; Kim 2012; Frost 2010; Laing and Crouch 2009, p. 193–194; Seaton 2002). From the interviews with extras, all respondents are clear about their favourite types of roles they would like to perform. The wish to be in the shoes of particular characters seems to be shared by both film tourists and extras. In this regard, film tourists collect memorabilia of places, characters and players (Beeton 2016, p. 75) and may photograph their re-enactment to capture and enhance their experience (e.g. Kim 2010). Many extras also keep their costume photos as memories, knowing these images are likely to appear in the productions.

A lot of respondents express that they want to give it a try in the film industry so that they will have no regrets, regardless of whether they can make it and become actors or not. They speak of being extras as a once-in-a-lifetime endeavour when they still have time to do this as an experiment before settling down. Sometimes, making such a once-in-a-lifetime endeavour needs a stimulus in the first place:

> The film 'I Am Somebody' inspired me a lot, and I know some people who came here because of this film, too. We are young and have never left our hometowns, like the protagonist. When he tells his parents about the plan, they don't support it at first. But he comes here anyway. I started my first job at the age of 21 and worked for three years, without any chances to go out. So I decided to go out for an adventure. (Meng, Henan Province, 24 years old, 2 months in Hengdian)

Several respondents, including Meng and Litian, have been induced by the film 'I Am Somebody' (Wo Shi Lu Ren Jia) by Derek Yee Tung-sing. Released in Mainland China, Hong Kong and Singapore in July 2015, the film offers a realistic portrait of Chinese young extras who work hard and live under poor conditions with the ambition of becoming actors in Hengdian. This bittersweet film pays tribute to the thousands of *HengPiao*, with real-life extras taking the lead in the film. For Litian, the film has introduced him to the unknown world of film studios and lives of extras. For some respondents, the film has inspired them to make the decision to move to Hengdian and start working there as an extra.

Just like film tourists who want to experience what characters do in the films, several fans of *I am Somebody* are deeply moved by the stories of the fictional extras and want to imitate those protagonists by becoming an extra themselves. Moreover, in both cases there is also a social dimension to their experience. Just like most film tourists like to share their knowledge and fondness of a story with like-minded people (Reijnders 2016), extras also search for like-minded souls – living together in Hengdian for a period of time and sharing their dream, ambitions and both victories or disappointments along the road.

11.5   Demystification and Insiderness

Many respondents still remember their feelings when they have just begun to participate in productions. The excitement firstly sprang from seeing the medium and the realization of appearing 'in the media':

> I didn't realize that the leading actors were behind me. They walked past. I was excited. So I will appear in that shot for sure. It was the first time in my life to face a real movie camera, which was recording directly towards me, and I walked past. (Tao, Henan Province, 24 years old, 1 month in Hengdian)

Tao is excited about seeing the medium from close by and the promise that he will be in the scene. A filming set is full of things and happenings that one cannot see and experience elsewhere. Although various things on set make many extras' hearts beat faster, such as seeing professional movie cameras, being close to famous actors and actresses as they play pedestrians, firing guns in war films, etc., their views may change as time goes by:

> I treat it as a job. So I don't find the whole thing 'magical' or anything special. On my first day, I was unfamiliar with things on set. I didn't stand in the right place as they required. It was noisy, and I missed the instruction. In the end, I was blamed for the mistake. (Fei, Guangxi Province, age unknown, 1 month in Hengdian)

It is common to regard the extra's practice as a normal job, as Fei suggests, especially among those who have been working for a while. In the interviews, most respondents say that they have gotten used to this job, and 'it is just like that and there is nothing special about it anymore'. What these extras seem to experience is a process of demystification. The media no longer appears special, as extras find out how things are mediated by participating 'in the media'. Meanwhile, extras obtain the 'inside' knowledge of filmmaking basics, such as how a camera works, framing, movement, settings, etc.:

> Now I have learned a lot, such as capturing different angles for a scene, ignoring everything outside the camera frame and just ensuring things inside are correct. I also realize how different the filming and images shown on screen can be, for many things are changed due to post-production. (Peng, Henan Province, 23 years old, 3 months in Hengdian)

> I recognize many things when I watch television now, like in TV series, people only eat nuts on the table and never try other main dishes. Why? I didn't know the answer until I participated in productions. Dishes are all props. They are uneatable and crews need to return props. During those days of film shooting, we had the same dishes every time. (Litian, Guizhou Province, 32 years old, 1 month in Hengdian)

Respondents have seen through the verisimilitude of the production process, including inconsistencies of things in and outside the frame, props, etc. This demystification leads some extras to view television productions with different eyes. Sometimes, the discovery of differences between the filming and images shown on screen may result in disappointment:

> I used to find watching television fun. But ever since I was here on set, I found it uninteresting. For example, we often see several people appearing in a scene on television. In fact, each person and each scene are shot separately and scenes are edited later. So I don't think television is special any more. […] Once, I laughed there after finishing the work, hahaha, when there was no camera on set. Actually there was nothing around. That was funny. (Meng, Henan Province, 24 years old, 2 months in Hengdian)

Peng, Litian and Meng all comment on certain techniques of filmmaking. Actions during the filming are different from how they look like on television or what audiences imagine them to be. In Meng's case, he is no longer attracted by television and doesn't think it's 'special' anymore, for he has found out that he used to be tricked by an illusion. The illusion consists of many elements, as Meng sees it, such as editing and filming locations. Without cameras and settings, the place is empty and common, where one can do whatever he or she wants. Meng witnesses the transformation of a space from being 'in the media' to 'outside the media', from artificiality, verisimilitude back to reality, and is amused by the change in that space.

They observe procedures of filmmaking and filming sets both during the filming and when there is 'nothing around', discovering all sorts of differences between 'on screen' and on the actual set. This has been noted before in studies on media pilgrimages: those who visit filming locations find differences between the set as seen on television and the actual set (Couldry 2003, p. 87; Reijnders 2010, 2011). Immersing 'in' the media, extras find differences between actions as seen on television and actual happenings on set, between results as seen on television and actual efforts and between sets on television and actual sets. Indeed, the process of demystification is partly also a process of differentiation, the 'parcelling out' suggested by Levi-Strauss, confirming the category differences on which the media ritual is based (Couldry 2003, p. 86).

The demystification during their media participation comes along with a sense of 'insiderness'. In this respect, although people take part in different shows and productions, they all more or less obtain a general knowledge of television making (Boross and Reijnders 2017; Shufeldt and Gale 2007). On the other hand, when discussing their experiences, it is hard for extras to ignore the practical things they undergo on set. In most interviews, respondents describe hardships that they have been through, and some of them recall the hardships as the most impressive experiences 'in the media'. They have to work in the outdoors until dawn in extreme temperatures, walk or run back and forth in wet boots, go out before dawn and stand for hours during the day, bear the anxiety and wait for the next role and depend on a low income, to name a few.

11.6 Progress and Transformation

In addition to aforementioned hardships during the filming, extras experience a hierarchical system in which actors and actresses are treated differently than extras in many aspects. However, many respondents show a humble attitude, accepting the hierarchy in the media mechanism positively rather than complaining about it:

> It is all about having a positive attitude. They are actors, and we are extras. But there are learning opportunities. So keep learning until we reach the high status. (Peng, Henan Province, 23 years old, 3 months in Hengdian)

Indeed, the locales of media production are at least available to extras. This access to the media world in a spatial term is an advantage for extras, something which media audiences do not have. Many respondents admit a very small chance of becoming 'real' actors, but even as an extra, one has the possibility to learn more about the film/TV industry. Some respondents have also decided to gradually shift their focuses to technical skills, aiming at opportunities to become crew members behind the cameras in the future.

At this point, when respondents are still working as extras, they do not think anymore that there is something to be proud of, just because they appear 'in the media'. More than half of the respondents have not shown their costume photos to families and friends or even told them about this job. Instead, they want to keep their experiences to themselves until they become actors:

> I prefer sharing normal photos of my real life to sharing embarrassing photos of working in TV productions. I just take some photos of myself in costumes and keep them for myself. (Xiaoming, Hubei Province, 24 years old, 1 month in Hengdian)

Xiaoming's awareness of embarrassment derives from the fact that he is doing ordinary things 'in the media', in his words, 'not successful enough yet'. For extras, the idea of doing extraordinary things in the media world is ever-present. Those who did show photos to friends reported similar conversations:

> My friends wowed. 'Are you becoming a star?' No, no, I just came to perform for productions. 'Which movies? In which productions can we see you? Which character did you play?' They are very curious about these. It is refreshing to them. (Wang, Henan Province, 23 years old, 6 months in Hengdian)

Wang's friends are more curious about the resulting films than about his personal experiences and want to know whether he is going to obtain stardom or not and when he will appear on television. Non-media people in the 'ordinary world' usually link the meaning of being 'in the media' to fortune and fame, while people in the media world, extras in particular, think differently and have the feeling that they know what it truly means to enter this industry. As the respondent Donglin remarks: 'people who become extras because they fancy glamor in the film/TV industry would leave after a few months'.

If this is the case, how do extras reflect on their experiences of participating in film and TV productions then? Apart from appreciating the learning opportunities, as discussed above, a few respondents realize changes in their personalities along the way:

> I wasn't used to expressing my feelings. Through acting, I have found myself. During the filming, there are many things going on, and I can act out my feelings that are left out in real life. For instance, I care about my family very much; yet, I never spoke about it. As I realize that it is a performance and I am acting here, I can express all my feelings. In this way, I am enriched. (Fei, Guangxi Province, age unknown, 1 month in Hengdian)

Fei is not alone in recognizing positive influences on his life. Xiaozhu says he used to have an introvert character but acting has changed that. Through playing different fictional roles and interacting with the film crews, he continues to expect further transformations in his life. Xiaozhu stays motivated and frequently says things such as, 'there is a long way to go' and 'try my best' during the interview.

In addition, some respondents remark that they have learned from fellow extras, either because of previous professional and life experiences in a variety of industries and places or because of other extras' efforts and dedication:

> Extras who participate in explosion scenes are really admirable. They took the roles, regardless of the danger. This is the attitude you have when you really love something, either a job or a girl. (Anqiang, Jiangxi Province, 24 years old, 1 month in Hengdian)

The dedication Anqiang describes can be seen in many other industries and is often regarded as a life lesson. Like Fei, Xiaozhu and Anqiang, respondents transfer the lessons they have learned during the course of their practices in the media world to the social world. For extras who have been working in Hengdian for some time, their experiences and reflections are more complicated than simply 'participating in the media'. In Couldry's case study (2000, p. 116–118), an interviewee desires to be on television for one time. After finally appearing on a talk show, he has feelings of empowerment because of the nature of television itself. Even though the appearance is ordinary and brief, that one-time experience is significant. For the respondents in the case study on Hengdian drifters, appearing 'in the media' does not necessarily provide them with empowerment, as many respondents have hesitations in announcing their practices to families and friends. Instead, acting and interactions with people are helpful to extras in actualizing certain *transformations in their characters*. Some become more extroverted, some get more comfortable with expressing feelings, while others learn to dedicate themselves on a new level.

11.7 Conclusion

This chapter has probed into the practices and experiences of 'ordinary people' participating in film and TV productions, focusing in particular on the lives and perspectives of 15 'Hengdian drifters'.

Based on a series of interviews, we conclude that most extras undergo a similar process, consisting of the following three steps. To start with, many respondents get 'in' the media with the wish to perform, to experience other roles or to express oneself through roles. Would-be extras assume that elementary jobs in film studios are different from other sorts of jobs, as a different lifestyle worthy to explore. Some believe that they can possess a double life by acting, one in the real world and the other in the media world. This idea resonates with film tourists' wishes to step into the shoes of their beloved characters. Prior to their media participation, people see the media world through rose-tinted glasses, expecting that it is different from anything else.

Second, as they participate in productions on a daily basis, extras tend to experience a gradual process of demystification. They gain knowledge that they could not have known without being 'in' the media. Similar to how *short-term* film tourists visiting filming locations find differences between the actual set and how it is seen on television, extras discover differences between 'on screen' and 'on set', witnessing and taking part in the process of how reality as well as fiction is mediated. This knowledge partly takes off the rose-tinted glasses and diminishes their dreams, but they are also welcomed as newly gained 'insider knowledge'.

Becoming extras is their first experimental step into the media world. For those who decide to stay longer and wish to take on more 'inside' jobs in the film/TV industry, they appreciate these kind of learning opportunities and strive to make progress. Some extras recognize the transformation to become expressive along the way, because of the realization that it is a performance instead of reality or daily interactions with others during their media participation.

In the first section of this chapter, we compared the experience of the extras with the experience of film tourists. Both groups consist of 'ordinary people' who cross the boundary between 'inside' and 'outside' the media while hoping to gain more insight into the media machinery and to get close to the 'magic' of the media. At the same time, there are obvious differences between the two groups, not the least in terms of the temporal character: while the tourist experience entails not more than one or 2 hours, the extras invest months if not years of their life. What then can be learned from their experiences? What possibilities are there to improve the existing, sometimes rather superficial, film tourist experience? First, film studios can be more engaging if they provide people with opportunities to be different characters and to engage in certain activities they are not used to in daily life. Like extras who treat performing 'in' the media as a way to create a substitute for reality or enrich their lives, film studio visitors may also enjoy doing things that are impossible in the real world. Moreover, fundamental knowledge of filmmaking can be introduced on site. By doing so, people can learn how media representations are produced, and the feeling of being 'in' the media world would be magnified. The vivid showcase of filmmaking can be combined with the first interactive way to engage further with visitors. Third, inspirational elements or possibilities of self-discovery can be incorporated as highlights.

Extras' reflections on the transformations in their characters seem to be parallel to two motivations of film tourists: ego enhancement and self-actualization (Macionis 2004). Earlier studies have shown how media tourists energize a particular way of thinking conveyed in a story by travelling to a specific place (Reijnders 2016). For example, male James Bond tourists visiting Bond-related locations are found to symbolically strengthen their own masculinity (Reijnders 2011).

Likewise, as it turned out during the interviews, the extras in Hengdian underwent a 'rite of passage' (Turner 1967). As they left one group to enter another with a change of status in society, they also went on a journey of finding the self of adulthood and a position in the social world. The individual's transition, from a young 20 something without deep understanding of the self or a goal of life to a mature person with a clear vision of life, is an essential meaning that many of the interviewed extras attach to their practices. Such a condition makes their participation in these kinds of media rituals more personal and meaningful and shows how media rituals can stimulate transformation from within.

More generally, what extras experience at China's Hengdian World Studios also fits in well with Dilthey's idea of a complete experience, 'living through' a sequence of events, involving 'moments' of 'performance', acts of retrospection and 'wishing forward' (Turner 1982, p. 18). The symbolic boundary between inside and outside the media plays an essential role in marking those 'moments' for media participants to live through, think back or make comparison between their expectations and reality and finally wish forward. In this way, 'ordinary people' generate meanings and gain experiences during their media participation that may be treasured for a lifetime.

These findings on extras' practices suggest several directions for future research. First, it is worth further exploring the temporal dimension of film tourism. As mentioned before, most studies done on film tourism are based on (extreme) short-term tourist experiences without explicitly acknowledging this. It is questionable whether current theories and findings are also applicable for other longer-term examples of film tourism. Secondly, in addition to focusing on short-term and long-term film tourism, it would also be worth exploring the midterm range of film tourism, e.g. film tourists who book their holidays in (film) theme parks, not seldom for more than 2 or 3 days. To a certain degree, these more lengthy encounters with the 'backstage regions' of theme parks (Beeton 2016, p. 268; see also Chap. 16 in this Volume) might be comparable with the experiences of the extras in Hengdian. Finally, while this chapter emphatically shifted the focus from Western examples to the role and experiences of extras in the Chinese film industry, we believe that even more can be expected from more elaborate projects based on international comparative research on comparing the similarities and differences between forms of media participation in different cultures.

Acknowledgements The authors would like to express their gratitude towards the editor Associate Professor Sangkyun Kim and anonymous reviewers for their constructive feedback and suggestions. The authors would also like to thank Leonieke Bolderman, Balázs Boross, Siri Driessen, Nicky van Es and Abby Waysdorf for helpful comments on an earlier draft of the manuscript.

Funding This study was carried out with the financial support of the China Scholarship Council.

References

Andrejevic, M. (2004). *Reality TV: The work of being watched* (p. 145). Lanham: Rowman & Littlefield Publishers.

Aslama, M. (2009). Playing House: Participants' experiences of Big Brother Finland. *International Journal of Cultural Studies, 12*(1), 81–96.

Beeton, S. (2016). *Film-induced tourism* (2nd ed.). Bristol: Channel View Publications.

Boross, B., & Reijnders, S. (2017). 'These cameras are here for a reason' – media coming out, symbolic power and the value of participation: Behind the scenes of the Dutch reality programme *Uit de Kast*. *Media, Culture and Society, 39*(2), 185–201.

Bryman, A. (2012). *Social research methods 4e* (pp. 578–581). Oxford: Oxford University Press.

Chen, Q.D. (2015). *Hengdian pilot reform plan released*. News in the Middle Area of Zhejiang. http://www.jhnews.com.cn/2015/1117/570175.shtml. Accessed 12 Mar 2017.

Couldry, N. (2000). *The place of media power*. London: Routledge.

Couldry, N. (2003). *Media rituals*. London: Routledge.

Couldry, N. (2005). On the actual street. In D. Crouch, R. Jackson, & F. Thompson (Eds.), *The media and the tourist imagination: Converging cultures* (pp. 60–75). Abingdon: Routledge.

Dyer, R. (1977). Entertainment and Utopia. *Movie, 24*(Spring), 2–13.

Frost, W. (2010). Life changing experiences: Film and tourists in the Australian outback. *Annals of Tourism Research, 37*(3), 707–726.

Holden, A. (2016). *Environment and tourism*. Routledge.

Kim, S. (2010). Extraordinary experience: Re-enacting and photographing at screen tourism locations. *Tourism and Hospitality Planning & Development, 7*(1), 59–75.

Kim, S. (2012). Audience involvement and film tourism experiences: Emotional places, emotional experiences. *Tourism Management, 33*(2), 387–396.

Kim, S., & Wang, H. (2012). From television to the film set: Korean drama Daejanggeum drives Chinese, Taiwanese, Japanese and Thai audiences to screen-tourism. *International Communication Gazette, 74*(5), 423–442.

Kvale, S., & Brinkmann, S. (2009). *InterViews* (pp. 135–136). Los Angeles: Sage.

Laing, J. H., & Crouch, G. I. (2009). Exploring the role of the media in shaping motivations behind frontier travel experiences. *Tourism Analysis, 14*(2), 187–198.

Ma, J. (2015). Visiting Hengdian drifters. Dongyang Daily. http://www.dongyang.gov.cn/dongyang/ztzj/jrhd/181763.shtml. Accessed 11 Nov 2016.

Macionis, N. (2004, November). Understanding the film-induced tourist. In *International tourism and media conference proceedings* (Vol. 24, pp. 86–97). Tourism Research Unit, Monash University, Melbourne, Australia

Reijnders, S. (2010). On the Trail of 007: Media Pilgrimages into the World of James Bond. *Area, 42*(3), 369–377.

Reijnders, S. (2011). *Places of the imagination: Media, tourism, culture*. Farnham: Ashgate.

Reijnders, S. (2016). Stories that move: Fiction, imagination, tourism. *European Journal of Cultural Studies, 19*(6), 672–689.

Seaton, A. V. (2002). Tourism as metempsychosis and metensomatosis. In G. Dann (Ed.), *The tourist as a metaphor of the social world* (pp. 135–168). Wallingford: CABI.

Shufeldt, M., & Gale, K. (2007). Under the (glue) gun: Containing and constructing reality in home makeover TV. *Popular Communication, 5*(4), 263–282.

Syvertsen, T. (2001). Ordinary people in extraordinary circumstances: A study of participants in television dating games. *Media, Culture and Society, 23*(3), 319–337.

Turner, V. (1967). *The forest of symbols*. Ithaca: Cornell University Press.

Turner, V. (1982). *From ritual to theatre: The human seriousness of play*. New York: Performing Arts Journal Publications.

Turner, G. (2015). *Re-inventing the media*. Abingdon/New York: Routledge.

Wei, J. (2016). "I'm the Next American Idol": Cooling out, accounts, and perseverance at reality talent show auditions. *Symbolic Interaction, 39*(1), 3–25.

Ying, H. (2012). China's 'Hollywood' shines in business. *China Daily*. http://usa.chinadaily.com.cn/business/2012-05/28/content_15400461.htm. Accessed 10 Mar 2017.

Zeng, Y.L. (2016). *A new record for Hengdian World Studios to welcome crews*. News of Hengdian World Studios. http://www.hengdianworld.com/NewsDetail.aspx?id=3978&channel=新闻资讯. Accessed 10 Mar 2017.

Zhao, H.D. (2017). *Hengdian World Studios welcomed 119,500 tourists during the 2017 New Year three-day break*. News of Hengdian World Studios. http://www.hengdianworld.com/NewsDetail.aspx?id=4060&channel=新闻资讯. Accessed 10 Mar 2017.

Part IV
Transcontinental Film Tourism

Chapter 12
Power of Dramas: A Comparison of Voluntourism Between Chinese and American Film Tourists

Jun Shao and Ulrike Gretzel

Abstract Neither the connection between film tourism and voluntourism nor the differences between Chinese and American film-induced voluntourists have been studied enough despite the potential importance of film-induced voluntourists for destinations. This research explores the phenomenon of voluntourism among fans of two very popular TV dramas in China and the US, *Soldier Sortie* and *Lost*, respectively, by conducting a qualitative 'netnographic' study on fans' online conversations. The study aims at investigating both the motivations and specific behaviours of film-induced voluntourists in different cultures. The study finds that *Soldier Sortie* fans in China act more like a virtual charity organisation, while *Lost* fans engage with an existing charity organisation. Volunteering programs initiated by *Soldier Sortie* fans have taken on an important role in propelling the development of some tourist destinations in rural areas of the province where the series was shot. Moreover, *Soldier Sortie* fans act not only as donors but also as organisers and auditors, choosing and determining which school to help. This reflects the much stronger level of connectivity and activism among Chinese fans.

Keywords Film tourism • Voluntourism • Cultural difference • Netnography • Fan activism • Social media

J. Shao (✉)
School of Landscape Architecture, Beijing Forestry University, Beijing, China
e-mail: ninashaojun@bjfu.edu.cn

U. Gretzel
Annenberg School of Communication and Journalism, University of Southern California, Los Angeles, USA
e-mail: gretzel@usc.edu

12.1   Introduction

TV series and films have the power to increase the number of visitors to destinations related to them (Beeton 2005; O'Connor et al. 2008; Hahm and Wang 2011; Shao et al. 2016; Li et al. 2017). Therefore, film tourism has received increasing attention from tourism operators and destination marketers (Riley et al. 1998). Inspired by TV dramas, more and more Chinese fans, similar to their American counterparts, use online communities to develop various fan movements, especially volunteering programs aimed at promoting the spirit embodied in their favorite TV dramas. As part of their volunteering efforts, Chinese fans also travel to the destinations connected with the TV drama, which can be locations where the drama was filmed or where events portrayed in the drama actually happened (Shao and Gretzel 2009). However, American fans seem to choose destinations close to the creative team of TV dramas (Scarpino 2008). This paper explores the phenomenon of voluntourism among fans of two very popular TV dramas in China and in the US, *Soldier Sortie* (SS) and *Lost*, respectively, by examining fans' online conversations. The study aims at investigating both the motivations and specific behaviors of film-induced voluntourists in different cultures. In doing so it explores how voluntourism emerges within fan communities and what factors (including culture) are relevant in shaping it. Such an investigation is important as neither film-induced voluntourism nor cultural differences are currently discussed extensively in the film tourism literature.

Netnography is selected as the methodological framework to guide the research as it aims at deriving deep cultural understandings of phenomena and offers guidelines as to how to approach research that seeks to take advantage of data available online (Kozinets 2015). Netnography has been applied in tourism research (Mkono and Markwell 2014) and specifically research on Asian tourists (Wu and Pearce 2014). This existing research illustrates the valuable insights netnography helps uncover from unmediated digital traces, i.e., unsolicited data, that individuals and organizations leave behind when engaging with others online.

12.2   Background: Understanding Film Tourists

Film tourism refers to "on-location tourism that follows the success of a movie (or set), television program, video or DVD in a particular region" (Beeton 2005, p. 9). Some studies have questioned the actual contributions of film to tourism in creating strong motivations to travel (Shao et al. 2011). For instance, based on a survey conducted on people who like watching films and traveling, Macionis and Sparks (2009) found that only 4% of the total respondents said the main reason for travel had been film related, while most just happened to visit a film location in the course of a trip motivated by other factors. Following this study, film tourism could be seen as an incidental tourist activity. Di Cesare et al. (2009) investigated different phases of the decision-making process starting with a desire to travel induced by films, searching for information about places seen in films, having or changing destination images and perceptions, choosing the travel destination, and the final purchasing of a tourist product. Although they confirmed a strong influence of film viewing on the desire to travel, the influence gradually weakens as the decision process goes on. Based on focus group interviews with Singaporean women who are avid viewers of Korean TV dramas, Chan (2007) found interviewees could be divided into those who were motivated by TV dramas and those who were interested in visiting Korea for other reasons. TV dramas warrant special consideration due to the degree to which they trigger emotional involvement in viewers (Chang 2016; Kim and Long 2012). The shooting and airing periods of TV dramas are longer than those of movies. Also, their theme can be repeated in each episode, leading to a more enduringly and deeply engaged audience. Such enduring involvement with a TV series can enhance travel motivations to screen sites (Chang 2016; Kim 2012a; Kim and Long 2012).

Regarding the motives of film tourists, Riley and Van Doren (1992), Beeton (2005), Macionis (2004), and Chang (2016) all believe that the push-and-pull factor framework is suitable for understanding them. In terms of destination attributes, the iconic attractions and scenery depicted in the settings of film or TV dramas are the primary pull factors for the viewers to visit the film set (Busby et al. 2013; Chan 2007; Hudson and Ritchie 2006; Singh and Best 2004). Film-specific factors such as stories and characters/actors (Kim et al. 2007; Kim 2012a) and emotional involvement in a drama push fans to visit places featured in the dramas (Shao and Gretzel 2009). Existing research has sought to align film tourism motivations with the personal seeking dimension of Iso-Ahola's (1982) model of tourism motivation (Singh and Best 2004). Based on the research of Kim et al. (2007), Lee et al. (2008), and Kim (2012a), it is proposed that people's involvement with a TV drama affects their perceptions of tourism destinations (familiarity, image, and visitation intentions). Kim et al. (2007) found that empathy with actors or actresses contributed to Japanese's preferences for and involvement in Korean TV dramas and desires to visit Korean locations associated with these TV dramas. Wong and Lai (2015) indicated that celebrity attachment to Korean TV dramas by Taiwanese audiences was positively related to behavioral intentions to visit South Korea. Shao and Gretzel (2009) found emotional involvement in a drama leads to strong desires to visit the place where the story really happened and that during their travels, fans often engage in meaningful activities such as volunteering and self-reflection.

12.3 Understanding Voluntourists

Volunteer tourism has been defined as "utilizing discretionary time and income to travel out of the sphere of regular activity to assist others in need" (McGehee and Santos 2005, p. 760). Existing research found the motives for volunteer tourists include both altruism and self-related perspectives. Altruistic motives are the distinct feature that differentiates voluntourism from other forms of tourism; they encompass helping others in need, restoring the environment, and helping the host people (Butcher 2003; Scheyvens 2007; Stoddart and Rogerson 2004). Self-related motives involve hedonic experiences and self-development. Self-development in particular, includes contemplating, fulfilling a dream, expressing individuality, enriching oneself, developing skills relative to university studies and future careers, engaging in meaningful experiences, or enjoying the feeling of being part of a team (Brown and Morrison 2003; McGchcc and Santos 2005; Mustonen 2005; Sin 2009; Stoddart and Rogerson 2004; Uriely et al. 2003; Wearing 2003; Wearing and Deane 2003; Wearing and Neil 2001). The question is whether film-induced voluntourists exhibit similar motives and, consequently, engage in similar behaviors such as helping others in need, restoring the environment, and helping the host people (Butcher 2003; Scheyvens 2007; Stoddart and Rogerson 2004). It is assumed that the empathy with film characters and involvement in film locations exhibited by fans spur true caring for featured places and people and/or lead to a desire to realize values communicated by films.

12.4   Cultural Differences of Film Tourists

Previous research on cross-cultural differences in tourism confirmed that tourist motivations (Kozak 2002; Lee 2000), destination image (Baloglu and Mangaloglu 2001), destination choice (McKercher and Du Cros 2003), perceptions and stereotypes (Pizam and Jeong 1996; Pizam and Reichel 1996; Pizam and Sussmann 1995; Reisinger and Turner 2002), as well as consumption patterns (Rosenbaum and Spears 2005) are subject to cross-cultural differences. In terms of cultural differences of film tourists, research has asserted that the influence of a film on travel motivations is unlikely to be homogeneous across audiences from different countries (Hudson et al. 2011; Kumar and Duang 2016). Such cross-cultural differences further determine the travel patterns of film tourists (Kim and O'Connor 2011; Kim 2012b).

Specifically, Busby and Klug (2001) found that various forms of film tourism exist, and each tourist is motivated by different factors to visit filmed locations based on different cultural backgrounds. Choosing the Motorcycle Diaries in which South America was portrayed evidently in the film, Hudson et al. (2011) conducted a survey on viewers from the USA, Canada, and Spain. They found that Canadians showed a significantly higher desire to visit South America than the US and Spanish participants. Kim and Richardson (2003) proposed that familiarity, including cultural familiarity, may lead to different views of the destination depicted in the film. Kim and O'Connor (2011) conducted a cross-cultural analysis of film tourists from China, Japan, Taiwan, and Thailand who visited a theme park associated with the South Korean TV drama *Daejanggeum*. The study found differences in screen product preferences and travel patterns based on traveler origin. Further, most Asian fans visit film sites with friends, colleagues, or family to form collective memories (Kim and O'Connor 2011), while the majority of *Lord of the Rings* fans visiting New Zealand participate in film location tours to encounter fellow fans and share their enthusiasm and passion (Buchmann et al. 2010). Despite these important studies, cross-cultural comparisons are still not extensively discussed in the film tourism literature. Further, the social dimension of fandom, and how culture influences it, has not been explored enough.

12.4.1 Soldier Sortie and Lost

The TV dramas chosen for this research were two popular TV series with a large number of fans, *Soldier Sortie (SS)* in China and *Lost* in America. Both include tourism by fans as well as fans engaging in charity-related activities.

SS was the most popular Chinese TV series produced and broadcast in 2007. It had 88,701 online fans in Baidu Tieba, which is extraordinary if compared with other TV series, which usually had no more than 1000 online fans each. *SS* talked about a young farmer who was forced to join the army by his father, gradually became the most outstanding soldier of his whole regiment, and found his true self in the army. The spirit of *SS*, *doing meaningful things*, inspired millions of Chinese fans. *SS* was recommended to Chinese Youth in 2013 officially by the Propaganda Department of the Chinese Central Committee, the Ministry of Education of China, and the Central Communist Youth League of China. The Chinese province, Yunnan in remote Southwest China is the filming location of *SS*. Rural regions in Yunnan are very poor, and there are increasing numbers of *SS* fans going to Yunnan for volunteering purposes (Shao et al. 2011). In response to a *SS* fan's initial call for establishing primary schools in rural areas as a way of doing meaningful things, *SS* fans created an online group named *Family of Seasons in the Sun (FSS)* in *Baidu Tieba*, which is dedicated to organizing charitable activities to establish primary schools in Yunnan. The name *FSS* originates from a famous line of a *SS* character, "Being Young and Frivolous during Seasons in the Sun." Though the story of *SS* is not directly related to establishing primary schools, *SS* fans thought volunteering in Yunnan was a meaningful way of helping the region depicted in the drama.

Lost is an American TV drama that originally aired from September 22, 2004 to May 23, 2010 on the US television network ABC. It is consistently ranked by US critics on their lists of top TV series (Schillaci 2012). *Lost* follows the lives of various individuals and groups of people, most importantly the survivors of the crash of a commercial passenger jet flying between Sydney and Los Angeles, on a mysterious tropical island somewhere in the South Pacific. *Lost* fans gathered in an online forum, thefuselage.com, hosted by the creative team behind the drama. Annually, *Lost* fans attended a fan party called "Destination L.A.," which was later named "Lost Weekend." It consists of a Friday night fan party, a Saturday night charity event that members of the show are invited to, and an optional Sunday brunch. The charity event benefits the *Children's Defense Fund (CDF)*, which advocates on behalf of children in education, health care, and other areas. *CDF* is irrelevant to the storyline of this TV drama. It is J. J. Abrams' (the director, scriptwriter and producer of Lost) favorite charity.

12.5 Methodology

12.5.1 Research Questions

In order to explore the volunteer activities, film-induced travel and motivations of fans, a qualitative "netnographic'" study (Kozinets 2002) using fans' online conversations from forums dedicated to the volunteer efforts of *SS* fans and *Lost* fans was conducted. Attention was paid only to those threads related to our research questions:

1. What kind of volunteer activities do *SS* fans and *Lost* fans discuss in their online conversations related to the dramas?
2. What kind of voluntourism occurs?
3. Why do they participate in volunteering activities as fans?
4. Why do they travel to the destinations rather than volunteering through donations and fan art contributions online from home?

12.5.2 Data Collection

Based on Kozinets' (2002) criteria for Web site selection, the forum dedicated to discussing *SS* fans' volunteering, *Tieba of Family of Seasons in the Sun* (*FSS* forum, https://tinyurl.com/gn6vpmk) and the *Lost* fans' dedicated forum (*Lost* forum, http://forum.thefuselage.com) were selected as the two online communities for our study due to the amount of fan activity and their centrality to fans' voluntourism.

In the case of the *FSS* forum, all 423 threads available prior to April 20, 2010 (the peak period of the drama) were extracted from the forum. They were classified by *FSS* forum administrators into eight groups. Among them, 185 threads were considered for the analysis of volunteering activities of *SS* fans including 35 threads of "*FSS* History" recording all the volunteering activities of *FSS* plus 130 threads of "Recommended Articles" and 20 threads of "Videos and Photos" showing further details of these activities. Another 164 threads were considered for the analysis of motives of *SS* fans participating in volunteering tours which include 91 threads of "*FSS* Essays" posted by *FSS* members individually talking about their stories, 33 threads of "*FSS* Data" and 40 threads of "*FSS* Promotion", containing transcripts of leading *FSS* members interviewed by public media. The remaining 37 threads of "*FSS* Announcements" and 6 threads of "*FSS* Donation List" were only used to get general information about the volunteering work of *FSS*.

In the case of the *Lost* forum, the sub-forum entitled "Caves and Beaches" was selected as it is dedicated to discussing fan events. We used the search engine provided by the *Lost* forum, inputting the keyword "charity" and searching within "Caves and Beaches" and its child forums. Using September 13, 2010, as the cutoff time (the show ended in 2010), 500 relevant postings distributed among 33 threads that encompassed 2975 posts were extracted.

12.5.3 Data Analysis

Coding the posts involved both data analysis and data interpretation (Kozinets 2002; Spiggle 1994). To investigate volunteer activities and motivations of *SS* and *Lost* fans, thematic analysis (Aronson 1995; Attride-Stirling 2001) was applied. Thematic analysis is the process of collecting, analyzing, and coding information into emergent themes (Merriam 1998; Strauss and Corbin 1998; Taylor and Bogdan 1984). Thematic analysis is relatively flexible compared to other qualitative methodologies, as it can be used both as an inductive approach and a theoretical or deductive approach (Braun and Clarke 2006). The research questions served as the initial coding framework. Each thread was coded by the initial message and this initial coding was later confirmed through analysis of subsequent comments. Then, individual comments were categorized based on the different themes. For example, all postings related to the charity activities of *SS* fans were categorized under the theme of "Volunteer Activities of *SS* Fans," while the postings describing their feelings about the volunteer tours were categorized under the theme of "Volunteer Motivations of *SS* Fans."

12.6 Results and Discussion

12.6.1 Volunteer Activities of Film Tourists

Postings from the *FSS* forum indicate that *SS* fans focus mostly on building schools in rural areas. From the 185 threads analyzed for volunteering activities of *SS* fans, it became apparent that *FSS* members have not only built schools for children but also organized several charity tours to interact with the children they have helped. In general, two types of voluntourism activities of *FSS* members were identified: onsite donation distributions at the *Seasons in the Sun Hope Primary School (SSHPS)* and onsite volunteering work during the drought disaster that occurred in 2010 in the Southwest of China.

SS fans were dedicated to building schools in rural areas in Yunnan, where *SS* was filmed. The main shooting site, a military field not open to the public, cannot be visited by the fans; they therefore focused on the region overall instead of a particular location. In October 20, 2007, a fan named "steel seven 5001" called for fans to donate jointly for establishing primary schools in rural areas of Yunnan. Though this is not directly related to the *SS* storyline or actors, *SS* fans thought this was consistent with the theme of *SS, doing meaningful things*. A week after the initial call, fans had already created *FSS* as their online community. They had online meetings to discuss the site selection of schools and agreed to name the schools "Seasons in the Sun" to honor the famous line in the drama. It signifies memorable times spent together as fans as well as blessings brought upon the children in poor rural areas. Within a span of only 4 months, *FSS* had raised RMB 250,000 (about US Dollars 36,500) to establish the first school (referred to as SSHPS) in Yunnan. In addition to direct donations, *FSS* members raised additional money through charity sales of fan art with signatures of the *SS* cast and *FSS* members. Up to April 20, 2010, SSHPS No.1 had been built; No.2 was under construction; and No. 3 was in the site selection process. *FSS* members traveled to rural locations to inspect sites for future SSHPS projects and visit the already completed SSHPS. From the forum threads we can see that during the onsite inspections, *FSS* also delivered donations to candidate schools, such as books, stationery, electric blankets, shoes, socks, clothes, and so on. *FSS* members posted numerous photos in the forum, sharing their meaningful experiences.

Fans also gathered to visit the first SSHPS school when it was established. On July 19, 2009, a large group of fans visited SSHPS No. 1 in Huize County. Many postings recorded this "meaningful meeting." Students and teachers at that school as well as officers of the local government hosted a celebration party for the establishment of SSHPS No. 1, welcoming the *FSS* members. More than 60 *FSS* members participated, played, and exchanged gifts with the children. What moved *FSS* members the most was a performance in which students reproduced the admission ceremony of the company of Steel Seven, a very classic scene in the TV drama. One fan said "I could not help bursting into tears when I watched the familiar scene reenacted by the children." Interestingly, one local officer who was in charge of promotion gave each *FSS* member a tourist brochure entitled "Charm of Huize." A female fan said she was touched by the brochure and interested in the attractions in Huize. Almost every fan expressed his or her disappointment and sadness for having to leave and looked forward to their next visit. It is of importance to note that fans also discussed their travel and tourism activities after visiting SSHPS No.1. After the group activities were over, a number of fans went to visit other attractions in the Yunnan Province.

In addition to voluntours to the donation schools, fans also worked onsite when their help was needed. A thread of the *FSS* forum posted on March 27, 2010 reported what *FSS* fans had done during the drought disaster that had occurred in the southwest of China, as the SSHPS schools were also affected by the drought. When the headmaster of SSHPS No.1 turned to *FSS* for help, the fans organized quickly. According to a fan, "the funding for rebuilding drinking water facilities was available on that very day!" *FSS* members near the school also organized to deliver water onsite with the help of local officers.

In summary, many *SS* fans donated money and materials online from home and a small portion of dedicated *SS* fans visited the donation locations. Even though not all fans had the opportunity to travel together, the volunteer work spurred a great desire to visit the actual locations within the fan community to see the difference that fan contributions could make and to realize the theme of doing meaningful things.

On the other hand, from the threads that represent what *Lost* fans discussed in the *Lost* Forum, we know they raised money by participating in charity auctions or participated in a raffle at the annual charity events. In addition, *Lost* fans also bought merchandise, such as T-shirts, graphic novels signed by *Lost* writers, as well as contributed time by being volunteers for the party. During the charity parties, fans could bid on autographed scripts and memorabilia from the show and mingle with cast and crew. All the benefits went to CDF.

Lost fans went to Los Angeles to attend charity parties annually from 2005 to 2010. The first two events named "Destination L.A." were held on April 16, 2005 and May 20, 2006. The third event named the "LOST Weekend Fan Party 2007" was held on the weekend of March 30 to April 1. The fourth event was scheduled for 2008 but was canceled due to the strike of the *Writers Guild of America*, as most Hollywood workers including *Lost* writers and other crew stopped working and refused to attend any events related to their work. Most attendees were true *Lost* fans. The cast and creative team whose schedules allowed attendance were also there, but the American Broadcasting Company was not involved. In regard to destination choice of fan meetings, different from the choice of drama-related sites by the Chinese *SS* fans, American *Lost* fans chose to meet in Los Angeles as it was close to most fans and the show-related VIPs.

Similar to Chinese *SS* fans, postings from the *Lost* forum indicated that all the parties were organized by *Lost* fans themselves. The most active ones volunteered to form a committee and recruited other fans to help. Unlike Chinese *SS* fans who interacted with charity recipients, checked donation results on site, even experienced part of the recipients' daily life by dining at school canteens and attending classes, and traveled within the broader region of the drama-related destinations, *Lost* fans met at the charity parties and interacted with each other just for fun and for charity, without any desire to connect with the drama-related destinations or the charity recipients.

12.6.2 Motivations of Film-Induced Voluntourists

On the *FSS* forum, one *SS* fan proclaimed: "It is the power of the drama!" The fans were especially moved by two lines from the drama which exemplify the spirit of SS – "Do something meaningful!" and "Don't abandon, don't give up!" They "want to express their feelings for SS" and an empathy-identification-altruism pattern appeared (Shao et al. 2011). At first, they feel moved by *SS*, "feeling they could find themselves or others in the drama." Next, they love and identify "with the emotional information and values delivered by the drama." Finally, they transfer this kind of feeling to altruism, and want to experience "the power of good examples from SS by achieving excellence, such as working hard and living seriously, treasuring families and friends, and producing warmness to everyone around them."

SS fans feel they can find friendship, trust, and self-enhancement by volunteering. A fan described his relationship to *SS* as follows: "To me, FSS is like my family. I have left FSS for a period due to personal reasons and I felt as empty as a drum at that time, similar to losing something. I recognized suddenly, FSS is so important to me, as it has integrated into my life and become an indispensable part of my life." Reflecting on self-enhancement by volunteering, the originator of FSS, a village teacher, said: "I now understand that we can live on a firm footing, life can show its glorious features without miracles, and we can nicely live and do things in meaningful ways." Other benefits related to personal development are described in the words of one *FSS* member: "Learn the power of commitment, learn the value of myself, learn the flexibility of work, and learn the power of gratitude and love."

SS fans organized volunteer activities as a nonprofit organization. When charity outcomes were related to money beyond just donating tangible objects or volunteering labor, *FSS* cooperated with the Yunnan Youth Foundation, an official charity organization that operates in the region of interest. However, *SS* fans monitored the usage of their charity fund and traveled together to check sites. Due to the empathy for the region and its people developed while watching the drama, *SS* fans felt personally responsible for the development of the schools.

In contrast, *Lost* fans wanted "to meet up and become closer friends under this great fandom" and attended events because it is "for a good cause" and can make them "ALL proactive in the world." *Lost* fans described the charity parities as "a celebration for charity, for fans and for fun", "a party and not a con, an opportunity to meet up, start new friendships, and have a fabulous time." Therefore, they wanted "a fabulous shindig and a nice check for charity." Thus, *Lost* fans show strong commitments to volunteering and to drama-related travel but neither exhibit the empathy nor the level of activism developed by *SS* fans.

12.6.3 *Comparison on Voluntourism Between SS Fans and Lost Fans*

The similarity of voluntourism between *SS* fans and *Lost* fans is that both voluntours of *SS* fans and charity parties of *Lost* fans are organized by the fans themselves and discussed via internet forums rather than initiated and managed by the destinations or the TV corporations. However, there are some differences between these two groups of fans. Due to space limitations, we only briefly list them in Table 12.1. It seems that in China volunteering programs initiated by *SS* fans have taken on an important role in propelling the development of some tourist destinations in rural areas, even though they are not the actual film locations.

Moreover, *SS* fans act not only as donors but also as organizers and auditors, choosing and determining which school to help. As such, *FSS* acts more like a virtual charity organization, while *Lost* fans engage with an existing charity organization and are much less active and involved. This reflects the intensity of Chinese

Table 12.1 Differences in voluntourism between *SS* fans and *Lost* fans

		SS fans	*Lost* fans
Motives		Developing the theme of *SS*, witnessing donation results, and helping others	Meeting with fans and VIPs, making *Lost* fans look good by doing good
Behavioral patterns	Destination choice	Schools in Yunnan near shooting sites	Hotels in LA, close to fans and VIPs (the cast and creative team)
	Charity choice	Discussed and decided by fans, not related to crew or creative team	A favorite of J.J. Abrams with fans' approval
	Attendees	Fans, donors, and local officers	Fans, some VIPs
	Activities	Interacting with donors, onsite donating, traveling within greater region, meeting with other fans	Participating in charity auctions, having fun together
	Relationship with charity funds	As donors, organizers, and auditors	Just as donors

fandom and the crucial role of online communities in supporting consumer activism in China.

12.7 Conclusion

In summary, based on the "netnographic" study of the two TV drama forums, this study found that the TV dramas created strong motivations for their fans to volunteer in order to live the values promoted by the shows. These volunteer activities, in turn, inspire travel. *SS* fans traveled to the volunteering sites and the greater region of Yunnan, and *Lost* fans traveled to LA to attend charity events. The actual volunteer work conducted by fans takes on different forms, depending on the specific themes promoted in the dramas. This is in accordance with Kim (2010), who argued that fans travel to contextualize and perform the themes of TV dramas. Overall, *SS* fans seem much more engaged and more connected to TV drama-related locations than *Lost* fans. We suggest that this is due to the strong feelings of empathy the TV drama evoked in them. However, there also seem to be cultural differences in that *Lost* fans clearly travel more to experience the fan fellowship described for *Lord of the Ring* fans by Buchmann et al. (2010). Further, the need for fans to take matters into their own hands and to carefully audit donations is a much stronger theme for Chinese fans due to their distrust in government and established charity organizations.

Understanding differences in volunteer tourist activities and their fandom-driven motives between Chinese and American fans in this chapter provides essential insights from theoretical and practical perspectives. The results of the study inform both the voluntourism as well as the film tourism literature in that they illustrate film-induced travel beyond the desire to experience places where TV dramas are filmed or take place. In addition to the altruistic motives of volunteering identified in past research, the research uncovered deeper levels of both activism and empathy in Chinese fans that motivated them to travel to local areas to make sure the desired results were achieved. Such fan activism and its connection to travel have so far not sufficiently been explored in the voluntourism and film tourism literatures. Future research should focus on fans' online self-organization capabilities and how they build internal trust and continuously maintain it. The research also shows that film-induced voluntourism can take on many forms. Future research that expands this topic to other TV shows and films is therefore needed to validate the findings for other fan cultures and different film contexts. Finally, the different needs for online and offline communion with fellow fans in the two cultures and show contexts have not been adequately addressed by past research. While the current study uncovered distinct behavioral patterns with regard to fan fellowship, the underlying factors that influence it should be explored in greater detail in future research.

Further, the findings of this research allow for an enhanced understanding of film tourists in different cultures, which is important for destination marketers looking to successfully connect to this very different group of travelers. The research results hinted at opportunities for Chinese destinations to encourage film-induced volun-tourists to travel beyond their actual volunteer work assignment. They also illustrate the necessity to support these travelers in living the spirit of the TV drama through their trips. Furthermore, being aware of the power of TV dramas and the volunteer-ing they can spur in addition to just travel to the area, destination governments may consider establishing official policies to encourage film shooting activities, espe-cially in poor areas in China.

Importantly, the research also illustrates the value of qualitative research and, specifically netnography, in revealing deeper meanings and unexpected activities and motivations. Survey research or quantitative content analyses might have picked up some of the themes but would have been unable to ground the findings in the lived experiences and communicative actions of the fans, which contributed greatly to the depth of understanding underlying meanings and cultural nuances.

References

Aronson, J. (1995). A pragmatic view of thematic analysis. *The qualitative report, 2*(1), 1–3.

Attride-Stirling, J. (2001). Thematic networks: An analytic tool for qualitative research. *Qualitative Research, 1*(3), 385–405.

Baloglu, S., & Mangaloglu, M. (2001). Tourism destination images of Turkey, Egypt, Greece, and Italy as perceived by US-based tour operators and travel agents. *Tourism Management, 22*(1), 1–9.

Beeton, S. (2005). *Film-induced tourism.* Clevedon: Channel View Publications.

Braun, V., & Clarke, V. (2006). Using thematic analysis in psychology. *Qualitative Research in Psychology, 3*(2), 77–101.

Brown, S., & Morrison, A. M. (2003). Expanding volunteer vacation participation an exploratory study on the mini-mission concept. *Tourism Recreation Research, 28*(3), 73–82.

Buchmann, A., Moore, K., & Fisher, D. (2010). Experiencing film tourism: Authenticity & fellowship. *Annals of Tourism Research, 37*(1), 229–248.

Busby, G., & Klug, J. (2001). Movie-induced tourism: The challenge of measurement and other issues. *Journal of Vacation Marketing, 7*(4), 316–332.

Busby, G., Huang, R., & Jarman, R. (2013). The Stein effect: An alternative film-induced tourism perspective. *International Journal of Tourism Research, 15*(6), 570–582.

Butcher, J. (2003). A humanistic perspective on the volunteer-recipient relationship. In P. Dekker & L. Halman (Eds.), *The values of volunteering* (pp. 111–125). New York: Springer Science+Business Media LLC.

Chan, B. (2007). Film-induced tourism in Asia: A case study of Korean television drama and female viewers' motivation to visit Korea. *Tourism Culture and Communication, 7*(3), 207–224.

Chang, D. Y. (2016). A study of TV drama series, cultural proximity and travel motivation: Moderation effect of enduring involvement. *International Journal of Tourism Research, 18*(4), 399–408.

Di Cesare, F., D'Angelo, L., & Rech, G. (2009). Films and tourism: Understanding the nature and intensity of their cause–effect relationship. *Tourism Review International, 13*(2), 103–111.

Hahm, J., & Wang, Y. (2011). Film-induced tourism as a vehicle for destination marketing: Is it worth the efforts? *Journal of Travel & Tourism Marketing, 28*(2), 165–179.

Hudson, S., & Ritchie, J. R. B. (2006). Promoting destinations via film tourism: An empirical identification of supporting marketing initiatives. *Journal of Travel Research, 44*(4), 387–396.

Hudson, S., Wang, Y., & Gil, S. M. (2011). The influence of a film on destination image and the desire to travel: A cross-cultural comparison. *International Journal of Tourism Research, 13*(2), 177–190.

Iso-Ahola, S. E. (1982). Toward a social psychological theory of tourism motivation: A rejoinder. *Annals of Tourism Research, 9*(2), 256–262.

Kim, S. (2010). Extraordinary experience: Re-enacting and photographing at screen tourism locations. *Tourism and Hospitality Planning & Development, 7*(1), 59–75.

Kim, S. (2012a). Audience involvement and film tourism experiences: Emotional places, emotional experiences. *Tourism Management, 33*(2), 387–396.

Kim, S. (2012b). A cross-cultural study of on-site film-tourism experiences among Chinese, Japanese, Taiwanese and Thai visitors to the *Daejanggeum* Theme Park, South Korea. *Current Issues in Tourism, 15*(8), 759–776.

Kim, S., & Long, P. (2012). Touring TV soap operas: Genre in film tourism research. *Tourist Studies, 12*(2), 173–185.

Kim, S., & O'Connor, N. (2011). A cross-cultural study of screen-tourists' profiles. *Worldwide Hospitality and Tourism Themes, 3*(2), 141–158.

Kim, H., & Richardson, S. L. (2003). Motion picture impacts on destination images. *Annals of Tourism Research, 30*(1), 216–237.

Kim, S. S., Agrusa, J., Lee, H., & Chon, K. (2007). Effects of Korean television dramas on the flow of Japanese tourists. *Tourism Management, 28*(5), 1340–1353.

Kozinets, R. V. (2002). The field behind the screen: Using netnography for marketing research in online communities. *Journal of Marketing Research, 39*(1), 61–72.

Kozak, M. (2002). Comparative analysis of tourist motivations by nationality and destinations. *Tourism Management, 23*(3), 221–232.

Kozinets, R. V. (2015). *Netnography: Redefined*. Thousand Oaks: Sage.

Kumar, A., & Dung, T. P. (2016). Film tourism and desire to travel: A cross National Study of India and China. In M. C. Dhiman (Ed.), *Opportunities and challenges for tourism and Hospitality in the BRIC nations* (pp. 203–219). Hershey: IGI Global.

Lee, C. K. (2000). A comparative study of Caucasian and Asian visitors to a cultural expo in an Asian setting. *Tourism Management, 21*(2), 169–176.

Lee, S., Scott, D., & Kim, H. (2008). Celebrity fan involvement and destination perceptions. *Annals of Tourism Research, 35*(3), 809–832.

Li, S., Li, H., Song, H., Lundberg, C., & Shen, S. (2017). The economic impact of on-screen tourism: The case of the Lord of the Rings and the Hobbit. *Tourism Management, 60,* 177–187.

Macionis, N. (2004, November). Understanding the film-induced tourist. In *International tourism and media conference proceedings* (Vol. 24, pp. 86–97). Tourism Research Unit, Monash University: Melbourne, Australia.

Macionis, N., & Sparks, B. (2009). Film-induced tourism: An incidental experience. *Tourism Review International, 13*(2), 93–101.

McGehee, N. G., & Santos, C. A. (2005). Social change, discourse and volunteer tourism. *Annals of Tourism Research, 32*(3), 760–779.

McKercher, B., & Du Cros, H. (2003). Testing a cultural tourism typology. *International Journal of Tourism Research, 5*(1), 45–58.

Merriam, S. (1998). *Qualitative research and case study applications in education.* San Francisco: Jossey-Bass.

Mkono, M., & Markwell, K. (2014). The application of netnography in tourism studies. *Annals of Tourism Research, 48,* 289–291.

Mustonen, P. (2005). Volunteer tourism: Postmodern pilgrimage? *Journal of Tourism and Cultural Change, 3*(3), 160–177.

O'Connor, N., Flanagan, S., & Gilbert, D. (2008). The integration of film-induced tourism and destination branding in Yorkshire, UK. *International Journal of Tourism Research, 10*(5), 423–437.

Pizam, A., & Jeong, G. H. (1996). Cross-cultural tourist behavior: Perceptions of Korean tourguides. *Tourism Management, 17*(4), 277–286.

Pizam, A., & Reichel, A. (1996). The effect of nationality on tourist behavior: Israeli tour-guides' perceptions. *Journal of Hospitality and Leisure Marketing, 4*(1), 23–49.

Pizam, A., & Sussmann, S. (1995). Does nationality affect tourist behavior? *Annals of Tourism Research, 22*(4), 901–917.

Reisinger, Y., & Turner, L. W. (2002). Cultural differences between Asian tourist markets and Australian hosts, part 1. *Journal of Travel Research, 40*(3), 295–315.

Riley, R. W., & Van Doren, C. S. (1992). Movies as tourism promotion: A 'pull' factor in a 'push' location. *Tourism Management, 13*(3), 267–274.

Riley, R., Baker, D., & Van Doren, C. S. (1998). Movie induced tourism. *Annals of Tourism Research, 25*(4), 919–935.

Rosenbaum, M. S., & Spears, D. L. (2005). Who buys that? Who does what? Analysis of cross-cultural consumption behaviours among tourists in Hawaii. *Journal of Vacation Marketing, 11*(3), 235–247.

Scarpino, M.R. (2008). *Young media-induced travelers: online representations of media-induced travel conversations.* Master Thesis, Texas A&M University.

Scheyvens, R. (2007). Exploring the tourism-poverty nexus. *Current Issues in Tourism, 10*(2–3), 231–254.

Schillaci, S. (2012). *Johnny Depp, 'The Dark Knight,' 'Lost' Named to IMDb's Top 10 of the Last Decade,* Retrieved from http://www.hollywoodreporter.com/news/brad-pitt-johnny-depp-dark-knight-lost-imdb-top-10-284912

Shao, J., & Gretzel, U. (2009, October). Online empathy response to a Chinese popular TV series: Implications for film-induced tourism. In *Proceedings of the 2009 Annual International Society of Travel and Tourism Educators (ISTTE) Conference* (pp. 224–235).

Shao, J., Scarpino, M., Lee, Y., & Gretzel, U. (2011). Media-induced voluntourism in Yunnan, China. *Tourism Review International, 15*(3), 277–292.

Shao, J., Li, X., Morrison, A. M., & Wu, B. (2016). Social media micro-film marketing by Chinese destinations: The case of Shaoxing. *Tourism Management, 54,* 439–451.

Sin, H. L. (2009). Volunteer tourism—"involve me and I will learn"? *Annals of Tourism Research, 36*(3), 480–501.

Singh, K., & Best, G.(2004). Film-induced tourism: Motivations of visitors to the Hobbiton movie set as featured in the Lord of the Rings. In *International tourism and media conference proceedings* (Vol. 24, pp. 98–111). Tourism Research Unit, Monash University: Melbourne, Australia.

Spiggle, S. (1994). Analysis and interpretation of qualitative data in consumer research. *Journal of Consumer Research, 21*(3), 491–503.

Stoddart, H., & Rogerson, C. M. (2004). Volunteer tourism: The case of habitat for humanity South Africa. *GeoJournal, 60*(3), 311–318.

Strauss, A., & Corbin, J. (1998). *Basics of qualitative research: Techniques and procedures for developing grounded theory* (2nd ed.). Thousand Oaks: Sage.

Taylor, S. J., & Bogdan, R. (1984). *Introduction to qualitative research methods: The search for meaning* (2nd ed.). New York: Wiley.

Uriely, N., Reichel, A., & Ron, A. (2003). Volunteering in tourism: Additional thinking. *Tourism Recreation Research, 28*(3), 57–62.

Wearing, S. L. (2003). Volunteer tourism. *Tourism Recreation Research, 28*(3), 3–4.

Wearing, S., & Deane, B. (2003). Seeking self: Leisure and tourism on common ground. *World Leisure Journal, 45*(1), 4–12.

Wearing, S., & Neil, J. (2001). Expanding sustainable tourism's conceptualization: Ecotourism, volunteerism and serious leisure. In S. F. McCool & R. N. Moisey (Eds.), *Tourism, recreation and sustainability: Linking culture and the environment* (pp. 233–254). Wallingford: CABI Publishing.

Wong, J. Y., & Lai, T. C. (2015). Celebrity attachment and behavioral intentions: The mediating role of place attachment. *International Journal of Tourism Research, 17*(2), 161–170.

Wu, M. Y., & Pearce, P. L. (2014). Chinese recreational vehicle users in Australia: A netnographic study of tourist motivation. *Tourism Management, 43*, 22–35.

Chapter 13
Paris Offscreen: Chinese and Taiwanese Tourists in Cinematic Paris

Yun-An Olivia Dung and Stijn Reijnders

> *To grasp its secret, you should not then begin with the city and move inwards toward the screen; you should begin with the screen and move outwards toward the city.*
>
> Baudrillard (1988, p. 56)

Abstract This chapter examines from a European-Asian perspective the relationship between media representations and the tourist's imaginations. We use the case of Chinese and Taiwanese tourists in Paris to investigate how these non-European tourists imagine Europe and how these imaginations are being realised, challenged and modified during concrete tourist experiences. Drawing on semi-structured interviews with tourists and field observations, this chapter shows how both the Chinese and Taiwanese tourist imagination of Europe is strongly influenced by popular representations from the media – American Hollywood films in particular. As it turns out, the Chinese and Taiwanese tourist experience of Paris is characterised by an ongoing negotiation between media-inspired fantasies and personal experiences of the 'real' Paris. As a result of this, the way these tourists imagined Europe before their visit is reinforced, but also challenged. Chinese and Taiwanese tourists tend to develop a hybrid perspective: they learn Paris in its complexity while reconstituting their own cultural identity vis-a-vis the European other.

Keywords European-Asian • Film • Imagination • Paris • Tourism

Y.-A.O. Dung (✉)
Institute for Area Studies, Leiden University, Leiden, The Netherlands
e-mail: y.a.dung@hum.leidenuniv.nl

S. Reijnders
Erasmus University Rotterdam, Rotterdam, The Netherlands
e-mail: reijnders@eshcc.eur.nl

13.1 Introduction

One afternoon in the spring of 2011, we followed the queue to enter the Louvre Museum in Paris. In front of us, there was a group of about 20 Chinese tourists listening to a man with a red flag on his bag, pointing out the spot where the actor Tom Hanks kneeled down in front of the glass pyramid in the movie *The Da Vinci Code*. Later that day, in the *Café les 2 Moulins*, two Taiwanese girls asked us to take a picture of them in front of the poster of the movie *Amélie*.

After a long period of national isolationism – following the declaration of the People's Republic of China in 1949 – Chinese outbound tourism started to take off in the early 1980s, at first mainly to Asian and Pacific regions. After the agreement "Approved Destination Status" in 2004, European Union and three Scandinavian countries opened up as new tourist destination to citizens of China. Over the last few years, rising incomes, cheaper flights, easing visa restrictions, as well as the depreciation of the euro have contributed to the rapid growth of Chinese citizens traveling to Europe. In 2010, 2.3 million Chinese visited Europe; and in 2014, the visits increased to 13.6 million (China Tourism Academy 2011, 2015).

Where do these "new" tourists go to? Without a doubt, France and in particular its capital Paris are on the top of the list. According to the Chinese official tourism statistics, France received 2.2 million Chinese visitors in 2014 (ibid, 2015). The numbers are expected to continuously increase. Large surveys conducted by private sectors suggest that France remains the most wanted visit global destination for Chinese citizens (Plowright 2015; Hotels.com 2017). According to Chen's report on Chinese tourist behavior in France, the average time Chinese tourists travel in France is 3.5 days, of which they usually spend 1.5 days in Paris (Chen 2006). France and Paris have also been the top preferred destination for Taiwanese tourists over the last few decades (Hsu 2013; Poh 2011). While "theme travel" being embraced by both the travel industry and younger Taiwanese, such as patisserie, literature, and architecture tourism are featured in travel guidebooks, online blogs, or traveling packages offered by tourist agencies (Lai 2011; Wu 2015).

How do Chinese and Taiwanese people imagine the city of Paris and from that choose this location – almost on the other side of the world – as their tourist destination? What are the crucial deciding factors in this process of destination decision-making? Part of the answer can be found in the omnipresence of Paris in (Chinese) popular culture. Of all foreign cities, Paris is one of the cities that are represented most in Chinese popular culture, with many recurring, well-known stereotypes of Paris city life, such as images of the Eiffel Tower, street corner cafés, and young couples walking the streets dressed in haute couture. For many Chinese and Taiwanese, Paris has become an adjective, a synonym of an exotic, cultural, artistic European bourgeois lifestyle (Liu 2004).

Although the precise effect remains unclear, numerous previous tourism studies have indicated that there is a strong connection between representations in the popular media and how tourists imagine their destination to be (Bolan and Williams 2008; Crouch et al. 2005; Iwashita 2006; Kim and Richardson 2003). In contemporary society, people receive a vast and complex amount of information, images, and representations of the world via visual media, particularly in the form of popular culture products such as movies and TV series. These all-pervading screen images constitute a system of understanding for individuals to imagine the world "out there" in their mind (Schofield 1996).

In recent years, the influence of the popular media on the tourist gaze has been acknowledged by the tourist industry, and diverse strategies have been developed with the goal of influencing this process, for example, by informing directors and production companies of the possibilities for shooting movies at a desired location. As Kavaratzis and Ashworth (2006, p. 185) describe, "managing the place brand becomes an attempt to influence and treat those mental maps in ways that is deemed favorable to the present circumstances and future needs of the place."

In this chapter, our intention is to show how Chinese tourists as the "newcomers" and the Taiwanese as the "individual explorers" to the European continent experience Paris when they walk through the doors of Charles de Gaulle Airport. More in particular, we will focus on the importance of popular media, cinematic representations in particular, in the process of Chinese and Taiwanese tourists' imaginations, constructions, and experiences. How do film representations contribute to the Chinese tourists' imagination of Paris? And how are these images being realized, challenged, and modified by their concrete experience of Paris? Before going into further, it is necessary to note that in the chapter, we will use the term "Chinese tourist" to include both the Chinese and Taiwanese visitors in Paris. That said, it is not our intention to dismiss existing differences between visitors from China and Taiwan (cf. Kim 2012a). Instead of representing the citizens of People's Republic of China exclusively, the term "Chinese" as used in this chapter is based on the English translation of the general term "Hua-ren" in Chinese language, which represents the group of people who share a Chinese cultural background and language and locate across nations and societies. However, where the sentence states "Chinese" next to "Taiwanese" tourists, the word "Chinese" refers more exclusively to citizens from the People's Republic of China.

13.2 Media Tourism

The observation that tourists are drawn to media locations is not new. There is a history of people going on trips to locations from famous novels. For instance, in *The Literary Tourist: Readers and Places in Romantic and Victorian Britain* (Watson 2006, p. 12), British literary scholar Nicola Watson describes how visiting locations from popular novels was a widespread phenomenon in nineteenth-century Britain. Oral folk culture also has a tradition of "legend trips": people traveling to locations – castles, bridges, and burial sites – that are tied in with popular folk or ghost stories (Ellis 1989, 2001).

Nevertheless, today, we are witnessing a popularization and wider-scale eruption of the phenomenon. Visiting "fictional" locations from "popular culture" has become an important economic activity, with a far-reaching impact on the towns and villages involved, their inhabitants, and the visiting tourists (Beeton 2005). For many cities, stimulating media tourism has become part and parcel of their city marketing policy. Hence, while nineteenth-century literary tourism was restricted to a small group of literary fans, contemporary examples lure tens of thousands of tourists every year.

This new development – variously labeled as "TV tourism," "movie tourism," "movie-induced tourism," "film-induced tourism," or simply "media tourism" – has been studied from the perspective of a wide range of disciplines, including tourism studies, media studies, and cultural geography. For example, there have been studies about the attraction of the set of *Coronation Street* at Granada Studios near Manchester (Couldry 2000) and the Manhattan TV Tour in New York (Torchin 2002). Other scholars have focused on the popularity of *Blade Runner* in Los Angeles (Brooker 2005), *Braveheart* hotspots in Scotland (Edensor 2005), The Sound of Music Tour in Salzburg (Roesch 2009), *Harry Potter* settings in the United Kingdom (Iwashita 2006), James Bond locations worldwide (Reijnders 2010), The Sopranos Tour in New Jersey (Couldry 2008), and tourism to sites where *The Lord of the Rings* was shot in New Zealand (Roesch 2009; Tzanelli 2004).

Unfortunately, much of the literature in this interdisciplinary research field has an Anglo-Saxon bias, both with regard to the study of media tourists and in terms of the societies and identities they are seen to have an impact on. There have been only a few exceptions where it concerned the relevance of non-Western tourists, for example, the investigation on the social and spatial consequences of the increasing presence of Indian Bollywood tourism in Switzerland (Frank 2011) and the studies on the popularity of South Korean television drama tourism in East Asia (e.g., Chan 2007; Kim and Wang 2012); in most of the earlier tourism studies, the gaze is usually from "the West" to "the rest."

Acknowledging this missing "Eastern gaze" in the study of tourism in general and media tourism in particular, there is an urge to identify the salient dimensions of the non-Western tourist in a Western destination. Furthermore, the boom of non-Western tourists challenges the general argument that tourism is a new form of neocolonial imperialism (Smith 2009). Such an argument is influenced by the work of Said (1995), in which the relationships between the Occident and the Orient are interpreted as part of the hegemonic nature of European culture. In Said's (1995) work, the relation between "the West" and "the rest" is defined in terms of "viewer" and "the viewed." However, different authors have shown how such a binary opposition between the West and the non-West is problematic in several ways: first, it disregards the variations within the non-Western world and the fact that each of those regions maintains different historical relations to the West; second, it denies the fact that "the rest" stereotypes the "West" as well, stereotyping is not a one way process; and, finally, the presumption of Western predominance in the interaction with other cultures leaves no room for dynamic discourse and, more generally, can be said to be at least problematic when confronted with the new political reality, for example, the economic rise of the BRIC countries (Brazil, Russia, India, and China) since the early 2000s (Bonnett 2004).

Yet, the emerging literatures on Occidentalism over the past decade have challenged such rigid affiliation (e.g., Bonnett 2004; Buruma and Margalit 2004). The non-Western narratives of the West aim to examine the image of the West from its own right, as intrinsically essential and as "possessing a degree of autonomy from Western global hegemony" (Bonnett 2004, p. 7). Although studies in Occidentalism have allowed a new dimension to inspect the relation between the West and the East, it is noticeable that most works remain historical and theoretical. There is a lack of empirical studies investigating how the idea and the image of the West have been constructed and how the non-West conceives the West in contemporary societies. What happens when "the rest" becomes the client and knocks on the door of the West?

Over the last two decades, the new tourist flow from the East to the West side of Eurasia brings us an opportunity to find out about how the West is defined, imagined, and experienced by the Easterners, within the context of tourism. How do the "exotic" differences Western society presents play out in the eyes of Chinese tourists? Are there significant differences with the standard literature of media tourism based on Western tourists?

13.3 Method

In order to understand how Chinese tourists form their image of Paris under the influence of film representations and how they experience, realize, and modify what they imagine in their actual visits, we have applied a multi-method approach, including individual interviews and ethnographic fieldwork on various film locations in Paris.

In order to recruit the interviewees, in April and May 2011 we posted the research information on various well-known Chinese-language travel-information-sharing websites that focus on Europe or France, including Backpackers (Taiwan), Eurotravel (Taiwan), PTT-Traveling (Taiwan), Tianya (China), GO2EU (China), Yododo (China), and Ziyou (China). We asked the members of the travel websites who had experienced media tourism in Paris to participate in an individual interview. Initially, we received 19 volunteers and, at the end, conducted 12 semi-structured personal interviews, based on the methodology described in Bryman (2004). In general, our respondents turned out to be young adults from urban settings with a high level of education. All respondents were interviewed via Internet telephone, except for two interviewees who preferred to do the interview via an Internet chat program – Windows Live Messenger. The aim of these interviews was to investigate in depth the role of popular media in the decision-making process of choosing the holiday destination, the tourists' imagination of Paris, and, following that, the respondents' travel experiences.

Studies of media tourism, especially on an international scale, have their limitations and difficulties. The methods we applied in this study also have their advantages and disadvantages. First, the use of online websites to recruitment offered us the potential to reach mass numbers of respondents in an efficient and cost-effective manner (Litvin and Kar 2001). Additionally, it enabled us to contact the respondents from various regions in China, Hong Kong, and Taiwan. However, the method of online recruiting could lead to the bias of limiting respondents to fervent Internet users, which could produce an unrepresentative sample frame (Litvin and Kar 2001, p. 309).

Based on the interviews with the respondents, we concluded that the experience of cinematic Paris by Chinese tourists can generally be understood as a continuous process, constituted of three stages: *the pre-visit stage* in which tourists consume destination images and construct travel intentions and expectations, *the on-site tourist experience* of the locations known from the media, and *the post-visit stage* in which tourists recollect their experiences and mentally connect the first two stages. In the next section, the results of the interviews are presented with these three stages serving as a framework.

13.4 Imagining Paris

"If you are lucky enough to have lived in Paris as a young man, then wherever you go for the rest of your life, it stays with you, for Paris is a moveable feast," Ernest Hemingway wrote in 1950. This sentence has become one of the most popular slogans about Paris. During the interviews, two respondents referred to this slogan to illustrate their initial impression of Paris, before they actually paid a visit to Paris. For most of the respondents, Paris is a city that represents nothing but itself – Parisian and French:

> How I imagined Paris is just … French! Very Parisian! There is no other word that can describe it except itself! (Wei, 24, male, Chinese)

Such "Frenchness" is contextualized by several terms the respondents used to describe the Paris from their imagination before they really traveled to Paris; this included terms such as romantic atmosphere, historical buildings, artistic culture, stylish and fashionable Parisians, the good life, and so on. These initial impressions, however, are strongly derived from their mediated experiences of popular culture, especially from movies. As we asked why they would imagine Paris in such a cultural and amorous way, two respondents mentioned the influence of French literature, but all the respondents referred to the Paris-related movies. Most popular among Paris-related films mentioned were *Amélie* (2001), *Paris, I love you* (2006), *Before Sunset* (2004), *The Da Vinci Code* (2006), and *Moulin Rouge!* (2001).

Interestingly, it has not been left unnoticed that most of these movies were American productions. The employment of stereotypical Frenchness in American Hollywood film productions is recognized by the scholars in film studies. American films tend to depict an image of France, Paris particularly, that is characterized by romance, femininity, historical representations, and unpredictability (e.g., Humbert 2003; Verdaguer 2004). With the exception of *Amélie*, the only French production in the Paris-related films mentioned most by the respondents, the Chinese tourists' image of Paris is as it turns out, to a certain level, highly influenced by American film representations. This triangular relation among the Chinese tourists, the city of Paris, and American movies reaffirms the significant power of the American movie industry, which has such an impact on global audiences and their perception of not only American culture, but the rest of the world as well.

Among the five films mentioned most, four were romantic comedies. The portrait of Paris in these films is closely related to a magical romantic aura of a daily city life where unusual things tend to happen. The movie *Paris, I love you* comprises 18 love stories set in the city of love, Paris. The movie *Amélie* features a girl who finds love after a series of heroic acts to help the people around her. In the movie, the director portrays the city of Paris as a colorful dreamscape by using computer-generated art (Mitchell 2001). This creates an exotic and unrealistically romantic atmosphere for the audience to experience and imagine the city. In the movie *Before Sunset*, Paris is a still picture with the golden light of sunshine and the flowing water of the Seine (Scoot 2004). Two lovers meet each other after 9 years of separation and enjoy various kinds of philosophical debate over life and society while sharing the view of the city within a limited timeframe. In these movies, Paris is a dreamland filled with romantic possibilities. This characteristic of Paris seems to provide an idealistic image for the tourists to fulfill the needs of romantic escapism and for extraordinary experiences.

According to the respondents, the scenery of Paris is not just a background for the story to take place. The city itself plays a major role in these movies, creating and sustaining the amorous atmosphere which is seen as a defining characteristic of romantic movies. As respondent Jia-Ling (35, female, Chinese) stated, "You cannot imagine the stories happening somewhere other than Paris. If you take Paris out of these movies, you take the magic out of them." A panoramic view of Paris is shown in all the movies selected. The picture of Paris in the Chinese tourist's mind is inextricably connected to the pictures on the screen.

Yet, not all the respondents shared the image of almost a romantic fairy-tale Paris before their trips. Hua-Dong (24, male, Chinese) perceived Paris as an "over-praised cosmopolitan city" that "because it is too popular and thus it loses its uniqueness and the adventurous spirit to travel to." In addition, some respondents were informed that Paris is not as civilized, clean, and romantic as seen on the screen. Most of the respondents found it hard to believe that a "dirty" Paris is also very much part of reality. This conflicting information gives the respondents the urge to clarify the truth themselves.

Other factors also contributed to the image of Paris, partly in line with the impact of French films. For example, five of the respondents mentioned they had French in school as a second foreign language. The familiarity with the language, for the respondents, not only reflects their image of French culture but also re-enhances their adoration of it:

> At the beginning I had been exposed to some French works, like translated French novels and films. So I started to show an interest in the language. But, well, I was also kind of already interested in French culture. That's why I watched those French movies ... I don't

know which comes first actually ... It's like chicken and the egg paradox. I just like its culture, I guess! (Shu-Jyuan, 29, female, Taiwanese)

The statements of Shu-Jyuan indicated the fact that the fondness for the French language and the reference to French films amounts to a reciprocal causation. But what we can assume is that language brings the respondents closer to a culture. Within these French-culture-favored surroundings, France, or the city of Paris, becomes a dreamland that is familiar in their mind's eye and that needs to be unveiled.

However, this leads us to the question of why French culture or, to be more specific, the "Parisian-ness" on screen is conceived as so "charming" that it attracts Chinese/Taiwanese people to travel almost halfway around the world to visit it? For most of the respondents, what they yearn to experience in Paris is the atmosphere, the "European" or "French" atmosphere that is different or even opposite to their Chinese cultural background and only appears within the media as "the distant other" (Silverstone 2007):

> I think what I expected the most was just to experience the atmosphere in Paris. It feels like the people there are kind of idle, relaxing, you know, like there's nothing to be in a hurry about or be busy about. They just seem to enjoy their lives. It's totally different from the way we are in China. All we do is just work, study and, pursue a socialized and successful life. (Jia-Ling, 22, female, Taiwanese)

> The city presents this feeling of ... For the Easterners, the typical elegance of European culture, a romantic, humanist, and artistic atmosphere. That's something different from where we are from. I think it is the reason that attracts me the most. (Huei-Wen, 23, female, Chinese)

The adoration of Paris was in line with the comparison between the self and the others. For both Taiwanese and Chinese respondents, Paris stood as an opposite other to their Eastern cultural identity. Paris is imagined by these travelers as a representation of Western culture, with the exterior of the classic European cityscape and an inner culture of bourgeois lifestyle that has a sharp distinction with East Asian society. Such an imagination, however, surprisingly does not differ between Taiwanese tourists and tourists from mainland China. To explain this shared similarity, we consider that first, the imaginations of Paris both from Taiwanese and Chinese tourists are influenced by the same source: American movies. In addition, as we have been arguing, the imagination of Paris results from the symbolic opposition between the self (Chinese culture) and the other (Western or European culture). Partly due to this binary opposition, small and subtle differences between Taiwanese and Chinese culture are underplayed.

To draw on the concept of collectivism or situation centeredness (Hung and Chen 2005) would further explain the self-perceived comparison between the East and the West by the respondents. According to Triandis (2001), people in societies characterized by collectivism give priority to the goals and values of the in-group, such as family, work, nation, and so on, instead of their own. In Chinese culture, self is generally defined by the relations an individual has with those around him or her, with a focus on others' needs and expectations (Gao et al. 1996).

This trait is mostly recognized when the respondents attempt to describe Frenchness in contrast to themselves. For example, respondent Jia-Ling expressed her adoration for the lifestyle of the French because "they know what they want, and they are living it. That's something different, different from me, from us [the Chinese]." In these Chinese tourists' eyes, Parisians live a "quality" life that is based on personal interest and taste, which is different from the ordinary life routine in East Asian society. The "exotic" images of Paris motivate the tourists to travel to the city and to experience this distinctive pleasure of life. Therefore, in their journeys, the Chinese tourists seek out particular images to confirm their imagination, for example, French people sitting in a street café on a random afternoon, young couples lying in the sun on the banks of the river Seine, or various bizarre performances by street artists. This romantic idea of Paris is constructed with the differentiation between the ordinary and extraordinary in mind, the East and the West, and the self and the other.

13.5 Experiencing Paris

According to the respondents, the most popular film locations visited by the Chinese tourists were the "Café les 2 Moulins" from the movie *Amélie*, "The Shakespeare Book Store" from the movie *Before Sunset*, the tomb of Oscar Wilde from the movie *Paris, I love you*, the Moulin Rouge from the movie *Moulin Rouge*, and the Louvre Museum from the movie *The Da Vinci Code*. For the respondents, their understanding of the city of Paris is in part a construct of representations from films. Therefore, those film locations functioned as anchors for the tourists to identify their expectations and imaginations and to experience Paris.

However, besides depicting their personal traveling map, the film locations also provide an affectionate connection for the tourists to experience the cityscape. By identifying and visiting the film locations, the Chinese tourists felt a sense of familiarity in the foreign city. In the context of media tourism, it is known that the audience tends to develop a personalized feeling of attachment toward the fictional characters as well as the filmed locations, and hence, the wish to visit them arises (Kim 2012b). One of the respondents, Shu-Jyuan, told us that the movie *Before Sunset* has a significant meaning to her, due to its relation to the relationship between her and her husband:

> My husband and I both like the movie a lot. What happened to the main characters is kind of like the story of my husband and me. We passed each other by but met again and decided to stay together. That's why we wanted to make Paris our honeymoon destination. We feel it's necessary to visit these scenes ourselves. (Shu-Jyuan, 29, female, Taiwanese)

In her story, Shu-Jyuan recognized herself and her husband in the characters from the film. In order to strengthen and realize such recognition, she and her husband visited various film locations of *Before Sunset*. Once there, they mimicked acts or scenes from the movie. For example, just like Jesse and Celine, the main characters in *Before Sunset*, Shu-Jyuan and her husband went to the Seine to walk along the riverbank. And, in line with *Before Sunset*, they also entered one of the boats. On the boat, they talked about their love as well as the love between Jesse and Celine. By visiting the places where this "fictional" romance happened, and by making a connection between the two love stories, Shu-Jyuan and her husband symbolically anchor their love to the city of Paris.

These experiences bring to mind Reijnders' study on "places of the imagination." According to Reijnders (2011), our world is full of locations that derive their significance from the fact that they were used as the background for popular narratives in literature, television, or cinema. These "places of the imagination" offer fans the possibility to have a transcendent experience between two worlds: an imagined world on the one hand and that which is considered to be the "real" world on the other.

However, in the current study, the respondents' experiences were often a little less symbolic and hyperreal than those in the work of Reijnders (2011). Although the respondents did feel the urge to visit the places that were once in their minds, and although they had personal connections to the locations, at the same time, many of the respondents denied a strong sense of a transcendent experience. For example, Jing and Wei both described how their experience at the location was rather superficial:

> When I had just got there I really felt so excited. It was like, after all the thousands of miles of travelling, I could finally see the place. But that's it. I took a picture, and thought: so ... this is what it looks like in real life. And I was gone. (Jing, 25, female, Taiwanese)

> I felt that when you were there, you wouldn't experience some kind of sensational, surreal, movie-ish feeling, but just the feeling that the surrounding gave to you at that moment, in the reality. Of course you will think about 'oh, that's where it happened in the film!' But most of feeling was current, what you really saw with your eyes. (Wei, 24, male, Chinese)

Take, for example, Jing. She stayed only a few minutes in front of Pont Neuf. She recognized the bridge from the movie and decided to take a photograph of the bridge to document this experience. But the engagement Jing had with the "real" Pont Neuf did not go beyond the level of recognizing and photographing the bridge. Whereas for some tourists visiting media sites can become a transcendent experience, Jing's experience was rather superficial and short-lived. The same can be said of Wei. When visiting a location from *Amélie*, Wei recognized the scene, but his attention quickly shifted to other aspects of this street location, most noticeably the street artists who were trying to sell their works there. Although it is difficult to generalize our findings based on such a small amount of respondents, the experiences of our Chinese/Taiwanese respondents do seem to differ from most existing studies on media tourism, where the experience of media tourists is characterized and described as an emotional and significant event (Beeton 2005; Reijnders 2011).

There are some possible explanations for this difference. First, in his work, Reijnders (2011) analyzes three case studies of media tourism which focus on serial products: the detective television series, the series of James Bond movies, and the numerous Dracula movies. Due to the fact that these serial media products have been available for a relatively long time and in various forms, it causes a deep degree of viewer involvement and a sense of emotional friendship/relationship to the fictional characters (Reijnders 2011). This finding is in line with what Kim and Long (2012) theoretically suggested: "personalized viewing experiences through gradually intensified identification, empathy, emotional connection, and parasocial interaction are associated more with TV soap operas than films" (p. 178).

Without the continuation of storylines and the consistency of themes throughout the Paris-related movies, two hours of movie watching gives less chance for the viewers to develop such close bonds with the fictional character or to know the details of the movie as opposed to themed media products. According to the respondents, there was hardly anyone who had watched a "Paris" movie more than three times. Instead of becoming acquainted with all features, designs, and details of the movies, only a few interesting moments in the movies as well as a holistic impression could be recollected. Clearly, the connections between the respondents and the various Paris movies are not of the same level as the ones between the fans and the TV series in Reijnders' (2011) study.

Besides familiarity with the movies' details, the wider history of the city of Paris also plays an important role in the respondents' different experiences of media tourism. Paris is one of the most popular tourist destinations in the world. The Moulin Rouge, the river Seine, the tomb of Oscar Wilde in the cemetery Père Lachaise, and the Louvre Museum are all famous for their own history and are visited by numerous tourists from all over the world. Given this, the symbolic meanings created by the movies are only part of a wider network of signifiers.

Moreover, most sites turn out to be rather crowded. Silent moments of private meditation could easily be disturbed by other tourists. Urry's (2002) theoretical concept of the gazes could help us to understand this process. In Urry's work, the tourist gaze is divided into two different types: the romantic gaze and the collective gaze. A romantic form of tourist gaze is one "in which the emphasis is on a private, personal and semi-spiritual relationship with the object of the gaze" (Urry 2002, p. 43). What people gaze upon are ideal representations that are being internalized from various media forms. The concept of the romantic gaze is very much in line with what Reijnders (2011) discusses about the transcendent experiences, which media tourists undergo when visiting the movie/TV series' locations. Both arguments contend that the objects of the tourist gaze are appreciated through an indirect experience of reality and via the images already in their mind. However, this very personal appreciation can be interrupted by the fact that there are too many people involved on the locations. Thus, it eventually becomes a collective gaze (e.g., Roesch 2009).

The collective gaze is a sort of tourist gaze that requires the presence of large numbers of other people to share the view. This sharing of the atmosphere with others takes away the unique connection between the objects and the viewer. For example, standing in front of the *Moulin Rouge*, respondent Yi-Ting noticed that she was not the only one there, but felt part of a large group of tourists. This sense of the mediocre broke the special connection between her and the film location. The romantic gaze transformed into a collective gaze:

> I was there ... with a lot of other tourists who were taking photos of the building. So I did too. And then I just went on to the next destination. (Yi-Ting, 25, female, Chinese)

The disruption of personal moments was not solely caused by other tourists. According to the respondents, the local people near the sites or the interactions with their travel companions could also decrease the possibility of experiencing the crossing between inside and outside of the media world:

> When I was in the Park, I tried to recall what happened here in the movie. But then, a police car passed by; a man sat down next to me. It was quite difficult to concentrate on your own thoughts since there were too many interesting things happening in reality. (Zhi-Cheng, 35, male, Taiwanese)

Transcendence between reality and imagination can be a delicate affair. It can be easily intruded by various occurrences. As Zhi-Cheng concludes, this transcendent moment cannot be forced; it is something that only happens "when it comes to you."

13.6   Recollecting Paris

According to the respondents, the trip to Paris offered them not only something they had already expected but also something new – a Paris beyond their imagination. Some of the respondents mentioned that before their trip, they were informed by other friends or by the messages on travelers' websites about the "dark side of Paris." However, one of the Chinese respondents, Fang-Yi, said most of the Chinese tourists "couldn't buy it" until they walked out of the airport.

For the Chinese tourists, this "unimagined" Paris is described as rubbish in the streets, smelly subways, horrible traffic, a non-English-speaking environment, and the presence of such large numbers of many former French-colonial ethnic minorities:

> It was just so dirty almost everywhere! It's nothing like you would imagine before you went there. It's Paris! How would anyone imagine that Paris is a dirty city? I think even my city is cleaner than Paris. (Zhi-Cheng, 35, male, Taiwanese)

Most tourists tend to understand a foreign society by viewing the public as a homogeneous mass. This is especially the case with Chinese tourists in Paris. For most of the respondents, Paris, or French in general, is the culturally and geographically distant other that was known primarily from the cinema screen. The imagination and understanding of the city was constructed based on its mediated appearances as classical, romantic, fashionable, and civilized. In Chinese eyes, Paris was the city which represented ideal Western/European culture, based on civilization, reason, bourgeois lifestyle and prosperity, and to some degree the ideal role model for contemporary Asian cities. However, experiencing "the other side of Paris" led the tourists to reconsider the culture of Western deification in China and Taiwan and to reconfirm with regard to their Chinese cultural identity that – in the words of Yi-Ting – "we are not so bad!" This comparison between their Eastern hometown and the Paris of the "Far West" was made by the Chinese tourists with respect to details from their trip. For example, according to the Chinese tourists, the French are more easily offended by other people staring at them, they are less polite when confronted with strangers, and they do not follow official regulations and so on. These unexpected views and experiences led the tourists to reevaluate their own cultural Chinese identity:

> I think Parisian people are just a little bit self-centered. They don't care what other people think. If they don't want to talk English, they just won't. If they don't want to pay for the metro ticket, they just jump over the gate. It really confused me. Maybe just because I'm Asian and we follow the rules. (Fang-Yi, 21, female, Chinese)

In this quote, Fang-Yi uses West/East cultural differences to explain the differences between her stereotypical view of Western society and the experienced reality. Recognizing the individualism within Western society led her to redefine her own "Asian" identity. Following this argument, the boundary between Eastern society and Western society was redrawn based on relatively cultural differences with fewer hierarchical relationships.

Another element of the "other Paris" – as highlighted during the interviews – consisted of the ethnic diversity of the Parisian street life. All the respondents mentioned the fact that they were surprised by the many "non-White" people in Paris, which was a kind of a cultural shock for them:

> It's like there were no French people in Paris. Maybe it's because of the immigrants. There are a lot of black people in Paris, with their tribal clothes. It was exotic, but not in the way that you had imagined. (Jyun-Ming, 22, male, Chinese)

This sense of unfamiliarity can be explained in two ways. First, from a historical perspective, we can see how the Chinese tourists tend to see the world in terms of China/Taiwan and its main counterparts, namely, Europe/United States and Japan, whereas, for example, Africa is hardly mentioned (e.g., Dikötter 2005). This is consistent with Liu's study that for most the cultural Chinese, European, or Western society is perceived as the White society (Liu 2004). Second, although there are 50 different ethnic minorities officially recognized in China, over 90% of the population is classified as Han, the ethnic Chinese (Dikötter 2005). In this sense, although there are many cultural, linguistic, and regional differences within China and Taiwan – as there are within Europe – there are relatively fewer differences in physical characteristics such as skin color. As a result, encountering "non-White" people in Paris was not what the respondents were expecting or, in a fundamental sense, familiar with. For most respondents, this created a sense of discomfort. A similar observation was also made by the Japanese psychiatrist Hiroaki Ota in the 1980s. He used the term "Paris syndrome" to describe the negative cultural shock experienced by the Japanese tourists (Viala et al. 2004).

The Chinese tourists are satisfied when they encounter the objects and settings which correspond to their preestablished imagination. These sights are usually related to views of European historical buildings, the banks of the river Seine, the artistic shops and cafés, the random street artists, the fashion on display in the Avenue des Champs-Élysées, and, last but not least, the Paris film locations. These contribute to the sense of familiarity and to the satisfaction derived from traveling. They confirm the romance, art, and history of picturesque Paris. Thus, it is fair to say that satisfaction seems to stem from anticipation, from seeking out the pre-configurations of the imagination.

At the same time, the observation of different scenes in different districts of Paris led some of the Chinese tourists to acknowledge the "real" Paris – a versatile, multifaceted city, beyond the stereotypes of the city of love. For these tourists, their journeys sparked a process of negotiation in realizing their imagination and at the same time in revealing and accepting the other side of Paris. This sense of reassured pleasure and adoration also made most of the respondents willing to travel back to Paris again.

13.7   Conclusion

Previous studies have indicated the strong relationship between representations in the popular media and the tourist imagination. However, these studies were largely based on the perspective of Western tourists. This chapter has used the case of Chinese and Taiwanese tourists in Paris to investigate Eastern media tourism to Europe. More in particular, we have focused on how popular media – film representations in particular – contribute to the Chinese and Taiwanese tourists' imagination of Paris and how these images are being realized, challenged, and modified during their actual experience of Paris.

To answer these questions, we have analyzed three aspects of the experience of Chinese and Taiwanese tourists in Paris: the imagination, the experience, and the recollection of cinematic Paris. First, regarding the imagination, the results of the individual interviews illustrate the crucial role that media representations play in forming a system of understanding for imagining the destination. For these tourists, Paris is not only an objective realm out there but also a place in their minds with strong symbolic meanings, created by a series of images, signs, and symbols represented on the screen. Regardless of the different levels of prior experiences associated with French culture or the city itself, the respondents shared a similar imaginary picture of Paris before their journey: an image of a bourgeois lifestyle, romantic atmosphere, and civilized culture. This image turned Paris into a dreamland for the Chinese and Taiwanese tourists and compelled them to visit it.

As the interviews showed, the Chinese imagination of Paris is based on a fundamental binary opposition between the self and the other, the ordinary and the extraordinary, and the East and the West. In these Chinese and Taiwanese tourists' eyes, Paris is imagined as a homogeneous city featuring characteristics fundamentally different from those in Chinese societies. What Paris represents is an opposite system of values: one of individualism, in which personal interest takes precedence over social obligations. On the one hand, this imagination of Paris is highly influenced by occidental stereotypical narratives of the East and the West. On the other hand, we recognized a third party that contributed to the formation of such an image:

the American view of Paris, as experienced by Chinese through the medium of American movies. Paris is seen and idealized by Chinese and Taiwanese people based on American visions.

During their stay in Paris, most respondents visited various film locations. These film locations are seen to serve as important physical points of reference, resulting in a perceptional framework for the tourists to examine "what they imagined" Paris to be. However, the Chinese and Taiwanese tourist experience of the movie sites turned out to be rather mundane, especially when compared to existing literature on media tourism. Most Chinese and Taiwanese tourists had little knowledge of the specific features, designs, and details of the movies. Nor did the respondents report any "spiritual" connection with the locations they visited. This is strikingly different from earlier studies on media tourism, where media tourists are sometimes referred to as "pilgrims" and are reported to have deep, emotional experiences while being at these "lieux d'imagination" (Reijnders 2011). Therefore, although the Chinese and Taiwanese tourists tended to visit various film locations in Paris, the experience of the Chinese and Taiwanese tourists at the individual sites was on that level remarkably different from those of "media pilgrims."

How did these Chinese and Taiwanese tourists recollect their journey, after having returned home? Most respondents mentioned the fact that their previous stereotypes of Paris, based on American movies, were partially confirmed but also challenged by visiting the "real" Paris. In their journeys, so the respondents said, they quickly discovered "the other side" of Paris, which was beyond the occidental stereotypes and their mediated imagination, one which was characterized by rubbish and dirty streets, arrogant people, and racially mixed populations. For them, their visit to Paris turned out to be an ongoing negotiation between media-inspired fantasies and personal travel experiences. At the end, having experienced the "real" Paris awoke these Chinese and Taiwanese tourists from their imaginations and gave rise to a new hybrid subjective perspective in evaluating and re-appreciating the city. Along their journey, these Chinese and Taiwanese tourists learned Paris in its complexity while reconstituting their own Chinese cultural identity vis-a-vis the European other. Consequently, the traditional relationship between Western society and the Asian home, based on the supposed idealization of the former, changed along the way.

Acknowledgments This chapter is the updated version of a paper publication in *Tourist Studies* (Dung and Reijnders 2013). Our thanks to this journal for their valuable reviews and their permission for (partial) reuse of the existing text.

References

Baudrillard, J. (1988). *America*. London: Verso.
Beeton, S. (2005). *Film induced tourism*. Clevedon: Channel View Publications.
Bolan, P., & Williams, L. (2008). The role of image in service promotion: Focusing on the influence of film on consumer choice within tourism. *International Journal of Consumer Studies, 32*(4), 382–390.

Bonnett, A. (2004). *Idea of the West-culture, politics and history*. London: Palgrave Macmillan.

Brooker, W. (2005). The blade runner experience: Pilgrimage and liminal space. In W. Brooker (Ed.), *The blade runner experience: The legacy of a science fiction classic* (pp. 11–30). New York: Columbia University Press.

Bryman, A. (2004). *Social research methods*. Oxford: Oxford University Press.

Buruma, I., & Margalit, A. (2004). *Occidentalism: The West in the eyes of its enemy*. New York: Penguin Group (USA) Inc.

Chan, B. (2007). Film-induced tourism in Asia: A case study of Korean television drama and female viewers' motivation to visit Korea. *Tourism Culture & Communication, 7*(3), 207–224.

Chen, Q. (2006). Guanyu "zhongguo gongmin fu faguo luyou shichang" de fenxi yu yanjiu [the analyses and research on Chinese citizens in the French tourism market]. *Shichang Luntan, 23*, 27–28.

China Tourism Academy. (2011). *Annual report of China inbound tourism development 2010*. Beijing: China Education Press.

China Tourism Academy. (2015). *Annual report of China inbound tourism development 2014*. Beijing: China Education Press.

Couldry, N. (2000). *The place of media power: Pilgrims and witnesses of the media age*. London: Routledge.

Couldry, N. (2008). Pilgrimage in mediaspace: Continuities and transformations. *Etnofoor, 20*(1), 63–74.

Crouch, D., Jackson, R., & Thompson, F. (2005). *The media and the tourist imagination: Converging cultures*. London: Routledge.

Dikötter, F. (2005). Race in China. In P. Nyiri & J. Breidenbach (Eds.), *China insideout: Contemporary Chinese nationalism and transnationalism* (pp. 177–204). Budapest: Central European University Press.

Dung, O., & Reijnders, S. (2013). Paris offscreen: Chinese tourists in cinematic Paris. *Tourist Studies, 13*(3), 287–303.

Edensor, T. (2005). Mediating William Wallace. Audio-visual technologies in tourism. In D. Crouch, R. Jackson, & F. Thompson (Eds.), *The media and the tourist imagination: Converging cultures* (pp. 105–118). London: Routledge.

Ellis, B. (1989). Death by folklore: Ostension, contemporary legend, and murder. *Western Folklore, 48*(3), 201–220.

Ellis, B. (2001). *Aliens, ghosts, and cults: Legends we live*. Jackson: University Press of Mississippi.

Frank, S. (2011). *When the rest enters the West: Bollywood in Switzerland*. Paper presented at the Society Internationale d'Ethnologie et de Folklore – International Conference, Lisbon, Portugal, 17–21 April.

Gao, G., Stella, T., & Gudykunst, W. B. (1996). *The handbook of Chinese psychology*. New York: Oxford University Press.

Hotels.com. (2017). *Chinese international travel monitor 2016*. Retrieved from http://www.citm-hotels.com

Hsu, R. W. (2013). *Taiwan luyou shu: yi bali weili* [Guidebooks in Taiwan: A case study on Paris] (Unpublished M.A. dissertation). National Taiwan Normal University, Taipei.

Humbert, B. (2003). Screening france. *French Politics, Culture & Society, 21*(2), 81–94.

Hung, L., & Chen, P. (2005). Taiwan zishang renyuan dui xifang zishang yu huaren wenhua xin-nian chongtu de zhuanhua jingyan [Cultural shock in counseling: The experiences of Taiwanese counselors]. *Jiaoyu Xinlixue Bao, 37*(1), 79–98.

Iwashita, C. (2006). Media representation of the UK as a destination for Japanese tourists: Popular culture and tourism. *Tourist Studies, 6*(1), 59–77.

Kavaratzis, M., & Ashworth, G. J. (2006). City branding: An effective assertion of identity or a transitory marketing trick? *Place Branding, 2*(3), 183–194.

Kim, S. (2012a). A cross-cultural study of on-site film-tourism experiences among Chinese, Japanese, Taiwanese and Thai visitors to the Daejanggeum Theme Park, South Korea. *Current Issues in Tourism, 15*(8), 759–776.

Kim, S. (2012b). Audience involvement and film tourism experiences: Emotional places, emotional experiences. *Tourism Management, 33*(2), 387–396.

Kim, S., & Long, P. (2012). Touring TV soap operas: Genre in film tourism research. *Tourist Studies, 12*(1), 173–185.

Kim, H., & Richardson, S. L. (2003). Motion picture impacts on destination images. *Annals of Tourism Studies, 30*(1), 216–237.

Kim, S., & Wang, H. (2012). From television to the film set: Korean drama Daejanggeum drives Chinese, Taiwanese, Japanese and Thai audiences to screen-tourism. *International Communication Gazette, 74*(5), 423–442.

Lai, H. S. (2011). *Woguo luxingye ouzhou zhuti luyou zhi yanjiu - yi MIT luxingshe weili* [Theme travel in Europe: A study of MIT Travel Service] (Unpublished M.A. dissertation). National Chengchi University, Taipei.

Litvin, S. W., & Kar, G. H. (2001). E-surveying for tourism research: Legitimate tool or a researcher's fantasy? *Journal of Travel Research, 39*(3), 308–314.

Liu, L. (2004). Masque et Mirror: L'image de Paris à travers un spot publicitaire. In *City and modernity international symposium paper collection* (pp. 169–185). Taipei: Department of French, Tamkang University.

Mitchell, E. (2001, November 2). Little Miss Sunshine as urban sprite. *The New York Times.* Retrieved from http://www.nytimes.com/2001/11/02/movies/film-review-little-miss-sunshine-as-urban-sprite.html

Plowright, M. (2015, April 30). The top dream destination for Chinese tourists: It's France. *Financial Times.* Retrieved from https://www.ft.com/content/fe668d18-ef1f-11e4-87dc-00144feab7de

Poh, S. B. (2011). *Taiwan nuxing haiwai zizhu luxing jingli zhi yanjiu* [A study of Taiwan women's overseas independent travel experiences] (Unpublished M.A. dissertation). National Taiwan Normal University, Taipei.

Reijnders, S. (2010). On the trail of 007. Media pilgrimages into the world of James Bond. *Area, 42*(3), 369–377.

Reijnders, S. (2011). *Places of the imagination: Media, tourism, culture.* Farnham: Ashgate Publishing.

Roesch, S. (2009). *The experience of film location tourists.* Bristol: Channel View Publications.

Said, E. (1995). *Orientalism.* London: Penguin Books.

Schofield, P. (1996). Cinematographic images of a city. *Tourism Management, 17*(5), 333–340.

Scoot, A. O. (2004, July 2). Reunited, still talking, still uneasy. *The New York Times.* Retrieved from http://www.nytimes.com/2004/07/02/movies/film-review-reunited-still-talking-still-uneasy.html

Silverstone, R. (2007). *Media and morality: On the rise of the mediapolis.* Cambridge: Polity Press.

Smith, M. K. (2009). *Issues in cultural tourism studies.* London: Routledge.

Torchin, L. (2002). Location, location, location. The destination of the Manhattan TV Tour. *Tourist Studies, 2*(3), 247–266.

Triandis, H. C. (2001). Individualism-collectivism and personality. *Journal of Personality, 69*(6), 907–924.

Tzanelli, R. (2004). Constructing the "cinematic tourist". The "sign industry" of The Lord of the Rings. *Tourist Studies, 4*(1), 21–42.

Urry, J. (2002). *The tourist gaze: Leisure and travel in contemporary societies.* London: SAGE.

Verdaguer, P. (2004). Hollywood's Frenchness: Representations of the French in American films. *Contemporary French and Francophone Studies, 8*(4), 441–451.

Viala, A., Ota, H., Vacheron, M. N., Martin, P., & Caroli, F. (2004). Les Japonais en voyage pathologique à Paris: un modèle original de prise en charge transculturelle. *Nervure Supplément, 17,* 31–34.

Watson, N. J. (2006). *The literary tourist: Readers and places in romantic & Victorian Britain.* Basingstoke: Palgrave Macmillan.

Wu, H. Y. (2015). *Bali tiandian meishi guanguang: Taiwan guanguangke de wenhua xiaofei shijian* [Patisserie tourism in Paris: On the practices of Taiwanese tourists] (Unpublished M.A. dissertation). National Taiwan Normal University, Taipei.

Chapter 14
Home Away *at* Home: Mediating Spaces of Tourism and Narratives of Belonging in the German Village of South Korea

Desmond Wee

Abstract Current research of film tourism has been garnering interest, but still mainly premises managerial perspectives on destination management, lacking more holistic approaches to critical implications of film tourism. It becomes pertinent to explore film tourism in terms of tourist experiences comprising the reliving and reconstitution of fictional events (not always) based on media narratives. This paper considers how tourism 'takes place' *in media* (as content) and *touring uses film* (as process) as inherent parts of spatial, liminal and mediated experience. It centres on the German village in Namhae, South Korea, which was built over a decade ago as a tribute to the Korean workers who lived in Germany as *Gastarbeiter*. It explores the question of identities of the 'locals' as portrayed in the film, 'Endstation der Sehnsüchte' by Cho Sunghyung and juxtaposes this alongside the huge influx of 'tourists' indulging in photographing experience on the film set of the Korean TV drama 'Couple or Trouble'. What surfaces in this research is a complex mediation of experiences that explore the nexus between the impacts of film and television on the cultural heritage of residents in film tourism locations and the convergence of mediatisation, globalisation and identity through film.

Keywords Media • Tourism • Identity • German village • South Korea

14.1 Introduction

Places are being embodied and reproduced through mediation in a constantly evolving world. They are performed on unstable stages as they are being imagined and reimagined. But what if these places constitute spaces of belonging? How do we then understand the significance of home in the material and affective lives of

D. Wee (✉)
Karlshochschule International University, Karlstraße 36 – 38, Karlsruhe 76133, Germany
e-mail: dwee@karlshochschule.de

© Springer Nature Singapore Pte Ltd. 2018
S. Kim, S. Reijnders (eds.), *Film Tourism in Asia*, Perspectives on Asian Tourism, DOI 10.1007/978-981-10-5909-4_14

people as home is being destabilized? How does one attribute identity if 'home' and 'away' are being diffused? How do we make ourselves at home through new forms of mobilities such as tourism? These questions underpin the importance of exploring the relation (and mediation) between narratives of belonging and spaces of tourism in terms of experiences. This chapter centres on the German Village on the island of Namhae, South Korea, that was built over a decade ago as a tribute to the Korean workers who lived in Germany as *Gastarbeiter*, as portrayed in the film 'Endstation der Sehnsüchte' (Home from Home) by Cho Sung-Hyung (2009). It explores the question of identity and what it means to be 'local' when these *Gastarbeiter* returned from Germany to live in Korea. This nostalgia of 'returning home' is juxtaposed alongside the huge influx of 'tourists' indulging in photographing an authentic 'German' experience in Namhae. What surfaces in this research are the impacts of film and television on the cultural identities of residents in film tourism locations and the convergence of mediatization, globalization and identity through film.

Film tourism does not need much explanation especially with the emphasis of films in connection to place branding and marketing by various DMOs, many notable cases being 'Lord of the Rings' in New Zealand, 'Brave Heart' in Scotland, 'Bollywood' in Switzerland (see also Chap. 3 in this volume) and 'Hallyu' in South Korea. Current research of film tourism has been garnering interest but still mainly premises managerial perspectives on destination management, lacking a more interdisciplinary approach to critical implications of film tourism. For example, Hudson and Ritchie (2006) approach film tourism from destination marketing perspectives, exploring product placement on destinations as product and its influence on tourism. In a similar vein, Beeton (2005) is concerned with the impact of tourism on destinations. However, in both cases, the analysis is focused on the visitation of a place based on the result of the representation of a destination on screen. This chapter provides a more holistic approach and aims to look at media and place from critical perspectives, in line with more recent work done on 'cinematic tourism' (Tzanelli 2007) and 'media tourism' (Reijnders 2011).

Tzanelli (2007) considers cinematic tourism as a condition of globalization incorporating both technological advancement that promotes at the same time, tourist synchronicity and hybridization alongside economic development. Following from this, it becomes pertinent to construct, more than just film tourism, a notion of media(ted) tourism in terms of how tourist experiences comprise the reliving and reconstitution of fictional events (sometimes, but not always) based on media narratives. Yet this tourism may also be *mediated* itself, in how media is *appropriated as experience* or, in other words, how tourism is experienced. Hence, cinematic representations of place are not only the lure of tourism but also a reflection of how tourism and the everyday are practised. We need to reconsider who the tourist and the local are based on encounters of other and the constant reconstructions of identity (see below on 'Endstation der Sehnsüchte'). Reijnders (2011, p. 17) describes how 'the phenomenon of media tourism derives its power and popularity from the symbolic contrast between imagination and reality' and how places of imagination involve not only physical locations but also the underlying processes in which the imagination 'takes place'. Jansson (2007, p. 8) in a similar regard also emphasizes a connection between media and tourism that 'takes place and produces space through texture', positing that society, spaces and places in tourism are incorporated into fundamental communication processes. The notion of 'taking place', as opposed to a static understanding of place or destination, is reproduced through spatialities in which embodied performances and practices are facilitated within complex infrastructure, networks and mobilities.

Film tourism is prevalent in South Korea as a unique cultural phenomenon, and this is, amongst a few other things, related to the growth of South Korea's culture industries, most visible being Hallyu or the Korean wave (Lee 2008; Shim 2008; see also Chap. 10 in this volume) and the cultivation of an avid following across Asia. However, Hallyu, and its association with mass hysteria, is only peripheral to this chapter since the aim is to explore intersections with an embodied creation of place, in which multiple meanings are constructed by various actors. Much less attention has been given to the study of media and its manifestation of meanings within the circuit of tourism and the circulation of imaginaries that reveals 'how cultural representations are mixed together, consumed, and interpreted' (Salazar 2012, p. 867). It is imperative to understand how viewers circulate amongst the mediated, symbolic goods, rather than the other way around (see Lash and Friedman 1992).

Mediation is hence the affordance of various modes of media, its circulation and its connection to the notion of home and tourism. Yet mediation is also the stuff that 'takes place' within and across people and space, providing deeper ways of understanding the circulation of people. This chapter considers how tourism 'takes place' *in media* (as content) and *in touring using film* (as process) through spatial, liminal and mediated experience. It provides a critical analysis incorporating reflexive and visual methodology to explore how identities are being configured through local narratives and practice in this era of transformative change as exemplified by the German Village in South Korea. To achieve this, an exploratory research based on secondary sources comprising of literature research and Internet discourses, alongside a visit to the German Village, was conducted. The following analysis shows how discursive ideas of identities are constructed in the light of everyday intimacies.

14.2 Mediation Taking Place, Making Home

'Endstation der Sehnsüchte' (Cho 2009) provided the basis not for film tourism per se but a tourism in which mediation took centre stage on several levels. It documented the process of mediation in reflexive ways, describing the conditions for the construction of the German Village in Korea as a physical place and, at the same time, a fabricated one in which the cultivation and displacement of identities were endemic. On another level, the film referred to the phenomenon of tourism, one in which Korean tourists became fascinated with a real German Village that suddenly appeared from nowhere on an island famed for its rustic charm, rural tranquility and garlic plantations. What was not alluded to in the film was the Korean drama series 'Couple or trouble' that provided a simultaneous impetus for visitation, this time in search of its film location and set. This more traditional idea of 'media tourism' colluded to further the greater tourism project, which in turn served to question the identity project of what it meant for the residents to have returned 'home'.

Media tourism is perhaps a better description of the phenomenon in the 'German Village', rather than film tourism because of the multiple intersections 'taking place' across various media. The making of place and the reflection on the making engage both deeper levels of sedimentation within narratives and, at the same time, their dispersal of meanings based on mediation. Jenkins (2006) reiterates this as the flow of content across multiple media platforms or a 'convergence' that premises not only the circulation of information and images created by media but also about audience reception of the media or mediascapes. This is aptly projected by Appadurai (1996, p. 35) when he states that '[t]he lines between the realistic and the fictional landscapes… are blurred, so that the farther away these audiences are from the direct experiences of metropolitan life, the more likely they are to construct imagined worlds that are chimerical, aesthetic, even fantastic objects, particularly if assessed by the criteria of some other perspective, some other imagined world'.

In the anthropology of tourism, Salazar (2012, p. 877) relates the circulation of tourism imaginaries with how attention needs to be focused on 'the relationships between the various elements and relations of tourism circuits, and the contradictions, anomalies, and paradoxes that these entail'. What is evident is that the circulation of images is, at once, also the stifling of mobility. Indeed, we need to question if media do create communities with 'no sense of place' (Meyrowitz 1985) or even a supermodernity of placelessness (Auge 1992). Appadurai (1996, p. 38) describes a *deterritorialization* 'in which money, commodities, and persons are involved in ceaselessly chasing each other around the world, that the mediascapes and ideoscapes of the modern world find their fractured and fragmented counterpart. For the ideas and images produced by mass media often are only partial guides to the goods and experiences that deterritorialized populations transfer to one another'.

Yet, two decades after Appadurai's (1996) profound work, one must reconsider the mass media as governing authority in the production of images, not to reduce its scope of power but to expose it as an inherent part of the deterritorialization process that Appadurai is so concerned about. It is probably useful to highlight that '[w]hile the migrant goes from place to place, moving with a resting place in mind, the nomad uses points and location to define paths. The nomad is never reterritorialized, unlike the migrant who slips back into the ordered space of arrival' (Cresswell 2006, p. 49).

The global flows of people, things and ideas in less global places need to accommodate mediation as constitutive of the disruption in meanings in place-making, especially homemaking, giving credence to a reflexive process of mediation that supports everyday currency. After all, it is the concept of home that 'often remains as the uninterrogated anchor or alter ego of all this hyper-mobility' (see Morley 2002, p. 3). Sara Ahmed (2000) characterizes a disembodied notion of home and the strangeness involved in its impossibility:

> Home is here, not a particular place that one inhabits, but more than one place: there are too many homes to allow place to secure roots or routes of one's destination. It is not simply that the subject does not belong anywhere. The journey between homes provides the subject with the contours of a space of belonging, but a space that expresses the very logic of an interval, the passing through of the subject between apparently fixed moments of departure and arrival. (p. 77)

Although it is important to acknowledge the sense of displacement, restrictions and immobilities, it is also helpful to see a more positive, creative and emergent sense of how belonging may evolve, or as Morley (2002, p. 6) suggests, 'a progressive notion of home, Heimat and community, which does not necessarily depend, for its effective functioning, on the exclusion of all forms of otherness, as inherently threatening to its own internally coherent self-identity'. Indeed the modern home can be said to be a 'phantasmagoric place, to the extent that electronic media of various kinds allow the radical intrusion of distant events into the space of domesticity' (Morley 2002, p. 9). It is no longer rooted in one particular physical place but is mobilized through social habits, small daily rituals, precious objects, mundane technologies and significant others (Germann-Molz 2008). Tuulentie (2006) sums it up as follows:

> Home can be seen as a complex concept that may include movement. Thus, when conceptualizing the home not as one centre but as something that is created in movements and can appear in several locations, the idea of being at home becomes closer to those modes of tourist experience that are characterised by strong enthusiasm for particular places. (p. 147)

Yet, tourist places are produced not only by the actual performance of tourists but also by 'the stabilising and intersecting flows of people, objects, memories and images' (Bærenholdt et al. 2004). Bærenholdt et al. (2004) reinforce that the 'attention to networks and flows, bridging the dualism of home and away, the cultural and material, physical space and social space, raises the question as to how to capture the mobile or fluid production of such tourist places'. Hence, 'returning home' is more than a 'homecoming', but a 'home(be)coming' (see Wee 2012) where the meanings of the German Village as home for the Korean *Gastarbeiter* are constantly being produced and reproduced.

In a way, Appadurai (1996, p. 29) envisaged the global flows of people and things before the coming of the German Village, filled with ironies and resistances, sometimes camouflaged as passivity, and a bottomless appetite in the Asian world for things Western. This is reminiscent of the 'Orient strikes back' (Hendry 2000) in which spatial theming of the 'West' in the 'East' poses a challenge to normative 'Western' notions of touristic consumption. New ways of interpretation need to be construed to understand how new homes will be constantly evolving, especially given the proliferation 'homes' that eventually lend themselves to 'theme parks' (see also Chap. 16 in this volume).

14.3   The Korean German Village

Known as *Gastarbeiter* in a German-Korean agreement matching the economic
boom of Germany with an impoverished South Korea, approximately 10,000
Korean nurses and nursing assistants and 8000 Korean miners came to Germany
between 1963 and 1977 as migrant workers (see Choe and Daheim 1987). Upon
returning to Korea after their prolonged exposure in Germany, the Korean migrants
realized that Korea in the twenty-first century was incomparable to Korea in the
1960s and 1970s when they had left; many felt like strangers as if the old Korea
existed only as imagination as much as the new Korea was intimidating (Garz 2015,
p. 166).

> Many returning migrants invest a great deal of hope and optimism in return, in no small
> measure because of the notion that they are going home. The word 'home', however, can be
> misleading, particularly when one has lived abroad for an extended period. Sometimes
> returnees fail to anticipate how much 'home' has changed. (Bartram et al. 2014, p. 122)

'Endstation der Sehnsüchte' (Cho 2009) told the stories of three German-Korean
couples who made the decision to move from Germany back to Korea and the struggles in constructing 'home', especially in terms of what it meant to be German,
Korean or somewhere in between. This liminality was further manifested with the
influx of tourism, where Koreans from around Korea would visit the island of
Namhae to seek the 'authentic' German Village, with real Germans living in it, at
least three of them.

The German Village or 독일마을 (Dogil Maeul) was conceptualized in 2002 as
a cultural exchange between Korea and Germany by a former district commissioner
in Namhae county (see Cho 2009); the idea was the provision of affordable land to
the former *Gastarbeiter* as incentive to resettle in South Korea, the motives being an
expression of gratitude for the efforts of the migrants who worked to send money
back, the rejuvenation of a declining rural area and the creation of a model example
of modern villages in the country (Onishi 2005; Garz 2015). Hence, the village was
to be built according to ecological measures and building requirements that adhered
to 'German standards'. To be specific, they had to be built to the specifications of
two floors with white walls and red-brick roofs as an archetype of 'typical German
village houses' (Chung 2008, p. 14).

The German Village was not slated for tourism; rather, tourism emerged as a
process of media channels, through a Korean drama series, word of mouth and various media rhetoric. Although 'tourism' per se was not factored into the equation as
it was mostly residential, the 'first German Village in Namhae County has become
a popular tourist destination over the past few years as word has spread about its
interesting look and feel' (Astudillo and Cha 2012). According to the Visit Korea
website:

> The German Village was built for Korean residents who returned from living in Germany.
> Many [Koreans] lived in Germany where they earned foreign currency during the modern-
> ization of Korea in the 1960's. The area is now a unique tourism spot related to German
> culture.... Korean residents in Germany directly imported materials from Germany to build

Fig. 14.1 Bonn House, 'Minbak' (image: Desmond Wee)

German-style houses. When residents are not living in the house while in Germany, the houses are used as tourist houses.

Tourism evolved rather 'organically' through the habituation of 'German identity' and its accompanying authenticity. This was evident in 'Endstation der Sehnsüchte' (Cho 2009) when Armin presented his reliable German machinery which he brought with him from Germany and expressed his utmost trust in it despite its age. Onishi (2005) reports:

It's about 90 percent German, 'said one of the German teachers, Kai Schroeder, 41, an assistant professor at Kyeongsang National University'. It's better, or more like a German village, than a German village, because the houses are new and big. It's an idealized expression of German living.

Astudillo and Cha (2012) interviewed Juliane Eirich, a professional photographer and native German who lived in Korea and related that she still found herself taken back at times, being able to 'talk German to everybody, you can buy great sausages and ham there', she adds, 'I was sometimes confused where I am and it did not feel like the Korean south coast at all'.

The 'tourist houses' that were mentioned above in the Visit Korea website reference the *Minbak* (민박), tourist apartments that are equipped with amenities (see Fig. 14.1). 'Citizens rent out rooms to curious guests who wish to see what "real German homes" look like' (Astudillo and Cha 2012). Yet the image reveals houses on the main drag which are solely Minbaks as written on the hanging plaque. In fact, Ludwig in 'Endstation der Sehnsüchte' (Cho 2009) explicitly stated (in the subtitles):

'The German Village' That name shouldn't be allowed. Only three real Germans live here…
Less than half of the houses are occupied. They're registered, but don't live here! Not even
half. Maybe one third. The other two thirds are just rented out! That's cheating! The rent
goes to Germany and nobody pays any taxes! The extent of this fraud is unbelievable.

From Fig. 14.1, the address of this *Minbak* can be read in Korean as Bonn House,
66 Germany Road. This seems to be the convergence of what German identification
may mean through materiality with an 'authentic' consumption through tourist
practice. With the hanging plaque uniform throughout the row of houses, one would
question if in Germany, this would be the case and, if so, if this is 'German' at all.

In the beginning of the film, one of the main protagonists, Willi, goes about doing
his household chores around his house, collecting his mail. In this scene, if one
looks carefully, above his mailbox are two plaques: one that reads 1145 (his house
number) and the other bigger one that reads '민박' (*Minbak*). It seems to beg the
question of who is the tourist: the man (German) and his family who own the house
and live in it, the family who will stay in it when he and his Korean wife go for a
'vacation' back to Germany or the others who try to open the door to go in, thinking
it is a walk-in attraction at the German Village.

The omnipresent *Minbak* in the village illustrates the nature of tourism, and at
the same time, it also questions how the residents articulate the notion of home. In
an article for the Spiegel entitled, Weisswurst and Beer: Tourists Flock to South
Korea's 'German Village', Ertel (2012) describes (with a sub-header entitled, 'We
Have No Home'):

> The German Village is an upside-down world. Many struggle with the idea of 'home'. 'My
> home is where my wife is', said Ulrich Ulmer. But his wife sees things differently. 'We have
> no home, there is always something missing', she said. Now, 40 years after she left
> Germany, she is finally back where she grew up and has her roots -- but it is still not her
> home. She speaks Korean, 'as it was spoken 40 years ago', she said. She doesn't really feel
> right in her home country, she said.

This point is reiterated by Chun-Ja in 'Endstation der Sehnsüchte' (Cho 2009) (in
the subtitles):

> I thought I'd live in Korea again at some point. But now that I've come to live here, I think
> of Germany as my homeland. We have no homeland and that's the tragedy of our lives. It
> was staggering. I felt a great sense of emptiness, although I was back in my homeland. I've
> lived here for six years, but the longer I live here, the more I think about Germany. It's odd.

Yet, Willi, her husband, who seems to reflect on his retirement, moves from Germany
to Korea in a more light-hearted way says (in the subtitles):

> Where can you find that in Germany? You live by the sea with mountains behind you. A
> house with a sea view, what big city has that?... It's better here. It's like being on holiday,
> every day. Sometimes you travel to take a break from your holiday. It's not my homeland in
> the traditional sense, but I still like it here.

Performing home in terms of 'away at home' premises changing spaces at home and
the adaptation of self: there is no need for a physical and subject-oriented sense of
being away because 'away' as the mobilities of home already encompass change,
movement and strings of othered processes. What is evident as portrayed by
'Endstation der Sehnsüchte' (Cho 2009) was the moulding of local identities through

greater cultural entanglements, involving what it meant to be German or Korean, local, resident or tourist. For the most part, the German Village comprised of people in between, where home is performed as much as tourism (see Wee 2012), as in the case of Willi, when he feels that he is on holiday every day. In this sense, places are becoming less about their static and immanent attributes but more about 'the webs of stories and narratives people produce when they sustain and construct their social identities' (Bærenholdt et al. 2004, p. 10).

14.4 Korean Tourists in the Korean German Village

Some years later after the emergence of the German Village, MBC screened an award-winning Korean drama in 2006 entitled 환상의 커플 ('Couple or Trouble') or its other manifestations such as 'Couple in Trouble' (Yun 2007), 'Couple of Trouble's' (Visit Korea, Korean TV Drama) and 'Couple of Fantasy' (see Lee 2015). According to Visit Korea, Korean TV Drama:

> The fast-paced yet comical drama became quite popular, consequently turning its film locations of Namhae Island into famous tourist sites.... Although the drama was filmed all around Namhae Island, its film location for the main neighborhood was at the 'German Village'. The main male character, Jang Cheol-Su's house still exists untouched. Furthermore, other film locations within the German-village such as the 'Mulgeon Port' set have been preserved.

The draw to the German Village seemed to be multifold. It comprised of a chance to be in an 'authentic' setting reeking with Germanness as described above. Yet there was a concurrent force at work: a film tourism that prompted the emotional and behavioural involvement of tourists and provided the stimulus for the tourists' on-site film tourism experience (see Kim 2012). After the filming of 'Couple or Trouble', 'the retired movie house is just a regular home. Unfortunately for the inhabitants, there is a continual bombardment each weekend by those who want to take pictures of the house, some even trying to make their way inside' (Astudillo and Cha 2012).

Because of its recent fame, the German Village is continuing to attract more and more visitors, especially during the fall when it hosts an annual Oktoberfest for 3 days (Astudillo and Cha 2012). In the Spiegel, Ertel (2012) writes (with a subheader entitled 'A Tourist Sensation'):

> The 'German Village' is a sensation in South Korea.... Locals are stared at, photographed, flooded with questions and their peace and quiet is disturbed. Uninvited visitors trample through their front yards, walk onto their terraces and sometimes even venture into their living rooms. 'It's like a museum village', said Engelfried. He, unlike some of his neighbors, can still see the funny side of the intrusions.

Figure 14.2 shows the house of Ludwig and Woo-Za Straus-Kim. The family of garden gnomes and the allusion to Snow White and the Seven Dwarfs contribute to the making of the 'German' landscape. The sign post right beside describes the

Fig. 14.2 Mainz House, home of Ludwig and Woo-Za Straus-Kim (image: Desmond Wee)

house in Korean that translates as Mainz House. The set-up does resemble an out-door museum indeed, and in 'Endstation der Sehnsüchte' (Cho 2009), a Korean tourist trespassed into the Straus's garden and started to take photographs there, much to the disdain of Woo-Za. She stops a police car and complains to the police about the tourists, how they infest the streets and how they come right into the house, 'I came here to live', she says, 'These Koreans don't care if we're dead or alive'.

To be fair, it would be difficult for 'these Koreans' to distinguish if the house was private property. In Fig. 14.2, it would appear that these houses are indeed artefacts of the German Village, somewhere between a theme park and an outdoor museum. The Straus family needs to deal with tourists trespassing, and they need to recon-sider, at the same time, their role within this German Village as actors and living artefact accompanying the other authentic objects of the German Village. This script was made apparent by Woo-Za Straus-Kim in her reference to 'these Koreans' as third person, distancing herself from 'being' Korean. Also, the fact that she 'came here to live', as opposed to saying that this is her home, implied her right as a resi-dent or a foreign resident rather than a Korean 'at home'.

Figure 14.3 reveals more tourists taking photographs with a backdrop of '[s] mall, narrow roads and alleys intertwine just as they do in Germany, while white fences surround colorful flower gardens and manicured lawns' (Astudillo and Cha 2012). In 'Endstation der Sehnsüchte' (Cho 2009), scenes of tourists packing the main street were interjected onto the cinematic text. Each of the tourist scenes always begins with a verbal countdown by the photographer, conveying less the practice of preparing the person for the final click, but how photography is practised in the German Village.

Fig. 14.3 Tourists taking photographs at the German Village (image: Desmond Wee)

14.5 Endstation der Sehnsüchte

It is interesting to note that the original title in German for Cho's (2009) film, 'Endstation der Sehnsüchte' (Home from home), is almost identical to the German translation 'Endstation Sehnsucht' for Tennessee Williams's acclaimed play, 'A Streetcar named Desire' (Williams 1947), and Elia Kazan's (1951) film adaptation of the same name. Even more interesting in this play-film transition is that Kazan directed the play before he directed the film, and Williams wrote the screen play for the film. Also, apart from Jessica Tandy who starred in the original Broadway production as the legendary Blanche Dubois, and replaced by Vivienne Leigh in the film, all the other three main protagonists were acted by the same people, both in the play and in the film: Marlon Brando, Kim Hunter and Karl Malden. The sync in both the play and the film, both in terms of plot, acting, set and mood seemed uncannily consistent. By extending this parallel to 'Endstation der Sehnsüchte' (Cho 2009), and inverting it, it would seem as if the film was also derived from a play, one that was full of complex, almost surreal characterizations and being acted out in the German Village of Namhae (See Fig. 14.3).

The characters in this play may feature various mobile modalities comprising of 'the Stranger' (Simmel 1950), 'the Nomad and the Migrant' (Cresswell 2006), 'The Cosmopolitan and the Local' (Hannerz 1990; Germann-Molz 2008), 'the Vagabond and the Tourist' (Bauman 1996), 'the Alien' (Ahmed 2000), 'the Driver' (Thrift 2004) or 'the Choraster' (Wearing et al. 2010). All these actors perform within a 'media environment', one that is material, in between and in the process of becoming mediatized (Lash and Lury 2007, p. 9). They consume media through convergence with participatory culture and collective intelligence, occurring when 'people take media into their own hands' (Jenkins 2006, p. 16). Be it 'Endstation Sehnsucht' or 'Endstation der Sehnsüchte', some kind of travelling is implied, both in the content of the films that they represent and also in the semantics of how one might comprehend the phrase. Yet this trip comes to an end at the last stop (Endstation), once again compared alongside a kind of desperate longing (Sehnsucht), paradoxically questioning the termination itself, if this is indeed the object of desire or the projection of a transfer onto another vehicle to take the protagonist onwards.

Jenkins (2006, p. 17) elaborates that '[e]ntertainment content isn't the only thing that flows across multiple media platforms. Our lives, relationships, memories, fantasies, desires also flow across media channels'. It is precisely these ever-evolving media channels and the mediation processes without needing remote controls that allow *us* to be, as Chaney (1993, p. 64) would assert, 'performers in our own dramas on stages the industry has provided'. Edensor (2000, p. 331) describes 'heterogeneous spaces' as 'a system of spatial ordering where transitional identities may be sought and performed alongside the everyday enactions of residents, bypassers, and workers'. Hence, the uncertainty and fluidity of how tourism is performed are dependent on the sort of performance that is enacted. In this sense, 'heterogeneous space is transcended through performative mediation' (Edensor 2000, p. 333), and tourism stages transform depending on the range of performances within the tourism sphere.

One of the ways in which this play is performed is through photography, a part of 'theatre' that 'enables modern people to enact and produce their desired togetherness, wholeness and intimacy. When cameras appear, activities are put on hold, and in posing people present themselves as a desired future memory...' (Haldrup and Larsen 2006, p. 283). Even though the cinematic media format was what enticed the tourists in Namhae, the recording of the process was still photographic for the most part. For some reason, tourists prefer to take photographs rather than film. Perhaps it has something to do with 'the process of taking photographs and analysing the photographs taken, [that] the cultural moment is captured inasmuch as it is discovered. This implies a sense of agency and subjective understanding unto which the self becomes embodied as subject (Wee 2012, p. 80) and acquires a sense of permanence, something a photograph does, both in symbolic and material means, better than a film.

Bruno (1997, p. 17) emphasizes that '[t]he film 'viewer' is a practitioner of viewing space – a tourist', meaning that the cinematic is already incorporated into the gaze, as well as the projection of that gaze. In a similar way, Sontag (1977) refers to the 'photographing eye' in which the eye is already trained to see as a camera. Her idea of representation is manifested in modern tourism characterized by a gazing upon and a picturing of the *already* pictorial. We can say that our reality is composed of a perpetual framing and photographing, captured on retina and selectively retained in memory all through representation. Thus, the interpretation of sight can only be culturally and historically specific (Classen 1993). Our very sight takes pictures, or another way of putting this is that we are always carrying a camera and the eye is an extension of the camera, rather than the other way around. Yet what surfaces is an interesting transfer of remediation and the filmic quality of experience in place, being projected back onto a static plane, that of photographs. By moving retrospectively from Bruno (1997) to Sontag (1977) and from film *back* to photography, we witness a fixed rendering of a moment in the way Sontag (1977, p. 86) references Paul Strand's pictures, 'when he turned from the brilliant discoveries of the abstracting eye to the touristic, world-anthologizing tasks of photography'.

If the landscape should stay constant, the cinematic quality shifts from a moving subject into a stationery one. Whether the image is then made into memes or posted onto Facebook or Instagram, the movement within the cinematic text is conveyed into movement across, and not only within, media. In other words, the moment the tourist encounters place (represented by or in the film), the film *decays* in order to accommodate the 'real' performance in place, in this sense, either as a play or photography or both. New mediation takes the place of, re(places) and feeds the imagination contrived by the film. It slows down from moving images to a silent, immobile rigour mortis of reality, a symbolic death (Barthes 1972). Perhaps this death must happen to usher in memory, something that the play tries to bolster and the photograph tries to sustain.

The activity of reminiscing is a performance to connect past with present and recollect how dreams have failed or faded from memory. Memories through stimulation or production are coherent with Lippard's (1997, p. 33) 'lure of the local' where 'finding a place for oneself in a story [is] composed of mythologies, histories and ideologies – the stuff of identity and representation'. The challenge then is to understand how people 'weave stories into and out of place so as to construct identities' (Mitchell 2001, p. 276). These are the kinds of narratives that 'engender journeying through the memory, traversing time and space, and displacing the boundaries of the actual and the imaginary, are representative of those that generate and are themselves activated by souvenirs' (Levell 2000, p. 36). These souvenirs can be mediated, as illustrated by Appadurai (1996, p. 30), 'The past is now not a land to return to in a simple politics of memory. It has become a synchronic warehouse of cultural scenarios, a kind of temporal central casting, to which recourse can be taken as appropriate, depending on the movie to be made, the scene to be enacted, the hostages to be rescued'. Hence, the 'reminiscing involves performance, both by those 'real' performers who are there to stimulate memories and by visitors who have to work, often cooperatively, with others in order to produce memories' (Kershaw 1993 as cited in Rojek and Urry 1997, p. 15).

The memories of the three couples in 'Endstation der Sehnsüchte' (Cho 2009) were reflected in some scenes in which photographs were used to narrate their experiences either in Korea before they left or in Germany where they lived. These photographs had a very poignant appeal, especially in that they provided a trace of history sedimented in time that spoke of emotional hardship. But how does one make meaning of the photography performed by the tourists (both the tourists who are there to experience the 'German Village' and the ones represented in the film) especially in ways that were highly frustrating for the residents? How did the photography and photographs of the tourists stand in contrast with the residents, in terms of material culture, social practice and cultural memory?

Salazar (2012, p. 869) contends that '[a]nalyzing the global circulation of images and ideas of tourism—a constant interaction between documents, devices, and people—and seeking to determine the local dynamics of this exchange is a complicated matter. Imaginaries often become the symbolic objects of a significant contest over economic supremacy, territorial ownership, and identity'. Hence, mediation is about being inherently part of a play, confined within a film set and its production and reproduced on a stage in which the 'German' homes in the film become as realistic alongside the tourism that it supports. On the other hand, mediation is also in a more forgiving manner, a kind of intercession, both processual and relational between the different actors thriving in the German Village. It exists as a complex fabric of in-between spaces in which identities and the practice of those identities are mediated, starting from the very founding of the village as a historical device of amelioration, in a move to entice Koreans back to Korea.

14.6   Conclusion

In the beginning scene of 'Endstation der Sehnsüchte' (Cho 2009), the landscape of Korea is made visible, from the bustling port of Busan leading to the island of Namhae, depicting the transitions from a modern to rural feel. A man is walking towards the camera, all in a single take, and the first words of the film are his words (from the subtitles), 'Are you measuring something?' directed at the filmographer. His question asked in the most unassuming way posits the ultimate question of the film and the greater question of mediation. Indeed, the film would seem to be measuring something: the interstices between what it means to have a home away *at* home. It begs the question of what identities mean in transnational mobilities and the complexities of repatriation in Korea after being *Gastarbeiter* in Germany.

In this chapter, we have furthered the conceptualization of touristic practices of Koreans occurring within the space of the German Village. It considers the lure of media tourism and how tourist performances such as photography are juxtaposed with displaced identities of what 'home' means to the inhabitants. In exploring the impact of media tourism on local communities and residents, the film 'Endstation der Sehnsüchte' (Cho 2009) becomes a reflexive medium to understand how globalization shapes belonging and the making and remaking of identity. However, it is not just the film but the enticement of the drama series, photography and its relation to permanence that question the role of mediation and its connection to belonging and the making of place.

The German Village on Namhae is not the only 'migrant' village. Its ramification is apparent as it is 'joined by a smaller and more reclusive American village that adds a Western touch to the Namhae county landscape' (Korea Herald 2016). The houses are supposed to look 'American' to cater for the Koreans returning from America. Figure 14.4 depicts the idyllic charm of the island, and in the foreground

Fig. 14.4 Bus stop at the American Village (image: Desmond Wee)

rests a bus stop in the shape of the bust of Mickey, looking outward and romantically incorporating into the distant landscape (see Lefebvre 2006) the American dream perhaps, or taking a moment's breath, if it is indeed the 'Endstation der Sehnsüchte'.

A second German Village is now in the process of being built elsewhere in Korea. It seems that these themed villages that exist as real homes will proliferate across the nation. Hence, it is increasingly important to ask even more so, how the notion of 'place' is reproduced through spatialities in which embodied performances and practices are facilitated within complex infrastructure, networks and mobilities. Hopefully this research will encourage other researchers to explore the multifaceted meanings that places are embedded in, involving informal encounters in the everyday and going beyond a limited focus on the tourist experience at a destination.

References

Ahmed, S. (2000). *Strange encounters: Embodied others in post-coloniality*. London: Routledge.

Anonymous (2016, March 9). Connecting cultures: Koreans returning from abroad make waves. *Korea Herald*. Retrieved from http://www.koreaherald.com/view.php?ud=20160309000794

Anonymous (n.d.-a). German Village. *Visit Korea*. Retrieved from http://english.visitkorea.or.kr/enu/ATR/SI_EN_3_1_1_1.jsp?cid=1941105

Anonymous (n.d.-b). Korean TV Drama. *Visit Korea*. Retrieved from http://english.visitkorea.or.kr/enu/CU/CU_EN_8_5_1_22.jsp

Appadurai, A. (1996). *Modernity at large: Cultural dimensions of globalization*. Minneapolis: University of Minnesota Press.

Astudillo, T-M, & Cha, F. (2012, August 14). Korea to build second German Village. CNN. Retrieved from http://travel.cnn.com/seoul/visit/korea-build-another-german-village-023609/

Auge, M. (1992). *Non-places: Introduction to an anthropology of Supermodernity*. London: Verso.

Bærenholdt, J., Haldrup, M., Larsen, J., & Urry, J. (2004). *Performing tourist places*. Aldershot: Ashgate.

Barthes, R. (1972). *Mythologies*. (A. Lavers, Trans.) New York: Hill and Wang.

Bartram, D., Poros, M., & Monforte, P. (2014). *Key concepts in migration*. New York: Sage.

Bauman, Z. (1996). From pilgrim to tourist–or a short history of identity. In S. Hall & P. D. Gay (Eds.), *Questions of cultural identity* (pp. 18–36). London: Sage.

Beeton, S. (2005). *Film-induced tourism* (Vol. 25). Clevedon: Channel View Publications.

Bruno, G. (1997). Site-seeing: Architecture and the moving image. *Wide Angle, 19*, 8–24.

Chaney, D. (1993). *Fictions of collective life: Public Drama in late modern culture*. London: Routledge.

Cho, S.-H. (Director). (2009) Endstation der Sehnsüchte [DVD]. Frankfurt: Zorro Medien GmbH.

Choe, J.-H., & Daheim, H. (1987). *Rückkehr- und Bleibeperspektiven koreanischer Arbeitsmigranten in der Bundesrepublik Deutschland*. Frankfurt a.M.: Peter Lang.

Chung, D.Y. (2008, November 20). *Das deutsche Dorf in Namhae*. Bestandsaufnahme, Hintergründe & Perspektiven. Lecture. Retrieved from http://www.daad.or.kr/Documents/Deutsches%20Dorf_Nov.2008.pdf

Classen, C. (1993). *Exploring the senses in history and across cultures*. London: Routledge.

Cresswell, T. (2006). *On the move: Mobility in the modern Western world*. London: Routledge.

Edensor, T. (2000). Staging tourism: Tourists as performers. *Annals of Tourism Research, 27*(2), 322–344.

Ertel, M. (2012, July 12). Weisswurst and beer: Tourists flock to South Korea's 'German Village'. Der Spiegel. Retrieved from http://www.spiegel.de/international/world/german-village-in-south-korea-draws-tourists-by-the-thousands-a-843438.html

Garz, D. (2015). Going away. Going home! Coming home? The Migration of Korean nurses and miners to Germany and their return in retirement to Korea's German village-together with their German husbands. *OMNES: The Journal of Multicultural Society, 6*(1), 161–183.

Germann-Molz, J. (2008). Global abode: Home and mobility in narratives of round-the-world travel. *Space and Culture, 11*(4), 325–342.

Haldrup, M., & Larsen, J. (2006). Material cultures of tourism. *Leisure Studies, 25*(3), 275–289.

Hannerz, U. (1990). Cosmopolitans and locals in world culture. *Theory, Culture and Society, 7*, 237–251.

Hendry, J. (2000). *The orient strikes back: A global view of cultural display*. Oxford: Berg Publishers.

Hudson, S., & Ritchie, J. R. B. (2006). Promoting destinations via film tourism: An empirical identification of supporting marketing initiatives. *Journal of Travel Research, 44*(4), 387–396.

Jansson, A. (2007). A sense of tourism: New media and the dialectic of encapsulation/decapsulation. *Tourist Studies, 7*(1), 5–24.

Jenkins, H. (2006). *Convergence culture: Where old and new media collide*. New York: NYU Press.

Kazan, E. (Director). (1951). A Streetcar named desire. [Motion picture]. New York: Warner Bros.

Kershaw, B. (1993). Reminiscing history: Memory, performance, empowerment. In C. Rojek & J. Urry (Eds.), *Touring cultures: Transformations of travel and theory*. London: Routledge.

Kim, S. (2012). Audience involvement and film tourism experiences: Emotional places, emotional experiences. *Tourism Management, 33*(2), 387–396.

Lash, S., & Friedman, J. (1992). *Modernity and identity*. Oxford: Wiley-Blackwell.

Lash, S., & Lury, C. (2007). *Global culture industry: The mediation of things*. Cambridge: Polity.

Lee, K. (2008). Mapping out the cultural politics of "the Korean wave" in contemporary South Korea. In C. B. Huat & K. Iwabuchi (Eds.), *East Asian pop culture: Analyzing the Korean wave* (pp. 175–190). Aberdeen: Hong Kong University Press.

Lee, S.A. (2015, March 5). Enjoy a bit of island life in Namhae. *Korea.net*. Retrieved from http://www.korea.net/NewsFocus/Travel/view?articleId=126014

Lefebvre, M. (2006). *Landscape and film*. New York: Taylor & Francis.

Levell, N. (2000). Reproducing India: International exhibitions and Victorian tourism. In M. Hitchcock & K. Teague (Eds.), *Souvenirs: The material culture of tourism*. Hants: Ashgate.

Lippard, L. (1997). *The lure of the local: Sense of place in a Multicentered society*. New York: New Press.

Meyrowitz, J. (1985). *No sense of place: The impact of electronic media on social behavior*. Oxford: Oxford University Press.

Mitchell, D. (2001). The lure of the local: Landscape Studies at the end of a troubled century. *Progress in Human Geography, 25*(2), 43–67.

Morley, D. (2002). *Home territories: Media, mobility and identity*. London: Routledge.

Onishi, N. (2005, August 9). In a corner of South Korea, a taste of German living. *New York Times*, Retrieved from http://www.nytimes.com/2005/08/09/international/asia/09korea.html?_r=o

Reijnders, S. (2011). *Places of the imagination: Media, tourism, culture*. Farham: Ashgate Publishing.

Rojek, C., & Urry, J. (1997). Transformations of travel and theory. In C. Rojek & J. Urry (Eds.), *Touring cultures: Transformations of travel and theory*. London: Routledge.

Salazar, N. (2012). Tourism imaginaries: A conceptual approach. *Annals of Tourism Research, 39*(2), 863–882.

Shim, D. (2008). The growth of Korean cultural industries and the Korean wave. *East Asian pop culture: Analysing the Korean wave, 1*, 15–32.

Simmel, G. (1950). *The Sociology of Georg Simmel*. (Kurt Wolff, Trans.) New York: Free Press.

Sontag, S. (1977). *On photography*. London: Macmillan.

Thrift, N. (2004). Driving in the city. *Theory, Culture & Society, 21*(4/5), 41–59.

Tuulentie, S. (2006). Tourists making themselves at home: Second homes as a part of tourist careers. In N. McIntyre, D. Williams, & K. McHugh (Eds.), *Multiple dwelling and tourism: Negotiating place, home and identity*. Oxfordshire: CABI.

Tzanelli, R. (2007). *The cinematic tourist: Explorations in globalization, culture and resistance*. London: Routledge.

Wearing, S., Stevenson, D., & Young, T. (2010). *Tourist cultures: Identity, place and the Traveller*. London: Sage.

Wee, D. (2012). Touring heritage, Performing home: Cultural encounters in Singapore. In L. Smith, E. Waterton, & S. Watson (Eds.), *The cultural moment in tourism: New perspectives on performance and engagement* (pp. 79–96). London/New York: Routledge.

Williams, T. (1947). *A Streetcar named desire*. London: Signet.

Yun, S. J. (2007). Essay on TV Drama as a storyteller in the digital era-focus on the MBC TV Drama Couple in trouble. *Korean Literary and Criticism, 11*(3), 101–126.

Chapter 15
Impact of Hindi Films (Bollywood) on the Indian Diaspora in Honolulu, Hawaii

Torsha Bhattacharya

Abstract This chapter investigates the impact of Hindi films (popularly known as Bollywood) on the Indian diaspora in Honolulu, Hawaii. Using a short survey and detailed interviews with a few members of the Indian diaspora on the island, it finds a subtle impact of Bollywood films on their travel decisions. Active engagements like dancing, and social community gatherings like Diwali and Holi celebrations, seem to provide the Indian diaspora with a connection to their homeland. While some in the community feel that Bollywood is reflective of urban India, others feel Bollywood only serves to paint a distorted picture of what India should look like, is much more Westernised, and takes away from their experience or connection with their homeland. While some members of the community are more likely to be influenced by Bollywood films and travel to new places in India, others are more likely to travel to their usual destinations, visiting friends and family.

Keywords Bollywood • Indian community • Diaspora tourism • Film tourism • Hawaii

15.1 Introduction

This chapter attempts to develop a greater understanding of the impact of Hindi films, popularly known as Bollywood, on the Indian diaspora in Honolulu, Hawaii. Punathambekar (2010) talks about "cultural citizenship" among the diaspora as delving deeper into the "emotional investment in the idea of India" (p. 46). According to Beeton (2016), the study of film tourism is complex, which is not just limited to narrow specializations like marketing but where we need to look at different fields such as sociology, psychology, finance, branding, etc., to get a complete picture of the impact of the film industry on tourist behavior. There is a range of perspectives and different ways to analyze film tourism and its impact. The controversial issues

T. Bhattacharya (✉)
School of Travel Industry Management, University of Hawaii, Manoa, Honolulu, HI, USA
e-mail: b.torsha@gmail.com

© Springer Nature Singapore Pte Ltd. 2018
S. Kim, S. Reijnders (eds.), *Film Tourism in Asia*, Perspectives on Asian Tourism, DOI 10.1007/978-981-10-5909-4_15

including actual or imagined benefits, authentic or inauthentic film sites, and fascination with the famous or infamous (Beeton 2016) have a significant impact on the diaspora, which views films as a connection to their homeland. As Bandyopadhyay (2008) rightly notes, in addition to having scarce research in the field of diaspora tourism, film tourism is also a fairly under-researched topic. Majority of literature on Indian film tourism focusses mostly on Indian outbound tourism to film locations worldwide, with specific studies on the USA, Australia, the UK, and Scotland (Singh 2003, 2004). There has been relatively less attention paid to diaspora tourism and the impact that Bollywood films might have on diaspora travel behavior.

This chapter, therefore, strives to fill this research gap and shed some light on the impact of Bollywood films on the Indians residing in Honolulu, Hawaii. There have been a few studies looking at Indian diaspora tourism as well as film tourism. But how does the Indian diaspora in the most isolated land mass maintain their connection to their homeland? What sustains their nostalgia, in a place thousands of miles away from home, as well as from other major cities? In this chapter the author strives to answer these questions by analyzing the social and cultural impacts of Indian films and how films have impacted the Indian diaspora in Honolulu, Hawaii, in terms of their travel decisions and social interactions. In addition, the author also tries to develop an understanding of the impact of these films on the event planning, especially the wedding planning market if any. This chapter also looks at whether the Bollywood Film Festival has influenced or has been influenced by the Indian diaspora in Hawaii.

15.2 Literature Review

People are constantly moving from one place to another, some in search of better opportunities, some to escape death and torture, others in search of novelty. Whatever the reasons for migrating, people tend to look back to their home country with nostalgia and longing. Therefore, ideas like "home away from home," "roots," and "identity" are very common in the diaspora (Appadurai 1990; Rapport and Dawson 1998). In trying to locate and situate one's sense of identity and belongingness, diasporas, irrespective of their present living situation, try to build their identity, in a new place with the available resources they might find on hand. These communities, looking back at the place that they still consider home, visit their "homelands," to rediscover their roots and find fulfilment (Basu 2004). This type of travel has been termed as "diaspora tourism" or "roots tourism" (Timothy 1997; Timothy and Teye 2004). The reasons why people travel back to their home country can be varied. Some visit their homeland for cultural or religious purposes, (Basu 2004) whereas others do so to quench their nostalgia (Lowenthal 1998, 2005; Timothy and Teye 2004; see also Chaps. 9 and 14 in this volume).

There has been some research on diaspora tourism that specifically looks into nostalgia's impact on travel behavior (Cohen 1988; Dann 1994a, 1994b, 1996, 2005; MacCannell 1973, 1989; Peleggi 2005; Urry 1996). Nostalgia captures the essence of diaspora tourism like no other term, since it serves to bring back tourists to their home country in search of intangible experiences, but has real economic implications (Lowenthal 2005). Timothy and Coles (2004) pointed out the complicated relationship that exists between the people and its places and between diaspora and tourism. Safran (2004) considers the Indian diaspora as being representatives of increasingly globalized world, as these communities are not merely minorities that have migrated and assimilated, but they have retained a very strong and influential connection with India. This dissolving of the Indian identity, yet not being completely assimilated into the western society, leads to newer identities (Hall 1992, 1996; Bhabha 1994).

Films provide the return to nostalgia, the strong connection to culture, the feeling of revisiting home, as well as updating oneself about the new and emerging young India (Mehta 2005). For some in the diaspora, the idea of Bollywood and India has become synonymous. The sense of joy, and belongingness, that films, songs, and dances provide in spite of the distance between the producer and the consumer is unparalleled. In the 2-h time frame, Bollywood manages to erase the distance between the diaspora and their homeland. According to Bhattacharya (2002), Indian films try to invoke nostalgia and retrospection. It is an active medium where viewers not only passively consume what is offered but also engage in imagination, creation, and production of cultural codes and identity, thereby feeling empowered. This is especially true for the diaspora population who remain physically away from their country but always long for the connection.

Dwyer (2010) observes that modern Indian films depict affluent and harmonious families and beautiful locations and try to build an image of India as it should be and not as it is. The image of the global Indian is deliberate and not only encourages economic and cultural allegiance from the Indian diaspora but also portrays a relatable lifestyle for the socially and economically mobile Indian middle class living in India. Sarkar (2008) talks about the "melodramas of globalization," which engulfs Bollywood and more broadly India, a country in a state of confusion over its identity, using films to reflect its hopes and dreams of the developed, progressive, and modern nation amid the unpleasant realities of poverty and social ills. Punathambekar (2005) notes that with liberalization and the cultural shift that took place in the 1990s, India emerged as an economic force to reckon with. This change is reflected in the growing pride that Indians living in and out of the country feel and in the positive portrayal of the image of the new India as successful and equal among its global peers. He also notes that Bollywood projects an environment which is mostly upper-class Hindu, normalizing prayers, religious rituals, and wedding ceremonies with no reference to important issues like religious intolerance, poverty, corruption, or politics. This trend, as Virdi and Creekmur (2006) point out, might be attributed to the rise of Hindu majority politics and increased sense of nationalism among the Hindus in India.

Punathambekar (2010) in his more recent work points out that the nonresident Indian, who was once ridiculed and looked upon with suspicion for being too westernized, has transformed into the ideal citizen in the increasingly globalized world. The characters in these films feel as much at home in New York as they do in

Mumbai and can wear traditional Indian and western clothes with equal ease and not look out of place or one bit uncomfortable dancing at elaborate Indian weddings or delivering a speech at a multinational corporate headquarter. They embody what he describes as the globalized "super Indian" at ease with their identity and culture and yet completely comfortable in a foreign setting. In Desai's (2004) opinion, films are very important cultural products through which diaspora identities are created, recreated, as well as contested over time.

As mentioned before, not a lot of attention was paid to diaspora tourism in the context of film tourism. Recently diaspora tourism in general and studying Indian diaspora in particular have gained a lot of prominence. The sheer diversity that exists in India, from language to food to religion and culture, provides a multitude of possibilities for research (Jain 1993, 1998). The globalized world, success of Bollywood films, rise of global stars, mainstreaming of Indian stories, and recognition of India as an increasingly growing influence in culture, including dance, music, food, and films, have raised the research potential of analyzing the Indian diaspora residing in the USA or UK (Singh 2003, 2004), and how they have been impacted by or in turn have impacted the film industry (Appadurai 1996; Dudrah 2006; Uberoi 1998). These authors utilized an interdisciplinary approach looking at the Bollywood film industry from the sociology, film, and media studies to gain a holistic understanding of the extent of influence that Indian films have had on the global population.

15.3 Evolution of the Indian Film Industry (Popularly Known as Bollywood)

In spite of existing for more than 50 years, Bollywood has emerged on its own as a global entity only recently (Aftab 2002; Childers 2002; Dudrah 2002, 2006). The Indian movie industry produces over 1000 films per year and sells over 3.5 billion tickets. That staggering number makes the industry a magnet for financial investors, both national and international, since there is an increase in confidence about the market and the type of business these films can end up doing. The major international markets for Indian films are the USA, the UK, Canada, and the Middle East. There is a growing appetite for regional language films, but most of the market is still occupied by Bollywood films, which are Hindi-language films. (Hindi is dominant in the central and northern part of India.)

The total number of Bollywood films that have an overseas release is growing every year but is still a small fraction of the total number of films that are produced in India. Production houses primarily utilize the star power or their enormous marketing and advertising budget to distribute and sell these films, but some production houses also make money from "repeat viewing" where older films are sold as a package or standalone in newer regions (FICCI Studies and Surveys 2013). The Indian diaspora has become so influential and profitable that Indian producers have started catering to the diaspora with their offerings (Desai 2004; Dudrah 2006; Gillespie 1995; Rajadhyaksha 2003). The Indian population has been one of the fastest growing groups in the USA, with a growth rate of roughly 70% (2.84 million in 2010, up from 1.68 million in 2000) in the last decade (US Census 2010). At the same time, the Indian movie industry is experiencing a growth rate of 15% per year, resulting in a projected revenue of 1.6 trillion in 2016 (FICCI Studies and Surveys 2013; see also Chap. 3 in this volume).

The Indian film festivals have also been making their presence felt every year, starting in 1952 with the International Film Festival of India (IFFI). There are similar festivals that are being hosted in major cities around the world celebrating the Indian film industry; festivals like London Indian Film Festival, Indian Film Festival of Los Angeles, and New York Indian Film Festival have become very popular (FICCI Studies and Surveys 2013). In Honolulu, Hawaii, the Bollywood Film Festival completed a decade in January 2017.

15.4 Indian Organizations and Diaspora in Honolulu, Hawaii

The city and county of Honolulu, on the island of Oahu, in the state of Hawaii, has a population of 998,714. It is a diverse place with 23.3% of the population white, 3.3% black, 42.2% Asian, and 9.3% Native Hawaiian. About 20% of the population is foreign born with over 27% speaking a language other than English at home (US Census 2010). Indians comprise only 0.20% of the population in Honolulu—the major city in the island state of Hawaii. The island chain is the most isolated land mass on Earth, its closest neighbor being California, which is 2400 miles away (NPS 2017).

The diversity and spirit of "aloha" make Hawaii an ideal place to encourage and cultivate arts, literature, culture, and language from all corners of the world. In Hawaii, everybody is part of one large family or "ohana" and is a protector of the "aina" or the land that nourishes the people (University of Hawaii 2016). It is no wonder then that in Hawaii there are several Asian, South Asian, as well as Indian diasporas coexisting peacefully, trying to contribute to the sense of ohana in Hawaii, at the same time holding on to their culture, traditions, and nostalgia.

The Indian diaspora in Honolulu is prominent in spite of their small size. There are a few local organizations that are relevant to this discussion. The first is LOTUS (Lord of the Universe Society) which was established in 1989 by a small group of Hindu devotees on the Island of Oahu, with a focus on promoting and enhancing "the understanding and practice of spiritual, cultural, and philosophical ideals through devotional activities and discourses" (SAADA 2016). The society is primarily focused on celebrating Hindu festivals like Holi and Diwali and organizing monthly worship/potlucks at a temple in Wahiawa. Although not overtly religious, it does have a Hindu learning perspective but is welcoming of all Indian and South

Asian population. LOTUS's main annual event celebrating Diwali has evolved into a venue to showcase Indian culture, music, Bollywood, and classical dance. It also enables the Indian diaspora on the island, isolated from other Indian expats on the mainland, to get a feel of home away from home.

The second organization is the Watumull Foundation established by the first Indian family who settled in Hawaii about a century ago. They helped in forging the understanding between eastern and western philosophies and cultures. They are patrons of the Indian Classical Music Circle in Hawaii, support the Bollywood Film Festival by the Honolulu Museum of Art, support scholars and programs at the University of Hawaii's Center for South Asian Studies (SAADA 2016; University of Hawaii 2016), and play a very vital role in bringing a taste of India to the Indian diaspora in Honolulu.

There are two other organizations that have helped promote Indian films in Honolulu. First is the Honolulu Museum of Arts that celebrates Bollywood films with its film festival, showcasing eight to twelve films every year. The Hawaii International Film Festival (HIFF) is another organization dedicated to promoting international films throughout the state of Hawaii. HIFF was created as an East-West Center project at the University of Hawaii, Manoa, in 1981 and has grown in popularity and attracts 70,000 film viewers from all over the world.

15.5 Methodology

In addition to the document review to gather information about the different organizations and their contributions to the Indian diaspora in Honolulu, Hawaii, the author collected primary data using two different methods. The first involved conducting short surveys among the Indian community in Hawaii regarding their perceptions about Bollywood films and how that might have impacted their travel decisions to India. The sample for this survey was selected from the movie goers to the 10th Annual Bollywood Film Festival held at the Honolulu Museum of Arts, between January 7 and January 10, 2017. The author designed a survey tool using University of Hawaii's SurveyShare which consisted of mostly open-ended questions to gain a better understanding about the impact of Bollywood on the respondents' travel decisions. This short survey is part of a study conducted by the museum to gauge the tastes, preferences, likes, and dislikes of the audience members that attend the Bollywood Film Festival every year. This is the first year that such a detailed survey has been conducted.

The link for the survey was sent to the Bollywood Film Festival attendees, but only those who are of Indian origin and residing in Honolulu were requested to complete it. Social media like Facebook invites, emails, and LISTSERVs were utilized to recruit survey participants. There was a total of 155 attendees at the opening film event among whom only 27 responded. After deleting the survey responses that were incomplete or had missing data, there were 20 completed surveys, with a response rate of 13%. It is important to note that not all 155 attendees were of Indian

Table 15.1 Profiles of the interviewees

Birth country	Gender	Race	Age	Education	Income	Name
India	Male	Asian	67	PhD	80,000	*Hari Shukla*
India	Male	Asian	72	MS	Retired	*Kedar Banerjee*
India	Female	Asian	44	PhD	70,000	*Sheela Bhatia*
USA	Female	Caucasian	36	MA	50,000	*Marie Chung*
India	Female	Asian	50	BS	40,000	*Meeta Iyengar*[a]
India	Female	Asian	35	MS	50,000	*Geeta Ghosh*[a]
USA	Female	Asian	27	MS	90,000	*Gurmeet Patel*[a]
USA	Female	Asian	29	MS	60,000	*Pramila Arora*[a]

[a]Members of Bollywood dance group Aaja Nachle Hawaii

origin and, therefore, the study sample was significantly smaller, resulting in a higher (but unknown) response rate. The survey included questions about the reasons, frequency, and venues, for watching Indian films, as well as impact of these films on their impressions of India and travel decisions to specific destinations in India.

In addition to the survey, the author conducted face-to-face interviews with a total of eight interviewees. These approximately 45-min-long interviews were structured as mostly open-ended discussion around the social and cultural impacts of Bollywood films on the Indian diaspora and impact of films on the interviewees' travel decisions. The interviewees included two prominent members of the Indian diaspora in Honolulu who play an active role in Indian cultural organizations, two organizers of the Bollywood Film Festival, and four members of the Bollywood dance group "Aaja Nachle Hawaii" (ANH). The setting for this face-to-face interview with ANH members was informal, with participants sitting in a group and sharing their experiences with the author as well as each other. The interviews took place in two rounds.

The first round consisting of four interviews was conducted during late November and early December, 2016. The second round consisting of four interviews was conducted in late February, 2017, as ANH was on a break due to the winter vacation from mid-December 2016 to mid-January 2017. These in-depth interviews provided a deeper and much better understanding of the Indian diaspora in Honolulu and how their travel decisions might or might not have been affected by Bollywood films. It also provided a glimpse into the deep social and cultural impact that Bollywood films have had on these interviewees. Table 15.1 below provides the interviewee profiles (names have been changed).

15.6 Results

The survey respondents were all above 30 years old: 50% had an annual income of at least $50,000, 70% were female, and 60% had a master's degree or higher. Among the interviewees, 75% were above the age of 30, 75% were female, and 87% had at least a master's degree or higher. In comparison, the general population in Honolulu is 49% female, 32% have a bachelor's degree or higher, with a median household income of $74,460. 21.5% of the population is below 18 years and 16% is above 65 years.

The results from the survey reveal that the most common reason respondents watch Bollywood films was to get a flavor of home and feel reconnected to their country or what researchers have termed "nostalgia" (see also Chap. 9 in this volume). Some of them mentioned that the recent films depicted a more beautiful, clean, and successful image of India, but that those images might not be close to the truth on the ground. Most of them watch Indian films at least once a month and are likely to watch it mostly at home with family and friends. All the respondents agreed that Bollywood helped them gain a better understanding of the changing India. The most common words the survey respondents used to describe India as a tourist destination are exotic, traditional, and beautiful (see also Chap. 2 in this volume). As for the frequency of travel, these respondents did not frequently travel to India but rather tried to recreate Indian traditions and customs here on the island. The travel destinations, as influenced by films, were Mumbai, Ladakh, Goa, Varanasi, Kolkata, and the states of Gujarat and Rajasthan. One respondent mentioned that after watching Bollywood films, they were more likely to visit Spain and Australia, not India.

The interviews provided interesting and rich insights into the minds of the interviewees in the Indian diaspora in Honolulu. Discussing the evolution of Bollywood films, Sheela Bhatia mentioned that she used to feel uncomfortable and even ashamed when watching Bollywood films in the early 1990s, but since then she has embraced the songs, dances, colorful costumes, as well as the melodrama. According to her these films serve as a conversation starter about Indian literature, culture, films, food, language, etc. She feels that Bollywood films provide a forum to share with others the wide variety of experiences and offerings from the Indian film industry. She also discussed the changing faces of Indian cinema, specifically how actors like Irrfan Khan and Priyanka Chopra have become global stars and not just Bollywood celebrities and that has helped Bollywood become more mainstream in the USA. According to Marie Chung, melodrama has the ability to transcend language barriers and encourage people to partake in another culture. She mentioned that with the evolution of Bollywood, the film festival in Honolulu has also evolved from just showcasing mainstream Bollywood films to providing a platform for regional and art house cinema. According to her, the primary audience for these films is the local Hawaiian community comprising of Japanese, Chinese, Whites, and only a handful of Indians. The film festival has not able to attract the Indian diaspora in Honolulu. This fact is also corroborated by the survey results.

Analyzing the social and cultural influence of Bollywood on the Indian diaspora in Hawaii, the responses of the interviewees ranged from nostalgia and love to indifference. Hari Shukla and Meeta Iyengar, both of whom moved to the USA about 25 years ago from India, consider Bollywood films as a means to look back to a time and place they grew up in and occasionally visit. Hari mentioned that he makes sure to watch older Bollywood films with his kids so that they can relate to the stories he narrates to them. Meeta mentioned that although they did not speak Hindi at home, her kids love Bollywood films, and these films have helped her pick up quite a bit of the language even after moving away from India. Both of them return to India to visit friends and family.

But similar positive sentiments were not reflected by another member of the Indian community. Kedar Banerjee mentioned that Bollywood films did not interest him. He felt that the westernized portrayal of the actors in these films did not represent the real India, one which he is familiar with. He mentioned watching regional films based on the rich literature of the country and is not a "fan" of Bollywood and prefers traveling to pilgrimages when visiting India. All four dance group interviewees mentioned that their group is a fun, open, and completely free platform where all community members, not just the Indian diaspora, can come together to create beautiful and energetic choreographies to Bollywood film as well as folk songs. Their weekly community gathering, they pointed out, is open to everyone who loves Bollywood, wants to reconnect with their homeland, wants to learn more about India, or simply loves to dance.

Another aspect of cultural influence of Indian films that came to the forefront was that both Gurmeet and Prameela, both of whom were born and brought up in the USA, were trained in Indian classical dances that require rigorous discipline and take years to master. They both mentioned that although they were born in the USA, their parents made sure to inculcate Indian culture and traditions from a very young age. They revealed that they love to watch Bollywood films and feel that they can relate with a lot of the recent films. Prameela said that her mother was concerned that it would be difficult for her to adjust to the different social and cultural norms when she visited her relatives back in India. But she felt growing up watching Bollywood films helped her develop a kinship with Indians, without having visited the country before. According to her, India was exactly what she had come to expect from the films. But unfortunately Gurmeet had a different opinion due to her experience while in India. She was in for a shock since India was filthy, smelly, and scary, very different from the image she had come to expect from the films. Instead of an amazing time of learning, having fun, and a spiritual and educational experience, she felt disgusted and incredibly sad for the conditions people exist in. She also mentioned that she felt unsafe and the trip to India was a major disappointment and culture shock for her.

When analyzing Bollywood's influence on travel behavior, the interviewees revealed different degrees of impact. Meeta agreed that Bollywood films have influenced her travel decisions when visiting India. She mentioned joining travel and tour groups to visit South Indian temples, Goa as well as Udaipur. She did mention that the influence might have been so subtle that she did not think about it before this interview. But Pramila Arora had a different opinion. She said that although she loved watching Indian films, she would never visit a place just because she saw it in a movie. There has to be some deeper connections to that place, given that she only gets to visit India once every 3 or 4 years. Geeta Ghosh said:

> Putting mehendi on my hands and feet are not a tradition in the state that I am from, but you watch the marriages in Hindi films, Oh My God! They are so elaborate and so much fun. When I return to India, I want to have a Bollywood type wedding celebration, maybe in a

palace in Rajasthan like in the movie Band Baaja Baraat. I don't have that kind of money,
but let's see what we can manage (laughing).

All of the people interviewed agreed that Bollywood films have played a major
role in maintaining the diaspora's connection to their homeland. While a few of the
interviewees named specific Bollywood films that have inspired them to travel
(Highway-Ladakh, Haider-Kashmir, and Raavan-Kerala), most agree that this influence is subtle and hard to gauge. Sheela put it this way:

I think there exists some type of a connection between the places I want to visit and these
films, but I don't exactly know what it is.

15.7   Conclusion

After analyzing the survey data, interviews of film festival organizers, a few members of the Bollywood dance group, and the Indian community organizations, the
author concludes that there is some impact of Bollywood films on the Indian diaspora's travel pattern and decisions. The Indian diaspora does not turn out in full
force at the theater to watch Bollywood films showcased at the film festivals, instead
opting to watch films at home with friends and family. Indian expats, born and
brought up in India, view Bollywood films as their connection to their homeland,
but one respondent felt that the recent films have become too westernized and fail to
deliver the same nostalgia that older films provided. The Indian American interviewees view these films as a connection to their parents, to their culture and roots,
to the more urban and modern India. The impact of Bollywood films on travel
behavior of the Indian diaspora can be described as subtle and subconscious. Some
members of the diaspora return to visit friends, relatives, and pilgrimages when in
India; there is generally no connection between their travel patterns and films. But
others are impacted by the Bollywood films and want to explore destinations showcased in these films. Bollywood films focus on family values, culture, songs, and
dances. Wedding ceremonies seem to bring all of these aspects together and are a
significant part of some films. It is no wonder then that some in the Indian diaspora
accept that depiction as ideal and want to replay a similar event in their own life
possibly at a location made famous by the films. Active community engagements
like the dance group seem to bring together people from all walks of life who share
a love of Bollywood films and by extension India. It creates a community space
where art is created and shared, helping the Indian diaspora feel connected to their
home in a fun, participatory, and tangible way.

Since Hawaii is such a diverse place, there is ample scope for Bollywood films
and their impacts to spread beyond the narrow confines of the Indian, South Asian,
or even Asian communities to include everyone who is interested in cross-cultural
engagement. The influence of films appears to be subtly present; it is not as conspicuous among the diasporas in their travel decisions. It could be due to Bollywood
films being so closely intertwined into the fabric of the diaspora that its impact on

specific decisions is hard to crystalize. Overall though Bollywood films tend to influence their understanding of the changing country and make them feel closer to their roots.

References

Aftab, K. (2002). Brown: The new black! Bollywood in Britain. *Critical Quarterly, 44*(1), 88–98.
Appadurai, A. (1990). Disjuncture and difference in the global cultural economy. *Theory, Culture, and Society, 7*(2), 295–310.
Appadurai, A. (1996). *Modernity at large: Cultural dimensions of globalization.* Minneapolis: University of Minnesota Press.
Bandyopadhyay, R. (2008). Nostalgia, Identity and Tourism: Bollywood in the Indian Diaspora. *Journal of Tourism and Cultural Change, 6*, 79–100.
Basu, P. (2004). My own island home: The Orkney homecoming. *Journal of Material Culture, 9*(1), 27–42.
Beeton, S. (2016). *Film-induced tourism: 2nd edition aspects of tourism.* London: Channel View Books.
Bhabha, H. (1994). *The location of culture.* London/New York: Routledge.
Bhattacharya, N. (2002). A basement Cinephilia: Indian diaspora women watch Bollywood. *South Asian Popular Culture, 2*(2), 160–183.
Center for South Asian Studies. http://www.hawaii.edu/csas/financial.html
Childers, H. M. (2002). *"You Go Girl!" Nationalism and women's empowerment in the Bollywood Film Kya Kehna.* A Master's Thesis in Art History at Louisiana State University.
Cohen, E. (1988). Authenticity and commoditization in tourism. *Annals of Tourism Research, 15*(3), 371–386.
Dann, G. M. S. (1994a). Tourism and nostalgia: Looking forward to going back. *Vrijetid en Samenleving, 12*(1/2), 75–94.
Dann, G. M. S. (1994b). Travel by train: Keeping nostalgia on track. In A. Seaton (Ed.), *Tourism: The state of the art.* Chichester: Wiley.
Dann, G. M. S. (1996). *The language of tourism: A sociolinguistic perspective.* Oxon: CAB International.
Dann, G. M. S. (2005). Nostalgia in the noughties. In W. Theobald (Ed.), *Global tourism* (pp. 33–50). Burlington: Butterworth-Heinemann.
Desai, J. (2004). *Beyond Bollywood.* London: Routledge.
Dudrah, R. K. (2002). Vilayati Bollywood: Popular Hindi cinema-going and Diasporic South Asian identity in Birmingham (UK). *The Public, 9*(1), 19–36.
Dudrah, R. K. (2006). *Bollywood: Sociology goes to the films.* New Delhi: Sage Publications.
Dwyer, R. (2010). Bollywood's India: Hindi cinema as a guide to modern India. *Asian Affairs, 41*(3), 381–398.
'Engaging Diaspora: The Indian Growth Story' - Eleventh Pravasi Bharatiya Divas: Tourism Sector: Current status and trends, policy status, acts and regulations. (2013). *FICCI studies and surveys,* Jan 22, 2013.
Gillespie, M. (1995). *Television, ethnicity and cultural change.* London/New York: Routledge.
Hall, S. (1992). Cultural identity and cinematic representation. In M. Cham (Ed.), *Exiles: Essays on Caribbean Cinema* (pp. 220–236). Trenton: World Press.
Hall, S. (1996). Ethnicities. In D. Morley & K. Chen (Eds.), *Stuart Hall: Critical dialogues in cultural studies.* London: Routledge.
Hawaiian Language. http://www.olelo.hawaii.edu/
Jain, R. (1993). *Indian communities abroad: Themes and literature.* New Delhi: Manohar.

Jain, R. (1998). Indian diaspora, globalization and multiculturalism: A cultural analysis. *Contributions to Indian Sociology, 32*(3), 337–360.

Lowenthal, D. (1998). *The heritage crusade and the spoils of history*. Cambridge: Cambridge University Press.

Lowenthal, D. (2005). *Past is a foreign country*. Cambridge/New York: Cambridge University Press.

MacCannell, D. (1973). Staged authenticity: Arrangements of social space in tourist settings. *American Journal of Sociology, 79*(3), 589–603.

MacCannell, D. (1989). *The tourist: A new theory of the leisure class* (2nd ed.). New York: Schocken.

Mehta, S. (2005) Welcome to Bollywood. *National Geographic*.

National Park Service. https://www.nps.gov/havo/learn/nature/index.htm

Peleggi, M. (2005). Consuming colonial nostalgia: The monumentalisation of historic hotels in urban South-East Asia. *Asia Pacific Viewpoint, 46*(3), 255–265.

Punathambekar, A. (2005). Bollywood in the Indian-American diaspora: Mediating a transitive logic of cultural citizenship. *International Journal of Cultural Studies, 8*(2), 151–173.

Punathambekar, A. (2010). 'From Bihar to Manhattan': Bollywood and the transnational Indian family. In M. Curtin & H. Shah (Eds.), *Reorienting global communication: Indian and Chinese media beyond Borders* (pp. 41–59). Urbana: U of Illinois.

Rajadhyaksha, A. (2003). The "Bollywoodization" of the Indian cinema: Cultural nationalism in a global arena. *Inter-Asia Cultural Studies, 4*(1), 25–39.

Rapport, N., & Dawson, A. (Eds.). (1998). *Migrants of identity: Perceptions of home in a world of movement*. Oxford: Berg.

Safran, W. (2004). Deconstructing and comparing diasporas. In W. Kokot, K. Tölölyan, & C. Alfonso (Eds.), *Religion, identity and diasporas* (pp. 9–29). London: Routledge.

Sarkar, B. (2008). The melodramas of globalization. *Cultural Dynamics, 20*, 31–51.

Singh, G. (2003). Introduction. In B. Parekh, G. Singh, & S. Vertovec (Eds.), *Culture and economy in the Indian diaspora* (pp. 1–12). London: Routledge.

Singh, S. (2004). Religion, heritage and travel: Case references from the Indian Himalayas. *Current Issues in Tourism, 7*(1), 44–65.

South Asian American Digital Archive. https://www.saada.org/

Timothy, D. (1997). Tourism and the personal heritage experience. *Annals of Tourism Research, 34*(3), 751–754.

Timothy, D., & Coles, T. (2004). Tourism and diasporas: Current issues and future opportunities. In T. Coles & D. Timothy (Eds.), *Tourism, diaspora and space* (pp. 290–297). London: Routledge.

Timothy, D., & Teye, V. (2004). American children of the African diaspora: Journeys to the motherland. In T. Coles & D. Timothy (Eds.), *Tourism, diaspora and space* (pp. 111–123). Routledge: London.

U.S. Census. https://www.census.gov/

Uberoi, P. (1998). The diaspora comes home: Disciplining desire in DDLJ. *Contributions to Indian Sociology, 32*(2), 305–336.

Urry, J. (1996). How societies remember the past. In S. Macdonald & G. Fyfe (Eds.), *Theorizing museums: Representing identity and diversity in a changing world* (pp. 45–68). London: Blackwell Publishers.

Virdi, J., & Creekmur, C. K. (2006). India: Bollywood's global coming of age. In A. T. Ciecko (Ed.), *Contemporary Asian cinema: Popular culture in a global frame*. Oxford: Berg.

Chapter 16
Creating Places and Transferring Culture: American Theme Parks in Japan

Sue Beeton and Philip Seaton

Abstract In this chapter, we consider the ways that elements of Japanese heritage have been incorporated into the contemporary Hollywood theme parks of Disney (Tokyo) and Universal Studios (Osaka), resulting in an attraction quite different from their US counterparts. This presents a significant change to the way in which these places have been traditionally developed, resulting in a glocalised tourist attraction that appeals to both Japanese and foreign visitors. By taking a cultural landscape approach, the authors uncover the cultural layers of these two theme parks, resulting in a deeper understanding of the relationship between Western and Asian culture, presenting a popular culture phenomenon that transcends a traditional monocultural approach. Consequently, theme parks should be seen as more than bland, 'placeless' places of Western cultural imperialism.

Keywords Cultural landscape • Film-induced tourism • Contents tourism • Glocalization

16.1 Introduction

The dominance of Hollywood cinema over the past century has pervaded much of the world, seemingly regardless of cultural differences among its audiences. Following on the heels of such popularity is the desire of viewers to visit the places and experiences represented in such movies and TV series (Reijnders 2009, 2011; Beeton 2001, 2006, 2015; Ji and Beeton 2011). But when the place is entirely fictional such as in many of the animated films, this is not possible. However, the Imagineers of Disney and creatives at Universal Studios have applied their imagination toward

S. Beeton (✉)
William Angliss Institute, Melbourne, VIC, Australia
e-mail: s.beeton@outlook.com

P. Seaton
Hokkaido University, Sapporo, Japan
e-mail: seaton@imc.hokudai.ac.jp

© Springer Nature Singapore Pte Ltd. 2018
S. Kim, S. Reijnders (eds.), *Film Tourism in Asia*, Perspectives on Asian Tourism, DOI 10.1007/978-981-10-5909-4_16

creating fantastical, hyperreal places where fans can experience these stories in a temporal space, namely, the theme park (Beeton 2015, 2016). As Hannigan notes in his discussion on what he refers to as the "fantasy city,"

> ... as motion picture and amusement park technologies merge to produce a new generation of attractions, the space between authenticity and illusion recedes, creating the illusion of 'hyper reality' described by such postmodern writers as Umberto Eco and Jean Baudrillard. (Hannigan 1998, p. 4)

While many of the attractions at these studio-based theme parks that are based around movies and TV series have actual destinations attached to them, such as the Disneyland attractions of the historical figure of Davy Crockett, there are rides and experiences at Disney based around fantasy (Fantasyland) and science fiction (Tomorrowland). At Universal Studios, the Marvel comic characters roam the park along side attractions such as *The Wizarding World of Harry Potter*. It is worth noting that, while most of the theme park rides are established after the movie or TV series has been released, there are some interesting exceptions, such as Disney's *Pirates of the Caribbean* and *Country Bears* movies, which were both based on the original Disneyland rides (Beeton 2016).

There are now several American theme parks in Asia, including Universal Studios (Singapore and Osaka), Disneyland (Tokyo, Shanghai, and Hong Kong), and DisneySea (Tokyo). This chapter focuses on those Hollywood theme parks in Japan, exploring their place in contemporary Japanese culture and how they have retained their popularity while other parks have fallen into trouble. In doing so, we consider the extent that local culture is incorporated into these Hollywood constructs, especially regarding their expansion into the realm of contents tourism (Beeton et al. 2013). This is reminiscent of "glocalization," a term that emerged from Japan in the 1990s to describe the numerous ways in which techniques were adapted to the Japanese environment. In fact, the term initially used was *dochakuka*, which is related to the adaptation of farming techniques to local conditions. It then expanded into the business world as "global localization" or glocalization (Khondker 2005). This implies that there is no simple imitation, but the fusion of ideas – a process that clearly resonates within the theme parks we studied.

In his study of the Daejanggeum Theme Park in Korea, Kim looks at the extent of audience involvement, and he found that the primarily Asian visitors related to notions of "...'prestige and privilege', 'intimacy and memory', and 'beyond screen, sensory experience and re-enactment'..." (Kim 2012, p. 394). While a most interesting study, and one that calls for more work relating to Asian theme parks, our focus here is not on the Asian-created theme park but those of Hollywood in Asia, which in turn adds to our overall knowledge of film tourism at theme parks.

A powerful way to consider this is through the lens of the cultural landscape, which enables the stories of a place and its people to come out, in particular those that have been imposed on the land as at the theme parks.

16.2 Cultural Landscape Approaches in Tourism

"In the course of generating new meanings and decoding existing ones, people construct spaces, places, landscapes, regions and environments" (Anderson and Gale 1992, p. 4).

While not a new term, "cultural landscape" came to prominence through the work of geographer Carl Sauer in the 1920s. In his essay on *The Morphology of Landscape*, Sauer stated that "…the cultural landscape is fashioned from a natural landscape by a culture group. Culture is the agent, the natural area is the medium, the cultural landscape is the result" (Sauer 1925, p. 46). More recent cultural geography studies have used it to investigate the multiplicity of meanings in the cultural landscape, offering "rich conceptual tools with which to recognise, understand and interpret our world" (Brown 2007, p. 34).

This approach has been applied to public land management, where it engages with the layers of stories embedded in that landscape as remembered and told by the people, which is often seen in indigenous communities (see Walter and Hamilton 2014; McNiven and Russell 2008). As Duncan and Gibbs (2015, p. 27) affirm, "Indigenous Australian and Pacific island communities encode and contain their ancestral cultural identity within their cultural landscape(s) and associated features, especially through the … retelling of tales associated with them."

In 1998, Ringer applied the concept to tourism, describing tourist destinations as "groups of people and their places of lived experience, whose cultural landscapes and local economies increasingly exhibit the influx of new ideas and changing patterns of social interpretation and communication associated with tourism's progress" (Ringer 1998, p. 2). Ringer introduced a more fluid concept of a destination or place which is integral to tourism.

While most of the cultural landscape literature focuses on the role of culture within the landscape, it is a little hard to grasp unless we can agree on a more precise definition. The manner in which we perceive "cultural landscape" in this chapter is the way that, just as with the layers of sediment and rock-trapped fossils in the land, humanity lays down its own fossils in the layers of history in the form of stories. What remains are our "cultural landscapes." So, to wrangle this into a definition, cultural landscapes comprise layer upon layer of intangible culture and heritage, identified through the intangible artifacts of storytelling.

Taking Rogers' tourism application and our definition, the cultural landscape approach can be used in several ways, including as a research tool, to identify tourism potential, marketing themes, or the links between elements of the destination. The key to this approach is in identifying the layers within the landscape, such as its history, the physical nature of the landscape, and what cannot be seen, and then tying them together with stories that thread their way between them.

Not extensively applied in Asian contexts, this approach is nevertheless sound in that it recognizes the complex nature of culture and landscapes and the way that stories link them, and Cunningham (2009), for example, has considered the cultural landscape of the indigenous peoples of Ogasawara in Japan. He found that "what the landscape represents for those who live there should play a prominent role in the identification and protection process, as well as in the construction, marketing and consumption of place" (Cunningham 2009, p. 224). Reeves and Long (2011) shed further light on the way that a cultural landscape approach can help in managing cultural resources in another Asian study based in Laos, noting that "[c]ultural landscapes reflect the way different people have valued land over time, and demonstrate how differently land has been and continues to be used by groups and individuals" (Reeves and Long 2011, p. 5). Beeton (2010) argues that often it is the landscape itself that becomes a major character in film and TV programs, either literally or metaphorically, inferring its place in culture.

Such a focus on stories resonates with movies and their associated theme parks. Jewell and McKinnon (2008, p. 160) suggest that "[m]ovies create new cultural landscapes, an interaction between and evolution of society's external and internal economic, cultural and social aspects." We have used this approach to understand how the culture of the Hollywood theme parks has been overlaid onto Japanese cultural landscapes and what has occurred at these sites, through numerous participant observation trips to these theme parks.

16.3   The Layers

During the course of our research, we found layers of the Hollywood-Japanese theme parks in their history, built landscape (the physical theme park), imagined landscape (the fantastical theme park), and the "Japanification" of Hollywood (through changes were made to the original). The layers can be linked by the many stories we witnessed based around themes of adventure, love, horror, and excitement.

In order to triangulate the study, fieldwork was undertaken separately over a period of 2 years at Tokyo Disneyland and Universal Studios Japan in 2014 (Beeton) and 2016 (Seaton) with a view to identifying ways in which the permanent attractions in the parks had adapted for the Japanese market. Visitation during the autumn also enabled comparison of a seasonal event, Halloween, which has been adapted in quite different ways according to the target market of the two parks. As with all of the Universal and Disney theme parks, both were originally built as replicas of the US originals. We look at how, from the original corporate blueprint (the initial foreign layer), both parks have undergone creeping cultural adaptation as layers of Japanese practice are added on to make the park more appealing to the Japanese market and consequently to foreigners. One crucial difference is that this process has been more guest-driven at Tokyo Disneyland and more management-driven at Universal Studios Japan.

16.3.1 Layer 1: The Historical Context

In Japan, there is a long history of travel behavior induced fully or partially by works of popular culture, a phenomenon known in Japan as *kontentsu tsūrizumu* or *contents tourism*. While this term dates from the 1990s, it can be identified from at least since the 1950s in terms of film and as far back as the seventeenth century or earlier for literary tourism (Seaton et al. 2017).

Up until the 1980s, film tourism was primarily to "related sites" (*yukari no chi*) or "on-location" as Beeton (2005, 2016) refers to it. For example, film tourism generated by the annual *Taiga drama* (epic historical dramas, typically lasting a year) was primarily at existing heritage sites related to the historical figures depicted in the drama (Seaton et al. 2017).

Yet, Japan's close relationship with Disney dates back to the 1950s when Walt Disney had a major influence on Japan's own animators, such as Tezuka Osamu, and Disney films and cartoons were widely watched in cinemas and on television. The various cinematic imports from the USA were watched initially with a mixture of *akogare* (admiration or longing for American lifestyles and affluence) and *konpu-rekkusu* (inferiority complex) in the wake of Japan's defeat in 1945 (Arai 2016, pp. 52–54). But a transition occurred around the mid-1960s when the Japanese economy was growing fast and the 1964 Tokyo Olympics marked the culmination of Japan's reintegration into the international community.

Amid Japan's high economic growth and growing consumer culture, as evidenced through changing car ownership and the growth of glocalization, there was a shift away from "mass tourism" to "new tourism" from the 1980s focusing on attracting independent travelers (Yamamura 2008, pp. 3–5). In addition, Japanese animation and manga industries were flourishing and developing the distinctive voices that form the foundations of the contemporary global popularity of Japanese pop culture. Communities tried to attract visitors through the construction of sites which, in the case of film tourism, included theme parks, open sets, and museums about famous local authors, directors, or characters (see also Chap. 5 in this volume). Toyoda Yukio (2014, p. 210) notes that 1983, the year Tokyo Disneyland opened, is typically called "year zero for theme parks" in Japan. From 1983 to the bursting of the bubble economy in the early 1990s, around 40 theme parks were built. Many were "foreign country theme parks," in which the park was themed on the history and culture of another country, for example, Nagasaki Holland Village, which also opened in 1983.

After Walt Disney died in 1966, Disney productions receded from Japan's public consciousness. After the park opened in 1983, the public's interest in Disney rekindled, largely thanks to Tokyo Disneyland but also because of popular hits in the 1990s such as the *Little Mermaid* and *Aladdin*. By the 1990s, Tokyo Disneyland was established as a wholesome family day out within easy travel distance of central Tokyo (Arai 2016, pp. 44–65). The park seemed immune to the financial woes affecting other theme parks following the bursting of the economic bubble, and its

1983	Tokyo Disneyland opens ('year zero for theme parks')
	1.97 million foreign tourists visit Japan
1987	The Resort Law facilitates large-scale resort development
1997	Disney's Halloween begins
2001	Universal Studios Japan opens
	Tokyo Disney Sea opens
2003	Japan government's 'Tourism Nation Declaration'
	5.21 million foreign tourists visit Japan
2010	Morioka Tsuyoshi moves to Universal Studios Japan
2011	11 March earthquake and tsunami
	Universal Studios' Halloween Horror Nights begin
2013	Tokyo Disneyland's 30th anniversary
	10.36 million foreign tourists visit Japan
2014	The Wizarding World of Harry Potter opens at Universal Studios
2015	First 'Universal Cool Japan' event
	19.74 million foreign tourists visit Japan

Fig. 16.1 Tokyo Disney Resort and Universal Studios Japan chronology

visitor numbers continued to grow in the 1990s (albeit slower than in the buoyant 1980s; see Figs. 16.1 and 16.2).

The second major year for theme parks was 2001 when Tokyo Disney Resort expanded with the opening of DisneySea adjacent to the Disneyland complex and Universal Studios Japan opened in Osaka. In line with its overseas operations, Universal Studios Japan was more of a park for teenagers and adults rather than young children (Beeton 2015). Its attractions included rides themed on Hollywood blockbusters such as *Jaws* and *Jurassic Park*. In 2001, a combined 33 million visitors entered the two parks. This coincided with the third main phase of Japanese tourism, "next-generation tourism," in which people were using travel to develop specific interests and develop personal networks (Yamamura 2008, pp. 3–5). It is this period in that contents tourism gained the attention of policy-makers, and the promotion of the "narrative quality" (*teemasei*) of regions via contents was formalized within national tourism strategies in 2005 (Beeton et al. 2013).

Consequently, Tokyo Disneyland in particular, but also Universal Studios Japan, occupies important and successful positions in the history of Japanese tourism. The fact that both parks are nominally sites of American film tourism poses interesting questions about what makes them successful in comparison with "Japanese" film tourism sites and theme parks. Toyoda (2014, p. 208) argues that the appeal of Tokyo Disney Resort for Japanese lies in it being a "comfortable space of self-contained fantasy that is both 'non-Japanese' and 'non-ordinary.'"

This works as a general conclusion, but the visitor numbers in Fig. 16.2 indicate considerable fluctuations. Amid overall success, both Tokyo Disney Resort and Universal Studios Japan have had rough periods. In particular, visitor numbers to Universal Studios Japan dropped from a peak of 11 million before rising and then dropping to a new low of between seven and eight million people in 2009–2010. By looking at this from a cultural landscape perspective, we can suggest another key causal factor, as discussed in the next section.

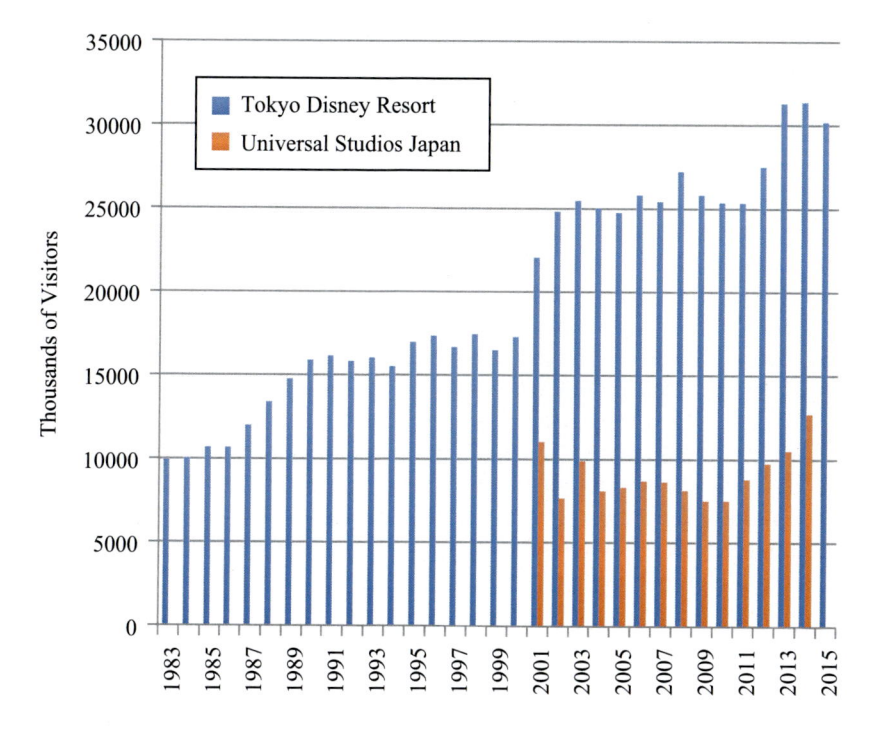

Source:http://www.yuuenchi.com/入園者数推移まとめ tdrusj/ (Accessed 4 January 2017).
Please note: From 2001, visitor numbers to Tokyo Disney Resort are the sum of visitor
numbers to Tokyo Disneyland and Tokyo DisneySea.

Fig. 16.2 Visitor numbers at Tokyo Disney Resort and Universal Studios Japan, 1983–2015

During the second decade of the twenty-first century, both parks successfully
introduced layers of Japanese culture onto the American foundations in the forms of
hospitality practices and attractions based around Japanese pop culture contents.
Furthermore, over the life spans of the parks, Japanese visitors have Japanized them
(albeit not enough to damage their "non-Japaneseness" and "non-ordinariness")
through fan behaviors typically seen among fandoms of Japanese contents, such as
cosplay. As discussed below, the fortunes of Universal Studios Japan after 2009
were turned around by the use of Japanese contents. A similar, albeit much less
obvious, transition occurred at Tokyo Disney Resort, where the success of the park
is primarily due to a dedicated group of repeaters called "Disneymaniacs" (Toyoda
2014, p. 214) or "Dizunī otaku" (Arai 2016, p. 30) who have transformed the park
from a site primarily of family entertainment (the Walt Disney ideal) to a site of play
for groups of female fans in their 20s and 30s.

Another important trend is the exponential rise in foreign visitors to Japan from
under two million in 1983 to over 20 million visitors in 2016. In an aging and

depopulating Japan, the massive rise in inbound visitors creates a potentially new market to be tapped. In 2014, 10% of visitors to Universal Studios and in 2015 6% of visitors to Tokyo Disneyland were non-Japanese (*Sankei Shinbun* 2016; OLC Group 2016); yet this market cannot necessarily be tapped further if all the parks offer is an American space. So, while both parks were built as "authentic" replicas of original sites in the USA, both have evolved into multilayered spaces blending American film and Japanese contents tourism and culture. It could be argued that the future success of the parks relies on them *not* being faithful replicas and instead offering a "uniquely Japanese" experience.

So, while Disney theme parks in particular have been regularly criticized for creating placeless places and removing cultural meaning from the landscape (Relph 1976) or for their "cultural imperialism," our conclusions reflect and update the findings of Aviad Raz (2000), who rejects criticisms of "cultural imperialism" and sees Tokyo Disneyland as "a 'case study' where the 'acculturated' - the Japanese - are not passively dominated but rather make an active and manipulative use of Western culture" (Raz 2000, p. 95). What we are considering here are the ways that imaginary places have been placed onto the landscape and then over a long period of changing socioeconomic conditions are reimagined and co-opted by the host culture in ways that are meaningful and beneficial. The parks, in effect, socially construct a place of the mind rather than mere physicality.

16.3.2 Layer 2: Language

The most obvious cultural layering or adaptation at the parks is linguistically. Place names, visitor information, regulations, and so on need to be given in Japanese on signs and in pamphlets, although English is also ubiquitous. Cast/crew members receive training in welcoming or guiding guests in the appropriate mixture of American and Japanese (Raz 2000). Glancing at the maps of both parks reveals that most attractions and locations are transliterations of the English names using the phonetic script katakana. So, at Disneyland, the Star Wars attraction "Star Tours: The Adventures Continue" is rendered "Sutā Tsuāzu: za adobenchāzu kontinyū." This preserves the "non-Japanese" feel. However, this language policy may also be seen in reverse at Universal Studios, where an attraction called *Tatari* was held as part of the Halloween events in 2016 and simply rendered in romanized transliteration (the translation is "evil spirits").

The words used to refer to staff at the parks also come from English. At Tokyo Disney Resort, staff are called *kyasuto* (cast), while at Universal Studios they are *kurū* (crew), which reflects how Disneyland conceives itself as a stage where guests enter a fantasy, make-believe world, while Universal Studios conceives itself as taking guests on an exciting, entertaining journey.

16.3.3   Layer 3: Japanification of Attractions

The *Tatari* attraction mentioned above is just one example among many of Japanese contents being used at Universal Studios. This phenomenon is far less visible at Tokyo Disney Resort, although in 2004 they did introduce an original Japanese character, Duffy the Disney Bear, which was a hit with Disneymaniacs (Arai 2016, p. 34). At Universal Studios, the Japanification of attractions seems to be the key to arresting the decline in visitor numbers.

In 2010, Morioka Tsuyoshi was appointed as the director of marketing, and the park saw a much-heralded "V curve" in visitor numbers that turned Morioka into a marketing guru. Morioka himself stresses that the turnaround was started by Glenn Gumpel (chief executive officer, 2004–2016). While much has been made in the media of the role of *The Wizarding World of Harry Potter* attraction in boosting visitor numbers from 2014, the turnaround began 5 years earlier when Gumpel took the initial decision to incorporate Japanese contents such as *Hello Kitty*. However, it was Morioka's knowledge of the Japanese domestic market that was decisive: Morioka succeeded in shifting the emphasis from the brand name (Universal) to the brand quality (world-class entertainment), opening the way for Universal Studios to use Japanese contents in addition to American contents (Morioka 2014, p. 43). This philosophy is now encapsulated in the park's slogan: *Sekai saikō wo, otodoke shitai* (Bring You the Best of the World).

The park's market has also gone global. It ran a "Universal Cool Japan" event in 2015, supposedly for one year, but in 2017 it returned for its third year. This attraction ties the park into the national government's "Cool Japan" strategy, which supports the marketing of Japanese contents internationally and has turned Universal Studios Japan into the largest de facto site of *Japanese film/contents* tourism for foreigners. This trend looks set to continue with the planned opening of Super Nintendo World in time for the 2020 Olympics. With its fortunes revived by a bold Japanese marketing director who understood how to get the most entertainment out of contents, regardless of national origin, Universal Studios is now effectively an American theme park in name only.

16.3.4   Layer 4: Seasonal Events (Halloween)

Visitor numbers at both Tokyo Disney Resort and Universal Studios are boosted by dedicated repeater guests who purchase annual passports. To encourage year-round repeat visitation, both parks offer numerous seasonal events. They have been key as they require little modification to the current built landscape but add temporary layers based around special/seasonal stories.

Raz describes New Year at Disneyland as "a blatant show of 'Japan' onstage" (Raz 2000, p. 94) with Disney characters in kimono enacting New Year customs. Indeed, the image of Mickey Mouse and other characters in kimono encapsulates

Fig. 16.3 Hello Kitty in a sari atop a float at Universal Studios Japan

the argument of this paper that these parks comprise layers of domestic cultural adaptations upon a foreign cultural sub-layer, and such glocalization creates comfortably familiar yet enticingly other worlds. This correlates with Reijnders' (2011) "places of the imagination" which "for certain groups within society serve as material-symbolic references to a common imaginary" (Reijnders 2011, p. 14). Further convoluting the layers, a parade at Universal Studios in October 2016 contained Hello Kitty in a sari atop a float shaped like the Taj Mahal, which placed Indian layers over a Japanese foundation amid a supposedly American park (Fig. 16.3).

However, our focus is on the Halloween events, which have been introduced at both parks in contrasting ways that not only appeal to Japanese visitors but also connect with the traditions of their Hollywood masters. These different stories told at Disney and Universal Studios highlight how diverse Japanese layers placed on diverse American foundations result in very different celebrations of the same event. Despite its Celtic roots, Halloween is seen as an American festival in Japan and the two US theme parks have played a central role in its popularization since the 1990s. Disney's Halloween started in 1997, and Universal Studio's Halloween Horror Night started in 2011. The parks reflect the two colors of Halloween in Japan: Disney is pumpkin orange and Universal is blood red.

The Disney event is the child-friendly world of jack-o'-lanterns, trick or treat, and witches' hats and reflects the Disney ethos of family entertainment (Fig. 16.4). Dressing up is part of Halloween, and it is the only time of the year when adults may enter the park in a full costume, which must be of a Disney character. Furthermore,

Fig. 16.4 Orange Halloween at Disneyland

on entry to Disneyland during Disney's Halloween 2016, pamphlets were being given out to warn that wearing "make-up that may frighten other Guests (fake injuries on the face or body, fake blood, etc.)" might result in people being asked to leave the park.

Halloween Horror Nights at Universal Studios are the polar opposite. Rather than family entertainment, Horror Nights draw on the history of Universal Studios, whose Universal horror films were famous from the 1920s to the 1950s, but added a J-horror twist. There were shops in the park doing horror makeup for cosplaying guests (Fig. 16.5), many of the attractions had age restrictions (such as the *Trauma 2 Experimental Hospital* attraction with an R-15 rating and warnings that those with needle and other phobias could not enter), and after-dark crew members dressed as zombies roamed designated zones of the park scaring people.

Mirroring the earlier conclusions relating to Universal Studios' introduction of Japanese contents, the attractions were themed on American (*Chucky's Horror Factory 3*), Japanese (*Tatari*), and generic horror (*Trauma* 2, zombies) contents, and the Chucky Hello Kitty goods on sale ("She wants YOU for a best friend") were a playful mash-up of Japanese/American and horror/cute. These attractions were particularly important in 2011, when they helped break the mood of self-restraint (*jishuku*) that had dampened tourism activity in the wake of the 2011 earthquake and tsunami; but in the longer term, they have turned the previously flat autumn season into a busy period (Morioka 2014, p. 68).

Halloween events demonstrate the power of these iconic theme parks to affect national culture. Orange Halloween has grown steadily in popularity since the 1990s,

Fig. 16.5 (**a**) Universal Studios guest in costume and with horror makeup (**b**) A board advertising horror make-up for guests

and each October a wide variety of themed goods from costumes to confectionary are available in shopping malls across Japan; and the growing popularity of red Halloween has effectively forced the Tokyo government to turn Shibuya Crossing into a pedestrian zone on the 31st of October each year as tens of thousands of revelers turn the iconic junction into a stage for often gruesome cosplay fun.

16.3.5 Layer 5: The Guest as Consumer

The adaptation of Tokyo Disney Resort and Universal Studios Japan for the Japanese market can also be seen in retail outlets and services within the parks. In the many cafeterias, restaurants, and stalls around both parks, there are many foods that are indistinguishable from the American originals from hamburgers to tubs of popcorn. However, Japanese portions are typically smaller than in the USA, and there are increasing numbers of outlets serving local food. In Tokyo Disney Resort, there are places serving rice balls and noodles, and as part of the participant observation for this chapter, it was necessary to try *meronpan* (melon bread, a popular sugar-coated roll in Japan) resembling the character Mike from *Monsters Inc.* (Fig. 16.6)

Fig. 16.6 Mickey Mouse senbei (rice crackers) on sale as souvenirs at Tokyo Disneyland

A clearer example of cultural differences exists when we look at souvenir shopping. The English term *souvenir* implies an object that helps the purchaser remember their visit. In Japan, purchasing mementoes for oneself is common, but there is also the quite different custom of *omiyage*, where travelers buy presents to take back to those family members or work colleagues who were not able to make the trip. The practice is rooted in the tradition of giving a gift of money to help with travel expenses to a traveler (historically a pilgrim), who then purchases a local specialty of half the value of the gift to take back to the donor (Graburn 1983, pp. 44–48). Today, people do not usually receive cash before travel, but it is still customary to take back a small gift. All Japanese souvenir shops are piled high with boxes of *omiyage*: boxes of ten to thirty individually packed cookies, sweet bean buns, or other local specialties ideal for people to take back as gifts. Comparison of the gift shops at Universal Studios in the USA and Japan revealed many identical souvenirs for Harry Potter fans, including clothing, wands, and Every Flavour Beans, but the boxes of individually wrapped Harry Potter cookies were for sale only in Osaka.

16.3.6 Layer 6: The Guest as Fan Tourist in the Digital Age

While the work practices of the management and cast/crew have placed Japanese layers on top of the American founding layer, the final and extremely important layer is driven by the visitors themselves. Here the cultural layer is not so much

"Japanese" as "digital" or "generational." Back in 1992, Michael Sorkin mused "... the Japanese family sitting in front of the Sony back in Nagasaki, watching their home videos [from their theme park experience] of the Animatronic re-creation of the creative geography of a Hollywood 'original' ... must be said to have achieved a truly weird apotheosis of raw referentiality" (Sorkin 1992, p. 229). A quarter of a century on, technology has transformed not only the devices on which experiences are recorded, replayed, and relived but also the people with whom the experience is shared.

In his somewhat mournful book, subtitled *The De-Disnification of Tokyo Disney Resort*, former cast member and now university professor Arai Katsuya describes the effects of the digital revolution on Tokyo Disney Resort. From the achievement of the Walt ideal in the 1990s of a park for a family day out, the park has become a different place in the new millennium. In 2014, the proportion of child guests (under 18) was 16.6% and falling (Arai 2016, p. 29). It is an adult park where 70% of guests are female (OLC Group 2016). This raises another discussion on the gendered aspect of the theme park and certain aspects of contents tourism, which is part of ongoing research. The Disneymaniac – predominantly young, female, single, financially independent, an annual passport holder, consumer-minded, fan, and a collector of cute – is the key visitor sustaining the park. She comes not with family but either a boyfriend or like-minded girlfriends with whom she keeps in touch via social media. Rather than a leisurely day out, each visit among the many that year takes her to specific points within the park to buy limited edition goods, consume limited edition food, and socialize with like-minded Disneymaniacs; and the experiences of the rides themselves are enhanced with the adventure of working out how to avoid the queues using the priority lanes. These fan-guest practices of the digital generation have developed against the backdrop of similar practices in other fandoms of the world of Japanese popular culture. For example, while costumes are quite restricted at Tokyo Disney Resort, it is common to see cosplayers at the Universal Studios, where they are openly welcomed subject to basic rules about not disturbing or offending other guests. The ability of technology to break down geographical and national cultural barriers has also made many such behaviors transnational in nature, rendering the distinction between Japanese and non-Japanese less important than the difference between the fan and casual visitor (Fig. 16.7).

Such technological layers are less visible at the Universal Studios, which has only existed in the digital age. If anything, Universal Studios has gone through the reverse process and reached out to families in a bid to broaden its customer base, a move vehemently opposed by some within the company as the "Disneyfication of Universal Studios" (Morioka 2014, p. 38). One problem identified by Morioka when he took over as marketing manager of Universal Studios was that the park was "too adult" and did not cater well to young children, which also excluded the young mothers market (Morioka 2014, p. 105). The solution was the *Universal Wonderland*, a zone aimed at three- to six-year-olds featuring Snoopy, Sesame Street, and Kitty Chan, opening in 2012 and sustaining the park's revival.

The fan-guest may be coming to the park to escape a socioeconomic and gendered reality temporarily and enter a fantastical world, but the theme park creator

Fig. 16.7 Guests/cosplayers taking selfies with mobile phones

aspiring to run a sustainable business cannot simply provide the dreams of their choosing presented in an unchanging imagined cultural time and space without regard for the changing socioeconomic realities that they are encouraging their guests to forget on passing through the park gates. Furthermore, technology does not stand still and in fact is often developed by the film studios themselves to tell their stories, so it is logical to see the fans also doing that for themselves.

16.4 Conclusion

The beauty of taking a cultural landscape approach is that it can handle complexity and richness, which are elemental to the study of film tourism, as it connects with our imagination as well as place (Reijnders 2011; Staiff 2014; Beeton 2015). When we add the theme park onto this, we have yet another form of cultural landscape with many intangible layers, further enhanced by the interplay between Asia and the West or, in this instance, Japan and the USA.

Duncan and Gibbs' (2015, p. 13) use of coastal cultural landscapes resonates with ours when they point out that "[l]andscape perceptions are not limited to visual stimuli and should include the other senses, such as smell, touch, sound and taste." Consequently, we are encouraged to look beyond the visual when seeking to understand visitors' responses to theme parks and their cultural complexities. Movies are all about stories, so using stories to appreciate a movie-based theme park is certainly logical and has provided us with some powerful outcomes.

By understanding these complexities, we have uncovered answers to our key question as to how the Hollywood theme parks have managed to retain their popularity in Asia while other parks have fallen on hard times. By looking at the cultural landscape layers and stories, we have identified the following four major trends that are not necessarily apparent in their original US versions.

First, both parks have found that the constant renewal of permanent attractions and staging of seasonal events are keys to attracting repeat visitors. Here, the rapidly evolving world of popular culture, as opposed to the more static nature of traditional culture, facilitates regular upgrades and renewals and thereby boosts repeat visits. The locations of both parks within close striking distance of the major Tokyo and Osaka conurbations make the day-tripping annual passport holder the key customer. In addition, by being "foreign" parks, both Tokyo Disneyland and Universal Studios enable high levels of escapism via imagining. Visitors can leave the real (Japanese) world as opposed to visiting another part of it, although the levels of familiarity retained through Japanized layers (such as language and hospitality) are key explanations for the popularity of the parks.

The parks also target less the social unit outside the park (primarily the nuclear family) and more the social group that wants to congregate within the park (friends and fandoms). The parks use both permanent and seasonal attractions to invite multiple fans (e.g., horror fans at Halloween to Universal Studios) to congregate within their spaces and cultivate their loyalty.

Finally, as the parks go global in their target audience simultaneously seeking to engage more with a shrinking domestic youth population, the parks (particularly Universal Studios) have increasingly integrated Japanese contents with American film in a hybrid cultural park. This presents us with a popular culture phenomenon that transcends the traditional monocultural view of theme parks, acknowledging their significant place within the host culture, rather than simply dismissing them as bland places of Western cultural imperialism.

References

Anderson, K., & Gale, F. (1992). *Inventing places: Studies in cultural geography*. Longman Cheshire: Melbourne.

Arai, K. (2016). *Dizunīrando no shakaigaku: datsu-Dizunīka suru TDR*. Tokyo: Seikyusha.

Beeton, S. (2001). Lights, camera, re-action. How does film-induced tourism affect a country town? In M. F. Rogers & Y. M. J. Collins (Eds.), *The future of Australia's country towns* (pp. 172–183). Bendigo: La Trobe University. Centre for Sustainable Regional Communities.

Beeton, S. (2005). *Film-induced tourism* (1st ed.). Clevedon: Channel View Publications.

Beeton, S. (2006). Understanding film-induced tourism. *Tourism Analysis, 11*(3), 81–188.

Beeton, S. (2010). Landscapes as characters: Film, tourism and a sense of place. *Metro, Special Feature Section on Landscape and Location in Australian Cinema, 166*, 114–119.

Beeton, S. (2015). *Travel, tourism and the moving image*. Clevedon: Channel View Publications.

Beeton, S. (2016). *Film-induced tourism* (2nd ed.). Clevedon: Channel View Publications.

Beeton, S., Yamamura, T., & Seaton, P. (2013). The mediatisation of culture: Japanese contents tourism and pop culture. In J.-A. Lester & C. Scarles (Eds.), *Mediating the tourist experience* (pp. 139–154). Farnham: Ashgate.

Brown, S. (2007). Landscaping heritage: Toward an operational cultural landscape approach for protected areas in new South Wales. *Australasian Historical Archaeology, 25*(4), 33–42.

Cunningham, P. (2009). Exploring the cultural landscape of the Obeikei in Ogasawara, Japan. *Journal of Tourism and Cultural Change, 7*(3), 221–234.

Duncan, B., & Gibbs, M. (2015). Introduction. In B. Duncan & M. Gibbs (Eds.), *Please God send me a wreck* (pp. 1–5). New York: Springer.

Graburn, N. (1983). *To pray, pay and play: The cultural structure of Japanese domestic tourism.* Aix-en-Provence: Centre des Hautes Études Touristiques.

Hannigan, J. (1998). *Fantasy city: Pleasure and profit in the postmodern metropolis.* London: Routledge.

Jewell, B., & McKinnon, S. (2008). Movie tourism—A new form of cultural landscape? *Journal of Travel & Tourism Marketing, 24*(2–3), 153–162.

Ji, Y., & Beeton, S. (2011). Is film tourism all the same? Exploring Zhang Yimou's Films' potential influence on tourism in China. *Tourism Review International, 15*(3), 293–296.

Khondker, H. H. (2005). Globalisation to glocalisation: A conceptual exploration. *Intellectual Discourse, 13*(2), 181–199.

Kim, S. (2012). Audience involvement and film tourism experiences: Emotional places, emotional experiences. *Tourism Management, 33*(2), 387–396.

McNiven, I. J., & Russell, L. (2008). Toward a postcolonial archaeology of indigenous Australia. In R. Alexander Bentley, H. D. G. Maschner, & C. Chippindale (Eds.), *Handbook of archaeological theories* (pp. 423–443). Plymouth: Rowman and Littlefield.

Morioka, T. (2014). *USJ no jetto kōsutā wa naze ushiromuki ni hashitta no ka.* Tokyo: Kadokawa.

OLC Group. (2016). Gesuto purofīru. Retrieved from http://www.olc.co.jp/tdr/guest/profile.html

Raz, A. E. (2000). Domesticating Disney: Onstage strategies of adaptation in Tokyo Disneyland. *The Journal of Popular Culture, 33*(4), 77–99.

Reeves, K., & Long, C. (2011). Unbearable pressures on paradise? Tourism and heritage management in Luang Prabang, a World heritage site. *Critical Asian Studies, 43*(1), 3–22.

Reijnders, S. (2009). Watching the detectives inside the guilty landscapes of Inspector Morse, Baantjer and Wallander. *European Journal of Communication, 24*(2), 165–181.

Reijnders, S. (2011). *Places of the imagination: Media, tourism, culture.* Farnham: Ashgate.

Relph, E. (1976). *Place and Placelessness.* London: Pion.

Ringer, G. (Ed.). (1998). *Destinations: Cultural landscapes of tourism.* Oxon: Routledge.

Sankei Shinbun. (2016, April 1) USJ sakunendo nyūjōshasū wa kako saikō no 1390-man-nin! *Sankei Shinbun.* Retrieved Dec 1, 2016 from http://www.sankei.com/west/news/160401/wst1604010044-n1.html

Sauer, C. O. (1925). The morphology of landscape. *University of California Publications in Geography, 2*(2), 19–53.

Seaton, P., Yamamura, T., Sugawa-Shimada, A., & Jang, K. (2017). *Contents tourism in Japan: Pilgrimage to 'sacred sites' of popular culture.* Amherst: Cambria Press.

Sorkin, M. (1992). See you in Disneyland. In M. Sorkin (Ed.), *Variations on a Theme Park* (pp. 205–232). New York: Noonday Press.

Staiff, R. (2014). Venice, desire, decay and the imagination: Travels into the 'dark side'. In G. Lean, R. Staiff, & E. Waterton (Eds.), *Travel and imagination* (pp. 213–228). Farnham: Ashgate.

Toyoda, Y. (2014). Recontextualizing Disney: Tokyo Disney resort as a kingdom of dreams and magic. *Social Science Japan Journal, 17*(2), 207–226.

Walter, R. K., & Hamilton, R. J. (2014). A cultural landscape approach to community-based conservation in Solomon Islands. *Ecology and Society, 19*, 1–10.

Yamamura, T. (2008). Kankō jōhō kakumei jidai no tsūrizumu (sono 1): kankō jōhō kakumei ron (jo). Web-Journal of Tourism and Cultural Studies. Retrieved November 1, 2016 from http://hdl.handle.net/2115/35005

Index

Printed in the United States
By Bookmasters